D1521772

TRIBES
of
INDIA

TRIBES of INDIA

The Struggle for Survival

Christoph von Fürer-Haimendorf

with contributions by
Michael Yorke and Jayaprakash Rao

UNIVERSITY OF CALIFORNIA PRESS
Berkeley · Los Angeles · London

University of California Press
Berkeley and Los Angeles, California

University of California Press, Ltd.
London, England

© 1982 by
The Regents of the University of California

Printed in the United States of America

1 2 3 4 5 6 7 8 9

Library of Congress Cataloging in Publication Data

Fürer-Haimendorf, Christoph von, 1909–
    Tribes of India. The Struggle for Survival.

    Bibliography: p.
    Includes index.
    1. Ethnology—India.   2. India—Social conditions
—1947-   I. Title.
GN635.I4F83   954   80-28647
ISBN 0-520-04315-4

To
N. V. Raja Reddi and Urmila Pingle
in memory of our journeys
in tribal country

Contents

Tables and Maps

TABLES

MAPS

Preface

THIS BOOK tells of observations among Indian tribal populations spanning the period from 1940 to 1980. Ever since 1936, when a study of the Konyak Nagas marked the beginning of my career as an anthropological field-worker, I have maintained contacts with Indian tribesmen. True, there were years when I concentrated on the study of the mountain peoples of Nepal, but even then I paid periodic visits to some of the tribal areas of India, and this enabled me to keep abreast of current developments.

When in 1976 I retired from the Chair of Asian Anthropology at the University of London and could devote more time to fieldwork, I decided to undertake a systematic investigation of social and economic changes affecting the tribal societies which I had studied in the 1940s. A grant from the Social Science Research Council of Great Britain, as well as subsidiary awards from the Leverhulme Trust Fund and the Wenner-Gren Foundation for Anthropological Research, provided the material basis for this project, which included also the funding of parallel research by my young colleague Dr. Michael Yorke. It is to be hoped that in future years Michael Yorke will return to the same tribal area, and thus extend the period of observation from forty to sixty or perhaps even seventy years. The School of Oriental and African Studies, which provided the administrative framework for the project, will preserve the documentation, storing all my field notebooks and diaries from the years 1940 to 1980, as well as photographic data.

Financial assistance from the Indian Council of Social Science Research enabled Mr. Jayaprakash Rao of the Osmania University in   *xi*

Hyderabad to participate in the project by undertaking a detailed study of the present condition of the Konda Reddis, a tribe of Andhra Pradesh which figured prominently in my research forty years earlier. His contribution to the volume (chapter 10) provides an Indian view of the problems of tribal populations. Both he and Michael Yorke, the author of chapter 9, are solely responsible for their contributions, which do not necessarily coincide in all details with my observations.

This book is the third of three volumes which have so far resulted from the project, the first two being *The Gonds of Andhra Pradesh: Tradition and Change in an Indian Tribe* (Delhi and London, 1979) and *A Himalayan Tribe: From Cattle to Cash* (Delhi and Berkeley, 1980), and it is planned that additional publications originating from the project will follow in due course.

Any realistic and unbiased analysis of the present situation of the Indian tribes must inevitably contain some references to the failures as well as the successes of government policies and include also some criticism of those responsible for the misfortunes of many tribal communities. Such outspoken criticism may be considered inappropriate on the part of an observer who throughout his fieldwork has benefited from the assistance of numerous government officials. Yet no good purpose can be served by turning a blind eye to corrupt practices and the resulting failures of policies, thereby distorting the picture of the true conditions of tribal populations. My decision to choose frankness rather than diplomacy and circumlocution in the assessment of the actions of government departments in no way diminishes my gratitude for the many facilities offered to me by the governments of Andhra Pradesh and Arunachal Pradesh.

I am particularly appreciative of the cooperation of the staff of the Tribal Research Institute in Hyderabad, whose Director Dr. D. R. Pratap furthered my work in many ways during the years my wife and I spent in Andhra Pradesh. I take this opportunity to express also our gratitude to Mr. N. V. Raja Reddi, whose generous hospitality we enjoyed both in his house in Bhimaram and on two tours in Maharashtra and the Bastar District of Madhya Pradesh. The interest and the pleasure of these tours were greatly enhanced by the company of Dr. Urmila Pingle, whose genetic and dietary research among the tribes of the area has opened many new vistas.

A detailed tribute to all those who helped our work in Arunachal Pradesh in 1978 is contained in the preface to *A Himalayan Tribe*. In 1980 we had the good fortune of returning to the Subansiri District, as well as of visiting part of Kameng District, including the Tawang Subdivision. In connection with this tour I would like to express our thanks to Mr. R. N. Haldipur, Lieutenant Governor of Arunachal Pradesh, and to Mrs. Haldipur, whose warm hospitality my wife and I enjoyed on more than one occasion. Equally cordial was the welcome of the present Collector of Subansiri District, Mr. L. Sharma, whose help greatly facilitated my work. A special word of thanks is also due to Mr. P. Ette, Circle Officer of Raga, who went out of his way to assist us in our investigations among the Hill Miris of his circle. In Kameng District we received the unstinting support of all the district officers and particularly of the Collector, Mr. O. P. Kelkar, who generously provided us with transport at a time when motor-fuel was in short supply throughout Northeast India. Once again Mr. B. B. Pandey of the Research Department accompanied us on our entire tour in Arunachal Pradesh, and it is a pleasant duty to express our gratitude for his assistance and companionship.

Finally, I wish to thank Mr. M. L. Kampani of the Ministry of Home Affairs and Mr. I. P. Gupta, Chief Secretary to the Government of Arunachal Pradesh, for piloting our application for permission to undertake research in the Subansiri and Kameng districts through the complicated official channels.

London
January 1981

Introduction:
The Ethnographic Scene

ONE PHENOMENON inherent in the nature of the plural society of the Indian subcontinent is the coexistence—often in a narrow space—of populations varying greatly in the level of material and intellectual development. Confrontation and eventual harmonization are the two possible outcomes of such a state of affairs, and this book focusses on the social problems created by the mounting influence of economically advanced and politically powerful groups on autochthonous societies which persisted until recently in an archaic and in many respects primitive life-style. A full understanding of the disruption caused by this impact within the whole fabric of tribal life cannot be gained from generalizations embracing the totality of the forty millions of Indian tribal populations. The diversity of ethnic groups and cultural conditions is so great that such an approach would be impracticable, and it is for this reason that I have concentrated on a series of microstudies, each dealing with a specific tribal society and with particular problems cognate to the process of social change.

While anthropologically interested Indian readers will have no difficulty in visualizing the tribes mentioned in the appropriate geographic and cultural context, those unfamiliar with the Indian ethnographic scene may well be confused by the kaleidoscopic pattern of tribal societies from which I have chosen concrete examples to illustrate contemporary developments among the tribesmen of the two regions best known to me, Andhra Pradesh and Arunachal Pradesh.

At the risk of repeating what I have written in earlier publications, many now out of print, I propose therefore to set the scene with a   1 catalogue raisonné describing briefly the various ethnic groups whose members appear as dramatis personae in the pages of this book. For the convenience of the reader wishing to probe deeper into the cultural background of the individual tribes, I have appended to each of the ethnographic vignettes a bibliography listing the main anthropological sources containing information on the group in question. To forestall any accusation of egocentricity, I may mention that in the case of several tribes, such as the Chenchus and Apa Tanis, few published ethnographic data are available apart from the results of my own field research.

TRIBES OF THE DECCAN

CHENCHUS

During the Palæolithic Age, the vast forests and park-lands of South India were inhabited by bands of nomadic people, who lived by hunting and the gathering of wild fruits, tubers, and edible roots. The only traces left by these ·early foodgatherers are crude stone implements found on the surface of many parts of the Deccan; so far no skeletal remains of the early races have come to light. Yet, in some isolated parts of the subcontinent, small groups of aboriginals persisted until modern times in a way of life which outwardly had changed very little since the Stone Age.

The Chenchus of Andhra Pradesh are one of these ethnic splinter groups, which were left behind by the material advance of the great majority of the South Indian population. Their present habitat is confined to the rocky hills and forested plateaux of the Nallamalai Range, extending on both sides of the Krishna River. Until 1947 this river formed the border between the princely state of Hyderabad, officially known as His Exalted Highness the Nizam's Dominions, and the Madras Presidency of British India. At that time Chenchus were found both in Hyderabad and in British territories, but today their entire habitat lies within the state of Andhra Pradesh, which contains the overwhelming majority of the speakers of the Dravidian tongue of Telugu, the language spoken also by the Chenchus.

Although in the census of 1971 more than 18,000 Chenchus were enumerated, only a few hundred persist today in their traditional lifestyle as semi-nomadic forest dwellers, and it is with the latter that we are mainly concerned in the context of this study.

In their physical make-up the Chenchus conform largely to a racial type described by anthropologists as Veddoid, a term derived from the Veddas, a primitive tribe of Sri Lanka (Ceylon). Like the Veddas, the

Chenchus are of short and slender stature with very dark skin, wavy or curly hair, broad faces, flat noses, and a trace of prognathism. Though no longer dressing in leaves like their ancestors, of whom the seventeenth-century Muslim chronicler Ferishta gave a poignant description, they normally wear but the scantiest dress: the men small aprons suspended from a fibre or leather belt, the end drawn in between the legs, and the women cotton bodices and a length of sari-cloth wound round their hips. There is no people in India poorer in material possessions than the Jungle Chenchus; bows and arrows, a knife, an axe, a digging stick, some pots and baskets, and a few tattered rags constitute many a Chenchu's entire belongings. He usually owns a thatched hut in one of the small settlements where he lives during the monsoon rains and in the cold weather. But in the hot season communities split up and individual family groups camp in the open, under overhanging rocks or in temporary leaf-shelters.

The basic unit of Chenchu society is the nuclear family, consisting of a man, his wife, and their children. For all practical purposes husband and wife are partners with equal rights, and this equality of status means that the family may live with either the husband's or the wife's tribal group. Each such group holds hereditary rights to a tract of land, and within its boundaries its members are free to hunt and collect edible roots and tubers. These used to be the Chenchus' staple food, though we shall see that in recent years there has been a change in their diet and ways of subsistence.

The Chenchus are characterized by a strong sense of independence and personal freedom. None of them feels bound to any particular locality, and the ability to move from one group to the other allows men and women to choose the companions with whom they wish to share their daily lives. Marriage rules are based on the exogamy of patrilineal clans. As long as they observe the rules of clan exogamy young people are free to marry whomsoever they wish. Spouses can separate without any formality, but the abduction of a woman still living with her husband is disapproved of as immoral.

In the sphere of religion the Chenchus evince certain characteristic traits which distinguish them from the surrounding Hindu peasantry. Though they worship some of the deities prominent in the cult of Telugu villagers, they accord much greater importance to a powerful goddess who has control over the game and the fruits of the forest. They also revere a sky god who shares some features, including name, with the Hindu supreme divinity Bhagavan and, though not believed to intervene very much in human affairs, is credited with power over life and death. The Chenchus' ideas of man's fate after death are vague, and it would seem that various notions adopted from their Hindu neighbours have not been incorporated into a consistent body

The Chenchu settlement of Pulajelma in 1940; during the dry winter season the round huts with conical roofs are being rethatched. In the background is the framework of a hut under construction.

of eschatological beliefs. There is no definite idea that a person's fate in the hereafter depends on his deeds in this life, even though some Chenchu stories contain references to reincarnation. More widespread is the belief that a person's life-force (*jiv*) is derived from the supreme god and returns to him after death. The whole concept of a life-force, a belief common to various Indian populations, very likely stems from casual contacts with Hindus, and thus represents a comparatively new element in Chenchu thinking.

Until two or three generations ago, the Jungle Chenchus seem to have persisted in a life-style similar to that of the most archaic Indian tribal populations, and their traditional economy can hardly have been very different from that of forest dwellers of earlier ages. In the following chapters we shall see that, despite recent developments and innovations, the Chenchus still stand out from all the other tribal populations of Andhra Pradesh.

In other parts of India, however, there are still some comparable groups of foodgatherers who have so far resisted the pressure to move out of the forests and change over to a more settled life. Several of these tribes inhabit the forested hills of the Southwest Indian state of Kerala. Anthropologists have studied the Kadars, who form the subject of a book by U. R. von Ehrenfels, and the Malapantaram, also known

A hut in the Chenchu settlement of Boramacheruvu in 1978. There has been no change in the structure of huts, but Chenchus have learned to grow marrows and to train them up the roofs of their huts.

as Hill Pantaram, whom I visited in 1953 and who were subsequently investigated in depth by Brian Morris. Of special interest are the parallels between the Chenchus and the Veddas of Sri Lanka, the first South Asian tribe of hunters and foodgatherers to arouse the interest of western scholars, notably C. G. Seligmann and P. Sarasin. The Veddas have virtually given up their traditional life-style, but during some brief encounters with groups of semi-settled Veddas I was struck by a physical similarity between Veddas and Chenchus so close that it would be exceedingly difficult to distinguish members of the two populations if brought together in one place. Though separated by a distance of hundreds of miles and a stretch of sea, the two groups may well be remnants of the most archaic human stratum of South Asia.

Bibliography
Ehrenfels, U. R. von. *The Kadar of Cochin.* Madras, 1952.
Fürer-Haimendorf, C. von. *The Chenchus—Jungle Folk of the Deccan.* London, 1943.
———. "Tribal Populations of Hyderabad: Yesterday and Today." *Census of India, 1941.* Vol. 21. Hyderabad, 1945.
———. "Notes on the Malapantaram of Travancore." *Bulletin of the In-*

Chenchu drawing his bow. Hunting used to be an important activity of the men, and though game has been depleted Chenchus are still in the habit of carrying bows and iron-tipped arrows.

ternational Committee on Urgent Anthropological and Ethnological Research, no. 3 (1960), pp. 45–51.

Morris, Brian. "Tappers, Trappers and the Hill Pantaram." *Anthropos* 72 (1977): 225–41.

Seligmann, C. G., and Brenda. *The Veddas,* Cambridge, 1911.

Sarasin, Paul und Fritz. *Die Weddas von Ceylon und die sie umgebenden Völkerschaften.* Wiesbaden, 1893.

Scott, Jonathan. *Ferishta's History of Dekkan.* Shrewsbury, 1794.

KONDA REDDIS

Among the aboriginal tribes of India there are many which persist on an economic level characteristic of the period in human history when man first abandoned the nomadic habits of hunters and foodgatherers and began to raise edible plants. In some parts of the world this revolutionary step occurred more than ten thousand years ago and was soon followed by further developments in agricultural techniques. In India, however, there exist tribal people who never advanced beyond a primitive type of agriculture, known as shifting or slash-and-burn cultivation, though most of them are now abandoning this way of life

Digging for edible roots and tubers remains an essential feature of Chenchu daily life. The iron spikes of the digging sticks are purchased from blacksmiths of the plains villages.

under the pressure of governments objecting to such tillage as wasteful of limited natural resources. Until half a century ago, tribes of slash-and-burn cultivators were found in many of the hill areas of Middle and South India, and in extensive regions of Northeast India shifting cultivation is still the predominant type of tillage.

The Konda (or Hill) Reddis of Andhra Pradesh are one of the tribal groups which depend to a great extent on slash-and-burn cultivation. They inhabit the wooded hills flanking the Godavari River where it breaks through the barrier of the Eastern Ghats. In the same way as the Krishna River separated the Nizam's Dominions from British territory, the Godavari formed the boundary between the erstwhile Hyderabad State and the East Godavari Agency of Madras Presidency. Today the great majority of Konda Reddis are found within Andhra Pradesh, though a few communities live in the adjoining Koraput District of Orissa. The Konda Reddis must be distinguished from the important Hindu caste also known by the name Reddi, which is politically the most powerful in the state and, at the time of writing, includes among its members the President of the Republic of India. The tribe of Konda Reddis has a strength of 43,609 and is divided into several sections differing in the manner of their assimilation to neigh-

Konda Reddis of a riverside village in the Godavari Valley; the men wear langoti *tucked into a belt of twisted creeper.*

bouring, economically more advanced Hindu castes. Like most other populations of Andhra Pradesh they speak Telugu, but in their racial composition, which includes primitive Veddoid as well as more progressive strains, they are clearly distinct from the majority of Telugu-speaking castes.

Traditionally the economy of the Reddis is based on the periodic felling of forest and the cultivation of various millets, maize, pulses, and vegetables in the resulting clearings. This type of tillage, in which the axe and not the plough is the primary instrument, is in Andhra Pradesh known as *podu*, in Madhya Pradesh as *bewar* or *penda*, and in Northeast India as *jhum*. But there are important differences among the various forms of shifting cultivation. While the Naga, Nishi, or Hill Maria uses a hoe to turn over the soil on his hill fields, the Reddi of the Godavari region broadcasts all small millets without so much as scratching the surface of the ground and dibbles the great millet (*Sorghum vulgare*), maize, and pulses into holes made with his digging stick. It can safely be said that Reddi agriculture represents as crude a form of cultivation as may be found anywhere on the Asiatic mainland. It is by no means efficient, and at some times of the year when their stores of grain have run out, Reddis subsist on wild forest produce, eating the sago-like pith of the caryota palm or the kernels of

Reddi woman and child of the hill village of Gogulapudi; Reddis buy cotton cloth and gilded nose ornaments from neighbouring plainsmen.

mango stones. They also hunt with bow and arrow, and those living on the banks of the Godavari add to their food supply by fishing, often from dug-out canoes.

Traditionally ownership of the land was vested in local groups whose members may hunt, collect, and cultivate anywhere within the territory belonging to the community.

The sense of unity based on a group's common ownership of a tract of land finds expression in joint ritual activities. Though not all the members of a group need live in one locality, they combine for the celebration of seasonal festivals and for the performance of sacrificial rites connected with the agricultural cycle. The atmosphere within such a local group is entirely egalitarian, but one man acts as head of the community. His position is usually hereditary in the male line, and his function lies mainly in the religious sphere. Acting as mediator between man and the local deities to secure the prosperity of the community, he inaugurates the sowing of the grain crops and propitiates the earth mother with sacrifices of pigs and fowls. This goddess is the only deity who is thought to be entirely and unalienably well-disposed towards humans, and is therefore regarded with gratitude and affection. The Reddi's attitude toward other deities and spirits is one of caution rather than reverence, for these supernatural beings are

Hills flanking the Godavari River bear the marks of the Reddis' slash-and-burn cultivation. The light patches are fields on which the crops have been harvested and only stubble is standing.

deemed potentially dangerous as well as helpful. The hills and forests are believed to be inhabited by a host of anthropomorphically conceived divinities, many of whom have their seats on mountain tops, and are hence referred to as *konda devata,* i.e. "hill deities." Ordinary people cannot see them, but there are magicians and shamans who can communicate with supernatural forces in dreams as well as in a state of trance.

The improvement of communications in recent years has made the Reddis' habitat accessible to outsiders, and we shall see that the commercial exploitation of forests has brought about a change in their style of living and has involved the loss of the freedom and independence of their traditional forest life.

The Konda Reddis are not the only tribe of slash-and-burn cultivators in the Eastern Ghats, and it is not unlikely that in the not very distant past the entire tangle of hills rising from the eastern coastal plains was inhabited by populations of a similar economic pattern. Even today the northernmost group of Reddis adjoins a small tribe known as Dire or Didayi, who occupy a hill tract inside Orissa but close to the border of Andhra Pradesh. The Dires speak a Munda language akin to that of the Bondos, but otherwise have much in common with the Reddis, whom they also resemble in racial type. The fact

Reddis of Gogulapudi dibbling millet on a plot newly cleared of forest growth; the seed is dropped into holes made with iron-tipped digging sticks.

that Munda- and Dravidian-speaking groups share similar cultural features suggests that the economic and social pattern characteristic of the primitive shifting cultivators of the Eastern Ghats cannot be associated with any one ethnic or linguistic group.

Bibliography

Fürer-Haimendorf, C. von. *The Reddis of the Bison Hills—A Study in Acculturation*. London, 1945.

———. "Notes on the Hill Reddis in the Samasthan of Paloncha." In *Tribal Hyderabad—Four Reports*. Hyderabad, 1945.

Thurston, Edgar. *Castes and Tribes of Southern India*. Vol. 3. Madras, 1909. P. 354.

KOLAMS

At a distance of some 250 miles from the habitat of the Konda Reddis lies the highland of Adilabad, the northernmost district of Andhra Pradesh. Until a generation ago a tribe known as Kolam (or in their own language, Kolavar) lived in this highland in a style very similar to that of the Reddis. We shall see in chapter 3 that the reservation of forests has largely destroyed the life-style and indeed the entire economic basis of Kolam society. In the 1940s, however, groups of Kolams still practised slash-and-burn cultivation, and their agricultural methods differed from those of the Reddis of the Godavari region only in minor details. Whereas the Reddis cultivate with digging sticks, the Kolams use a small hoe with an iron spike affixed by means of a socket to a knee-shaped shaft. It is a poor instrument compared to the broad hoes of such tribes as the Maria Gonds or Saoras, and does not turn over the soil but only scratches it. The same iron point can be hafted alternatively on hoe and digging stick, the latter being used for dibbling sorghum and maize, while the hoe is frequently used also for digging up edible roots.

Unlike Chenchus and Konda Reddis, who speak only Telugu, the Kolams have a language of their own which belongs, like Gondi, to the intermediate group of Dravidian languages. When talking to Gonds or Pardhans, Kolams generally speak Gondi, in which tongue most of them are fluent. In the eastern part of Adilabad District there are some groups of Kolams who have lost their original language and speak Telugu, and some groups in the Kinwat Taluk of Maharashtra speak Marathi. In these cases the loss of the tribal language means that Kolams living in adjoining regions can no longer communicate with each other, for members of the somewhat detribalized groups do not necessarily speak Gondi either.

The social organization of the Kolams is based on a system of exogamous patrilineal descent groups, each of which is associated with an ancestral territory and a common cult centre. Several of such lineages are grouped together in larger equally exogamous units which bear names identical with those of some Gond clans. Intimately linked with the system of localized patrilineal clans is the cult of a deity known in Kolami as Ayak, but referred to by speakers of Gondi as Bhimal and by those of Telugu as Bhimana. Within the territory which the members of a Kolam clan consider as their ancestral homeland there is a shrine of Ayak. In the chaos created by the expulsion of Kolams from areas of reserved forest, these Ayak shrines remain the only focal points of clan unity, for all Kolams, unless totally detribalized, return to their ancestral Ayak shrine for the performance of important rites, when the living members of the clan are united in worship and the dead of the clan are propitiated with offerings. The care of each Ayak shrine is the responsibility of a clan priest whose office is hereditary in the male line. Once in every three or four years the symbols of an Ayak may be taken on a circuit and visit Kolam and Gond villages within a radius of twenty or even more miles. Ayak is considered a benevolent god, accessible to the prayers and offerings of men. Though all Kolams emphasize the one-ness of Ayak, he is worshipped under different names derived from localities containing shrines of Ayak.

The Kolams are renowned for their skill in divination and the propitiation of locality gods. This reputation has led many Gond communities to entrust the cult of certain local divinities, and particularly of the gods holding sway over forests and hills, to the priests of nearby Kolam settlements, and it is because of this sacerdotal function of Kolams that Gonds refer to the entire tribe as Pujari.

Bibliography
Fürer-Haimendorf, C. von. "Tribal Populations of Hyderabad: Yesterday and Today." *Census of India, 1941.* Vol. 21. Hyderabad, 1945.
———. "The Cult of Ayak among the Kolams of Hyderabad." *Wiener Beiträge zur Kulturgeschichte und Linguistik* 9 (1952): 108–23.
Russell, R. V. *The Tribes and Castes of the Central Provinces of India.* Vol. 3. London, 1916. Pp. 520–26.

NAIKPODS

The wooded hills and secluded valleys of Adilabad District which were the habitat of the Kolams also served some groups of Naikpods as a refuge area, where until the 1940s they practised slash-and-burn cultivation with hoe and digging stick. Like the Kolams, whom they resemble in many respects, the Naikpods fell victim to the policy of forest reservation, and today only insignificant numbers of Naikpods live in hill settlements. Most of them are found in villages of the plains, where they work as tenant farmers or agricultural labourers. Few of them own the land they cultivate. They are scattered over a large area, and communities of Naikpods are found also in the districts of Karimnagar and Warangal. Naikpods originally had a language of their own which closely resembles Kolami, but today only a few small groups of Naikpods in the western part of Adilabad District and the adjoining taluks of Maharashtra still know this ancient tongue. The majority of the tribe speak Telugu as their only language and have largely been assimilated within the Hindu social order. They are regarded as a caste of low status but as superior to the polluting castes. Unlike the Kolams, the Naikpods have no institutionalized link with Gonds.

Bibliography
Fürer-Haimendorf, C. von. *The Raj Gonds of Adilabad.* London, 1948. Pp. 37–39.

GONDS

Among the tribal populations of India the Gonds stand out by their numbers, the vast expanse of their habitat, and their historical importance. No exact figures for the present size of the group of Gond tribes is available, for the census of 1961 was the last in which all individual tribes were enumerated. At that time 3,992,905 persons were returned as Gond, and there can be little doubt that by now the number of Gonds must long ago have exceeded the four million mark. Figures for the speakers of tribal languages are still being published, and in 1971, 1,548,070 Gondi-speakers were recorded. But this does not give an indication of the present strength of the ethnic group embracing the various Gond tribes, for more than half of all Gonds speak languages other than Gondi, such as Chhattisgarhi Hindi, an Aryan tongue which must have replaced the Dravidian Gondi.

The majority of Gonds are found today in the state of Madhya Pradesh. Their main concentrations are the Satpura Plateau, where the western type of Gondi is spoken, and the district of Mandla, where the Gonds have adopted the local dialect of Hindi. The former princely state of Bastar, now included in Madhya Pradesh, is the home of three important Gond groups, namely, the Murias, the Hill Marias, and the so-called Bisonhorn Marias, all of whom speak Gondi dialects. The states of Maharashtra and Andhra Pradesh also contain substantial Gond populations, and the majority of these have traditionally been described as Raj Gonds, though in their own language they call themselves *Koitur*, a word common to most Gondi dialects. The term *Raj Gonds*, which in the 1940s was still widely used, has now become almost obsolete, probably because of the political eclipse of the Gond rajas. The rulers of Chanda, situated now in Maharashtra, were until 1749 powerful princes whose dominion included a large part of the Adilabad District of Andhra Pradesh. The rule of the Gond rajas of several princely states in Chhattisgarh lasted until 1947, when the British withdrew from India and the Gond states were merged with Madhya Pradesh.

There exists little accurate information on the early history of the Gonds, and it was not until Mughal times that Gond states figured in contemporary chronicles. But the ruins of forts ascribed to Gond rajas suggest that in past centuries the Raj Gonds did not live in the isolation typical of many other tribal communities but entertained manifold relations with other populations whose style of living their rulers imitated. Until comparatively recent times, a feudal system prevailed also in the highlands of Adilabad, and myths and epics depict the life of Gond chieftains who were not subject to any outside power. The Gonds were then already settled farmers who cultivated their land with ploughs and bullocks. Land was plentiful, and individuals could freely move from one settlement to another. In the following chapters we shall see that this mobility has now come to an end, and with this the entire life-style of the Gonds has changed.

Gond society has both its vertical stratification and its horizontal divisions, and while with the decline of the raja families the stratification based on hereditary rank has been reduced in relevance, the division of society into exogamous patrilineal units has retained its importance. The basis of the social structure is a system of four phratries, each subdivided into clans, and the origin of this system is attributed to a divine culture hero. The members of each clan worship a deity described as *persa pen* ("great god"), and in some cases the shrine of this deity lies within the ancestral clan land. Today the clans are widely dispersed, but they still form a permanent framework which regulates marriage and many ritual relations.

Closely linked with each individual Gond clan is a lineage of Pardhans, bards and chroniclers, who play a vital role in the worship of the clan deity and many other ritual activities. The Pardhans, though themselves not Gonds and of a social status lower than that of their Gond patrons, are nevertheless the guardians of Gond tradition and religious lore. The recent deflection of their interests and energy to other enterprises will undoubtedly have an adverse effect on the preservation of Gond traditions.

A role similar to that of Pardhans is being played by another and much less numerous group of bards and minstrels known as Toti. These too have hereditary ritual relations with individual Gond lineages and act as musicians and story-tellers.

The Gonds of Andhra Pradesh, whose fortunes in recent years are the subject of a large part of this book, are only one of the many sections of the Gond race, and differ in cultural characteristics from the various Gond groups inhabiting the hill country of Bastar, which lies due east of Adilabad.

The Gond tribes of Bastar are themselves by no means uniform. The Hill Marias, a population of some 15,000 concentrated in the Abujhmar Hills, are slash-and-burn cultivators, and their agricultural methods resemble those of Konda Reddis and Kolams. Each group occupies a territory within which its members shift their settlements as well as their fields every few years, returning after some time to the same village sites. A few communities of Hill Marias have moved across the state boundary into the Bhamragarh region of Chandrapur District. Those who live in the high hills continue their traditional way of life, but in recent years quite a number have migrated to lower ground. There they have learnt plough cultivation from the local plains people, and now grow rice on rain-fed fields.

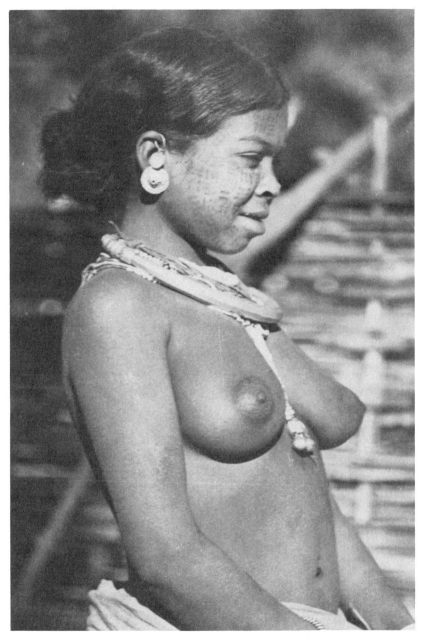

Hill Maria woman with extensive face tattoo wearing a hollow necklace of white metal and silver ear-rings.

Hill Maria girl wearing silver nose-studs and ear-rings, and several strings of glass beads.

Bisonhorn Maria girls of Bastar during a dance, wielding sticks with rattles attached; their necklaces and armlets are made of white metal.

Bisonhorn Maria dancer with a mask of cowrie shells playing a large cylindrical drum.

Far more numerous than the Hill Marias of the Abujhmar Hills are the Dandami, or Bisonhorn Marias, with a population of over two hundred thousand, spread over a large part of Southern Bastar, including the hills of Dantewara, the forest lands of Bijapur, and the low country of the Kutru, Sukma, and Konta regions. The designation *Bisonhorn Marias,* which has become current in the ethnographic literature, is derived from a distinctive head-dress adorned with the horns of wild bison and worn at marriage dances. These Marias are more settled than the Hill Marias and farm their land in a manner similar to that prevailing among the Raj Gonds of Adilabad. Like the latter they have a cult of clan gods, each of whom is connected with a traditional clan territory. The system of phratries subdivided into clans, so characteristic of the Raj Gonds, extends also to the Bisonhorn Marias.

Distinct from Hill and Bisonhorn Marias are the Murias, a Gond tribe spread over an extensive region in Northern Bastar. The most distinctive feature of the Murias is the *ghotul* or youth dormitory, and it is due to this institution, reminiscent of the youth dormitories of the Oraons in Bihar and most Naga tribes, that the Murias have a special place in anthropological writings on Indian tribal societies. Their compact villages are distinguished by spacious houses more solid than the dwellings of most other Gond groups. Their principal crop is rice, cultivated on permanent fields, usually embanked and irrigated, but where level land is scarce they also practise slash-and-burn cultivation on hill slopes, and much speaks for the probability that this was the original type of tillage before the Murias acquired ploughs and bullocks. Today the Murias of the Narainpur Taluk are among the most prosperous Gond communities.

The Koyas, a tribal population largely, though not exclusively, concentrated in Andhra Pradesh, are the southernmost section of the great Gond race. Known also as Dorla Koitur, they merge on the southern border of Bastar with the Bisonhorn Marias, and some groups of Koyas, notably those in the lower Godavari regions, also possess bisonhorn head-dresses. In that area Koyas still speak a Gondi dialect, but the majority of Koyas have lost their own language and now speak the Telugu of their Hindu neighbours. In the districts of Khammam and Warangal, Koyas make up the majority of the tribal population. There they have suffered a fate similar to that of the Gonds of Adilabad District, in the sense that they have lost much of their best land, which they used to cultivate with ploughs and bullocks, and are largely reduced to the role of tenants and agricultural labourers. The process of detribalization has progressed further among Koyas than among any other Gond tribe.

Bibliography
Elwin, Verrier. *Maria Murder and Suicide.* Bombay, 1943.
———. *The Muria and Their Ghotul.* Bombay, 1947.
Fürer-Haimendorf, C. von. *The Raj Gonds of Adilabad.* London, 1948.
———. *The Gonds of Andhra Pradesh.* Delhi/London, 1979.
Grigson, Sir Wilfrid. *The Maria Gonds of Bastar.* London, 1949.
Jay, Edward J. *A Tribal Village of Middle India.* Calcutta, 1970.
Rao, P. Setu Madhava. *Among the Gonds of Adilabad.* Hyderabad, 1949.

SAORAS

The Saoras (also spelt *Savaras*) are one of the principal Munda-speaking tribes and are widely spread over hill regions within Orissa, Madhya Pradesh, Andhra Pradesh, Bihar, and West Bengal. Their main concentrations are in the Ganjam District of Orissa and the Srikakulam District of Andhra Pradesh, and their total numerical strength exceeds 450,000. There are cultural and economical distinctions between the various sections of this large autochthonous population, but Saoras are conscious of their ethnic identity wherever and in whatever conditions they live. Communities inhabiting rugged hill regions practise mainly slash-and-burn cultivation, using hoes as their main agricultural implements. In lower and more level country they use ploughs and bullocks, and they also terrace fields wherever the terrain lends itself to irrigated rice cultivation. Saora settlements are characterized by parallel lines of houses standing opposite each other in long streets. Many Saoras erect megalithic monuments, in the style of the menhirs and stone platforms of the Gadabas, another Munda-speaking tribe of Orissa also represented by a few small communities in Srikakulam District.

The Saoras' material standards are lower than those of such neighbouring tribes as the Jatapus, and they give on the whole the impression of considerable primitivity. Their ritual and religious life, on the other hand, is extraordinarily complex, and Saora shamanism, in particular, is based on very complicated ideas about the interrelations between men and spirits and the possibility of human beings entering the spirit world and closely associating with its denizens.

Bibliography
Elwin, Verrier. *The Religion of an Indian Tribe.* Bombay, 1955.
Mazumdar, B. C. *The Aborigines of the Highlands of Central India.* Calcutta, 1927.
Thurston, Edgar. *Castes and Tribes of Southern India.* Vol. 6. Madras, 1909. Pp. 304–47.

JATAPUS

In the hills of Srikakulam District, Jatapus live in symbiosis with Saoras, members of both tribes either dwelling in adjoining villages or sharing the same village site. As a rule Jatapus prefer the lower valleys where there is level land for wet rice cultivation, while the less fertile higher hill slopes are left for cultivation by Saoras. Although the Jatapus are held to have originally been a Kond subtribe, few of them speak a dialect related to Kui, the language of the Konds, and most have adopted Telugu as their only tongue. They are settled plough-cultivators and practise slash-and-burn cultivation only in localities where they do not have sufficient flat land for permanent cultivation.

Jatapus extend over several districts of Andhra Pradesh and the adjoining regions of Orissa. Their total strength exceeds eighty thousand.

Bibliography
Thurston, Edgar. *Castes and Tribes of Southern India*. Vol. 2. Madras, 1909. Pp. 453–54.

TRIBES OF ARUNACHAL PRADESH

The tribal populations of Northeast India, which will be discussed in chapter 11, belong racially, linguistically, and culturally to a sphere totally different from that of all the aboriginal tribes of Peninsular India, and their present political situation contrasts fundamentally with that of tribals in states such as Andhra Pradesh.

Arunachal Pradesh, the union territory previously known as the North East Frontier Agency, is a mountainous region extending between the Brahmaputra Valley, whose eastern part it encloses like a horseshoe, Tibet to the north, Burma to the east, and Bhutan to the west. With the Tibetan region of China it has a common frontier, from the Bhutan border eastward to the tri-junction of India, Burma, and China in the extreme northeast. The border with Tibet/China is about 1,000 kilometers long and runs along some of the highest mountains of the eastern Himalayas. Arunachal Pradesh occupies an area of 81,436 square kilometers (31,438 square miles), and the population at the time of the 1971 census—the latest available enumeration—was 467,511. This means that the average density of population per square kilometer is only 6, whereas the comparable figure for the whole of India is 178 and that for Assam, 153.

Arunachal Pradesh comprises ethnic groups of great cultural diversity, but in many respects there is an overall uniformity. All tribes are of basically Mongoloid stock, and they all speak Tibeto-Burman languages. Many of these languages are not mutually understandable, but there are also large areas within which people can communicate by each speaking his own language, which is more or less understood by those speaking other dialects. British administration extended over only a small part of the present territory of Arunachal Pradesh, and the populations of large areas lived then in virtual isolation, although those of the northern border areas maintained occasional trade contacts with Tibet, while those of the foothills were dependent on some barter trade with Assam. Since 1947 strenuous efforts have been made to bring the entire territory under the effective administration of the Government of India, and in 1978 a democratic form of government based on universal franchise was introduced. Today Arunachal Pradesh has a legislative assembly and a cabinet of ministers consisting of members of this assembly.

The following ethnographic notes relate only to communities discussed in chapter 11, for in this context a description of all the tribal groups would serve no useful purpose.

Nishis

A large population of closely related tribal groups extends over the southern and western part of the Subansiri District and across its western border into the Kameng District. As long as little was known about the people of these districts, the members of this population were called Daflas, a name coined by the Assamese of the adjoining plains, which has the somewhat derogatory connotation "wild man." With the development of contacts between the people of the hills and those of the Brahmaputra Valley and particularly with the spread of education among the tribesmen, this term appeared objectionable to the people concerned, and they insisted on being referred to as Nishi, a term which is derived from the word *Ni* meaning "man." Today the name Dafla has been discarded and Nishi (or in relation to some groups Nishang) is used in conversation and all official publications, though some Assamese persist in their old habit of referring to the hillmen as Daflas. In the 1971 census 33,805 Nishis, 15,462 Nishangs, and 8,174 Hill Miris were counted, but it is not clear what criteria were used to distinguish between Nishis and Nishangs.

According to tribal tradition all Nishis are descended from one mythical ancestor by name of Takr, and it is also believed that his sons became the forefathers of three branches of the tribe, respectively known as Dopum, Dodum, and Dol. Each of these branches is divided into a number of phratries, which are exogamous units subdivided into several named clans. This system is spread over an extensive area,

Nishi man of Jorum village. Cane hats and hair-knots pierced by a brass pin are part of the traditional Nishi attire, and served as protection as well as decoration.

Miri woman of the Raga Circle. The disks worn in the ear-lobes are made of silver; the necklaces are partly of glass beads and partly of more valuable stone beads.

Nishi war leader speaking during peace negotiations to end a long-standing feud in 1944.

and there are few men whose knowledge of its ramifications extends further than their own phratry. Though the Nishis' mobility is high and there is evidence of extensive migrations, it appears that the three major branches and also some of the phratries had at one time a regional dimension.

But neither phratries nor clans are political units, nor in traditional Nishi society did the members of a village cooperate in the pursuance of political aims. We shall see in chapter 11 that in recent years there have been considerable changes in the system of social control, but in the conditions which prevailed until well into the 1940s (in many remote areas, into the 1950s and even the 1960s) the primary social unit was the household. Most Nishis lived and still live in long-houses comprising several families. It is only the members of such a giant household who have the duty to support each other in any dispute with outside adversaries, for Nishis lacked a tribal organization capable of maintaining law and order.

The instability of Nishi society was linked with the system of land tenure. As no one had individual rights to land and the inhabitants of a settlement were free to cultivate wherever they chose, wealth could not be invested in land, and movable possessions, be they cattle or valuables, were liable to fall into the hands of powerful opponents. A

Nishi men discussing the terms of a peace settlement.

concomitant of the general insecurity and frequency of armed hostilities was the distinction between free men and slaves. The latter were mainly people captured in war and either kept by their captors or sold. Their children became members of their owner's clan, but their status was that of dependants rather than slaves, and in time they could gain their freedom and acquire property. Thus there existed among Nishis no permanent slave class, barred for all time from a rise in social status.

Like most other tribes of Arunachal Pradesh, the Nishis were traditionally slash-and-burn cultivators. They cleared the forested slopes lying at altitudes between one thousand and six thousand feet and grew rice, millet, and pulses on these hill fields. Hoe and digging stick are their principal agricultural implements, and though they breed cattle, particularly *mithan* (*Bos frontalis*), they use neither the plough nor any form of animal traction. In recent years, however, the cultivation of rice on permanent, irrigated fields has been introduced in many villages possessing some level land, and this change in agricultural methods has caused economic as well as social changes.

Barely distinguishable from the Nishis of the western part of Subansiri District is a tribal group about 8,200 strong officially referred to as Hill Miris, which is settled in the hills to both sides of the lower course of the Kamla River. The two groups merge and overlap, and any line drawn between them would be entirely arbitrary, for there is no bar to intermarriage and many so-called Hill Miris describe themselves as Nishis when speaking their own language.

Equally blurred is the distinction between the Nishis of the upper Kamla Valley and the tribes living to the north of that area and spreading into the Sipi Valley and that of the upper Subansiri. They are usually referred to as Tagin, but as so far no anthropological research has been done among this ethnic group, little information of an ethnographic nature is available.

In the Kameng District the people identical with the Nishis of the Subansiri District but separated from them by a high though not impassable mountain range are known as Bangni. Their life-style is similar to that of the Subansiri Nishis, and in the days before the establishment of Indian administrative control they were as warlike as their eastern fellow-tribesmen and used to terrorize the less martial local tribes.

Bibliography
Bower, Ursula Graham. *The Hidden Land.* London, 1953.
Fürer-Haimendorf, C. von. *Ethnographic Notes on the Tribes of the Subansiri Region.* Shillong, 1947.
———. *Himalayan Barbary.* London, 1955.
Pandey, B. B. *The Hill Miri.* Shillong, 1947.
Shukla, B. K. *The Daflas of the Subansiri Region.* Shillong, 1959.

APA TANIS

Whereas Nishis, Hill Miris, and other related groups merge imperceptibly one into the other, there is one people, known as Apa Tani, which constitutes a separate endogamous community with its own territory, language, customs, and traditions, and an economy fundamentally different from that of all other tribes of Arunachal Pradesh. In a single valley with an area of approximately fifty-two square kilometers, close to 13,000 Apa Tanis live in seven villages ranging in size from 160 to 1,000 houses. The fact that roughly 300 tribal people can make a living on one square kilometer would be unusual anywhere among primitive subsistence cultivators dependent on their own resources, but in an area where no other tribe had until recently any idea of intensive cultivation, the achievement of the Apa Tanis is truly astonishing. Both Nishis and Apa Tanis are agriculturists, but their systems of cultivation differ fundamentally. While the Nishi slash-and-burn cultivator seldom tills a piece of land more than two or three years in succession, the Apa Tani tends every square yard of his land with loving care and the greatest ingenuity. Until the economic revolution of recent years, land was to him the source and essence of all wealth, and only the possession of land gave a man material independence. All cultivated land is jealously guarded property, and good irrigated fields fetch prices that in the plains of Assam would be considered fantastic. Rice cultivated on irrigated terraced fields is the Apa Tani's main crop, but on dry land millet, maize, potatoes, and vegetables are grown. All cultivation is done with iron hoes, digging sticks, and wooden batons, for not only were ploughs unknown in the past, they also failed to gain acceptance in recent years when Apa Tanis eagerly took to bicycles and other products of modern technology.

While most Nishis live in dispersed settlements, the Apa Tanis dwell in crowded villages where hundreds of houses stand eave to eave in long streets and narrow lanes. The villages are divided into wards, and each of these contains several exogamous clans. The villages are administered by councils of elders, but there has never been any overall authority controlling the entire tribal community or determining its relations with neighbouring Nishi villages.

A characteristic feature of Apa Tani society is its rigid stratification. There are two classes differing in status: an upper class whose members own the larger part of the land and wield political power in clan and village, and a lower class which used to consist of free men owning their own land as well as of domestic slaves. The latter have now been freed, but the endogamy of the classes persists, though nowadays it is occasionally breached.

Priests and shamans maintain communications with the world of gods and spirits, whom they propitiate with animal sacrifices and food offerings. There is a strong belief in an underworld, where the dead lead a life resembling in all details life on earth.

Bibliography
Bower, Ursula Graham. *The Hidden Land.* London, 1953.
Fürer-Haimendorf, C. von. *The Apa Tanis and Their Neighbours.* London, 1962.
————. *Morals and Merit—A Study of Values and Social Controls in South Asian Societies.* London, 1967.
————. *A Himalayan Tribe: From Cattle to Cash.* Berkeley and Los Angeles/New Delhi, 1980.

KHOVAS

The Khovas are a small tribe of slash-and-burn cultivators inhabiting ten villages in the Bomdila Circle of Kameng District. In their own language they call themselves Bugun, but this name is not used by any of their neighbours. Their social organization is based on a system of exogamous clans distributed over all the ten villages. The tribe is strictly endogamous, and there is no intermarriage with any neighbouring tribe, such as the Akas and Mijis, whose life-style is similar, or the Sherdukpens, with whom the Khovas have long-standing ritual and economic relations. Though the Khovas' traditional religion consists of the worship of numerous deities and nature spirits, which involves sacrifices of cattle, they are now influenced by Tibetan Buddhism and have begun to employ lamas for the performance of rituals. The Khovas used to have trade relations with Monpas as long as the latter were in a position to trade with Tibet. In the 1971 census only 703 Khovas were returned, but this may be an underestimate due to the fact that the small community is known under different names.

Bibliography
Elwin, Verrier. *Democracy in Nefa.* Shillong, 1965. Pp. 77–80.

SHERDUKPENS

The small tribe of Sherdukpens, numbering about 1,600 souls, inhabits a single valley of the Kameng District, where most of the population is concentrated in the two principal settlements of Rupa and Shergaon, each of which has several satellite villages. In their own language the Sherdukpens refer to themselves as Senji-Thonji, but the neighbouring Monpas call them Sherdukpen, and this name has been adopted in official records. According to local tradition the Sherdukpens are the descendants of a Tibetan prince and his followers who came originally from Beyalung in Tibet and first settled in Bhut, a village near Dirang Dzong, where the ruins of their first fort are still standing. Like Apa Tani society the Sherdukpen community is divided into two unequal and endogamous classes, known as Thong and Tsao, each of which comprises several exogamous clans. The Thong class is supposed to be descended from the legendary princely ancestor, whereas the inferior Tsao class stems from his attendants who immigrated at the same time. The Sherdukpens have long-standing political and trade relations with the plains people of Assam, and in one locality on the fringe of the plains there is still an area of 103 acres which is under the control of Rupa and serves as the site of an annual festival celebrated jointly by Sherdukpens and Assamese. Similarly, people from Assam send gifts to support the celebration of a festival at Rupa. The tribal god worshipped at this festival has no connection with Buddhism, and the priests ministering at the rites are local men elected by the people of Rupa. Yet, there is in Rupa a large Mahayana *gompa* decorated in a style influenced by Bhutanese and Tibetan prototypes. Like many populations on the periphery of the Tibetan culture sphere, the Sherdukpens practise two religions: an old tribal cult as well as Mahayana Buddhism. The Buddhist rituals are performed by lamas who are of Bhutanese origin or have been trained in Bhutan.

The Sherdukpens have some level land which they plough, using crossbreeds of *mithan* and ordinary cattle for traction. On hill slopes they practise shifting cultivation in the same way as Khovas and many Monpas.

Bibliography
Sharma, R. R. P. *The Sherdukpens.* Shillong, 1961.

MONPAS

All along the northern border of Arunachal Pradesh there are populations influenced by Tibetan culture or of Tibetan origin. In Kameng District, a population of 23,319 Monpas was returned in the 1971 census, but it seems that 1,716 Dirang Monpas, 1,046 Lish Monpas, and 826 Tawang Monpas listed separately are not included in that number. However this may be, in the Bomdila and Tawang subdivisions Monpas form the majority of the population. All of them speak languages akin to Tibetan, but not all of the local dialects are mutually understandable. Yet, culturally the various groups of Monpas have much in common. They differ fundamentally from such non-Buddhist tribes as Bangnis (as the Nishis are called in Kameng), Akas, Mijis, and Khovas, but share the Buddhist heritage of the Sherdukpens.

Most Monpas are high-altitude dwellers, and their economy has far more in common with that of such Himalayan populations as the northern Bhutanese or most Bhotias of Nepal then with the economy of most tribal groups in Arunachal Pradesh. For the cultivation of their level land they use ploughs and bullocks or yak-hybrids, though here and there they also practise slash-and-burn cultivation on hill slopes too steep for ploughing. Barley, wheat, and buckwheat are their main crops, though in sheltered valleys at an altitude below eight thousand feet rice is also grown. Monpa society is divided into several strata of different social status, but there is no developed system of exogamous clans comparable to that of Nishis, Khovas, or Sherdukpens.

Buddhist beliefs and traditions dominate cultural life, and monasteries and nunneries play an important role in the fabric of Monpa society. But side by side with Buddhist institutions there persists a cult of tribal deities conducted by priests who are openly described as representing an old religion related to the Tibetan pre-Buddhist Bon faith.

It is this coexistence of Buddhism with tribal religions which suggests the possibility of a fertilization of local cults by the more sophisticated ideology of Mahayana Buddhism, which was at one time the mainspring of Tibetan civilization.

Anthropologists concerned with India have for some time debated the problem of the distinction between autochthonous tribal groups and Hindu castes. Those speaking of a tribe-caste continuum hold the view that it is impractical to draw a sharp line between tribes and castes, whereas others feel confident of their ability to decide in concrete cases whether a given community should be classified as a tribe or a caste.

The notification[1] of tribal groups as "scheduled tribes" by the Indian Parliament clarifies, in most cases at least, the legal position. Yet there remain borderline cases. Political reasons may motivate a state government to include a particular community in the list of scheduled tribes, whereas in a neighbouring state more resistant to pressure groups the same community may not be notified as a scheduled tribe, and hence may not enjoy the privileges granted to kinsmen on the other side of the state boundary (see chapter 8). Insofar as the tribes included in the foregoing list are concerned, there can be little doubt that they deserve the politically advantageous classification of scheduled tribes.

In Arunachal Pradesh the notification of an ethnic group as a scheduled tribe is not of great relevance because in this union territory tribals constitute the majority of the population and power lies in their hands. It becomes important only for those tribesmen who pursue studies or a career outside Arunachal Pradesh and benefit from the reservation of a percentage of places in universities as well as of jobs in government service for members of notified tribal communities. In Andhra Pradesh, the autochthons are now a minority, even in areas where not long ago they constituted the main population, and the privileges granted to scheduled tribes play a vital role in their struggle for economic and cultural survival.

1. *Notification* is a legal term used in India—as in other previously British territories—for the promulgation of laws and government ordinances in the official gazette. Tribes notified as belonging to the "scheduled tribes" and notified tribal areas are those whose special legal status was established by a "notification" in the government gazette.

1 Relations between Tribes and Government

THE CO-EXISTENCE of established states and independent tribal communities living according to their own rules and customs dates back to the earliest times of recorded Indian history. In an age when the subcontinent was sparsely populated and beyond the limits of centres of higher civilization there were vast tracts covered in forests and difficult of access, populations on very different levels of material and cultural development could live side by side without impinging to any great extent on each others' resources and territories. Even at times of the greatest efflorescence of Hindu culture there were no organized attempts to draw aboriginal tribes into the orbit of caste society. The idea of missionary activity was then foreign to Hindu thinking. A social philosophy based on the idea of the permanence and inevitability of caste distinctions saw nothing incongruous in the persistence of primitive life-styles on the periphery of sophisticated civilizations. No doubt, there were areas where the infiltration of advanced populations into tribal territory resulted in a closer interaction between aboriginals and Hindus. In such regions, cultural distinctions were blurred, and tribal communities became gradually absorbed into the caste system, though usually into its lowest strata. Thus the untouchable castes of Cheruman and Panyer of Kerala were probably at one time independent tribes, and in their physical characteristics they still resemble neighbouring tribal groups which have remained outside the caste system. Aboriginals who retained their tribal identity and resisted inclusion within the Hindu fold fared better on the whole than the assimilated groups and were not treated as untouchables, even if they indulged in practices, such as the eating of beef, which Hindus considered polluting. Thus the Raj Gonds, some of whose rulers vied in power with Rajput princes, used to sacrifice and eat cows without debasing thereby their status in the eyes of their Hindu neighbours. The Hindus recognized the tribes' social and cultural separateness and did not insist on conformity to Hindu patterns of behaviour, and this respect for the tribal way of life prevailed as long as contacts between the two communities were of a casual nature. The tribal people, though considered strange and dangerous, were taken for granted as part of the world of hills and forests, and a more or less frictionless coexistence was possible because there was no population pressure, and hence no incentive to deprive the aboriginals of their land.

This position persisted during the whole of the Mughal period. Now and then the campaign of a Mughal army extending for a short spell into the wilds of tribal country would bring the inhabitants briefly to the notice of princes and chroniclers, but for long periods the hillmen and forest dwellers were left undisturbed. Under British rule, however, a new situation arose. The extension of a centralized administration over areas which had previously lain outside the effective control of princely rulers deprived many of the aboriginal tribes of their autonomy, and though most British administrators had no intention of interfering with the tribesmen's rights and traditional manner of living, the establishment of "law and order" in outlying areas exposed the aboriginals to the pressure of more advanced populations. In areas which had previously been virtually unadministered, and hence unsafe for outsiders who did not enjoy the confidence and goodwill of the aboriginal inhabitants, traders and moneylenders could now establish themselves under the protection of the British administration. Often they were followed by settlers, who succeeded in acquiring large tracts of the aboriginals' land. In chapter 2 the process of land alienation will be illustrated by concrete examples, and it will become apparent that by imposing on tribal populations systems of land tenure and revenue collection developed in advanced areas the government unintentionally facilitated the transfer of tribal land to members of other ethnic groups. The deterioration of the aboriginals' position, which in many parts of Peninsular India began as early as the middle of the nineteenth century and continued into the twentieth century, occurred despite the fact that many British officials sympathized with the tribesmen and some of the most fervent advocates of tribal rights were found among the officers of the Indian Civil Service. Yet, the recommendations for reforms contained in numerous reports were seldom implemented in full, and even where they were incorporated in legislation they did not always prove effective.

Unable to resist the gradual alienation of their ancestral land, the aboriginals of many regions either gave way by withdrawing further into hills and tracts of marginal land or, if no such refuge areas were left, had no other choice than to accept the economic status of tenants, sharecroppers, or agricultural labourers on the very land their fore-fathers had owned.

There was only one part of British India where a policy of non-interference and protection enabled the tribal populations to retain their land and their traditional life-style. In the hill regions of North-east India which enclose the Brahmaputra Valley in the shape of an enormous horseshoe tribes such as Nagas, Mishmis, Adis, Miris, Apa Tanis, and Nishis were the sole inhabitants of a vast region of rugged mountains and narrow valleys into which the peoples settled in the plains of Assam had never penetrated. A small volume of barter trade between hills and plains was carried on by tribesmen from the foothills, but most of the hill people never set foot in the Brahmaputra Valley. When in the second half of the nineteenth century and during the first decades of the twentieth century the British extended their administrative control over part of the hill regions, they did not en-courage the entry of plainsmen, but devised a system of administra-tion which allowed the hillmen to run their affairs along traditional lines. As late as the 1930s the entire administration of the Naga Hills District, for instance, was in the hands of one deputy commissioner stationed at Kohima and one subdivisional officer, whose headquarters was Mokokchung. With the help of a few clerks and a small force of Assam Rifles, these two officers maintained peace and order in a large hill region where bridle paths were the only means of communica-tions. No plainsman was allowed to acquire land in the hills, and the indigenous system of land tenure was retained virtually unchanged. This policy protected the hill people from exploitation and land alien-ation. It is not surprising that the introduction of a much more elabo-rate and less flexible system of administration in the years following 1947 sparked off a great deal of unrest, for tribesmen used to running their own affairs reacted violently to interference from a host of minor officials lacking in understanding of local customs. This is not the place to discuss the cause of the rebellions of Nagas and Mizos, which at the time of writing have by no means completely ended, but no analysis of the relations between aboriginal tribes and the govern-ments in power can be complete without consideration of at least some of the rebellions by which tribal populations tried to shake off the yoke of those who had invaded their habitat, usurped their an-cestral land, and mercilessly robbed them of the fruits of their labours.

Anyone familiar with the oppression and exploitation aboriginals of regions such as the Telengana districts of Andhra Pradesh have suf-fered at the hands of landgrabbers, landlords, unscrupulous traders

and moneylanders, and, regrettably, many minor officials must be surprised not by the fact that now and then tribal groups rose against
their oppressors in violent outbursts but that organized rebellions
were so few and so short-lived. If any of the tribes of Arunachal Pradesh or even of such settled hill regions as the Garo or Mikir hills had
been exposed to injustices as severe as those suffered by Gonds,
Kolams, Koyas, and Reddis, murder and violence would have been the
order of the day, but most of the tribes of the Deccan are on the whole
so gentle and inoffensive that extreme provocation is necessary before
they take the law into their own hands.

Rebellions of aboriginal tribesmen against the authority of the government are among the most tragic conflicts between ruler and ruled.
Whatever course the clash may take, it is always a hopeless struggle of
the weak against the strong, the illiterate and uninformed against the
organized power of a sophisticated system. There may be loss of life
on both sides, but it is always the aboriginals who court ruin and economic distress. I do not refer here to the past risings of martial frontier
tribes whose aims were basically political, but to the rebellions of
primitive aboriginal tribes of Peninsular India, such as the Santal Rebellion in Bihar, the Bhil Rebellion in Khandesh, and the Rampa Rebellion in the East Godavari District. All these uprisings were
defensive movements; they were the last resort of tribesmen driven to
despair by the encroachment of outsiders on their land and economic
resources. As such they could all have been avoided had the authorities taken cognizance of the aboriginals' grievances and set about
to remedy them, not as it happened in most cases *after* the rising, but
before the pressure on the tribesmen made an outbreak of violence
unavoidable.

The Santal Rebellion of 1855–56, with which we are here only marginally concerned, was mainly an effort to undo the steady loss of land
to non-tribal immigrants, but E. G. Mann, writing in 1867,[1] listed also
a number of specific grievances as having caused the Santals to rise
against an inefficient and lethargic government, totally inexperienced
in dealing with primitive tribes. Among the causes of the rising were:
the grasping and rapacious manner of merchants and moneylenders
in their transactions with the Santals, the misery caused by the iniq-
uitous system of allowing personal and hereditary bondage for debt,
the unparalleled corruption and extortion of the police in aiding and
abetting the moneylenders, and the impossibility of the Santals obtaining redress from the courts. The causes of the Santals' uprising,
one of the greatest rebellions in the annals of tribal India, were very
similar to the circumstances which led to outbreaks of violence in

1. *Sonthalia and the Sonthals.*

other tribal areas. An insurrection which occurred in an area now part of Andhra Pradesh involved the Hill Reddis, a tribe whose present situation will be discussed in the following chapter. This uprising occurred in 1879 and is commonly known as the Rampa Rebellion, after an area which now falls within the Chodavaram Taluk of the East Godavari District.

At the time of the cession of the Northern Circars by the Nizam to the East India Company, the Rampa country was in the possession of a ruler alternatively styled *zamindar, mansabdar,* or *raja.* This feudal lord was not a Reddi, but we do not know how he had originally gained possession of the country and by what means he controlled the independent and elusive hill people. He appears to have leased his villages to certain subordinate hill chiefs known as *muttadar,* and from these he received an annual income of Rs 8,750 per annum, an amount equal to at least Rs 800,000 according to the present value of money. This *mansabdar* was succeeded first by his daughter and subsequently by an illegitimate son. The latter's oppressive rule led to several minor insurrections, but the last straw was an excise regulation forbidding the drawing of palm wine for domestic purposes and leasing the toddy revenue to contractors entitled to collect taxes at their own discretion. Their illegal extortions and the oppressiveness of a corrupt police were the immediate causes of the Rampa Rebellion in 1879. The operation of the civil law of the country was an additional grievance of the tribesmen, whose trustfulness and ignorance of court proceedings enabled traders from the lowlands to make unfair contracts with them, and if these were not fulfilled according to the trader's own interpretation, to file suits against them, obtain ex parte decrees, and distrain as much property as they could lay hands on. The hill people laid the blame for all this injustice on government and government regulations and thought that their only remedy lay in rising against the authorities.

The rebellion started in March 1879 with attacks on policemen and police stations in Chodavaram Taluk, and it spread rapidly to the Golconda Hills of Vishakapatnam and to the Rekapalli country in the Bhadrachalam Taluk, which had recently been transferred from the Central Provinces to Madras Presidency. While under the previous administration shifting cultivation (*podu*) had been virtually unrestricted, the Madras government trebled the land revenue and excluded the tribal cultivators from certain areas. Because of these restrictions the Rampa leaders found adherents in the Rekapalli country, and soon five thousand square miles were affected by the rebellion. In the ensuing guerilla war the government forces comprised several hundred police drafted from neighbouring districts, six regiments of Madras infantry, two companies of sappers and miners, a squadron of cavalry, and a wing of infantry from the Hyderabad contingent. Despite these formidable forces the rebellion was not entirely suppressed until November 1880.

In this context the history of the Rampa Rebellion is relevant for two reasons. It shows first that aboriginal tribes, even if inherently not of a warlike character, are capable of considerable efforts if driven to extremities, and second that the grievances which had led to the rebellion were basically similar to the injustices and the exploitation under which tribal populations of Andhra Pradesh labour up to this day.

In the East Godavari Agency of Madras Presidency the conditions of the tribal populations were considerably improved as a result of the Rampa Rebellion. The necessity of instituting special methods of administering primitive populations had been forcefully brought before the eyes of the authorities, and steps were taken to protect the aboriginals from the encroachment of outsiders.

The various orders passed from time to time with the view of ameliorating the conditions of the tribal population of the East Godavari Agency were ultimately consolidated in legislation known as The Agency Tracts Interest and Land Transfer Act, 1917. The regulations of this act formed a model for similar legislation in other tribal areas, and I shall therefore quote some of its main sections. In order to save the tribals from the exploitation of moneylenders, the act laid down that "a) interest on any debt or liability shall not as against a member of a hill-tribe be allowed or decreed at a higher rate than 24% per annum nor shall any compound interest or any collateral advantage be allowed against him; b) the total interest allowed or decreed on any debt or liability as against a member of a hill-tribe shall not exceed the principal amount."

Even more important were the sections restricting the transfer of land from tribals to outsiders. The relevant section (4) contained the following provisions:

> 1) Notwithstanding any rule of law or enactment to the contrary any transfer of immovable property situated within the Agency tract by a member of a hill-tribe shall be absolutely null and void unless made in favor of another member of a hill-tribe or with the previous consent in writing of the Agent or of any other prescribed officer. [Agent was the revenue officer comparable to the collector of a normal district.]
>
> 2) Where a transfer of property is made in contravention of sub-section (1) the Agent. . . . may on application by anyone interested decree ejectment against any person in possession of the property claiming under the transfer and may restore it to the transferor or his heirs.

These sections of the Act of 1917 should, if fully implemented, have put a stop to all alienation of tribal land, and it is a sobering thought that sixty-one years later large areas in what was the Godavari Agency are no longer in the possession of their previous tribal owners, even though the provisions of the Act of 1917 remained in force till the promulgation of the Andhra Pradesh Scheduled Areas Land Transfer Regulation, 1959.

It is only fair to admit, however, that in the period 1917–47 the condition of the tribal populations in the East Godavari Agency Tract was relatively favourable, and that the massive invasion of tribal land by outsiders occurred after 1947.

The need for special protection of aboriginal tribes was not confined to the areas notified as Agencies, and in 1919 an act known as the Government of India Act, 1919, provided "that the Governor-General in Council may declare any territory in British India to be a 'Backward Tract' and that any act of the Indian Legislature should apply to such Backward Tracts only if the Governor-General so directed."

The legislation of 1919 was a forerunner of the Government of India Act, 1935, and the Government of India (excluded and partially excluded areas) Order, 1936. "Excluded areas" were backward regions inhabited by tribal populations to which acts of the Dominion Legislature or of the provincial legislatures were to apply only with the consent of the governor of the province. The intention of this provision was to prevent the extension of legislation designed for advanced areas to backward areas where primitive tribes may be adversely affected by laws unsuitable to their special conditions. Though at the time Indian nationalists saw in it a device to retain British control over selected areas, after the attainment of independence the government of India adopted a somewhat similar policy in regard to several territories on the North East Frontier.

The Indian Constitution of 1950 also provided for the notification of "scheduled tribes" and their protection by special legislation. Regarding the administration of the scheduled areas the governor of each state which includes a scheduled area is bound to submit a report to the president annually or whenever required. The states periodically prepare lists of scheduled tribes, and these have to be confirmed by parliament. As scheduled tribes are in receipt of various benefits, there has been considerable pressure from backward classes for inclusion in this list, and as late as 1977 new additions were proposed by various states and confirmed by parliament.

As this volume is largely concerned with the changing fortunes of tribal populations in parts of Andhra Pradesh which used to be part of H.E.H. the Nizam's Dominions, we will now turn to the situation as it prevailed in Hyderabad State, both in the days of the Nizam's rule and after the incorporation of the state in the Republic of India in 1948.

In contrast to the administration of adjoining provinces of British India, the government of Hyderabad State had not provided for any special privileges for tribal communities. Indeed it was not until the 1940s that the condition of the aboriginal tribes received serious attention from government. In his foreword to my book *The Chenchus* (vol. 1 of *The Aboriginal Tribes of Hyderabad*) the late Sir Wilfrid Grigson, then Revenue Minister of Hyderabad State, commented on the ignorance of the average Hyderabad official in regard to the tribal communities in the following words:

> This ignorance tends to blind him to the suffering and the loss of land and economic freedom that results in the backward areas when Hindu, Rohilla or Arab cultivators, contractors, traders and money-lenders are allowed freely to exploit the aboriginals. In such records therefore as can be traced of dealings between the governing classes of Hyderabad and the aboriginal and backward tribes little will be found of deliberate oppression or of positive policy. *Laissez faire* has been the governing principle, but, as everywhere in India, and not least in Hyderabad, *laissez faire* more than anything else has ruined the aboriginal and turned him into a landless drudge and serf.

In the following chapters we shall see that indifference to the plight of the aboriginals, be they Gonds, Koyas, or Konda Reddis, is as much the usual attitude of the dominant classes of Andhra Pradesh as it was that of the ruling classes of Hyderabad State. Yet today no one can claim the excuse of ignorance. Ethnographic accounts and published reports are found in libraries, and the files of government departments are crammed with reports on conditions in the tribal areas; moreover, administrative action taken during the last years of the Nizam's government pointed clearly to the type of policy which could have prevented the present decline in the aboriginals' fortunes.

But let us return to the situation in the early 1940s when I began the study of the tribal populations of Hyderabad State. At that time there were in the districts of Warangal (which then included the present Khammam District) and Adilabad large forest areas where tribal communities persisted in relative isolation from more advanced populations. However, these areas had already begun to shrink, and the alienation of tribal land by members of non-tribal communities was an on-going process. Moreover, the reservation of forests, often decreed with scant regard for the needs of the tribal forest dwellers, had begun to encroach on the traditional habitat of such tribes as Reddis, Kolams, Koyas, and Gonds.

There were at that time no officials specifically concerned with the welfare of the tribes and no legislation protecting tribal interests comparable to the Agency Tracts Interest and Land Transfer Act, 1917, of the neighbouring Madras Presidency. The position of the tribes of Hyderabad State was hence rapidly deteriorating. In the course of anthropological research, initially undertaken without any thought of providing data to be utilized in the planning of administrative reforms, I discovered a great many cases of exploitation and oppression of tribal communities and subsequently incorporated my findings in a series of reports submitted to the Nizam's government. Several of these reports were published by the Revenue Department under the title *Tribal Hyderabad*, with a foreword by W. V. Grigson, who held the portfolios of Revenue, Police, and Forest, thus being in charge of the departments most vitally concerned with tribal problems. The very positive reaction of the government to these reports—a reaction one could hardly imagine coming in that form from any minister in 1979—can best be outlined by quoting some passages from Grigson's foreword:

> The problems of the Hyderabad aboriginal areas are in kind exactly similar to the problems of aboriginal areas elsewhere in India. . . . Conditions in fact in the tribal areas of Hyderabad differ only from those in the Central Provinces in that in the Hyderabad areas till recently no determined effort had been made by district officials to keep their subordinates in check and prevent the extortion by them from the aboriginals of *mamul, begar, rasad* and bribes or to fight the exploitation (with their connivance) of the aboriginals by cleverer immigrants, such as the Banjara, the Maratha, the Brahman, the Muslim, the *sahukar* and the *vakil*, the less scrupulous among whom have long found in the tribal areas a happy hunting ground. . . . The lessons [of these reports] should also be felt in non-tribal areas elsewhere in the State where villagers suffer from the unchecked oppression of that bad minority of the *deshmuks, watandars* and *sahukars* who thereby bring discredit on their order as a whole. The press and political bodies have in recent months drawn attention to such tyrannies in various parts of Telingana. But the tribal areas, where the local bully has the freest scope, are less in the public eye and have less news-value, and the offender there is perhaps more often a subordinate official than a *watandar* or a *sahukar*. . . . In backward forest tracts where men are poor and ignorant and distances great, justice delayed or justice that is not cheap is justice denied. What are needed are touring officers combining executive and judicial powers, able to punish the tyrant or the exploiter on the spot.

Reading these comments thirty-five years after they were written, one cannot help feeling that the problem of the exploitation and oppression of tribals exists today as much as it existed then and that neither *sahukars* nor minor government officials have mended their ways to any great extent.

As a result of the interest shown by Grigson in the conditions in the tribal areas of Hyderabad State a number of ameliorative measures were taken which in a short time transformed the atmosphere, at least in Adilabad District, where as recently as 1940 ten Gonds had been killed in a bloody clash between tribals and policemen. A detailed account of this mini-rebellion will be given in chapter 2; here it suffices to say that the measures instituted by government soon changed the tribesmen's mood of gloom and despair to one of hope and confidence in the future.

A beginning was made in 1943 when a scheme for the training of Gond teachers and the establishment of special schools for Gonds (see chapter 6) indicated a new concern by government for the welfare of the tribesmen. This was followed by the appointment of a special officer for the tribal area of Adilabad and the allotment of land on permanent tenure (patta) to numerous aboriginals, both Gonds and Kolams, who until then had no legal titles to the land they and their forefathers had been cultivating, and who therefore had always been liable to eviction on various pretexts. These administrative measures were followed by the preparation of comprehensive legislation designed to afford protection to tribal populations. It was recognized that rights to land were of crucial importance. Only by placing aboriginals in a position in which they were safe in the possession of their land was it possible to free them once and for all from the threat of economic enslavement by moneylenders and landlords. Even before legislation recognized the aboriginals' prior rights to land, administrative measures and the instructions given to the officers entrusted with the task of looking after the tribals' welfare brought about a change in the whole attitude to the aboriginals. The extortion of illegal fees which minor government servants, such as forest guards or police constables, used to collect from the villagers was stopped or at least greatly reduced simply by the enforcement of stricter discipline, and, while it was clearly impracticable to eradicate all cases of corruption, a great improvement in the situation was soon noticeable. By 1946 the conditions of the Gonds in most parts of Adilabad District had changed out of all recognition, and a community which used to be seriously underprivileged became suddenly the "most favoured" ethnic group in the region.

In recognition of the need for the creation of a special agency for the implementation of the new policy vis-à-vis the tribals of the state, the Nizam's government established a new department known as the Social Service Department, attached to the Revenue Department and headed by the adviser for tribes and backward classes. This department consisted of a number of gazetted officers, as well as of social service inspectors and organizers, all of whom were posted in tribal areas. Existing special tribes officers, who were in the rank of deputy collector and had been drawn from the Revenue Department, were incorporated in the cadre of the Social Service Department, whereas the more junior posts of inspectors and organizers were filled by graduates with qualifications in social anthropology or sociology. After gaining experience in administration many of these directly recruited graduates were promoted to gazetted posts and ultimately replaced the special tribes officers drawn from the Revenue Department.

The culmination of the entire tribal policy of Hyderabad State was the promulgation of an act known as the Tribal Areas Regulation 1356 Fasli (1946 A.D.). This regulation empowered the government to "make such rules as appear to them to be necessary or expedient for the better administration of any notified tribal area in respect of tribals and of their relations with non-tribals." The substance of this regulation was incorporated in the Tribal Areas Regulation 1359 Fasli (1949 A.D) and the rules giving effect to its provisions were issued by the Revenue Department under the title Notified Tribal Areas Rules 1359 Fasli on 16 November 1949. A schedule annexed to the Tribal Areas Regulation notified as "tribal" 384 specified villages in Adilabad District plus all the 169 villages of Utnur Taluk, and 156 specified villages in Warangal District plus all the villages of Yellandu Taluk minus 3 named villages and all the villages of the Taluk and Samasthan of Paloncha minus 6 named villages. The schedule described the area to which the Notified Tribal Areas Rules were to apply.

These rules vested the administration of the Notified Tribal Area in the first *talukdar* (collector) as agent, in the special social service officer as assistant agent, and in a *panchayat* to be established by the agent.

From among the fifty-five rules applicable to the notified tribal area the following may be quoted as the most important:

RULE 4   The Agent shall be competent to appoint such person or persons as he considers desirable to be members of a Panchayat for such village or villages as he may specify and to entrust to such Panchayat any or all of the duties specified in these Rules.

RULE 5   No court of law or revenue authority shall have any jurisdiction in any Notified Tribal Area in any dispute relating to land, house or house-site occupied, claimed, rented or possessed by any tribal or from which any tribal may have been evicted whether by process of law or otherwise during a period of one year preceding the notification of such an area as a Notified Tribal Area.

RULE 6   All suits of proceedings relating to matters covered by rule 5 pending before any court of law or revenue authority on the date of the notification of such area as tribal area shall be transferred to the Agent concerned.

RULE 8   The Panchayat shall decide all cases in open Durbar in the presence of both the parties and at least three independent witnesses.

RULE 10   No legal practitioner shall be allowed to appear in any case before the Panchayat.

RULE 11   No legal practitioner shall appear in the court of the Agent or Assistant Agent except with the Agent's permission.

RULE 13   This rule provides that criminal justice in respect of certain offences in which a tribal is involved shall be administered by the Agent and the Assistant Agent. A number of offences and the relevant sections of the Hyderabad Penal Code are listed. [The list includes such offences as affray, assault, theft, house trespass, adultery, criminal intimidation, etc.]

RULE 16   The Agent may authorize a Panchayat constituted under rule 4 to try the following offences in which a tribal is involved as a party, and the Panchayat shall be competent to impose fines not exceeding Rs. 50, may also award payment in restitution or compensation to the extent of the injury sustained and enforce it by distraint of the property of the offender. [The appended list of offences contains most of the offences listed also under rule 13].

RULE 26   Civil justice in cases involving the rights of any tribal shall be administered by the Agent, the Assistant Agent and the Panchayat, if any authorised under these Rules, subject to the condition that the Agent shall be competent to exercise the powers of any court subordinate to the High Court.

RULE 27   The Panchayat constituted under rule 4 shall be competent to try all cases without limit as to amount in which both the parties are tribals and live within their jurisdiction.

RULE 29   All the proceedings shall be *viva voce* and the Panchayat shall not be called upon to make either record or registry of their decision. After hearing both parties, and their witnesses, if any they shall pronounce a decision forthwith.

RULE 32   Agent and Assistant Agent shall not ordinarily hear suits triable by the Panchayat but they shall have discretion to do so when they think right.

RULE 53   No land at present cultivated by a tribal or in respect of which he claims that he has a right to hold it, shall be sold in execution of any decree or order of any civil or revenue court whether made before or after the coming into force of the said Regulation.

RULE 55   The Agent shall be competent to recommend to Government the abolition of Patel and Patwari Watans in any notified tribal area and the appointment of tribal village officers in such area.

Anyone familiar with conditions in tribal areas will realize the great benefits conferred upon the tribes of Hyderabad State by these rules.

Instead of having to deal with a multitude of officials and depending on the judgements of distant courts whose proceedings were utterly unfamiliar and incomprehensible to them, the tribals were now in the care of officers of the Social Service Department who were sympathetic to their cause and vested with sufficient powers to prevent the alienation of tribal land as well as the exploitation of tribals by unscrupulous moneylenders and others.

The establishment of tribal *panchayat* backed by the authority of government gave the tribesmen confidence that they could run their own affairs without outside interference. Some of these *panchayat*, whose proceedings I was able to observe when revisiting Adilabad District in the early 1950s, worked extraordinarily well, and though the rules did not prescribe the keeping of records, cases and decisions were carefully recorded. In one village of Utnur Taluk, Mankapur, which had a powerful and greatly respected headman, such a *panchayat*, attended by members from several villages, was still functioning in 1980, even though the Tribal Areas Regulation which had invested it with authority had long been repealed.

The Gonds of Adilabad District still speak with nostalgia of the time when the Tribal Areas Regulation was in force and officers of the Social Service Department worked among them, for at that time they were secure in the possession of their land, and exploitation by outsiders had been greatly reduced. The presence of officers of the Social Service Department acted as a check even on the high-handedness of forest guards and *patwari*, who knew that corrupt practices and the extortion of illegal fees would be reported to their superiors.

Even after the partition of Hyderabad State in 1956 and the merging of the Telengana districts with the Andhra districts in the new State of Andrah Pradesh, the Hyderabad Tribal Areas Regulation of 1949 remained in force for seven more years. Unfortunately for the aboriginals of the Telengana districts, this regulation was repealed in 1963 and replaced by the Andhra Pradesh Scheduled Areas Land Transfer Regulation, 1959. While the latter regulation also protected the land of tribals, prohibiting any transfer to non-tribals, it did not contain any provision for the maintenance of tribal *panchayat*, and more importantly stripped the social service officers of the authority and judicial powers with which the Hyderabad regulation and rules had invested them.

The enforcement of the laws prohibiting the transfer of tribal land to non-tribals was now left to the ordinary revenue officials, who had neither the inclination nor the time to concern themselves with the welfare of the tribals. They were also much more exposed to the pressure of vested interest than the officers of the Social Service Department had been. Moreover, the authority of the civil courts, which the

Hyderabad Tribal Areas Regulation had set aside in all cases involving tribal land, was now fully restored, and any non-tribal whose occupation of tribal land was challenged by a revenue official could, and still can, lodge an appeal in a civil court. The immediate consequence of all these changes was the alienation of large areas of tribal land in several of the taluks of Adilabad District.

Some relief to the tribals threatened by non-tribal landgrabbers was subsequently provided by amendments of the Land Transfer Regulation, 1959, enacted in 1970 and 1971, which prohibit all transfer of land in scheduled areas, not only from tribal to non-tribal but even from non-tribal to non-tribal, by providing for conducting *suo moto* enquiries into non-tribal occupations of lands in tribal areas and for the restoration of such land to the tribal owner if the non-tribal is an illegal occupant, and by prohibiting attachment of tribal land in execution of money decrees. However, we shall see in chapter 2 that despite the absolute ban on transfer of immovable property in scheduled areas to non-tribals from a tribal or non-tribal except in the case of partition or devolution by succession, large areas of tribal land were in fact illegally occupied by non-tribals in the years 1970 to 1979.

Protection of the tribesmen against the alienation of their land, which in Hyderabad State was the cornerstone of tribal policy, seems to have taken second place in the thinking of planners as soon as tribal development was merged with the multisided activities of programmes known as Community Development and extending throughout India as part of the first Five Year Plan, which commenced in 1952. Community projects were not particularly geared to tribal needs, and in Andhra Pradesh only one out of four pilot projects covered tribal areas. In the second Five Year Plan there was a greater concentration on specific tribal areas, and the projects were now renamed Multipurpose Projects. In Andhra Pradesh four such projects covered predominantly tribal areas: one in Utnur Taluk of Adilabad District, one in Narsampet Taluk of Warangal District, and two in Vishakhapatnam District.

The effectiveness of these projects was assessed in the Government of India Report of the Committee on Special Multipurpose Tribal Blocks, 1960, in which Verrier Elwin played a leading role. This committee found that the programmes lacked a specific tribal bias, with the result that non-tribals residing within the project areas benefited from the funds expended more than the tribals. Officials in charge of the projects were more concerned about spending the allocated funds, often on inessential and elaborate buildings, than on meeting the urgent needs of the tribals. The committee recommended a change of priorities and emphasized that officials in charge of projects in tribal areas should not be transferred for a minimum of three years.

In the third Five Year Plan period, Multipurpose Projects were renamed Tribal Development Blocks, and twenty-four of these were located in Andhra Pradesh, covering most areas of tribal concentration. There was no major change in strategy during the fourth Five Year Plan, but it was during this period that in several tribal areas, notably that of Srikakulam District, the eruption of politically motivated violence reflected the shortcomings of the state's tribal policy. While these eruptions were undoubtedly sparked by a widespread revolutionary movement commonly known as Naxalite, their initial impact and support by large numbers of tribesmen showed very clearly the latter's resentment of the unrelenting pressure which advanced populations exerted on their resources.

The response of the government to the Naxalite-led tribal unrest was a repetition of official reaction to earlier rebellions. Ruthless suppression by police freely using automatic arms against tribesmen wielding bows and arrows and the occasional outdated gun was followed by remedial measures, long overdue but never implemented as long as the tribals were docile and law-abiding. Enactment of debt relief, restoration of tribal land, and various welfare measures such as nutritional aid for children were intended to placate the restive tribals.

With the commencement of the fifth Five Year Plan in 1977 an administrative setup known as the Integrated Tribal Development Agency was inaugurated. In this, high priority is being given to agricultural development, largely by provision of minor irrigation schemes. At the same time communications are to be improved and electricity brought even to backward areas. In order to provide employment for landless tribals, the establishment of minor industries is envisaged, and the Girijan Cooperative Corporation is supposed to provide improved marketing facilities for minor forest produce and to supply to tribals many of their basic needs. In pursuance of these aims Integrated Tribal Development Projects were prepared for specific areas of tribal concentration, or in some cases for individual tribal groups.

The successes and failures of the integrated approach will be discussed in the following chapters, but anticipating such an analysis it may be stated that many of the plans under the Integrated Tribal Development Agency are admirable on paper, but have suffered from grave deficiencies in their implementation.

The administrative machinery designed to carry out the various development schemes consists in each of the districts containing tribal blocks of a project officer and a tribal welfare officer, both of whom are usually posted at the district headquarters. There are no officers of the Tribal Welfare Department at taluk or block level, and the implementation of most of the development schemes falls thus to the block development officers and the village development officers, neither of whom have been trained in the treatment of specifically tribal problems. The attitude of many of them ranges therefore from conscientious but unimaginative application to outright lethargy. Many good schemes break down because of the disinterest of local officials, while, on the other hand, an active and dedicated project officer can inspire officials at block level to evince commitment and real efficiency. Yet frequent transfers among the officials at all levels have proved damaging to programmes however well funded and well-thought-out they may have been.

It is inherent in any plan for the protection and support of tribal minorities that whatever benefits are envisaged for tribesmen must adversely affect the interests of some more advanced sections of the population. Alienation of tribal land cannot be prevented without depriving non-tribal landowners of the chance to enlarge their holdings, a curb on exploitation by moneylenders interferes with the activities of local businessmen, and any attempt to eradicate corrupt practices of minor officials diminishes the income such persons are accustomed to derive from dealings with ignorant and illiterate tribals. Thus any policy of tribal rehabilitation arouses the opposition of vested interests. When the Nizam's government embarked on schemes for the betterment of tribals, there arose a good deal of resentment among members of the landlord and business community in districts such as Adilabad, and this resentment led to attacks on the policy in the press. But a system of benevolent autocracy could easily dismiss such attacks by vested interests, whereas nowadays similar vested interests can influence members of the Legislative Assembly and through them even ministers, with the result that measures designed to benefit tribal minorities tend to be watered down or abandoned altogether. In such situations officers sympathetic to tribals and assiduous in the protection of their interests are likely to be transferred and replaced by officers more pliable to the wishes of locally powerful pressure groups. It is therefore no exaggeration to say that only an administration of high integrity can successfully implement a policy of tribal development, and it would seem that the failure of many plans for tribal betterment is due to the lack of such integrity in high places and not to any inherent fault in the plans worked out by civil servants.

A few quotations from a report prepared in 1975 by D. Bandyopadhyaya, Joint Secretary, Ministry of Labour, Government of India, and B. N. Yugandhar, Special Assistant to the Deputy Chairman, Planning Commission, will indicate that government officials are fully aware of the reasons for the justified sense of grievance felt by so many tribal populations. The two civil servants visited the Parvathipuram Agency of Srikakulam District at a time when the activities of Naxalite rebels had passed their climax. After several meetings with groups of local tribes they wrote:

> The Girijans came in touch with the administration only in a state of confrontation when they were tackled for infringement or infraction of one or the other regulation which in fact abridged, annulled or tinkered with their customary rights and privileges. Thus the Girijans of the Parvathipuram agency tract found themselves totally alienated from the administrative machinery and newly set up self-governing institutions and were denied opportunities of gainful economic activities. They suffered not only from poverty but also from a deep sense of insecurity. They found themselves deprived at each point and at each front. A deep sense of grievance and injustice enveloped the entire tribal population through decades of neglect by the local administration. The indifference and the neglect was so much that when the agency tracts were redefined large areas of hill tracts inhabited by the tribal Girijans were left outside the agency through an administrative mistake.... Later attempts by some energetic district officials to bring them within the fold of the agency tracts have not met with any success.... The Girijan is suspicious of every move of the administration. He cannot rely on it. Today after the experience he had of [the Naxalite] movement and its consequences, he is slightly confounded but not cowed down. He has a sullen look and defiance is apparent.[2]

When I visited Srikakulam in 1979 the atmosphere had greatly changed. By the restoration of thousands of acres to their erstwhile tribal owners and the expenditure of large amounts of money on various welfare measures the government had gained the confidence of the majority of the tribals, while the former exploiters, intimidated by the violence of the Naxalite movement, had not dared to resume their domineering role. Thus the Naxalite rebels had in a way achieved their aim by stimulating the government to tackle the tribal problem and by breaking the power of those who used to exploit and oppress the tribals.

In other districts of Andhra Pradesh, where there has been no spontaneous uprising against the tyranny of landlords, moneylenders, and oppressive petty officials, the position of the tribal populations is far less happy. In the following chapters I shall trace the various stages in the decline of tribal freedom and prosperity in greater detail.

The contrast between the fortunes of the tribes of Andhra Pradesh and those of Arunachal Pradesh, to be discussed in detail in chapter 11, demonstrates incontestably that tribal populations can progress only if during the initial phases of any development programme they enjoy complete protection against exploitation by and competition from non-tribals. The total ban on any permanent settlement of mem-

2. Reprinted in *Social Life in Rural India*, ed. M. K. Pandhe, pp. 210–12.

bers of non-tribal communities in Arunachal Pradesh has enabled the local tribesmen to achieve truly miraculous progress, whereas in Andhra Pradesh the unholy alliance of vested interests, political pressure groups, and venal officials has frustrated most of the plans for tribal welfare despite the outlay of many millions in public funds.

2 The Fate of Tribal Land

WITH THE EXCEPTION of some small communities of hunters and foodgatherers, all tribal populations of Andhra Pradesh depend for their subsistence primarily on the cultivation of land. For centuries, if not millennia, they had free access to as much land as they could cultivate, and it was only at the beginning of the twentieth century that in some areas tribal communities encountered the competition of materially more advanced populations infiltrating into areas which had previously been the preserves of such tribes as Gonds, Kolams, Koyas, or Konda Reddis. Some of these tribes were slash-and-burn cultivators whose main implements were axe, hoe, and digging stick, while others had practised plough cultivation for countless generations and were living in permanent villages. The former, who tilled hill slopes cleared of forest growth, did not hold land attractive to other populations and were able to pursue their traditional method of tillage until the time when much of their ancestral territory was declared state forest, and newly introduced rules of forest conservancy limited the areas available for shifting cultivation. The fortunes of such primitive tribes depending on slash-and-burn cultivation will be discussed in a separate section at the end of this chapter; here I propose to deal with problems of land tenure as demonstrated by the Gonds, one of the major tribal groups of Andhra Pradesh.

THE HISTORY OF THE LAND PROBLEM IN ADILABAD

The main concentration of the Gonds is in Adilabad District, a region which until less than a hundred years ago was rich in forests, poor in   51

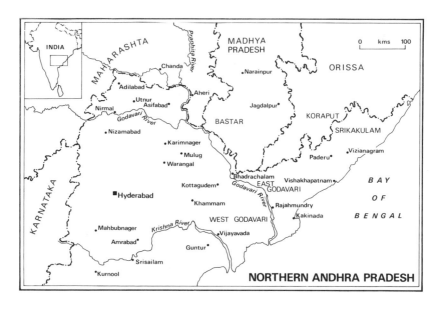

communications, and of little economic and political importance. There can be no doubt that the larger part of the district was then inhabited almost exclusively by aboriginals, among whom Kolams were probably the oldest population. But long before the rise of Muslim and later Maratha power, Gond chieftains, styled rajas, were established in the area. Several forts, such as the magnificently built Manikgarh Fort, suggest that Gond rajas lived in a style not inferior to that of Hindu rulers, and it would seem that even when the Gond chieftains had to acknowledge the sovereignty of the Nizam of Hyderabad a feudal system persisted among the majority of the Gonds of Adilabad District. They continued to be the principal holders and tillers of the land, and the administration established by the Nizam's government did not at first affect the condition of the tribal population. Small colonies of traders and craftsmen existed in market places such as Jangaon, later renamed Asifabad, but a major change in the tribals' position seems to have occurred only in the first years of the twentieth century with the improvement of communications between Mancherial and Rajura on the eastern side of the district and between Nirmal and Adilabad on the western side. Along these two lines non-tribal populations flooded into the district both from the south and from the north, and occupied such land as became easily accessible. The subsequent construction of a road linking Nirmal and Mancherial encouraged Telugu cultivators from the neighbouring district of Karimnagar to settle in the riverain tract and acquire land on the left bank of the Godavari, and at about the same time many Maratha peasants, mainly of Kunbi caste, moved from the adjoining districts of Berar across the Penganga River and occupied large parts of the northern plains.

To understand the process of the Gonds' gradual displacement by other and more dynamic populations, it is necessary to consider their system of cultivation as it existed before changes in the administrative system and the introduction of forest conservancy forced them to abandon their traditional agricultural methods. In the 1940s there were still old people alive who spoke of the time when the Gonds of the highlands mainly cultivated the light, red soils of the plateaux and slightly inclined slopes, but not the heavy, black soils in the bottom of the valleys. At that time Gond farmers were in the habit of shifting their fields every two or three years, abandoning each plot before the soil showed signs of exhaustion. It was mainly during the monsoon that they grew small millets and oilseeds in these light soils, where ploughing was easy and there was little danger of water-logging, while in the autumn and winter they cultivated only small plots growing sorghum and pulses in the vicinity of the villages. Yet, despite the restriction of the main agricultural activities to one season, the yield of crops grown during the rains on soils kept fertile by frequent periods of fallow seems to have equalled that of the combined monsoon and winter crops of later days. While in the hills the transition to modern conditions occurred so late that there still exist eyewitness accounts of the old economy, less certain information is available for the plains tract. But it is likely that there too Gonds cultivated their land in rotation, preferring the light soils to the heavy black soils and relying mainly on the crops grown during the rains.

The Gonds' practice of frequently shifting their fields and sometimes also their settlements was appropriate to a situation in which they were virtually the only inhabitants of large expanses of cultivable land and forest, and there were no other claimants to land temporarily abandoned by Gond cultivators. But as soon as agricultural populations from neighbouring areas moved into Adilabad District, the Gonds' habit of cultivating their land in rotation became a source of weakness, for fields left fallow with the intention of resuming cultivation after a number of years could easily be occupied by new settlers, who then managed to obtain title deeds for the occupied land. At the turn of the century, it was government policy to open up the district and to encourage the influx of new settlers, and to grant them *patta* free of charge for as much land as they could make arable. At first, no doubt, the Gonds too had the possibility of obtaining individual *patta*, and some Gonds were actually given *patta* documents, but the whole concept of having permanent rights to individual plots was foreign to the tribesmen, and they were slow to realize the necessity of obtaining title deeds to land which they had always considered communal property. Later, when pressure on land became acute and they did realize the value of *patta*, they were not sufficiently well versed in dealing with revenue officials to compete successfully with newcomers from more progressive areas. Consequently, they frequently failed to obtain recognition of their claims to the land which they and their forefathers had cultivated.

With the gradual improvement of communications and the influx of experienced cultivators such as Kunbis and Kapus the country became valuable and attractive to investors, and Brahmins, Komtis, and Muslims living in places such as Adilabad, Asifabad, and Nirmal began acquiring villages to be managed on a commercial basis. As few Gonds had *patta* rights this was not difficult, and absentee landlords could obtain whole villages by applying for the auctioning of government land and outbidding any tribal who tried to retain his land. In many cases the tribal cultivators were not even informed of the auctioning of the land they were tilling, and became aware of the change of ownership only when the new landlord demanded to be paid rent.

By 1940 most of the villages near such administrative or commercial centres as Asifabad had already fallen into the hands of non-tribals. Thus of the twenty villages within a distance of approximately three miles from Asifabad twelve no longer contained any tribals, five had a partly tribal population but were owned by non-tribal landlords, and there were only two villages in which Gonds and one in which Kolams cultivated government land, but in these villages, too, other land was held by non-tribals.

Similar conditions prevailed in the valleys running westwards and southwards from Asifabad. In the southern part of Asifabad Taluk, particularly in the Tilani area, a great deal of land was acquired by landowners of Velma caste who lived in the neighbourhood of Lakshetipet and in the neighbouring district of Karimnagar. The way in which these Velma gradually eliminated the indigenous tribesmen is illustrated by the following story, which Kotnaka Maru of Dugapur told me in 1941:

> I was born in Dugapur and cultivated there until some ten years ago, when there were so many tigers in the neighbourhood that all of us went to live in another village. When five years later the tigers disappeared, we returned to Dugapur, where the land had lain fallow in our absence and applied to the *tahsildar* for permission to clear again forty acres. When I and my brothers had felled all the small growth on these forty acres, the revenue inspector came and said that we could only cultivate eighteen acres and that the rest would be cultivated by

the Velma Dora of Mandamari. This Velma Dora acquired some land in Gamairapet only ten years ago and there he keeps a bailiff, but before we had cleared the land in Dugapur he never raised a claim on it. The revenue inspector assigned eighteen acres to me and for four years I cultivated these eighteen acres but last year the Velma Dora took three acres of my land. This year I had already sown maize and millet on the remaining fields when the Velma's bailiff brought twenty men with ploughs from Gamaraipet and ploughed up three acres of my sown fields. I have given many applications to the *tahsildar* but because the Velma Dora is so rich and powerful no official will help me.

Soon after Kotnaka Maru had told me this story, he became the victim of another outrage. He was watching his millet crop when the Velma's bailiff brought twenty-five men of Gamaraipet all armed with sticks, and they reaped Maru's crop in front of the owner's eyes and carried the grain away. Maru reported the matter to the police *patel*, who came to Dugapur and saw the reaped field, but advised Maru to keep quiet lest the Velma Dora drive him out of the village.

The plight of Kotnaka Maru was only one of the innumerable cases of oppression, the accounts of which filled my note-books of the years 1941–43. It would be pleasant to record that such blatant violations of tribal rights could no longer occur, but as we shall see presently, almost identical cases of the exercise of brutal force in the dispossession of Gonds were told to me when I visited the area in the years 1977–80.

In the 1940s the weakness of the Gonds' position was mainly due to the fact that few of them possessed title deeds (*patta*) to the land they were occupying. The majority of the tribals then cultivated according to a system of land tenure known as *siwa-i-jamabandi*. The land they tilled remained government land, and although they had permission to cultivate and annually paid the land revenue they were not registered as owners (*pattadar*) in the village register. The allotment of land on *siwa-i-jamabandi* tenure was within the powers of the *tahsildar*, who normally endorsed the actions of *patwari* and revenue inspector without investigating the rights and wrongs of individual cases. The transfer of government land from one cultivator to the other was then the order of the day, and every year many tribals were evicted from land which they had been cultivating on *siwa-i-jamabandi* tenure, only because an affluent non-tribal, able to bribe the revenue subordinates, had cast his eye on the same land and had been given preference over the tribal cultivator.

The system of *siwa-i-jamabandi* tenure, which by definition allowed a great deal of flexibility, provided the lower revenue staff with incomparable opportunities for enriching themselves by the shuffling of land from one cultivator to another, and even when government began allotting *patta* to Gonds and Kolams, large areas of land continued to be cultivated on *siwa-i-jamabandi* tenure. Figures quoted in my report *Progress and Problems of Aboriginal Rehabilitation in Adilabad District* (Hyderabad, 1946, p. 14) show that at that time the total of *siwa-i-jamabandi* land was 43,729 acres, of which 21,354 acres were occupied by tribals and 22,205 by non-tribal cultivators. Many of the non-tribal *pattadar* held, in addition to their own land, a substantial acreage on *siwi-i-jamabandi*. Thus in Utnur Taluk there were altogether 893 non-tribal *pattadar*, and they held on *patta* a total area of 27,869 acres and cultivated in addition 3,289 acres on *siwa-i-jamabandi*. Moreover, there were 698 non-tribals who owned no *patta* land but held 7,755 acres on *siwa-i-jamabandi* tenure.

In 1944 the Nizam's government was faced with two alternatives. It could follow a policy of laissez-faire and allow the deterioration in the tribals' status to continue, with the result that within a few decades the majority of Gonds would have become a floating population of landless agricultural labourers and sub-tenants devoid of any occupancy rights, or it could settle the tribesmen as a stable peasant community, secure in the possession of the land they tilled. The government decided on the second alternative and embarked on a bold policy of tribal rehabilitation. This involved above all a solution of the land problem by the grant of *patta* to as many of the tribals as could be accommodated on land under the control of government.

It was then calculated that at the most 10 percent of all tribal household heads were already *pattadar* and that hence a total of about ninety thousand would have to be covered by the operation of resettlement. As in some areas, such as the taluks of Both and Kinwat, little land was available for allocation to tribals, a transfer of substantial populations from the plains to the highlands and from the non-tribal area to the newly notified tribal area became inevitable. The task before the district officers and above all the special tribes officer was all the more daunting, as many of the would-be beneficiaries of the new policy were too ignorant and inexperienced or too much under the sway of landlords and moneylenders to grasp the implication of the new regulations for the grant of *patta* and to apply for land in the manner prescribed by the rules. Hence a systematic settlement of each group of villages had to replace the usual procedure according to which the revenue officers act only on individual applications for specific pieces of land. A particular problem was created by the lack of a detailed survey of land in many of the less-developed regions, and the grant of *patta* on land not clearly demarcated created difficulties in later years and gave a handle to non-tribal landlords trying to encroach on the tribals' newly assigned land. Some opposition to the tribal rehabilitation policy came as no surprise to those who knew what profits absentee landlords and moneylenders had derived from the exploitation of the uneducated and helpless tribals. There was resentment among the members of the landlord class because, since the notification of the tribal area and the suspension of all ordinary land allotment in that area, land made arable by Gonds or Kolams and cultivated by them on *siwa-i-jamabandi* tenure could no longer be acquired simply by applying for its auction and by then bidding against no other competition than that of inpecunious tribals. Obstacles were put in the way, not so much of the allotment of land to tribals, but of the occupation of the land by the new *pattadar*. In many cases, non-tribal landowners and *patel* tried to prevent Gonds by threats and even by physical violence from occupying the lands allotted to them by the special tribes officer. The village officers, the lower revenue staff, and the minor police were often in sympathy with locally important landowners, and the tribals could not count on their whole-hearted support. Indeed revenue inspectors and *patwari* often took unduly long in demarcating the new holdings and handing them over to the new tribal *pattadar*, and thereby gave the non-tribal landowners time to put forward claims to the lands in question. We shall see that precisely the same type of opposition was impeding the restoration of tribal land in 1977 and 1978.

Despite all such obstacles the allocation of land to the tribals of Adilabad which began in 1944 made good progress. By 1945 a total of 45,417 acres of land had been granted to 3,144 tribals, and by 1949 the amount of land assigned on *patta* to tribals had risen to 160,000 acres and the number of beneficiaries to 11,198. The work continued until about 85 percent of the tribal householders of Adilabad District were in possession of adequate holdings of cultivable land.

At that time sympathetic observers seemed justified in assuming that the economic basis of the tribal populations of Adilabad was reasonably secure, and even in 1960, when I revisited the district, there appeared to be no serious erosion of the Gonds' hold on their land. We shall see, however, that any optimism one might then have expressed was premature and that the gains achieved in the 1940s were largely lost in the 1970s.

RECENT DEVELOPMENTS IN ADILABAD

In a note submitted to the Government of Andhra Pradesh in 1960 at the end of a visit to Adilabad, I commented on the situation of the Gonds as follows: "There appears to be at present no acute land-problem, and as far as I could see there has been no serious encroachment on the tribals' land. The position will have to be watched, however, when the road-link Utnur-Kerimeri-Asifabad is completed, for the most isolated part of the highlands will then become more easily accessible to outsiders."

The last sentence of this comment proved prophetic, for since this motorable road was constructed a great wave of non-tribal immigrants has swept over the highlands, and many of the Gonds and Kolams who had been settled and provided with *patta* in the 1940s were once again deprived of their land. When in 1976 I began an intensive re-study of the Gonds of Utnur, I found a scene completely transformed by the presence of innumerable settlers, most of them emigrants from Maharashtra. There were Marathas, Hatkars, Mahars, members of various merchant castes, and many Muslims, mainly from the districts of Nander, Osmanabad, and Parbhani, as well as newly arrived Banjaras from Berar. It is not quite clear what triggered this invasion, but local Gonds as well as officials tell of the long columns of bullock carts on which the immigrants carried household goods and grain stores, and of the herds of cattle which they brought with them. It seems that this movement of non-tribals into the tribal area of Utnur reached its climax between 1965 and 1975, but even at the time of writing, i.e. 1980, it has not completely stopped. It coincided with widespread illegal fellings of forest, which resulted in the almost complete deforestation of most of the land along the road between Gudi Hatnur and Utnur.

It seems that a few senior district officers made some feeble attempts to stop the flow of immigrants, but on the whole neither revenue nor forest officers succeeded in stemming the tide. As many of the newcomers were able to occupy cultivable land, there can be no doubt that the minor revenue officials, and particular *patwari* and revenue inspectors, were won over by the immigrants, many of whom were wealthy enough to pay large bribes. The laws prohibiting the acquisition of tribal land by non-tribals were obviously ignored. Otherwise it would have been impossible for recent immigrants with no claim to tribal status to acquire house sites and arable land at the expense of Gonds who lost all or most of their land within a span of a few years. The methods used to achieve this aim were similar to those which forty years earlier were used to dispossess the tribals of the lowlands. Apart from outright trickery and the bribing of *patwari* and members of the revenue staff fraudulently to change entries in the land register, the newcomers deliberately led Gonds into debt, then induced them to lease their land for limited periods, and finally refused to return the leased land to the owner. With the connivance of *patwari* and revenue inspectors, it was then not difficult to enter the new occupier's name as "owner" in the village and *tahsil* records.

The results of this process of large-scale land alienation are obvious to anyone familiar with the area. Villages on or near the motorable roads, which in the 1940s and 1950s had still a purely tribal population and consisted of the usual thatched huts, are now teeming with new-comers, whose shops and large masonry houses, often painted in garish colours, have completely transformed the scene. Many of these villages no longer contain any Gonds, whereas in others small clusters of Gond houses in traditional style form incongruous accretions to the modern settlements. Thus Indraveli, once the seat of a Gond raja, has grown into a large commercial centre with brick houses and cement structures lining both sides of the road. Jainur, which in 1946 was a small Gond hamlet surrounded by forest, now contains a market cen-tre with many shops and masonry houses, all owned by non-tribals who settled there less than ten years ago.

Visual impressions of the process of ethnic and cultural change are supported by demographic figures. While in 1951 the population of Utnur Taluk was only 34,404, the majority of whom were tribals, by 1961 it had risen to 55,099 and by 1971, to 93,823. No official census figures are available for later years, but according to a malaria survey of 1977 the population of the taluk had then reached a total of 112,000. This phenomenal increase is clearly due to immigration, and all the newcomers are non-tribals. The change in the composition of the pop-ulation is reflected in the figures for tribals in individual circles. Thus in the Marlavai Circle, which in 1941 was almost totally tribal, the percentage of tribals in 1961 was still 90.38 percent, but by 1971 it had dropped to 65.52 percent, a figure which undoubtedly has diminished since then.

A similar, though perhaps less rapid, displacement of tribals by re-cent immigrants occurred in Asifabad Taluk, as described by Michael Yorke in chapter 9. There too the mechanism of land alienation fol-lowed the pattern observed in the 1930s and 1940s.

Neither in Utnur nor in Asifabad Taluk are figures for the tribal land alienated in recent years available, but the population figures for Utnur alone speak in very clear terms. To enliven these figures and illustrate the process of the exploitation and dispossession of tribals by members of advanced communities, I propose to quote from entries in my notebooks written in 1976, 1977, and 1978, when numerous Gonds approached me with stories of oppression by non-tribals and minor government officials.

On 7 December 1976, Kumra Boju of Kerimeri came to see me in Kanchanpalli and told me the following story:

My father Somu owned fifteen acres of *patta* land, but for the last thir-teen years Rama Gauru of Asifabad [a man of toddy-tapping caste] has been cultivating this land. When my father died I was a small child, and Rama Gauru occupied our land. Some time ago I applied to M.

Narayan, the special deputy collector, for restoration of my father's land. The deputy collector decided the case in my favour and restored the land to me. I was very happy and ploughed the land in preparation for sowing *jawari*. But when I was ready to sow Rama Gauru, supported by some villagers of Keslaguda, stopped me cultivating. Then the *tahsildar*, the revenue inspector, and the *patel* came to the village, and told me that my father's land was mine by right. But at the same time they advised me not to cultivate that land, but to occupy instead the adjoining field which belongs to a Muslim. How could I do this? Then Rama Gauru brought some men and sowed on my land. Moreover Rama Gauru had reported to the police that I had illegally ploughed his land. So the subinspector of police came to my house with some constables and wanted to arrest me. But in the end they did not take me to Asifabad. Rama Gauru has occupied also the *patta* land of three other Gonds, who are my mother's brothers. They all died but they have sons who have a claim to their land. Now none of us has any land of our own because Rama Gauru has all of it taken away.

This story, which recalls the days of the worst oppression of tribals in the early 1940s, is typical of the way in which corrupt minor officials frustrate the intention of government and fail to carry out the clear decisions of superior officers. It also demonstrates the partiality of the local police officers, who almost invariably side with locally powerful non-tribals.

The latter point is highlighted even more clearly by a case which I recorded a few days later. On 14 December 1976, Purka Maru of Ballanpur in Asifabad Taluk told me the following story:

I own eighteen acres of *patta* land in Sautiguda, which is a hamlet of Ballanpur. Three years ago a Muslim of Asifabad, Mohammed Isuf, drove me from my land. He repeatedly assaulted me and used to come at night to my house. I complained to the subcollector, and after some time the *tahsildar* and the revenue inspector came to Sautiguda. They did not give me back my land, but told me to cultivate a piece of land which was then cultivated by Kotnaka Somu. My own land they gave to Mohammed Isuf. For the next year I cultivated Somu's land and reaped some crops. I stored the grain in bags in my house. Then Mohammed Isuf with four other Muslims armed with axes and knives broke into my house at night. I managed to escape and hid in the jungle. When I returned next day I found that the Muslims had robbed me of my grain and all my valuables. They took 2½ quintals of *jawari*, 1 quintal of castor and all other stores, and stole also 1 tola of gold, 60 tolas of silver, and several brass pots.

Next day I complained to the subcollector and the subinspector of police in Asifabad. The subinspector then came to Sautiguda, went to a Muslim's house and made inquiries. After several hours he came to my house, blamed me for wrongly accusing Mohammed Isuf, and beat me. He then said that he would not allow me to stay any longer in Sautiguda.

Purka Maru had to leave his house and the place where he and his forefathers had lived and go to the main village of Ballanpur. There he found work as an agricultural labourer. Mohammed Isuf remained in occupation of his land, and Kotnaka Somu's land was not cultivated at all. M. Isuf had one house in Asifabad and another in Sautiguda. He owned twenty-one acres of *patta* land and cultivated eight acres of *parampok* land, as well as Maru's eighteen acres. He also occupied ten acres of *patta* land belonging to Kodapa Maru, whom he had frightened away and who had gone to live in Madura. He had also usurped nine acres of Dhurwa Moti Bai's *patta* land.

This, as well as the case of Kumra Boju, shows how by threats, bullying, and the unashamed use of force non-tribals are able to occupy tribal land, and that the tribals cannot rely on getting redress from the officers of government, many of whom, instead of upholding the law, make common cause with the exploiters of the tribals.

However, physical force is not always needed to dislodge a tribal from his land. In many cases non-tribal creditors take over a tribal's land and never return it to the owner, or the accidental loss of a tribal's *patta* documents is used to gain possession of his land. The following case is typical of many such tricks:

> In 1945 Soyam Sone Rao of Hasnapur in Utnur Taluk, a village swamped by non-tribals, had been given fifteen acres of land under the scheme for land assignment to Gonds. In 1951 his house burned down, and all his papers were destroyed. For many years he did not worry about this loss, but fifteen years after the fire an Inkhar immigrant from Maharashtra, who had been living for some time in the village, induced the *patwari*, a man of goldsmith caste, to connive at his occupation of Sone Rao's land. When Sone Rao complained to the *tahsildar*, the revenue inspector came to the village and told Sone Rao that he would be alloted five acres of land somewhere else, but Sone Rao did not agree to accept five acres instead of the fifteen acres to which he was entitled. In the meantime he maintained himself by working as a daily labourer.

The land of Gonds is also in jeopardy if a *pattadar* dies leaving a widow and young children. This is demonstrated by the following example:

> Maravi Ganpat, a Gond of Pochamlodi in Utnur Taluk, owned twenty acres of *patta* land. When he died the *patwari*, Abdul Rahim of Jainur, who had come to the locality only eight years previously, attached all the land on the plea that at the time of his death Ganpat had owed him Rs 3,500. Ever since, Abdul Rahim has cultivated the land and

Ganpat's widow and children cannot regain possession of it, for Abdul Rahim is a rich man and his position as *patwari* enabled him to manipulate the land register.

In Utnur Taluk a great deal of Gond land has passed into the hands of Banjaras, an immigrant community who had moved into Adilabad District from Berar only at the turn of the century. Well organized, aggressive, and often affluent, they succeeded in dislodging many Gonds from their holdings. A recent case, in which even the intervention of the special deputy collector (tribal welfare) had no lasting effect, demonstrates the methods by which Banjaras acquired much of their land:

Ara Lachu of Balanpur in Utnur Taluk owned fifteen acres of land. In repayment of a loan this was given to a Banjara on lease for three years. But when the lease expired the Banjara refused to give up the land. In 1973 the special deputy collector restored the land to Ara Lachu, but when Lachu and his brother started sowing on the land they had just ploughed, fifteen Banjaras armed with sticks and whips beat them and prevented them from sowing. Then the Banjaras cultivated the land. In 1976 Ara Lachu again applied to the special deputy collector, and in June of that year the latter restored the land to the Gond and told him that he might start ploughing. When he did so the Banjaras came and beat Lachu so severely that he had to be taken to the hospital. In the meantime, the Banjaras sowed cotton on the field. Subsequently the *tahsildar* came to the village and directed the revenue inspector to give possession of the land to Lachu with the standing crops.

When the cotton was ripe for picking, the Banjaras came and started picking the cotton. The Gond owner and his two sons protested, and there was a quarrel. In the course of this, thirty Banjaras set upon the three Gonds and broke Aru Lachu's arm. Lachu was admitted to hospital in Adilabad.

The next time I heard about the case, the Gond owner had not been able to regain effective possession of his land.

In the 1970s there were innumerable cases of illegal occupation of Gond land by Banjaras, but at that time there was at least the theoretical possibility of restoring the land to the Gond owners because the Banjaras were not notified as a scheduled tribe. In 1977, however, the Banjaras were included in the list of scheduled tribes (see chapter 8), and ever since then there has been no legal bar to the transfer of land from Gonds to Banjaras, for such transactions are permitted between tribals.

The foregoing examples of the alienation of Gond land are only a small selection of the innumerable cases which I recorded in 1976 and 1977. They show that the stabilization of the Gonds' position brought about by the efforts undertaken in the years 1944 to 1949 has been largely undone. Indeed it seems that, notwithstanding the existence of legislation apparently adequate for the protection of tribal interests, the position of the Gonds is as precarious and insecure as it was in the 1930s and early 1940s. There is, however, one important difference. In those years there was still some vacant land in the forested highlands where Gonds evicted from their holdings could find at least temporary refuge. This possibility no longer exists, and many Gonds are once more threatened by the likelihood of being reduced to the state of landless labourers.

It would be unfair to the officers charged with the protection and restoration of tribal land to give the impression that nothing was done to counteract the powerful forces engaged in the ongoing process of the illegal alienation of tribal land. The records of these officers reflect the magnitude of the problem and allow us to assess the progress made so far.

The following statistics compiled by the special deputy collector (tribal welfare) in December 1979 relate to the acreage of originally tribal land occupied by non-tribals, the number of cases registered for restoration procedures, and the decisions reached.

From the beginning of the scheme of restoring alienated tribal land to the original tribal owners in 1976 until the end of November 1979, 3,985 cases involving an acreage of 31,943.15 acres were booked. Of these, 2,296 cases involving 19,386.15 acres were decided, including those rejected because of the inapplicability of the Land Transfer Regulation. Of the total cases, 1,642, involving 13,639.5 acres, were decided in favour of the tribals. These include causes in which an appeal by the non-tribal parties resulted in a stay-order issued by a higher authority, and such stay-orders covered a total of 1,270.3 acres.

The cultivators evicted from tribal land illegally acquired can be divided into three categories:

Scheduled castes: 108 persons evicted from 1,075.8 acres.
Backward castes: 1,273 persons evicted from 10,339.7 acres.
Forward classes: 261 persons evicted from 2,224 acres.

The scheduled castes concerned include Mahar, Mala, and other Harijans; the backward castes include such Sudra castes as Kapu, Perka, Golla, Gaur, and Besta; and the forward classes include Brahmin, Komti, Reddi, Velma, and Muslim.

In October 1980 there was a balance of 1,536 undecided cases involving an area of 11,051.38 acres, and it stands to reason that, even with the help of a modest staff of assistants, a single special deputy collector would not be able to dispose within a reasonable time of so many hundreds of cases, investigate the circumstances of the alienation, and follow up his verdicts to restore possession to individual tribals. This assessment of the situation is confirmed by the fact that, despite strenuous efforts by the special deputy collector in the first nine months of 1980, only 54 cases involving 454 acres could be decided in favour of tribals. It is obvious that the administration would have to adopt more effective measures to redress the loss of tribal land, and it is regrettably not at all likely that this will happen in the foreseeable future.

Indeed, there are ominous portents that mounting pressure by vested interests and political groups is eroding the government's determination to implement the legislation designed to protect tribal rights to land. Thus, in August 1979 the Revenue Secretariat issued instructions to district officers that further evictions of non-tribals from tribal land should be carried out only in cases relating to encroachments by persons owning more than five acres of irrigated land or ten acres of dry land. By the end of 1980 these instructions, which legal experts regard as conflicting with existing legislation, were still operative, and this leads one inevitably to the conclusion that the policy of restoring alienated tribal land no longer enjoys the support of the Government of Andhra Pradesh, even though protective legislation has so far remained on the statute book.

WARANGAL DISTRICT

The land problem of the Koyas in the region now included within the Warangal District shares many aspects with the situation of the Gonds of Adilabad. In both areas there were until half a century ago large stretches of country where tribal populations were the only inhabitants. Whereas in some parts of Adilabad the hilly character of the terrain contributed to tribals' isolation from advanced Hindu populations, in the taluks of Mulug and Narsampet of Warangal District, dense forests constituted the tribesmen's main defense against the infiltration of land-hungry outsiders. No doubt, there too were at one time centres of Hindu civilization, and the exquisite carvings in the thirteenth-century Kakatiya temple of Palampet and the existence of such irrigation works as the Ramappa Lake, also stemming from Kakatiya times, show beyond doubt that in these great forests there were enclaves inhabited by people of sophisticated culture. But as the Kakatiya dynasty, which ruled for two hundred years from the middle of the twelfth century onwards, relinquished its hold on the region, tribal populations most probably akin to the present Koyas asserted themselves, and there is every likelihood that for several centuries the eastern part of the present Warangal District remained tribal territory similar in character to the adjoining tribal areas on the left bank of the

Godavari and in the highlands of Bastar. The fact that after the capture of Golconda by Aurangzeb Warangal came under Mughal rule had as little effect on the Koyas of the forest areas as the Mughal conquest had on the Gonds of the Adilabad highlands. After 1724, Warangal was part of the Nizam's Dominions, but it seems that only in the last fifty years of Hyderabad rule were there any serious attempts to open up and develop the forest tracts of Mulug and Narsampet Taluks. By 1940, when I first visited the areas, motorable roads led only as far as the western fringe of the tribal area, and the majority of Koya villages could be reached only on foot or by bullock cart.

The acquisition of tribal lands by immigrant Hindu and Muslim cultivators from other parts of the district had then already begun, and the Koyas and Naikpods of the villages near Palampet no longer owned any land, though they were engaged in the cultivation of irrigated land belonging to non-tribal landlords, many of whom were of Reddi caste.

The same measures of tribal rehabilitation which had proved effective in Adilabad were resorted to in the tribal areas of Warangal, and between 1946 and 1950 special social service officers allocated thousands of acres on *patta* to Koyas and Naikpods. But the beneficial effects of this policy initiated in the last years of the Nizam's rule were of even shorter duration than in Adilabad District. When I visited the area in 1960, I found that in the taluks of Mulug and Narsampet tribal land was once again under attack by non-tribal settlers. Immigrants from Guntur and other Andhra districts, many of whom were of Kamma caste, had infiltrated into tribal country. Even then many Gunturis had settled in such roadside villages as Chelvai and Pasra. They had begun by buying up quite legitimately the land belonging to local non-tribals, but once established they ousted their Koya neighbours by various more or less devious means. Though the Koya owners' names were still entered in the *patwari* and *tahsil* records, non-tribals were firmly in occupation of the land. Koyas had little chance of ever regaining it, and many of them worked as labourers for the Gunturi settlers who had usurped their land.

By the time I returned to Mulug Taluk in 1978, the process of land alienation had progressed even further. Chelvai, which in 1940 had been a purely tribal settlement of twenty houses of Koyas, was now a large village with a mixed population. There were many masonry buildings of non-tribals, shops, a brand new Hindu temple, and even a cinema. Only fifteen out of fifty-two Koya families possessed land of their own. Many had been allotted land in the 1940s but were induced, presumably because of indebtedness, to sell that land, though such transactions were illegal, as Chelvai is scheduled as a tribal village. Some cases falling under the Land Transfer Act had been booked, and in three cases orders for the restoration of the land to the tribal owners were issued, but the illegal occupiers obtained stay-orders from the high court and remained in possession.

Where there had been forest a large expanse of land was irrigated from the Laknavaram Lake, and all this wet land is now in the hands of non-tribal new settlers. In the nearby village of Pasra, now also on the motor road linking Mulug with Eturnagaram on the banks of the Godavari River, the situation is similar, and new settlers have occupied most of the cultivable land.

Koya villages at some distance from the motor road have fared better. Thus in Kamaram, a village of fifty-two Koya and four toddy-tapper houses, all the Koyas, with the exception of two newcomers, still held their land, and the Koya *patwari* had even succeeded in acquiring a holding of 30 acres. Some disputes over land between Koyas and non-tribal toddy-tappers were in 1978 still unresolved. Of 350 acres of land in the possession of Koyas, 150 acres were irrigated, 100 acres were used for the cultivation of rain-fed rice, and the rest were under such dry crops as maize and sorghum.

A complete contrast to this situation was provided by the village of Chinnaboyenapalli, a few miles further on the motor road to Eturnagaram. Not long ago this village was a small, purely tribal settlement, but in 1978 I found twenty Koya families outnumbered by eighty non-tribals, most of whom had within the past ten years immigrated from Nalgonda District. They had sold the land they had owned there and with the money obtained land from Koyas of Chinnaboyenapalli for Rs 200–300 per acre, whereas by 1978 the market value of land in the area had risen to Rs 3,000–5,000. Only six of the twenty Koya families had retained all their land. Of the remaining fourteen families, three had sold all their land, six had sold between four-fifths and two-thirds of their land, and five had sold between one-fifth and one-half of their land. The reasons they gave for this depletion of their capital varied from the need to repay loans obtained for such enterprises as the digging of a well to the expenses of a wedding or a funeral, or to the need to meet household expenditures. Inability to cope with the hazards arising from the change-over from a subsistence agriculture to a cash economy seems to be the underlying cause in all these cases of land alienation. The local officers were unable to enforce the law prohibiting the transfer of tribal land because the new settlers had political support and threatened to use force in resisting the implementation of restoration orders.

In two neighbouring villages, Shivapur and Gogpalli, similar conditions prevail, though there the Koyas have retained relatively more of their land, and some decrees for the restoration of tribal land have been carried out. Koyas and non-tribal settlers live there side by side, and settlers not only employ Koyas as agricultural labourers, but occasionally themselves work for wages on the land of Koyas. Such a situation makes the implementation of land-transfer laws particularly difficult, for politicians favouring the new settlers argue that both communities are of similar economic status, and Koyas should not be given preferential treatment.

In the riverain tract north and south of Eturnagaram, there has been heavy infiltration of settlers from other districts, and the same process can be observed on both banks of the Godavari in Khammam District. As the Godavari is navigable during part of the year, it acted like a road in facilitating the influx of newcomers into the tribal area. Experience has shown that legislation alone is not enough to safeguard the rights of the local tribal population and to stem the advance of settlers backed by influential politicians. Only continuing practical support for tribal communities can give them the strength to resist the pressure of affluent newcomers intent on acquiring tribal land. A few miles upstream from Eturnagaram lies Buttaram, a Koya village which the officers of the Integrated Tribal Development Agency (ITDA) have selected as an object for development work. There the agency has established a "colony" by constructing twenty-eight solidly built living quarters and in addition has provided agricultural advice and improved seeds, as well as distributing on a basis of 50 percent subsidy twenty-five milch buffaloes. The constant attention of officers of the Tribal Welfare Department protected the village against encroachment by non-tribal settlers. In 1978 there were thirty-two Koya families owning on an average two acres of irrigated and one acre of dry land. Though the yield of their fields did not satisfy all their food needs, they could make ends meet by collecting and selling minor forest produce and working occasionally for contractors or landlords in neighbouring villages. The cement houses constructed by the government did not so much improve housing standards as act as a visible sign of official interest in the village and also as a warning to potential land-grabbers. As a matter of fact few Koyas actually lived in the modern houses. Most families built next to the "colony" house a dwelling in traditional Koya style, and used the cement building as a store house for grain and other agricultural produce.

A few minutes' drive brings one from Buttaram to the large village of Rohir, and there the results of a lack of official protection become apparent. Rohir is not a scheduled tribal village, and 35 Koya and 25 Naikpod families are entirely overshadowed by 185 immigrant families belonging to non-tribal communities. Most of the land belongs now to caste Hindus and Harijans, and the Koyas are either entirely landless or own an average of about two acres. Twelve Koya families had cleared the forest on government land and started cultivation, but in 1967 the same land was assigned to non-tribal landlords resident in Eturnagaram, and these landlords then sold some of this land to Harijan families of the village. This is a common process we have observed also in Adilabad: tribals undertake the heavy work of making wooded land arable, only to be evicted when the covetous eyes of non-tribals are cast on their land and venal officials fall in with the plan to dispossess the tribals.

While in the 1940s there were many purely tribal villages tucked away in the interior of the forests of Warangal, by 1978 one had to go a long way over rough cart tracks to reach any village where Koyas still lived undisturbed by the claims of aggressive outsiders. The streams which throughout the monsoon impede access to such settlements are the last bulwark against the infiltrations of prospective settlers, and every bridge or causeway constructed on such forest tracks constitutes a breach in the natural defenses of the tribals' traditional habitat.

In November 1978, I visited three villages where one could still savour the tranquil atmosphere of a traditional Koya settlement. One of these was Korsela, which I had last seen in 1940. At that time the village consisted of fifteen Koya houses and one household of Madigas, but by 1978 the number of Koya houses had increased to forty-two, not only owing to natural growth but also because some families from less favoured villages had joined their kinsmen in Korsela. A tank recently constructed by the Integrated Tribal Development Agency at a cost of Rs 535,600 provided irrigation for 100 acres and could irrigate 200 acres if the Forest Department would agree to release 100 acres from the Reserved Forest. The houses stood in small clusters in between vegetable plots and rice fields, and a few *mahua* trees were scattered over the cultivated area. Here the Koyas had nothing to fear from encroachment of outsiders, and in the surrounding forest they could find edible roots and tubers to supplement their food supply. The villagers owned altogether 300 head of cattle, and a few families who had no bullocks used cows for ploughing. There was an ashram school where sixty-five boys from various villages were taught by a Koya teacher.

In Narsampet Taluk, which adjoins Mulug Taluk, the condition of the Koyas has developed on very similar lines. Wherever motorable roads touch previously tribal villages, part of the land has been occupied by advanced Hindu castes and in some cases also by Banjaras. Much of this immigration occurred in the 1960s and 1970s. The village of Sitanagaram provides a good example for this process. Here as elsewhere Koyas were the original inhabitants, whose forefathers had cleared the land of forest growth and established cultivation. Some time in the days of the Nizam's government, a Muslim by name of Abdul Aziz was granted a *maqta* for the whole village. He did not reside in the locality and left the Koyas in possession, charging only a moderate rent. After the break-up of Hyderabad State the owner of the *maqta* estate was approached by Reddis and Telegas from other parts of Warangal District who offered to purchase parts of his land in Sitanagaram, and he agreed to the sale regardless of the fact that Koyas had been in occupation for at least three generations. However, some of the Koyas, too, offered to buy some of the land they were cultivating, and they borrowed money to raise the purchase price. They did not realize, and the local revenue officials certainly did not tell them, that according to the law they were *shikmedar*, i.e. shareholders, and could have obtained *patta* free of cost if they had applied for them. In the end they could not repay the debts they had incurred to buy the land, and had to sell it to Reddis in order to pay off their loans. The result of all these largely illegal transactions was that by 1978 forty-four Koya families held only 53 acres out of a total of 1,240 acres, and that sixty-two Reddi families, thirty Telega families, and a number of other non-tribals cultivated the bulk of the land. Though the village is notified as a tribal village, the complication of the one-time existence of a *maqta* gave the non-tribals the possibility of contesting the Koyas' right to claim restoration of the land according to the Land Transfer Act.

In the nearby village of Chinnayelapuram the position of the Koyas was even more unfavourable. Their forefathers, too, had made the land arable, but within the past twenty years, i.e. at a time when the Hyderabad Tribal Areas Regulation and subsequently the Andhra Land Transfer Act were in force, Gollas occupied most of the land, and in 1978 there were only eight Koya families left, each of whom owned about half an acre of land.

Only in the interior of Narsampet Taluk, in villages far from motorable roads, have the Koyas been able to retain their land and their independence. In such villages as Madagudem and Gangaram, close to the borders of Yellandu Taluk of Khammam District, the Koyas hold virtually all the land. Their large and well-built houses reflect a prosperity such as most tribals used to enjoy before the invasion of settlers from other regions deprived them of their ancestral land. It is their misfortune that plans are afoot to link Pakhal with Yellandu by a motor road cutting right through the tribal area and undoubtedly bringing in its wake the petty traders, moneylenders, and land-grabbers who in other parts of the district have established themselves along all motorable roads.

The examples chosen from a cross-section of villages which I re-visited in 1978 show that, despite stringent rules prohibiting the transfer of land from tribals to non-tribals, alienation of tribal land has progressed at an alarming rate. This development is all the more surprising as administrative machinery for the restoration of alienated tribal land was established at the same time as in Adilabad District. A special deputy collector (tribal welfare) is in charge of these protective measures, and is assisted in each of the taluks of Mulug and Narsampet by a deputy *tahsildar*. But official figures on the alienation and restoration of land tell their own story about the effectiveness of the legislation and the machinery for its implementation. According to the information available up to November 1975, about 5,025 non-tribals were illegally holding 32,790 acres in scheduled areas by the alienation of tribal land. In 1,924 cases enquiries were initiated under section 3(2) of the Land Transfer Regulation, covering an area of 3,244 acres, and about 1,494 cases involving 2,358 acres were disposed in favour of tribals, yet only 1,313 acres were actually restored to tribals. The reasons for the failure to protect and restore tribal land are basically the same as in Adilabad, i.e. lacunae in the legislation and the imprecise drafting of the orders regarding the transition from the Hyderabad Tribal Areas Regulation to the Andhra Pradesh (Scheduled Areas) Land Transfer Regulation, lack of zeal on the part of some of the officials entrusted with the implementation of the regulations, and above all frequent interference by politicians and particularly members of the Legislative Assembly supporting non-tribals against tribals ousted from their land.

THE LAND PROBLEM IN KHAMMAM DISTRICT

In the areas adjoining Narsampet Taluk to the south, the position of Koyas and Naikpods is very similar to that of the tribals of Warangal District. In the villages close to the main motorable roads, Koyas have retained little of their land, but in the forest areas of Yellandu Taluk there are still villages with a majority of Koyas who own the land they cultivate. In 1977 I visited Gundela for the first time since 1940. The composition which I had noted then had remained much the same, with Muslims, Komtis, Ayars, Gaondlas, and service castes occupying the main village and Koyas living in the surrounding hamlets. The number of non-tribals had considerably increased, and a Komti had built a pretentious masonry house with two towers. Much of the village land was in the hands of non-tribals, who employed Koyas as agricultural labourers, but many of the Koyas in the hamlets also had land of their own.

In the southern part of Khammam District, roughly between Paloncha and Ashwaraopet, there is also a mixture of Koya settlements and the villages of non-tribals. The ability of the Koyas to retain their land stands in inverse relation to the accessibility of their villages. Where there are no or only recently constructed motorable roads, one still finds Koya villages where all, or nearly all, the land is in tribal hands.

A totally different situation prevails in the villages on the banks of the Godavari. Whereas before 1947 only the right bank belonged to Hyderabad State and the left bank formed part of the Agency Tracts of Madras Presidency, now both sides of the river are comprised in Khammam District. Originally the entire riverain region was inhabited mainly by tribals, though the small temple town of Bhadrachallam has long had a population of Brahmins and merchants.

Within the past thirty years, however, the character of the riverbank villages has been completely transformed. The alluvial soil found there is ideally suited for the cultivation of tobacco and chillies, two commercial crops yielding very high profits. In 1977 an acre under either tobacco or chillies could yield a crop worth Rs 3,000–4,000, and the labour charges were only about Rs 1,000. The prospect of such profits, far greater than those attainable by the cultivation of food crops, attracted many people from the coastal districts, such as Guntur, Krishna, and West Godavari. They came with some capital, and succeeded easily in securing the land of Koya villagers who had used the land for subsistence farming, growing food crops rather than tobacco and chillies. The Land Transfer Act of 1917 stood in the way of outright purchases, but did not prevent the leasing of tribal land, and leases often turned into permanent occupation by non-tribals.

Most of the riverside villages between Bhadrachallam and Kunavaram are now inhabited almost entirely by non-tribals, the original Koya inhabitants having withdrawn away from the river. But in the vicinity of Kunavaram the process of land alienation can still be observed. In Repaka, for instance, a village some ten kilometers inland from Kunavaram, nearly all of the 125 householders are Koyas, but 30 percent of the land is leased to non-tribals. The largest leaseholder is a Muslim who cultivates sixty acres. In the late 1960s he came as a penniless pedlar to Kunavaram, where he opened a small grocery shop and sold goods to tribals on credit. By 1977 he had become rich, and had built a two-storeyed house in Kunavaram, part of which was—ironically—rented by the Integrated Tribal Development Agency. His self-assurance and arrogance were so great that he publicly reproached the block development officer for having taken me to Repaka, where I had collected information on the land problem.

The process of land alienation has also affected Arkuru, a village of 187 Koya and 3 non-tribal households. There 40 percent of the land was cultivated on lease by non-tribals residing in Kunavaram. There I

Thrashing paddy with bullocks in a Koya village in the Godavari Valley; the pal-myra palms are used for tapping palm wine, and their leaves are used for thatching.

talked to the Koya headman and his educated young son, the former in a loin-cloth (*langoti*), the latter in a pair of smart trousers and a patterned shirt. "Until ten years ago," said the headman, "when the first newcomers began to take land on lease, none of the people of this village had to borrow money. Our needs were modest and easily satisfied by what we grew on our fields. But now people want all sorts of new things which the men from the coastal districts have introduced, and so they lease out their land for cash, getting an annual rent of Rs 300 per acre."

Downstream from Kunavaram are the Godavari gorges, an area which I described in my book *The Reddis of the Bison Hills*. There the riverbank villages are accessible only on foot or by boat, and in 1941 the population was almost exclusively tribal. Some villages were inhabited only by Konda Reddis, while in others Konda Reddis and Koyas lived side by side. They cultivated the hill slopes by the slash-and-burn method—which will be discussed presently—but used ploughs for the cultivation of the flat land close to the Godavari, and on this they grew mainly sorghum and pulses.

One of the villages with a good deal of fertile flat land between the riverbank and the wooded hill slopes is Koida. Here the land was owned by Reddis and Koyas who were also engaged in bamboo cutting for wages. In 1946 the Social Service Department established a

Koyas of the Godavari region at a weekly market, where they barter agricultural produce for commodities such as salt, kerosene, cloth, and metal implements.

bamboo-felling cooperative society, which also ran a shop to supply the tribal members with their basic necessities. But after the winding up of this society in 1962 (see chapter 4), the Reddis and Koyas worked for the agents of the Sirpur Paper Mills, who had taken a contract for the exploitation of forest coups (i.e. specific areas of bamboo forest demarcated for felling).

Up to then contractors and merchants had not been interested in acquiring land, but in the late 1950s a man from the coastal area, Kodiala Venkatswami, came to Koida and established a liquor shop. Soon Reddis and Koyas got into the habit of consuming distilled liquor, while previously they had drunk only palm wine. The shopkeeper supplied liquor on credit, and soon many of the tribesmen were indebted to him, and one by one mortgaged their land. K. Venkatswami was then joined by his brother-in-law and several other relations, and by 1977 forty families of non-tribals, mostly from the coastal area, had settled in Koida. They occupied the greater part of the land, some cultivating as much as forty acres, whereas most Reddis and Koyas were left only with small plots of one or two acres. The non-tribal settlers supplied them with grain at exorbitant rates of interest. Thus a man borrowing one bag of millet during the rains, which is a lean season because there is no work in the bamboo coups, had to return two bags after the harvest. If a Reddi could not repay a debt, the merchants took away his cattle or attached his land.

It is not surprising that the tribals got deeper and deeper into debt and that more and more land passed into the hands of the non-tribal settlers. Throughout this process the revenue and police officials supported the merchants, and the dominant man among the settlers was appointed as police *patel*, displacing the previous tribal incumbent. Even funds allocated by the Tribal Welfare Department were diverted to the use of the non-tribals. Thus a well constructed with tribal money was situated in such a way that it irrigated only the tobacco field of the non-tribal *patel*. The merchants' power is so great that when accompanied by an officer of the Tribal Research Institute I collected information on the economic position of the Reddis and Koyas, they threatened to cut off supplies of grain from all those tribals who had given us information.

It seems that all the gains achieved by the Social Service Department in the 1940s and 1950s have been lost and that the tribesmen have slipped back into a bondage as oppressive as that which I described in some detail in *The Reddis of the Bison Hills* and *Tribal Hyderabad*. But at that time this region was extremely difficult of access and moreover was situated in the Samasthan of Paloncha, and hence not under the direct control of the Nizam's government, which had remained ignorant of the tribals' plight but hastened to take remedial action when alerted by my reports. Now, the exploitation and tyranny of non-tribal settlers, whose occupation of tribal land is clearly in breach of protective laws, occurs under the eyes of the local officials and largely with their connivance, exemplified by the appointment of the chief exploiter as police *patel* of Koida.

Yet the picture is not one of unrelieved gloom. In Katkur, a village within an hour's walk from Koida, the Reddis freed themselves from the dominance of an outsider by their own efforts. There over one hundred acres of their land had been acquired by an immigrant Muslim, who leased the fields suitable for the cultivation of tobacco and chillies for as little as Rs 100–150 per acre, mainly from people indebted to him. Inspired by a tribal leader (and subsequent member of the Legislative Assembly) from the left bank of the Godavari, the Reddis of Katkur revolted against the Muslim landlord and forcibly occupied the land he had unfairly taken from them. In this case the special deputy collector supported this act of self-help and formally restored the land to its rightful owners.

The position of the Konda Reddis in the Godavari Valley as well as in other areas is the subject of a separate case study contained in chapter 10, and a further detailed discussion is therefore redundant.

THE PROBLEM OF SHIFTING CULTIVATION

There are many areas in Andhra Pradesh, as indeed in other parts of India, where the terrain offers little scope for agriculture other than shifting cultivation on hill slopes. This type of tillage, also known to anthropologists as slash-and-burn, or swidden, cultivation, is described in Telugu as *podu*, a term equivalent to *bewar* in the usage of Madhya Pradesh and *jhum* in that of Northeast India.

Several tribes of Andhra Pradesh were traditionally *podu* cultivators, and it is only in the last fifty years that considerations of forest conservancy led to various measures aimed at the restriction or total elimination of *podu*. In Adilabad District *podu* was practised as late as the 1950s by Kolams and Naikpods, but has now been completely suppressed. In the districts of Khammam, West Godavari, East Godavari, Vishakapatnam, and Srikakulam, however, slash-and-burn cultivation is still the main method of tillage of a number of tribal communities and is carried on side by side with plough cultivation wherever tribals are in a state of transition between the two systems. In the hills on the border between Khammam and West Godavari, there are communities of Konda Reddis who practise *podu* as their only type of cultivation and whose manner of land use has hardly changed during the past thirty-eight years. Two villages typical for their traditional *podu* cultivation are Gogulapudi and Motagudum, both of which I visited in 1941 as well as in 1979.

The system prevailing in 1941 is described in detail in *The Reddis of the Bison Hills* (pp. 79–85), and this description applies largely to present conditions also. However, there is one difference. Referring to the practice in the 1940s I mentioned that a Reddi seldom simultaneously worked fields cleared in different years, but that he usually cultivated a field adequate for his needs for one, two, or even three successive years, according to the fertility of the soil, and then abandoned it altogether and cleared a new *podu*. In 1979 the area open to the people of Gogulapudi had been limited by the forest officials, who allowed them to clear the forest on the hill slopes to one side of the village, but not to the other. Hence the Reddis had adjusted their cycle of rotation and cultivated each year a piece of old *podu* as well as a newly cleared plot. Thus a man would every year abandon a plot after two years of cultivation, continue to cultivate on the area cleared the year before, and cut the forest on a part of the hill slope adjoining that cleared the previous year. Wherever possible all these plots were adjoining, and only when such a sequence of clearings on one hill slope was completed would a man return to another slope where the forest had grown up sufficiently since the land had last been tilled. As long as a man resided in the village, his right to re-occupy land last cultivated by him would not be contested by any other villager. Thus certain individual claims to land were recognized, though parts of the village land not recently cultivated by men still living in the village were regarded as common property which anyone was free to clear subject, of course, to new restrictions imposed by forest officials. On an average every householder had a total of about two acres of old and new *podu* under cultivation, and from this he could expect an average yield of about eight quintals of grain of various kinds, mainly sorghum and small millets as well as some pulses, all sown as mixed crops. (See also chapter 10.)

In East Godavari District the areas under slash-and-burn cultivation are far larger, and, particularly in the hills of Chodavaram Taluk north of Maredumilli, *podu* is the predominant form of tillage. Restrictions imposed by forest officials are here not very rigorous, and, particularly in villages where no or very little level land is available for cultivation, it is clearly impracticable to forbid *podu*. Whereas the Reddis of the Godavari region use only digging sticks for the cultivation of their *podu*, in Chodavaram the Reddis dig over their *podu* with iron hoes.

Thirty years ago most villagers had only *podu* fields and did not use ploughs, but within the past ten to fifteen years many Reddis prepared paddy fields and began using ploughs. It was mainly the *muttadar*, hereditary chieftains recently deprived of their special status as collectors of revenue (see chapter 6), and some of the village headmen who developed flat land near their villages as paddy fields, usually rain-fed but in some cases also irrigated by hill streams. They had the advantage of already possessing cattle, even though the yoking of bullocks to the plough was new to them. In Perikivalasa of the Mohanpuram *mutta*, for instance, there were only *podu* fields in 1941, but by 1979 flat land had been cleared of forest and used for rice cultivation. The villagers said that in the old days they reaped sufficient grain on their *podu* fields because land was plentiful and they could cultivate as much as they liked, growing mainly small millets and oilseeds, whereas nowadays they grow paddy for their own consumption and castor to sell for cash.

The cultivation of paddy was not introduced by any outside agency, but with the improvement of communications Reddis became used to visiting markets at Chodavaram and Addatigala, and there they became familiar with the sight of paddy fields and ploughs drawn by oxen.

Wherever the terrain lends itself to the cultivation of rice and hill streams facilitate irrigation, the transition to such permanent cultivation relieves the pressure on land used for *podu*. Such pressure has arisen where the Forest Department has claimed large parts of the land for plantations of commercial species, such as teak or eucalyptus, but a shortage of land has also come about in certain hill villages owing to the natural growth of population. An example of the latter situation is provided by the village of Kanivada. When I visited this village in 1941 I remarked that "a growing though by no means serious pressure on land has brought about the curtailment of the individual's freedom in the choice of cultivable land. Here the consent of the headman must be sought before a piece of jungle is taken under the axe" (*The Reddis of the Bison Hills*, p. 79). By 1979 the village had grown from thirty-five to eighty houses, and the shortage of land had become serious. There was no possibility of extending the boundaries of the village land into areas still well wooded, and the villagers complained that even timber for building houses was no longer easy to obtain. Such examples demonstrate the limitations of slash-and-burn cultivation, which is a system of land utilization practicable only where small populations have access to large forest areas.

The argument, often put forward by forest officials, that *podu* cultivation is inherently wasteful and detrimental to the preservation of forests is nevertheless not without flaws. In the areas inhabited for centuries if not millennia by shifting cultivators, there are some of the largest natural forests, whereas the expansion of intensive plough cultivation has nearly everywhere led to a disappearance of forests. This becomes obvious in many parts of Andhra Pradesh. In Adilabad, where Kolams and Naikpods were practising *podu* cultivation and even the plough-cultivating Gonds frequently shifted their fields and then allowed forest to grow up on the abandoned land, there were vast stretches of forest as late as the first decades of the twentieth century. The same applies to the tribal areas of Warangal and Khammam, and in East Godavari District, the habitat of the *podu*-cultivating Konda Reddis, there are some of the most extensive areas of natural forest in the whole of Southern India.

The largest areas under *podu* cultivation to be found in Andhra Pradesh are in Srikakulam District. There most of the hills in the blocks of Sitampeta and Bhadragiri, close to the border of Orissa, are covered with the typical patch-work pattern of current *podu*, abandoned *podu* fields, and secondary jungle. The tribals most dependent on *podu* cultivation are the Saoras, whose small villages lie mainly in the high hills, where level land suitable for plough cultivation is very limited or non-existent. Even very steep slopes are being cleared of jungle growth, and small millets and pulses are broadcast or dibbled in the ashes of the burnt trees and brushwood. As the tree stumps are left standing, there is little erosion. Moreover, some of the stumps sprout again and thus facilitate the growth of secondary jungle after the *podu* has been abandoned. Even slopes covered in rubble are used for cultivation, the crops being dibbled in between the stones, which are said to protect the soil from the heat of the sun and thus help to preserve moisture. Saoras usually cultivate a *podu* field for two years and then allow it to remain fallow for several years. Yet the period of fallow is sometimes no more than three years, and it is surprising that so short a cycle of rotation is sufficient to retain the fertility of the soil.

Wherever suitable terrain and sources of water make rice cultivation possible, Saoras construct irrigated terraces, and though *podu* seems to be the traditional basis of Saora agriculture, some Saoras evince considerable skill in the construction and maintenance of terrace-fields. The combination of slash-and-burn cultivation with the raising of rice on irrigated terrace-fields reminds one of the agricultural system of the Bondos of nearby Orissa, like the Saoras a Munda-speaking people.

The Saoras share their habitat with the Jatapus, the second largest tribal community in Srikakulam District. While in some villages Saoras and Jatapus live side by side, though each community is in a separate street, the Jatapus favour the broader and lower valleys. They hold more flat land than Saoras, and this they till with ploughs and bullocks; yet many Jatapus practise in addition *podu* cultivation on nearby hill slopes.

The government, which in the past eight years has pursued a very effective policy of tribal rehabilitation, recognizes the part *podu* is playing in the economy of such tribes as Saoras, Jatapus, and Konda Doras. Relatively small plots have been assigned to tribals on *patta* on the assumption that the occupiers augment the yields by crops grown on *podu* fields. Whereas in Adilabad the Forest Department has fought a relentless battle against *podu* cultivation and ousted innumerable Kolams from the valleys and hills they and their forefathers had inhabited since time immemorial, in Srikakulam only limited areas have been declared reserved forest, and the majority of the hill slopes are open for *podu* cultivation. Here the government has accepted the fact that the tribesmen have an inherent right to the hills and valleys of their ancient homeland, while in the forest areas of Adilabad the tribals were at best tolerated, but often ruthlessly evicted from land claimed by the Forest Department without regard for the Kolams' long-standing occupation.

To some extent the difference in official attitudes is undoubtedly due to the fact that in Srikakulam the tribesmen, instigated and led by Naxalite revolutionaries, had risen in armed revolt against oppression by outsiders, whereas the tribesmen of Adilabad are now too cowed and docile to take up arms in defense of their rights.

3 Tribes and Forest Policy

ALL THE tribal populations of Andhra Pradesh were traditionally closely associated with forests, and there are some who even today spend the greater part of their lives in the proximity of trees. It is for this reason that aboriginals were often referred to as *jangali*, today a derogatory term standing for "uncouth" or "uncivilized" but literally meaning "forest dweller." Tribal communities living in settlements surrounded by forest regarded these woods as much their own as old-style pastoralists considered the grass-lands over which their herds were ranging as their own preserves, to be defended if necessary against the inroads of neighbouring tribes. In Northeast India there are to this day tribes among whom specific forest tracts with clearly defined boundaries are claimed as clan or village property, where only members of the clan or village in question are allowed to hunt or cut firewood. Ownership over forests is there clearly defined and generally recognized.

In the tribal areas now forming part of Andhra Pradesh, similar conditions prevailed until the beginning of the twentieth century. Communities living near forests depended on them for building material, fuel, fodder, and often also food in the shape of wild fruits and tubers. Preservation of the resources on which they relied for so many of their needs was in the tribesmen's own interests, and as long as there was no interference by advanced populations the ecological balance was usually well maintained.

A new situation was created, however, when the demands of modern industries situated outside the tribal areas led to the commercial   79 exploitation of forests. These became then an important source of revenue in the state, and to regulate the extraction of timber and other produce large forest areas were designated as "reserved" and put under the control of a government department. Tribal communities dwelling in enclaves inside the forest were either evicted or denied access to the forest produce on which they had depended for many necessities. Thus arose a conflict between the traditional tribal ownership and the state's claim to the entire forest wealth. Numerous revolts, one of which will be described later in this chapter, were the direct result of the denial of the local tribals' right in the forests which they had always considered their communal property. While they were forbidden to take even enough wood to build their huts or fashion their ploughs, they saw contractors from the lowlands felling hundreds of trees and carting them off, usually with the help of labour brought in from outside. Where tribals were allowed access to some of the forest produce, such as grass or dead wood for fuel, this was considered a "concession" liable to be withdrawn at any time. The traditional de facto ownership of tribal communities was now replaced by the de jure ownership of the state, which ultimately led to the exploitation of forest resources with total disregard for the needs of the tribal economy. In recent years many projects have been started which change the character of forests in such a manner that they serve exclusively commercial interests and no longer benefit the original forest dwellers. The natural mixed forests, which provided the tribesmen with the raw materials for many of their household implements, cane and bamboo for baskets, and such items of food as mangoes, tamarinds, jack fruits, *mahua corollae,* and edible berries, are being replaced by plantations of teak, eucalyptus, and various coniferous trees.

An extreme example of such a commercialization of forests at the expense of the local tribal population is a project in Madhya Pradesh where Rs 46,000,000 are to be spent on converting 8,000 hectares of forest in the Bastar Hills to pine forests to feed the paper pulp industry.

In a recent symposium on "Forests, Tribals and Development," Dr. B. D. Sharma, who is Tribal Development Commissioner, Government of Madhya Pradesh, stated the position very clearly when he said:

> As the ownership of the State gets consolidated and formalised and the decision making recedes farther away from the field, the special relationship of the tribals with the forest is not appreciated. Their rights are viewed as a 'burden' on the forests, and an impediment in their scientific and economic exploitation. . . . Since the forest produce is treated as nature's gift, the State stakes its full claim over it. At the best, the tribal may be allowed a reasonable wage for the labour which he may put in for the collection of minor forest produce or extraction

of major produce. Thus, the de-facto and conventional command of the tribal over resources is completely denied in this perception and he is reduced to the status of merely a casual wage-earner.

Dr. B. D. Sharma included in his exposition a detailed plan for a reconciliation of the interests of tribal communities and forestry development, largely by the economic involvement of tribals in the management and utilisation of forest resources. He summarises the basic principles of this plan as follows:

> It is clear that the development of the people and development of the forests, as two co-equal goals, are fully consistent. Certain basic needs of the local community must provide the solid foundation for rational utilisation of forest resources. The socio-economic conditions of tribal communities must be accepted as an important boundary condition for determining the level of technology and intensity of operations in an area.... The plan for tribal development must take the forest resources as the base on which tribal economy can progress with greatest confidence.... Planning without participation of the people and their active involvement cannot be expected to be realistic. The tribal should become a co-sharer in the new wealth created in these areas and should become an active participant in their management.[1]

In this context I am not concerned with plans for the future, but with recording the past and present conditions of the tribal populations of Andhra Pradesh, and we shall presently see that there is a great gap between these conditions and the idealistic vision of Dr. Sharma.

In an assessment of the forest policy of the former Hyderabad State and present-day Andhra Pradesh in its effect on the tribals, we must distinguish between three categories of populations: foodgatherers and hunters, shifting-cultivators, and settled farming populations.

The only tribe in Andhra Pradesh falling clearly into the first category is the Chenchus of the Nallamalai Hills. Since time immemorial they have inhabited the forest-clad hills to both sides of the Krishna River, and even today the forests are their true habitat. Hunting and foodgathering are the Chenchus' traditional occupations, and when I studied them in 1940 those living on the upper Amrabad Plateau in Hyderabad State and many of those in the neighbouring district of Kurnool subsisted almost entirely on wild fruits and tubers and the occasional game hunted with bow and arrow. Their small settlements, situated in the depth of the forest, consisted of round huts and leaf shelters, and they frequently shifted from one collecting ground to another. Foodgatherers in the true sense of the word, the Chenchus of

---

1. B. D. Sharma, *Tribal Development: The Concept and the Frame*, p. 83.

those days only rarely obtained grain, by barter in exchange for honey or other minor forest produce.

For centuries the inaccessibility of the upper Amrabad Plateau, ascent to which was only by foot-paths, had protected the Chenchus from any sudden inroads of outsiders, and it was left to them to seek barter contacts in the villages of the adjoining lowlands. The notification of the plateau as a forest reserve, first in 1894 and with some modifications in 1930, as well as the subsequent extraction of timber from the forests, brought the Chenchus' isolation to an end.

By 1940 roads suitable for wheeled traffic had been driven into the forest, and forest contractors brought hosts of labourers, partly to fell and cart trees, and partly to collect minor forest produce which had been auctioned by the Forest Department. The competition in the collection of such produce hit the Chenchus particularly hard, for by bartering honey, gum, certain nuts, and wild fruits they used to obtain metal tools, cloth, and some household goods. Forest guards recruited the Chenchus for work in nurseries and the demarcation of forest coups, but being badly paid such work was not popular. All the innovations resulting from the commercial exploitation of forests had come so rapidly that the Chenchus had no time to adjust mentally and materially to the new conditions. They felt baffled and helpless when watching the ever-increasing inroads into the forests which they had always considered their undisputed domain.

As a result of my reports to the Nizam's government at the conclusion of my fieldwork in 1940, administrative action was taken to protect the Chenchus from exploitation and to safeguard their rights to the forest produce on which they depended for their livelihood. Some 100,000 acres on the upper plateau were established as a Chenchu Reserve, in which they were enabled to continue their traditional lifestyle. The rules governing this reserve are contained in an appendix to my book *The Chenchus* (pp. 377–81). They provided for the Chenchus' right to collect for their domestic use all minor forest produce without payment, and established a procedure by which the Forest Department would purchase at fixed prices any forest produce the Chenchus would offer for sale. The auctioning of minor forest produce to contractors was to be discontinued. The Chenchus were also given grazing rights within the reserve free of charge, and were allowed to cultivate small plots of land near their settlements. Hunting with bow and arrow was permitted irrespective of whether the area of the reserve was included in a game sanctuary or not.

Already in 1940 a number of Chenchus owned buffaloes which they used for milking, and in view of their apparent skill in herding, the Social Service Department, which had established a centre in Mananur, provided some more female buffaloes free of cost. The idea was then that the Chenchus' semi-nomadic life-style would be compatible with the development of pastoral pursuits. However, contact with cattle brought into the forest area by Banjara graziers resulted in epidemics of foot-and-mouth disease which wiped out most of the buffaloes in the possession of Chenchus. Hence in 1977 the Chenchus of the upper plateau owned fewer cattle than the previous generation had possessed.

The most important change in the economic position of the Chenchus is the transition from gathering roots, tubers, and wild fruits for consumption to the collection of minor forest produce on a large scale for sale. This entry of the Chenchus into a cash economy has come about mainly by the activities of the Girijan Cooperative Marketing Society, an organization set up by government for the benefit of tribal populations. Without having changed their style of life, the Chenchus are now no longer concentrating on the gathering of wild plants for consumption, but gather marketable commodities and take them to Girijan depots, where they are paid for in cash. With that cash they then buy grain for their daily consumption. The sums obtained from the sale of minor forest produce are very considerable. Thus the Girijan Cooperative Marketing Society at Mananur purchased between January and November 1977 minor forest produce worth Rs 547,216. The main items were: gum, worth Rs 310,495; soapnuts, worth Rs 62,970; *nux vomica*, worth Rs 11,729; *mahua* seed *(Bassia latifolia)*, worth 75,412; *pungam* seed, worth Rs 98,066; and honey, worth Rs 26,724. Some of these commodities may have been irregularly bought from persons other than Chenchus but even if one allows for such malpractices the genuine purchases from Chenchus—say 80 percent of the total—must have made a decisive impact on their economy.

The Chenchus represent thus the unusual case of a forest tribe of semi-nomadic collectors and hunters who notwithstanding close contact with advanced populations and the agents of a regular administration have remained gatherers even though the bulk of the produce they gather is no longer food for their own consumption.

Until 1979, forest conservancy and the pursuance of the Chenchus' traditional life-style were not in conflict, and in view of the value of the produce collected for pharmaceutical and other industries there was every reason to believe that this situation could persist for the foreseeable future. However, in 1980 a development occurred which threatens to undermine the very basis of Chenchu economy. When I revisited the upper Amrabad Plateau in November 1980, I noticed large-scale inroads into the bamboo forest, and learned that the Sirpur Paper Mills, whose activities had already destroyed the greater part of the bamboo forests of Adilabad District, had been awarded a contract for the exploitation of bamboo on the upper Amrabad Plateau. The agents of the Sirpur Paper Mills had brought in hundreds of forest labourers, many of them recruited in distant Madhya Pradesh, as well as a fleet of trucks. The local forest officers told me that they were not in a position to control the extent and the manner of the exploitation of bamboo, and whereas there is a method of cutting bamboo which safeguards future regeneration, it was obvious that the felling was carried out without any regard for the conservation of the stocks of bamboo.

For the Chenchus, the destruction of bamboo in their habitat will be catastrophic. They depend on bamboo not only for the construction of their huts and for making many of their utensils, but above all for the manufacture of baskets and mats, which they traditionally sell or barter for agricultural produce. It is no exaggeration to say that the depletion of the stocks of bamboo in the forests of the Amrabad Plateau would make the area virtually uninhabitable for its original denizens. The fact that the prospect of such a development is by no means a figment of the imagination is demonstrated by the fate of other forest dwellers of Andhra Pradesh, whose life has been totally disrupted by a forest policy unmindful of the rights and needs of tribal populations.

THE FATE OF KOLAMS AND NAIKPODS

Tribes who in the past forty years have suffered such a fate are the Kolams and the Naikpods of Adilabad District. Both these tribes long have shared the habitat of the far more numerous Gonds, but both stood always on a lower level of material development and resembled in their life-style some of the Konda Reddis of Khammam District. Their traditional method of tillage was slash-and-burn cultivation (*podu*) on hill slopes, and for this they used digging sticks and very primitive hoes. When in 1941 I first came in contact with Kolams and Naikpods, most of them possessed no cattle and usually did not even possess goats, sheep, or pigs. Only a very few Kolams and Naikpods had at that time taken to plough cultivation. Compared with their Gond neighbours, most Kolams and Naikpods were very unsophisticated and limited in outlook. They had little idea of the functions of the various government officials, were vague about such revenue terms as *kharij khata, parampok,* and *patta,* and did not know the meaning of "reserved forest." Their reaction to any kind of difficulty was either flight or submission. Kolams of a disbanded village, whose inhabitants were scattered, easily lost all contact with each other and were ignorant of the whereabouts of close relatives. They had very few aspirations other than to be left in peace and allowed to find a bare livelihood. Many Kolams seemed to be content to live in the villages of landlords whose *patta* land included a few hill slopes where they could cultivate in their old style, and if the landlord sheltered them from threats of expulsion by forest officials, they submitted to any demands for unpaid labour.

The standard of living of most Kolams was much lower than that of Gonds, and their settlements were much smaller than Gond villages. Even in 1941, they seldom consisted of more than twelve houses on one site, while in the days before the reservation of forests, hamlets of only three or four houses were scattered over the hills at points convenient for *podu*. Kolams shifted their houses almost as often as they shifted their fields; their houses were small, often containing only one room, and so to rebuild was not much trouble. Their economic resources were much more limited than those of the Gonds. The crops sown and reaped, consisting mainly of small millets, sorghum, maize, and certain vegetables such as beans, taro, and marrows, provided a family with sustenance only for about seven or eight months a year, while during the remaining months wild fruits, herbs, and roots formed the mainstay of the diet. Neither Kolams nor Naikpods grew any cash crops such as cotton or oilseed; for their cash requirements they depended on the sale of jungle produce and baskets, in the manufacture of which they were expert.

Where Gonds and Kolams lived in close proximity, the Gonds usually settled at the foot of the higher ridges and cultivated the valleys, plateaux, and gentle slopes, while the Kolams built their hamlets on ridge tops and cultivated the steep hill-sides below.

At the time of the first demarcation of forest boundaries, many Kolam and Naikpod villages were disbanded and the inhabitants compelled to leave their houses and the hill slopes they used to cultivate. Other settlements, particularly those in the immediate vicinity of Gond villages, were established as enclaves in the forest, and in these were included the hill slopes then actually under cultivation. Though nominally *podu* was here allowed to continue, the restriction of the land left to Kolams to that under cultivation at the time of demarcation virtually ended their traditional type of economy. After a very few years the slopes included within the enclaves were utterly exhausted, and the Kolams were prevented from clearing any more forest. Consequently they had to move away unless they were able to obtain some level land and learn from their Gond neighbours the art of ploughing. There were in 1941 some Kolam settlements where most inhabitants practised plough cultivation; the bullocks, however, were usually not their own, but were hired from either Gonds or merchants.

The extent to which the Kolams' economy and social organization was broken up by the forest policy of the late 1930s and early 1940s can be judged from the developments in the Tilani State Forest. This massif of hills, in many parts broken up by deep ravines, used to be dotted by numerous settlements of Kolams, who could subsist in areas too rugged for the Gond type of plough cultivation. But the policy of forest reservation compelled the disbanding of settlements, and many Kolams moved to Rajura Taluk, where at that time conditions were slightly more favourable.

The fate of those who had remained is exemplified by developments in the cluster of hamlets known as Boramgutta, near Pangri Madra.

In July 1942 Boramgutta consisted of three settlements: A, B, and C. None of the inhabitants had ploughs or cattle. In settlement A, which had existed for more than twenty years, there were eight houses. In 1939 a forest line had been drawn round the village, and only four *podu* fields were included within the enclave. Settlement B lay two furlongs from A, but outside the enclave. It consisted of four houses, whose inhabitants had moved there from settlement A and cleared a piece of jungle outside the enclave, because they said it was impossible for them to subsist any longer on the small area within the enclave, which after three years of cultivation had become exhausted. But hardly had they sowed on their new *podu* when the forest guard and the *patwari* ordered them to go back to settlement A. Tekam Burma, the nominal head of a whole group of Kolam villages, told me about his and his people's plight:

> My father was headman [*dodomankal*] of eight settlements including Boramgutta, but now most of them are deserted, for the forest officials do not allow the Kolams to stay there. The people of these settlements, who were all our relatives, were scattered here and there, and now we do not even know where they live and which of them are alive.

Settlement C was about a furlong from B and consisted of four houses. Atram Gangu told me of the inmates' experiences:

> We used to live in the hills near Revalgudem and Goinna, cultivating now on this and now on that hill. But the forest officials stopped us cutting *podu*. Then we went to Mangi and cultivated with some Naik-pods, but after one year we were once more made to leave. So one year ago we came to Boramgutta and the *patwari* collected Rs 12 revenue for four households. He did not tell us that we won't be allowed to stay. But a few days ago he and a forest guard came and said that we must leave. Why did they not tell us that before? If they had said so in the hot weather we might have been able to move elsewhere, but now with the maize sprouting and no chance of cultivating anywhere else—what shall we do?

Similar was the fate of the Kolams of Pangri Madra, the site of one of the most sacred shrines of the Kolam deity Ayak, known to the Gonds as Bhimana. The hereditary priest of that shrine, where every year a festival attended by hundreds of people was held, told me that at the time of the demarcation of the forest lines the village site and all the land of Pangri Madra were included in the reserved forest, and the Kolams expelled. The priest of the shrine felt he could not desert the sanctuary, and he and some families were permitted by Gonds of Chintel Madra to settle on their land. But this was only a temporary arrangement, and when the Gonds needed their land the priest and eighteen Kolam families built a settlement close to the Gond village. But in 1942 the forest officials told them to vacate that site, threatening to burn their houses. These Kolams had neither bullocks nor ploughs, and since they were forbidden to do *podu* cultivation, they subsisted precariously by doing casual labour for Gonds and selling baskets.

In some places Kolams and Naikpods were able to remain in the reserved forest with the connivance of forest subordinates and *patwari*, but the price they had to pay for this concession in the form of bribes was usually high, and they knew that they could be told to leave their village and standing crops at a moment's notice.

Forest officers often complained about the Kolams' obstinancy in sticking to *podu* cultivation, but even those who took up permanent cultivation with ploughs and bullocks did not meet with the encouragement they deserved. This may be demonstrated by the example of Chinna Jheri in the Pedda Vagu Valley.

Chinna Jheri used to be a Kolam village of ten families who all cultivated with ploughs. They owned altogether 250 acres, and Tekam Bhima, who told me the story, possessed a *patta* and paid land revenue of Rs 35. When the forest lines were drawn he was told by the forest officers that unless he paid them Rs 100 he would have to give up his land. As he could not pay what was then a very large amount, they took away his *patta* document, and he and all the other households were forced to evacuate Chinna Jheri, without being given any alternative land.

The irony of this case lies in the fact that Chinna Jheri, like all the neighbouring villages in the Pedda Vagu Valley, is now in the hands of non-tribal settlers who have erased the entire forest and established intensive cultivation. No doubt they were rich enough to bribe the forest officers concerned.

Today *podu* cultivation is a thing of the past throughout Adilabad District, and nobody is concerned about the suffering and misery which the eviction from their ancestral homes and subsequent disper-

Shrine of the Kolam god Ayak in the forest near Dantanpalli in Adilabad District. Idols and votive offerings stand in the shrine; at the back are wooden posts erected in memory of departed members of the community.

sal has caused to the Kolams, an inoffensive primitive tribe whose right to live in the wooded highlands was cancelled with a stroke of the pen. Far away from the people whose whole life-style was to be destroyed, the areas to be notified as reserved forest were entered on some map, only too often without any local inspection, which would have revealed that whole villages, inhabited since time immemorial, were thus included in the reserve and turned into forbidden territory.

In the years 1944–47 some Kolams were also allocated land on *patta*, and there now exist villages where ever since Kolams have lived as settled cultivators. But unlike Gonds, who were already in occupation of permanently cultivated land, Kolams qualifying for grants of land were not easily identified. They themselves did not know how to apply and were not as aware as the Gonds of the facilities then offered to the tribals of the scheduled areas. Hence, many were left out of the distribution of land, and it is these who even now are pushed around by the Forest Department whenever they try to settle in localities where their fathers or grandfathers had lived. When I visited Adilabad District in 1976 and 1977, I met many Kolams who for years had been driven from pillar to post, without finding any land where they could make their home. Two cases may briefly illustrate their conditions.

Kolam priest with the symbols of the god Ayak: carved wooden staves holding peacock feathers. Various ritual objects lie in a heap at his side.

In December 1976 several Kolams of Raurnur came to see me in Kanchanpalli. There had been fourteen households of Kolams in Raurnur, who had lived and cultivated there for more than fifteen years. Though they had paid land revenue to the *patwari,* there was no record of their occupation in the *tahsil* office, and in 1973 the Forest Department evicted them and turned their land into a teak plantation.

The fate of the Kolams of Pauarguda was similar. They had cultivated the village land since the mid 1950s, but most of them were evicted by forest officials, with the explanation that their land had been included in the reserved forest. A few of them had money to bribe the forest guard, and they were allowed to continue cultivating, but all the others had to move away, and have since drifted about as casual agricultural labourers.

Another group of Kolams driven out of Yellapatar and Jamuldhara, which used to be old haunts of Kolams, settled in 1959 in Wankamadi and cultivated vacant land lying outside the reserved forest. However, in 1964 their village site and fields were included in the reserved forest, and they were evacuated to other villages. Yet the land in

Wankamadi which they had cultivated now remains fallow, and the Forest Department has not used it for plantations.

In 1980, when I last toured Adilabad District, there were no major concentrations of Kolams left, and although some were settled in villages of their own, such as Pannapatar and Lendiguda, most were dispersed and subsisted as landless labourers, working for Gonds or non-tribal landowners.

THE IMPACT OF FOREST POLICY ON GONDS

The effect of the reservation of large expanses of forest on the Gonds was not quite as catastrophic as it had been for Kolams and Naikpods, but it disrupted their agricultrual system by restricting the cultivation of light soils in rotation. The demarcation of forest lines drawn round the villages did not take place at the same time in the whole district, nor were the same principles everywhere applied. But the general idea was to include in the reserved forest all those areas which were not actually under cultivation. Thereby a great deal of land which had been cultivated on *siwa-i-jamabandi* tenure and was lying fallow at the time of demarcation was included in the reserve, and the Gonds were thus deprived of its future use. The grave disadvantage of this for the cultivators did not become apparent at once, but after some years when the Gonds wanted to follow their old routine of re-occupying the fallow lands, they could not do so, as in the meantime the land had been claimed by the Forest Department. In villages with a fair amount of permanently cultivated heavy black soil, this curtailment of the land with light soil did not result in very great hardship, but the Gonds had to lean more and more on the yield of the heavy soils cultivated in the *rabi* season. But there were other villages, situated on the tops of ranges, where the interference with the cycle of rotation created a very serious problem, for the Gonds of some of these villages, who used to move backwards and forwards between two or three village sites, alternatively cultivating the surrounding land, were now pinned down to the one site which they happened to occupy at the time of the forest reservation. In Konikasa, for instance, I found cultivated land which lay on the highest point of a ridge, so stony that it was hard to imagine how a plough could be drawn through the rubble, and the inhabitants told me that previously they used to cultivate there only occasionally and that land of much richer soil lay further down the hill, but just when the forest line was drawn they happened to be cultivating on the upper plateau, and now they could not move back to the better site and lands.

There is little doubt that the demarcation of the forest lines was done in a very haphazard way and depended to a large extent on the amount of money the villagers were able to pay to the forest officials. The Gonds of Harapnur, for instance, described the need of bribing the forest officials as follows:

> When the forest officers came they promised to draw the line very far from our village if we gave them Rs 200 (equivalent to circa Rs 3,000 according to money values in 1979). To this we agreed and they set to work while two of us went to our *sahukar* to fetch the money. But we had had a bad harvest and he would not give us any money. When the two men returned empty-handed the forest officers, who had already drawn the line far from the village, became very angry, changed all the marks, and drew the line right through our fields.

While villages in which at least part of the cultivated land was held on *patta* were established as enclaves, a number of Gond villages which comprised no *patta* lands were included in the reserved forest and the inhabitants given a time limit to evacuate the village lands. In pursuance of the policy of forest conservancy, large-scale evacuations occurred in the 1920s, and mopping up operations continued until 1940, creating an atmosphere of unending insecurity.

This policy of clearing large tracts of forest of all human habitation, including old, established villages inhabited for many generations, led to the only case of armed resistance by Gonds in the annals of Adilabad District. That mini-rebellion, as it may be called, is known as the Babijheri incident after the locality in which it occurred. As it clearly reflects the relations between the tribal population and the forest authorities and has found a place in Gond folklore, it merits description in some detail.

The leader of the Gonds at Babijheri was Kumra Bhimu, whose home village was Sankepalli, about five miles from Asifabad. He, like other Gonds of the area, felt a deep resentment that at that time any outsider, whether Brahmin, Muslim, or Komti, could get *patta* land, but Gonds could not obtain *patta* rights. Kumra Bhimu, who was an intelligent young man able to read and write, had repeatedly tried to get some land. In his home village most of the land had fallen into the hands of non-aboriginals. After staying for some years in various villages of Muslim and Brahmin landlords, he finally settled in Babijheri. This village was subsequently established as an enclave in the Dhanora State Forest, but those inhabitants who had no *patta* were told that they must vacate the place. As they had not left by the date fixed, all their houses were burnt by forest guards. Some Gonds and nine families of Kolams got permission to settle at Jhoreghat, a site east of Babijheri, and some land was measured and allotted to individual families by the revenue inspector and the *patwari*. The forest guard then came and told the Gonds and Kolams that they could clear as much forest as they liked if they paid him Rs 500. The Gonds and Kolams borrowed the money, paid it to the forest guard, and cleared some more land. But after some time the same forest guard came again and said that the Rs 500 was only for himself; if the Gonds wanted to stay they would have to pay Rs 2,000 for the forester and the forest ranger, otherwise they would be driven away and their houses burnt as had happened in Babijheri. (It must be remembered that in 1940 Rs 500 and Rs 2,000 were enormous sums for tribals.)

Then Bhimu and four other Gonds went to Hyderabad, and they are believed to have obtained there permission to cultivate fifty-seven acres at Jhoreghat. But when they showed the paper to the forest guard, he still insisted on the payment of Rs 2,000, and again threatened to burn all their houses. Bhimu therefore tried once more to approach higher authorities, and he sent by registered post a petition to the divisional forest officer, with a copy to the second *talukdar* (subcollector), in which he applied for permission to be allowed to stay and cultivate at Jhoreghat. But the forest ranger sent without the knowledge of the divisional forest officer a party consisting of the forester, several forest guards, and an Arab with a gun to enforce the evacuation of Jhoreghat.

As the party approached Jhoreghat they burned without warning several outlying settlements, and some cattle tied up in sheds were trapped and perished in the flames. The Gonds, enraged by the firing of the hamlets, opposed the party, but without fire-arms. The Arab, however, threatened to shoot Bhimu, and shot him through the hand. At that the assembled Gonds fell upon the party and gave them a good beating. Yet, all the forest officials made their escape and walked home.

It seems that Bhimu and the other Gonds of Jhoreghat decided to resist evacuation by force and that several hundred malcontent Gonds rallied to their support. This was a symptom of bitterness against the forest subordinates comparable to the exasperation of exploited and harassed tribals in Srikakulam District, who in the 1960s and 1970s joined the Naxalite uprising.

Bhimu and his supporters had no revolutionary aims, and their demands were simply freedom from harassment and extortions by forest subordinates, and the right to live undisturbed in their ancestral homeland.

Negotiations with Bhimu and his supporters by the district officers were clearly mismanaged, and were abortive because there was no one on the side of government who had the confidence of the tribesmen. Bhimu refused to give himself up, and when a police party advanced into the hills, where he and his followers had gathered, Bhimu fired a shot without wounding anyone. Thereupon the police opened fire, killed Bhimu and ten other Gonds on the spot, and wounded many more.

The incident left the Gonds deeply resentful of the policy of government and particularly of the forest officials, who intensified their oppression and exploitation, using the example of Bhimu's fate as a threat whenever Gonds resisted their exactions.

It was not until four years later that the measures taken for the rehabilitation of the tribals described in chapters 1 and 2 improved the atmosphere in Adilabad and restored the Gonds' confidence in the good faith of government.

At the time when the revenue and social service officers kept a close watch on the subordinates of all departments, harassment of tribals and the extortion of money and farm produce by forest officials diminished considerably, and the discipline then enforced shows that oppression of tribals by minor officers is not an irremediable aspect of Indian village life. It is depressing to record, however, that the period of freedom from exploitation was relatively short and that in the years 1976 to 1979 I heard of many cases of high-handedness and corruption of forest officials similar to those I had observed and reported in the 1940s.

A particularly brutal action by forest officials occurred in February 1979 in Utnur Taluk. Five families of Gonds had settled at Gari Sitakarra, a hamlet of Adesara. The site on which they had built their houses was allegedly in the reserved forest, but for five years they lived and cultivated there without being disturbed. On 23 February a team of forest officials, including the divisional forest officer, came to Gari Sitakarra and rounded up the five Gond families. Without allowing any of the Gonds to enter their houses, the forest officials set fire to the five houses, burning them to the ground. The Gonds had recently sold minor forest produce, such as gum, to which they are entitled, and hence had Rs 1,500 in cash in their houses. As the forest officials prevented them even from re-entering their houses, this money was lost in the flames. When a few days later I talked to the Gonds, they were destitute and were camping under trees.

One of the reasons for the tension between the tribal population and the forest officials is the uncertainty about the status of a considerable amount of land allotted to tribal cultivators on *patta* by the local revenue authorities but claimed by the Forest Department as reserved forest. Whenever I visited Utnur Taluk in recent years, many Gonds and some Kolams showed me documents on official forms headed "Final Patta" which had been regularly issued by the Utnur *tahsildar*, but which the Forest Department did not recognize. For years cultivation on much of this disputed land was tolerated provided the tribal occupant bribed the forest guard or forester. But in 1978 the forest authorities started a campaign to evict tribals from such land and collected fines of Rs 200 per acre on land on which cash crops had been sown and Rs 100 per acre on land under sorghum. These fines were collected irrespective of whether there was any yield and also irrespective of the economic position of the tribals fined. As this campaign coincided with the almost complete failure of the *kharif* crops and very poor yields of *rabi* crops, the inevitable result was that the Gonds had to take loans from moneylenders. Nearly all such fines related to land which for years had been in the possession of tribals and for which they had regularly paid revenue. Even some land held on *patta* long before 1940 has been included in the reserved forest during recent adjustments of the forest lines. Thus, eighteen acres at Marlavai which were the *patel's patta* land as early as 1941 may no longer be cultivated, but no compensation in either cash or kind has been granted to the owner. It is clearly not possible for illiterate tribals to understand the reason why one government department issues them *patta* and collects year after year the revenue for the land in question while another department fines them for cultivating such land. Hence they feel themselves to be victims of gross injustice and have lost all faith in the fair-mindedness of government.

An example of the confusion created by the claims of the Forest Department to land long cultivated by tribals is the case of Jamuldhara, on the eastern edge of Utnur Taluk. The Gonds of this village, which I first visited in 1942, have not been given permanent rights to the land they have cultivated for decades, and the Forest Department is disputing the legality of their possession. In an appeal to the magistrate's court in Both, the Gonds won their case, but the Forest Department appealed to the High Court, and there too the decision went in favour of the Gonds. However, no action to legalize the possession of the Gonds by the grant of *patta* was taken, and the forest officials continued to threaten the Gonds with eviction. It seems that the Forest Department picks on the weakest section of the population and leaves the big non-tribal despoilers of forests in possession of their ill-gotten gains.

The sense of injustice felt by Gonds and Kolams is all the greater as within the past twenty years thousands of acres of forest have been cleared and occupied by affluent non-tribals, most of whom had only recently immigrated into Adilabad District.

Thus in Jamni, a village refounded in 1945 by the Gond Maravi Moti and since then inhabited by about fifty Gond families, people from Maharashtra, mainly Marathas but also some Muslims, occupied part of the village land in 1962 and cleared a great deal of forest. Though they encroached on reserved forest the forest officials accepted substantial bribes and did not object to the illegal felling of forest. A similar situation has arisen in the nearby village of Gauri. There fifty Muslim families recently immigrated from Udgir in Maharashtra, settled next to the original Kolam village, and now cultivate land in the reserved forest from which the Kolams had been evicted by the Forest Department. The Muslims were presumably affluent enough to buy the good will of the local forest officials.

The discrimination in favour of non-tribals is borne out by figures provided by the Forest Department in 1976. In the Forest Division including Adilabad, Utnur, and Both taluks, 43,330 acres had been found under illegal cultivation, and of these 39,856 acres had been released from the reserved forest. As hardly any tribals had recently been given new land in forested areas, this large area must have been released to accommodate the large influx of settlers who came from Maharashtra. From 3,474 acres cultivators had been evicted. These were largely Gonds and Kolams; no cases of Marathas, Banjaras, or Muslims being evicted have come to my notice.

ILLEGAL EXACTIONS BY FOREST OFFICIALS

Apart from the problem of tribal land claimed by the Forest Department, which is a frequent source of friction between tribals and forest officials, there is also the continuous irritation of illegal fees collected by forest guards from the villagers. It is an old practice of forest guards to demand from the cultivators annual contributions, usually calculated according to the number of ploughs a man uses for cultivation. In Hyderabad State there was until 1944 a tax on ploughs collected by the Forest Department on the grounds that wood had been taken from the forest for the making of ploughs and other agricultural implements. Though this tax was abolished as part of the liberalisation of the government's policy vis-à-vis the tribals, forest guards continued to extort from the cultivators annual fees which went into their own pockets. The amount of these illegal fees varied from area to area and from forest guard to forest guard. In 1976–77 the forest guard of Kanchanpalli demanded Rs 17 per plough and some small contributions of grain, but the forest guard of Hasnapur exacted much higher fees, demanding for each plough Rs 40 and in addition from each household twenty-five kilograms of sorghum, twelve kilograms of red gram, five kilograms of black gram, and ten kilograms of paddy. Those who did not have these grains had to buy them in order to satisfy the forest guard's demands. Anyone who refuses to pay the illegal fees is certain to be harassed by the forest guard, who can prevent those in his bad books from collecting even legally permitted forest produce and may charge the defaulter with forest offences which had never been committed. Today the tyranny of forest guards is certainly as bad as it was in 1940, and there is no indication of any action on the part of the higher forest officers to curb the illegal activities of their subordinates. Much of the Gonds' hard-won cash has to be used to pay such illegal fees to forest subordinates and other minor government servants habitually preying on tribals, as the weakest and least articulate sections of rural society.

In the districts of Warangal, Khammam, and East Godavari the exactions by forest guards are very similar to the practices in Adilabad. It is only in Srikakulam, the district most affected by the Naxalite insurgency, that tribals have become conscious of their rights. There minor government officials are very careful not to arouse the resentment of the tribesmen by illegal demands, and the tribals now have enough self-confidence to resist this type of oppression.

Another form of exploitation of tribals by officials of the Forest Department is recruitment for virtually unpaid labour, both in plantations and for clearing the forest lines. Thus in Tekluru, a Konda Reddi village in the Rekapelli Block, the Reddis told me in 1978 that every year thirty men of the village have to work for several weeks in the teak plantations and that in the end they are given only Rs 30–40 to be shared between all of them. The forest officials exact this unpaid labour under the threat that any Reddi refusing to work would be charged with the offence of having cleared the forest for *podu* cultivation, which in this area has to be tolerated because its total abolition would condemn the Reddis to virtual starvation. The case of the Reddis of Tekluru was by no means isolated, and I heard similar stories from several other Reddi communities.

It is ironic that the state has not only asserted its absolute right to the forest which its traditional inhabitants always considered their own tribal property, but that the servants of the state, such as the officials of the Forest Department, have no compunction in compelling the original owners to work for a pittance in the forests of whose resources they have been largely deprived. From such a position it is a long way to the scheme envisaged by B. D. Sharma, who suggests that "the local tribal community which provides the labour should be accepted as a partner in the management and sharing of profits. They should not be taken merely as casual wage-earners whose services can be dispensed with at will."[2] It is obvious that the realization of such an arrangement would require a complete change of heart on the part of forest officials, most of whom evince little consideration for the interests of tribals.

2. *Tribal Development: The Concept and the Frame*, p. 75.

4 Economic Development

WITH THE exception of the foodgathering Chenchus, all the tribal pop-ulations of Andhra Pradesh are traditionally subsistence farmers. As long as they lived in their ancestral habitat, protected from the outside world by hills and forests, they produced food grains and reared animals almost exclusively for their own consumption. Contacts with the market economy of more advanced populations were few and of limited importance, consisting mainly of the barter of some items of agricultural or forest produce for supplies of the few necessities, such as salt and iron, which they were incapable of producing with the resources of their own environment. Small groups of artisans, living in symbiosis with the aboriginal farmers, provided them with such items as pots, metal implements, and certain ornaments, but the relations between cultivators and craftsmen were basically also on an exchange basis, and their mutual interdependence operated outside the market economy of neighbouring more advanced areas.

Among shifting-cultivators such as Konda Reddis and Kolams an undiluted system of subsistence farming could be observed as late as the 1940s, and in some remote pockets of primitivity it persists to this day. More advanced ethnic groups, such as Gonds and the majority of Koyas, had then already emerged from total self-sufficiency, but even they consumed most of the grain which they produced, and their need of commodities which had to be purchased with money was very limited. Change came to them in the first decades of the twentieth century, when outsiders acting as agents of the wider money economy penetrated into tribal regions, and governments with their systems of taxes payable in money compelled the tribals to acquire at least some small amounts of the official currency. Self-sufficiency came to an end, and tribal communities were sucked into a cash economy which had its roots in materially advanced and socially complex spheres outside the tribal regions.

Even in the 1940s there were still many tribals who had only a vague idea of the units of currency, and who easily fell victim to any unscrupulous outsider trading on their ignorance and trustfulness. A phenomenon which today is the bane of many a tribal society, namely that of indebtedness, arose only with the incorporation of the tribal economy within the money economy of neighbouring advanced populations. The primitive subsistence farmer had lacked the means of drawing on outside resources to tide him over a crisis, such as crop failure, or to acquire goods of a value exceeding that of his accumulated resources. The Konda Reddis in remote hill settlements, for instance, did not borrow money or grain if their crops failed to last them for the whole year, but eked out their food supplies by gathering wild tubers, roots, and forest plants.

GONDS AND KOLAMS

At the same time, the Gonds of the Adilabad highlands had already become used to meeting a shortage of their food grain by borrowing from merchants and moneylenders dwelling on the periphery of the tribal area. Thus had started the vicious circle of repaying borrowed grain by delivering to the creditor one and a half times the borrowed quantity as soon as the next harvest was reaped. Unless that harvest was exceptionally good the repayments usually resulted in the recurrence of the need to borrow grain for consumption later in the year.

Yet not all Gonds were compelled to depend on merchants to tide them over lean periods, and many reaped sufficient grain crops, mainly millets, to meet their domestic needs throughout the year. Food grain was then rarely sold, and cash requirements, such as the money needed for paying land revenue or buying clothes, were met by the sale of cash crops, usually grown only in small quantities. Oilseeds and castor were the main cash crops, for the large-scale growing of cotton is a relatively recent phenomenon. In Gond myths and epics there is no mention of cotton, whereas millet and rice both figure prominently.

A fundamental change in the agricultural pattern of the Gonds occurred in the first half of the twentieth century. Until then the Gonds had mainly cultivated the light, reddish soils on the high plateaux and gentle slopes on which they grew monsoon crops during the so-called *kharif* season. As these soils could not be cultivated year after year, periods of fallow had to alternate with the periods of cultivation. So long as there was ample land available, this system of frequent fallows allowed the Gonds to grow adequate crops on light soils, and to leave the heavy, black soils in the wooded valley bottoms largely uncultivated. Some farmers, however, used stretches of black soil for growing rain-fed rice during the monsoon and wheat, sorghum, and pulses in the post-monsoon season known as *rabi*.

The reservation of forests and the shrinkage of the tribals' habitat caused by the incursions of non-tribal settlers compelled most of the Gonds to abandon the practice of frequent fallows and to take more and more of the heavy, black soils under cultivation. Shortage of land and the official policy of granting to individuals *patta* rights to clearly delimited plots of land, in the choice of which they often had no decisive say, led, moreover, to changes in cropping patterns and to the diversification of the economy of Gond farmers. The man whose *patta* land consists mainly of light, reddish soil has no other choice than to depend mainly on *kharif* crops, whereas the owner of heavy, black soils must inevitably concentrate on *rabi* crops. There are, of course, landowners whose holdings include both red and black soil, but few have sufficient land to permit them to continue the traditional practice of interspersing periods of tillage with extended periods of fallow.

Another change in the farming economy of the Gonds was caused by the allocation of individual holdings to the adult sons of farmers who had previously cultivated a large area with all the resources of manpower available in a joint family consisting of several married couples. Such farmers had been able to cultivate with as many as six or seven ploughs, and this had enabled them to spread their agricultural operations both spatially and chronologically, and to grow a variety of crops on their extensive holdings. Individual farmers cultivating about ten to fifteen acres are marginally less efficient, mainly because they cannot afford to take risks but must concentrate on the cultivation of the food crops on which they depend for their domestic consumption.

Yet another change occurred some ten to twenty years after the allocation of land on permanent *patta* to individual householders. This change was triggered by the establishment of commercial centres in the heart of the tribal area. Wherever non-tribals engaged in trade and moneylending settled, a cash-oriented economy was brought right to the door-step of many Gonds. The availability of novel commodities displayed in the newly established shops created among the tribals a craving for such goods. The only way of satisfying this craving was the production of crops of a high cash value.

Within the span of a few years, the entire cropping pattern of Utnur

Gond village in the Adilabad highlands: the houses built of wood and bamboo are thatched with grass; free-standing cylindrical grain bins are made of wattle and covered with a mixture of mud and cow dung.

Taluk underwent a dramatic change. High prices paid for cotton and the possibility of speedily moving large quantities of this crop by lorry to the cotton market and rail-head at Adilabad transformed a food-producing area into a region concentrating on the growing of cotton. The availability of this valuable commodity brought increasing numbers of merchants, some from states as distant as Gujarat, to a region which twenty years earlier had been a tribal backwater.

One of the new commercial centres owing its rapid growth to the cotton boom is Jainur on the Utnur-Asifabad road. Until 1944 this locality was a deserted site in the midst of forest, and was then resettled by a few Gond families, who had moved there from such nearby villages as Marlavai and Ragapur. Within the past ten years it has turned into a flourishing market centre inhabited by numerous Hindu and Muslim merchants.

In the cotton-picking season in 1979–80, six trucks, each carrying one hundred quintals of cotton, left Jainur daily for Adilabad, and earlier in the year each of the six major cotton merchants had brought ten to twelve truck-loads of sorghum from outside the taluk for the purpose of giving advances of grain to the tribal cotton-growers. As a result of the good harvest, the price of cotton had dropped from the

Circle of Gond worshippers during the annual rites in honour of their clan god, symbolized by a black yak's tail erected on a stave in the centre of the circle.

previous year's rate of Rs 450–500 per quintal to only Rs 330–50.

The merchants dealing in cotton were the same shopkeepers who supplied the Gonds throughout the year with sundry commodities, and their methods of trading deprived the tribals of the full profits from the change-over to cotton. For cotton brought to Jainur in cart-loads, they gave the current price of Rs 330–50. Yet they did not pay cash on the spot, but gave the Gonds receipts and the promise to pay in two or three weeks' time after selling the cotton at Adilabad. Often they procrastinated the cash payment and tried to persuade the Gonds to accept part-payment in cloth or other consumer goods, and for these they asked prices much higher than those current in such towns as Adilabad or Mancherial. Those Gonds who had taken advances of grain, moreover, never received the entire cash value of their cotton when they delivered their crop. An even less favourable treatment had to be accepted by the numerous Gonds who had only small quantities to sell and brought the cotton by head-loads. Such loose cotton fetches a much lower price, which in 1979–80 was about Rs. 2.40 per kilogram, corresponding to a price of Rs 240 per quintal.

The replacement of food crops by cotton affects most parts of Utnur Taluk, and this is reflected in the very substantial imports of sorghum into an area which not long ago was self-sufficient in grain. Thus in

Gond woman of the Adilabad highlands; her forehead is tattooed, and suspended from a solid silver necklace is a bundle of keys. Gond wives have the keys to the store boxes and grain chests of the household, and carry them always on their persons.

Gond of the village of Marlavai in Utnur Taluk; a white or red turban is the tradi-tional head-gear, but tailored cotton shirts, now universally worn, are a modern innovation.

1979 in Narnur, another cotton market, alone two merchants between them brought 1,700 truck-loads of sorghum to their go-downs and from this stock supplied their Gond clients with the grain the Gonds now require because of their shift to the growing of cash crops.

The rapid change in the whole character of the agricultural economy has by no means brought only benefits to the Gonds. While those who possess ample land with heavy, black soil are likely to profit from devoting a large proportion of their holding to the raising of cotton, some Gonds owning only land of lighter soil are also tempted to grow cotton but may reap only a meagre crop. By growing the traditional food crops they would probably fare better. The cultivation of food crops, such as sorghum, also has the advantage that Gonds can estimate their domestic needs and if at all possible keep a store of sorghum to last them throughout the year. The cash obtained from the sale of cotton, on the other hand, is seldom spent for the purchase of a year's supply of grain but may partly be used up in buying luxuries previously beyond the reach of Gonds. After an exceptionally good harvest, there may be no harm in spending part of the cash received for cotton on items other than food grain, but in average and below-average years most Gonds just cannot afford to buy much more than essential clothes and food stuff sufficient to augment their own production of grain and pulses if this is inadequate to feed their families throughout the year.

The easy availability of such commodities as sugar, tea, cigarettes, and spirits in shops within walking distance of many villages, or even in small shops inside tribal villages, acts as a continuous temptation. While a generation ago tea and sugar were luxuries reserved for special occasions, many Gond families nowadays regularly purchase tea and sugar, and men who used to smoke their home-grown tobacco in leaf pipes now buy *bidi* or cigarettes. Wealthy men even own bicycles, and transistor radios are found in many of the larger villages. The cost of batteries alone for such radios and for the commonly used electric torches is a drain on a Gond's budget justifiable only in years when cash crops yield a good harvest.

The family budgets for 1976–77 set out in my book *The Gonds of Andhra Pradesh* (pp. 417–21) show that a wealthy man, such as Kanaka Hanu of Marlavai, had a cash expenditure of Rs 3,676, which included payments for land revenue and taxes, fertilizers, and wages for daily labourers. After the very bad harvest of 1978–79, only Kanaka Hanu and four other men of Marlavai expected to be able to balance their budgets, while all the other villagers foresaw that they would have to take loans of grain to meet their domestic needs until the next harvest. Kanaka Hanu was in a relatively favourable position because his holding contains several fields of heavy, black soil on which he grew ade-

quate crops of cotton and wheat, whereas those villagers whose land
was of lighter soils saw both their food crops and their cotton crop fail.

In the following year there were good crops, and Kanaka Hanu
reaped in *kharif* twenty quintals of rice, ten quintals of sorghum, two
quintals of black gram, half a quintal of maize, half a quintal of
oilseed, and twenty-five quintals of cotton. In January 1980 the *rabi*
crops looked promising, too, and Hanu expected a yield of about
thirty to forty quintals of sorghum and thirty quintals of wheat. As his
domestic requirements of cereals were about fifteen quintals, he had a
surplus of grain and could use the income from the sale of cotton—
about Rs 8,250—to meet all his cash requirements. Hanu's land-holding, as well as his skill in managing the farm work, are exceptional,
and the majority of Gonds have no surplus even in a good year.

A budget representative of a Gond of much more modest means is
that of Kodapa Jeitu of Marlavai. Jeitu owns five acres in Marlavai and
twelve acres in Jainur, which his brother cultivates on share. Jeitu
cultivates with two ploughs; he owns one pair of bullocks and hires
another from his brother Kasi, who lives in Jainur.

In 1976–77, he reaped the following crops:

Sorghum	7½ quintals
Rice	5 quintals
Maize	2 quintals
Red gram	10 kilograms
Green gram	10 kilograms
Castor	½ quintal
Cotton	1½ quintals
Chenna dhal	½ quintal

His share of the field cultivated by his brother amounted to two
quintals of cotton.

The sorghum lasted his family of seven heads for 11 months and
the rice for 10½ months. He sold castor at a rate of Rs 250 per quintal,
and cotton for Rs 450 per quintal. He spent Rs 440 on clothes, Rs 250
on oil and spices, and Rs 240 on tea and sugar.

He took a loan of Rs 400 from a cooperative society, and he did not
employ farm servants.

Tumram Lingu, one of the wealthiest and oldest men of Marlavai,
who died in 1978, had owned nineteen acres of *patta* land in Marlavai
and ten acres in Ragapur. His two married sons and one married
daughter, deserted by her *lamsare*-husband, had lived in his house and
cultivated with him. He had owned eight bullocks, eighteen cows, and
four buffaloes.

In 1976–77, Tumram Lingu reaped the following *kharif* crops.

Sorghum	20 quintals
Cotton	2 quintals
Ballar dhal	10 kilograms

His *rabi* crops amounted to:

Wheat	8 quintals
Chenna dhal	5 quintals

In Tumram Lingu's household there were then six adults and four children, and there was hence a surplus of grain over the family's needs. Gonds reckon that 1¼ quintals (i.e. 125 kilograms) of grain is sufficient to meet the average annual needs of one person.

The budgets of Kolams in possession of land are not different from those of Gonds, but there are relatively few Kolams who own economic holdings. One of these is Kodapa Jeitu of Muluguda (near Kanchanpalli), who owns twelve acres and cultivates with two ploughs. There are six persons in his household, including children.

In 1976–77, he reaped the following crops:

Kharif:	Sorghum	2 quintals
	Rice	5 quintals
	Maize	½ quintal
	Castor	½ quintal
	Oilseed *(til)*	25 kilograms
Rabi:	Cotton	3 quintals
	Chenna dhal	2½ quintals
	Wheat	2½ quintals

The domestic consumption of grain was ten quintals, i.e. the grain crop reaped, and the sale of cotton (Rs 1,200) and castor (Rs 125) more than covered the household's cash needs. Rs 700 had been spent on clothes, Rs 300 on oil, salt, spices, tea, sugar, etc., and Rs 31 on land revenue and tax on cash crops.

Besides those Gonds and Kolams who can balance their budget or even have a surplus, there are many who are seldom free of debt because their production of grain does not meet the family's consumption. Kanaka Dhami, a Gond of Kanchanpalli, for instance, was frequently in trouble. In the year 1975–76 he had to borrow from a merchant 2½ quintals of rice. In 1976–77, his harvest was again inadequate, mainly because he had been ill and had hence delayed the sowing of the *rabi* crops, which consequently failed.

In the *kharif* season he reaped:

Sorghum	1½ quintals
Maize	20 kilograms
Rice	5 quintals
Ballar dhal	½ quintal

His cotton had failed completely and he had sown no other cash crop. The normal grain consumption of the household of six adults and children was ten quintals, and the shortfall was made up by earnings from casual labour. As Dhami had only one bullock he had hired one, and for this he had to pay sixty kilograms of sorghum as rent. But he had still to repay the previous year's loan of rice, and as he had no rice to give, his merchant demanded Rs 320 in cash. To raise this money he sold his only bullock for Rs 600. With the remaining money he bought a young untrained bullock for Rs 150.

The chances of a man like Dhami to free himself from indebtedness are slim, because after repaying the previous year's debt he has probably to borrow again to meet his family's needs for food and essential clothes.

No recent statistics regarding the incomes of Gond cultivators are available, but a study of seventy-four agriculturists in four sample villages of Utnur Taluk was undertaken in 1972 by D. R. Pratap,[1] and if we allow for inflation the findings retain some relevance. The average holding of the families investigated was 13.26 acres, and the cash incomes of the seventy-four agriculturists of the sample were as follows:

19.0 percent of farmers	Rs 400–600
16.2 percent of farmers	Rs 601–1,200
43.2 percent of farmers	Rs 1,201–3,000
21.6 percent of farmers	Rs 3,001 and above

Attached labourers (farm servants) were paid an annual wage of Rs 400 plus five quintals of sorghum in the villages of Mutnur and Indraveli, and Rs 250 plus six quintals of sorghum in Lakkaram and Jainur.

Most agricultural labourers, who worked free-lance, had incomes between Rs 600 and Rs 1,400 per annum.

The average family income from all sources was calculated to be Rs 2,036.96, and the average per capita income was Rs 209.90, which compared unfavourably with the Andhra Pradesh average of Rs 545.29 in 1970–71.

The low incomes were explained by an analysis of the yield of the fields belonging to a random sample of Gond cultivators. The average yield of an acre under sorghum was 1.41 quintals, the yield of rice per acre was 2.36 quintals, and the average yield of cotton approximately 72 kilograms. Most Gonds do not have the capital to increase the yield of their land by applying chemical fertilizers and sowing improved hybrid seed. Hence agricultural production remains poor notwith-

1. *Occupational Pattern and Development Priorities among Raj Gonds of Adilabad District.*

standing various development programmes, which have either remained on paper or been channelled mainly to the non-tribal
inhabitants of the project area because these had greater pull with the
officials responsible for the distribution of benefits.

We have seen that Gonds have become used to purchasing a number of consumer goods in shops or markets, and this may give the
impression that their standard of living has risen in the past thirty
years. This impression is partly deceptive, however, for the parents of
the present generation had similar resources but spent them in different ways. While they bought few items of outside manufacture and
no Gond would have aspired to owning such a thing as a bicycle, they
were more lavish in entertaining and in the celebration of festivals
and rites. The expenditure of food stuff on weddings and funerals was
far greater than it is today, and the occasions for the employment of
Pardhan bards were more numerous. Moreover, the rewards these art-
ists received for their performances were much more generous than
they are nowadays. The very fact that on many ritual occasions cows
or bulls were slaughtered to provide meat for the entertainment of the
participants indicates a different type of consumption, and the present
addition of tea and sugar to the Gond diet must be weighed against
the diminishment of the protein content by the exclusion of beef. This
change also has a social aspect. Whereas the slaughter of a bullock
provided meat for a large gathering drawn from several villages, a
goat substituted as sacrificial animal can feed only a small circle of
relatives and close friends.

A change-over to different but not necessarily more valuable items
purchased by affluent Gonds is not an indication of a rise in living
standards either. Previously Gonds would buy their wives and daughters heavy silver ornaments fashioned by local craftsmen, and many
wealthy men wore embossed silver belts. Such items were not necessarily luxuries, because silver jewelry retained its value and in a crisis
could be used as security for a loan from a moneylender. Today Gonds
with cash to spare buy such articles as wrist-watches, electric torches,
or the like, or they spend their money on pilgrimages to Tirupati, an
unheard-of adventure thirty years ago. While some Gonds now possess bicycles, men of the previous generation often owned ponies
which they used exclusively for riding. These examples show that the
change in the consumption pattern does not necessarily amount to a
substantial rise in the standard of living.

A development which has caused a decline in living standards for a
substantial percentage of Gond families is the loss of land to non-tribal
settlers. In the 1940s, the great majority of Gonds were independent
farmers, whether they held their land on *patta* or not, whereas today
many have no land and no possibility of cultivating government land

on temporary tenure. Their only way of maintaining themselves is to work as farm servants or casual labourers on the land of non-tribal settlers who have displaced the original tribal population. This is a phenomenon not peculiar to Adilabad District or even to Andhra Pradesh alone, but is found in many parts of India. Thus a comparison of the data contained in the census reports of 1961 and 1971 shows that during the relevant decade the percentage of independent tribal cultivators fell from 68 percent to 57.56 percent, while the number of agricultural labourers went up from 28 percent to 33 percent largely, no doubt, owing to the mounting land alienation and eviction of tribals from their land.

It is obvious that the economic position of an agricultural labourer is greatly inferior to that of an independent cultivator, and that even Gonds who in the 1940s did not own land but cultivated government land on *siwa-i-jamabandi* tenure were far better off than agricultural labourers are today. Those landless Gonds who live in a purely tribal village and work for Gond landowners enjoy at least a social status not fundamentally different from that of other villagers, but Gonds working for non-tribal employers in villages where there are only a few other Gonds are among the most underprivileged tribals and in fact are no better off than Harijans.

The situation of the Gonds, Kolams, and Naikpods in Adilabad District, particularly in Utnur, has all the elements of a collective tragedy. Just at the time when the demand for cotton and the phenomenal rise in its price could have ushered in a period of mounting prosperity throughout the region of heavy, black soil which was so recently in tribal hands, the invasion of outsiders and a change in the political climate have shattered all hopes that the tribals would reap the benefit from their transition to cash crops. The transformation of a sorghum-, wheat-, and rice-growing area into an almost continuous expanse of cotton fields has brought about so rapid a commercialization of the whole economy that the conservative and largely illiterate Gonds cannot keep pace with the change-over to an entirely new system.

The very fact that land uniquely suitable for the growing of cotton is a magnet for advanced cultivators as well as merchants of all types makes it virtually impossible for tribals to remain in control of the land and its produce. Apart from the alienation of land discussed in chapter 2, there is also the penetration of the agents of commercial interests into the remotest villages. Traders who have their open shops and purchasing depots in such places as Jainur or Narnur have a network of agents, usually members of their own family, settled in many tribal villages. These agents keep small shops in which they stock matches, *bidi*, soap, tea, salt, and similar basic commodities, but each of them also gives advances for deliveries of cotton and castor, and in this way secures for his principal the crops grown by the villagers, often well below the market price. Such petty shopkeepers also encourage barter transactions such as the exchange of cotton for groundnuts. In March 1979, when the Gonds were short of food after an unusually bad harvest, traders gave one kilogram of groundnuts for one kilogram of cotton, thereby obtaining cotton for about half the price current in Adilabad. The victims of such tricks were naturally not the substantial cotton growers who had several quintals to sell and found it worth their while to take their crop to Jainur or Adilabad, but the small Gond farmers, who had reaped perhaps only twenty or thirty kilograms of cotton and were easily duped to dispose of this as close to their homes as possible.

In Jainur, where a ginning mill has recently been installed, there are at the time of the cotton harvest huge mountains of the precious crop. Truck after truck, loaded with cotton, leaves for Adilabad. Here big business has gained a foothold in what only fifteen years ago was a purely tribal and economically backward area. Insofar as business acumen is concerned most Gonds and virtually all Kolams have remained "backward," and they are not yet capable of taking advantage of the possibilities which the cotton boom has brought to the area. Profits are largely mopped up by the middlemen and by traders to whom many Gonds have mortgaged their crops long before the cotton is even picked.

The unequitable division of profits can be gauged by the contrast between the life-style of the non-tribal businessmen settled in Utnur, Jainur, Narnur, and Indraveli and that of the average Gond villager. The former live in houses built of bricks and cement, fitted with electric lights and fans, own motor vehicles, and are at home in the district headquarters as well as in Hyderabad, while the Gonds continue to live in thatched huts with mud-plastered wattle walls and to wear simple clothes not very different from those their parents used to don.

The affluence of the merchants of Jainur becomes explicable if we compare the prices they charge tribals for their wares with those current in the market towns of other parts of the district. In the following list of prices in Jainur in January 1980, the prices for items of similar quality current in Chennur are given in parentheses:

Cotton cloth, 54 inches by 90 inches	Rs 22	(Rs 13)
Cotton cloth, 48 inches by 80 inches	Rs 20	(Rs 12)
Dhoti	Rs 40	(Rs 22)
Sari	Rs 36	(Rs 23)
Cotton shawl	Rs 40	(Rs 20)
Kerosene, per kilogram	Rs 3	(Rs 1.20)
Unrefined sugar, per kilogram	Rs 3.50	(Rs 1.50)

The willingness of the Gonds to pay these excessive prices is surprising considering the fact that a cheap bus ride would take them to places where they could make their purchases at much more reasonable rates. It can only be explained by their relative unfamiliarity with money transactions, which places the greater number of tribals at a disadvantage in their dealings with shrewd members of traditional trading castes.

The phenomenon of the growing exploitation of the tribal farmers by a class of immigrant nouveaux riches abetted in their domination of the local population by venal or lethargic petty officials is not peculiar to Adilabad. Similar situations have been observed in many areas and over long periods, and in some regions, such as Srikakulam District, violent reactions occurred when the long-suffering tribal peasantry saw their salvation in political movements led by Naxalite extremists. A gradually widening gap between the rich and the rural poor has been demonstrated by many investigations based on official All-India statistics which show that the percentage of rural households living below the extreme poverty line rose from 38 percent in 1960 to 53 percent in 1968.

The impossibility of ascertaining with any accuracy the extent of the land actively controlled and utilized by traders and moneylenders, even if not owned by them in law, is largely due to the connivance of minor revenue officials in illegal land transactions which make a mockery of the protective legislation to which the government is officially committed. Even visual examination of the undisguised accumulation of wealth by non-tribals in commercial centres such as Indraveli and Jainur and the equally blatant poverty of many a tribal settlement gives the lie to the official assumption that economic growth, even if initially set in motion by non-tribal agents, must ultimately also benefit the tribal populations. In Adilabad most tribals were in 1980 far worse housed than in the 1940s and early 1950s, and their chances of survival as independent cultivators have greatly diminished.

While the decline of the tribal prosperity is hardly surprising in an area exposed to a development by recent settlers which can only be described as "colonial," it is strange that this should have occurred at a time when, at least on paper, the government of Andhra Pradesh had sanctioned very large sums intended exclusively for tribal welfare, and was publicly committed to a policy of protecting the interests of the so-called "weaker sections" of the population.

KOYAS

The development of the economy of the Gonds of Adilabad is paralleled by that prevailing among the Koyas of Warangal and

Khammam. In chapter 2 we have seen that in these districts, too, the local tribal population has suffered from the alienation of much of their land by members of immigrant, economically and politically more powerful populations. Within the past forty years many Koyas have been reduced to the position of landless agricultural labourers, and it is only in villages remote from motorable roads that Koyas have retained all of their land and preserved a relatively high economic status. One of the few islands of Koya prosperity, remnants of a former widespread condition, is the village of Madagudem in Narsampet Taluk. There 129 Koya families and a few families of Harijans share 398 acres of cultivated land, 30 acres of which are already irrigated by a newly constructed tank and 100 acres will shortly come under irrigation. Twenty Koya families who came from other localities to join kinsmen settled in Madagudem have no land of their own but cultivate on share with local Koyas who possess land. Half of the produce goes to the owner of the land, and the rest to the sharecropper, provided he cultivates by himself. But if the owner takes part in the cultivation, the yield is divided according to the input of each of the partners. Thus if owner and sharecropper each work with one plough, the owner gets half the produce for his land and one quarter for the labour contributed. In such a case the sharecropper is entitled only to one quarter of the yield. This arrangement is less generous than the system of sharecropping of the Konda Reddis, who divide the produce only on the basis of the number of ploughs contributed by each partner irrespective of the ownership of the land (see the following section of this chapter). Some Koyas of Khammam District follow a similar system. In Ankapallam village, for instance, the owner does not get a share for his land, but if he provides plough bullocks he is given one bag of grain for the bullocks, and the rest of the yield is shared according to each partner's input of labour. The land revenue is shared in any case.

The prosperity of the Koya community of Madagudem, so far unaffected by rapacious outsiders, finds visible expression in the comfortable and spacious homesteads characteristic of this village. In front of each of the well-built houses there is an open structure of the same size as the home itself. Massive teak-wood pillars rise from a raised mud platform, and a thatched roof, as high as that of a dwelling house, provides shelter from rain and scorching sun. In this open hall much of the housework, such as the pounding of grain, can be done in comfort, and hence there is no need for the members of the family to cram into the dark interior of the main house. Many of the villagers have vegetable gardens, often irrigated by wells from which water is drawn in buckets, and here and there are small groves of mango trees. Besides cattle, the Koyas keep pigs, and the headman even owns some guinea fowls. This idyllic atmosphere of rustic peace and well-being stands in stark contrast to the shabby huts of Koyas crowded together at the outskirts of settlements where non-tribal newcomers have occupied the centre of the village site.

ECONOMIC DEVELOPMENT AMONG KONDA REDDIS

In chapters 2 and 3 we have seen that the fortunes of the Konda Reddis in recent decades have been determined largely by two factors: the occupation of land suitable for plough cultivation by non-tribal newcomers and the restriction of shifting cultivation by the Forest Department. Within the limitations set by these two factors, Reddis are adapting themselves in different ways to a situation in which few of them can any longer pursue the life-style natural to their grandparents and parents. No doubt, there are even now isolated communities, each consisting of a small number of families that live in the depth of the forest as yet undisturbed by outsiders or even the control of the Forest Department. One such community I encountered in 1978 in a remote corner of Rekapalli Taluk, to the north of the Godavari River. There six houses then stood in a small clearing surrounded by high trees, but only two of them were inhabited at the time of my visit. A cyclone had done much damage to the sorghum crop, breaking many of the high stalks. The owners of the small cultivated plots had nevertheless saved some of the ears, and these were drying on a small wooden structure. For immediate consumption the men were boiling some wild roots, which had to be soaked in running water for two days before they became edible. Apart from a few cooking vessels, hatchets, bows and arrows, digging sticks, and home-made baskets these Reddis had few possessions, but they seemed cheerful and content because no one disturbed them, and in the forest they found sufficient food to supplement the grain grown on their hill fields. The other inhabitants of the small hamlet had left their houses and moved to temporary huts built on hill slopes among the crops, which had still to be watched.

It is undoubtedly in such an environment that the practice of sharing all land has developed. Where there was no shortage of cultivable hill slopes, the members of a small community considered all the land in the vicinity of their settlement as their joint property, accessible to anyone who wanted to clear a piece of forest. Among the Konda Reddis of the villages on the left bank of the Godavari, communal ownership of the land was practised until some twenty years ago when the leasing of land to non-tribals began and land became a scarce commodity. Yet the principle of sharing whatever land there is left seems deeply ingrained in Reddi custom. When in villages on both sides of the Godavari title deeds *(patta)* to land were somewhat haphazardly granted to Reddis by government officials, it happened that some families were left out. But cooperation between the villagers was so good that those without *patta* land were nevertheless allowed to share in whatever land was available. When I revisited Kakishnur in 1977, some thirty-seven years after my first fieldwork, I found that several men who had very modest holdings, which they and the members of their family could easily have cultivated by themselves, nevertheless allowed other men to whom they were not bound by kinship ties to cultivate with them as sharecroppers. The yield was divided equally among all workers without an extra share being set aside for the owner of the land. I found an example of similar cooperation in Motagudem, a small Reddi village in the hills of West Godavari District close to Gogulapudi (see chapter 10). There one Reddi, Boli Chinna Gangaya, originally of Gogulapudi, had spontaneously achieved the transition from slash-and-burn cultivation to permanent cultivation with ploughs and bullocks. He owned four bullocks and nine cows, all the off-spring of a calf bartered by his father for a pig. By never selling any cattle he built up this small herd and then cleared some flat land and started ploughing, while all other villagers continued with their digging stick cultivation on *podu* fields. Another man, who had come from a neighbouring village, joined him in this enterprise, but although the plough bullocks all belonged to Gangaya, who had also made the land arable, the two partners shared the yield equally. Jointly they also cultivated a *podu* field and divided the crop in the same manner.

A truly cooperative spirit, natural to primitive societies regarding all land as communal property, survives here into an age when governments recognize no other ownership than that of individuals. But where competition for land with non-tribal newcomers increases and land becomes a marketable commodity, the generosity of landowners vis-à-vis indigent co-villagers tends to fade. We have seen that among Koyas of Khammam landowners already charge sharecroppers for the use of their land, and the Gonds of Adilabad have given up the free sharing of land ever since individuals were allotted separate holdings.

Among the Reddis of the Godavari region, agriculture has for some time ceased to be the sole basis of the economy. The reasons for this development are two-fold. The restrictions on slash-and-burn cultivation described in chapter 3 forced the Reddis to seek other sources of subsistence, and the arrival of forest contractors in need of labourers capable of felling and transporting bamboo provided an alternative to the old order. While previously the Reddis had been free to fell the forest for their own purposes, they could now use their skill in woodcraft and familiarity with the hill forests by working for those who had begun to exploit the forest for commercial use.

In my book *The Reddis of the Bison Hills,* I discussed in detail the process which had turned many Reddis from self-sufficient cultivators into forest labourers, who often had to neglect their fields because of the demands of their new occupation. A brief recapitulation of the situation as I found it in the early 1940s will therefore suffice in this context.

Judging from local tradition and some remarks of G. F. C. Wakefield, who travelled in the Samasthan of Paloncha in the early decades of the present century,[2] the Reddis of Hyderabad State lived then mainly "in the heart of the jungle in primitive huts. . . . each hut, containing one family only living on the products of the jungle helped out with small patches of cultivation of a giant species of *jowari."* This picture drawn by Wakefield applies today only to a very few groups of Reddis, such as those of Kutturgata (see chapter 6), but even in the 1940s most Reddis had abandoned their traditional forest life. With the extension of an effective administration into the hill tracts, the Reddis had become liable to money payments for the use of their land and certain forest products, and in order to meet these obligations, they had to supplement their income by selling their own labour. Contact with lowlanders also instilled in them a taste for previously rare or even unknown commodities, such as spices, more substantial clothes, and metal and glass ornaments. The cash required for the purchase of such goods could be obtained by accepting employment offered by forest contractors who had begun to exploit the rich timber and bamboo growth in the hills flanking the Godavari. Contact with other castes also familiarized the Reddis with the practice of plough cultivation, and in some of the fertile alluvial pockets of the Godavari Valley, they began to plough with bullocks on permanently cultivated fields. Both regular forest labour and plough cultivation fostered a greater stability of settlement, and this led ultimately to the formation of relatively large villages on the banks of the Godavari, whose inhabitants depended only partly on slash-and-burn cultivation and the gathering of wild jungle produce, for they gradually had gotten used to the provisions received from merchants in payment for their labour in the forest.

The transition to an economy largely dependent on wage labour was by no means beneficial, for already in the early 1940s most Reddis of the Godavari zone had become entirely dependent on merchants and enmeshed in a web of indebtedness from which they could not

2. "Note on a Visit to the Prehistoric Burial-Grounds of Janampett, in the Paloncha Taluka of Warangal District of H.E.H. the Nizam's Dominions."

extricate themselves by their own efforts. In order to drag bamboos to the riverbank, from which they were floated down to the timber market at Rajahmundry, they needed bullocks, and these they obtained mainly on credit. Moreover, merchants provided their labourers with provisions the cost of which was set against wages earned. Payment was by piece-work, and in 1941 merchants were supposed to pay their men Rs 2 for felling one hundred bamboos and transporting them to the riverbank. This worked out at a daily wage of Rs ¼, corresponding in purchasing power to about three to four kilograms of millet. In practice, however, the merchants paid only a fraction of the fixed rates, and the majority of the Reddis' earnings were withheld on the pretext of old debts and the interest accruing. The merchants took advantage of the Reddis' inability to make any but the simplest calculations or to check on any transaction. To all intents and purposes most Reddi forest labourers were bond-servants entirely at the mercy of their employers. This situation is illustrated by the fact that it was not unusual for a group of Reddis to be "sold" by one contractor to another who then took over their debts.

In several reports to the Nizam's government,[3] I exposed this tyranny of the big timber contractors, and as a result of the action then taken by the administration the power of the principal merchants was curtailed for the time being. A cooperative scheme, first launched by a Swami, resident in a hermitage at Parantapalli, enabled the Reddis of several villages to draw fair wages, and free themselves from the oppression of unscrupulous contractors.

Subsequently the government department concerned with tribal welfare took over the organization of the cooperative exploitation of the forest coups in the Godavari area. A cooperative society located in the riverbank village of Koida took the coups in auction from the Forest Department, and worked them for the sole benefit of the tribesmen, both Reddis and Koyas, who were also supplied with provisions at fair prices. This society operated from 1947 till 1962, and the Reddis of the area are still talking nostalgically of the prosperity and security which they enjoyed while it was functioning. Unfortunately and inexplicably this cooperative venture came to an end when in 1962 the Forest Department leased out all the bamboo coups to the Sirpur Paper Mills at a rate lower than the cooperative society had paid. Inter-departmental frictions and the often demonstrated indifference of the Forest Department to the interests of tribal populations are the probable causes of this development, which destroyed with one stroke all the welfare work done among the local Reddis for several years.

3. See *Tribal Hyderabad*, "Notes on the Hill Reddis in the Samasthan of Paloncha," pp. 1–35.

When I visited Koida and other Reddi villages in 1978, conditions had largely reverted to a state of affairs as unfavourable to the Reddis as that which I had observed in the early 1940s. The Reddis were once again under the domination of non-tribal merchants, to whom most of them were indebted. But while in the forties merchants had resided in Rajahmundry and had come to the Reddi area only occasionally during the bamboo-cutting season, many have now built houses in Reddi villages and live there most of the year. In chapter 2 I have already discussed the way in which such merchants have acquired the de facto use of land which still belongs nominally to Reddis. Today they are only indirectly involved in the bamboo-cutting business, but by utilizing much of the village land for the highly profitable cultivation of tobacco and chillies, they force the Reddis to rely for their livelihood mainly on forest labour.

The Sirpur Paper Mills has established an organization with a staff of supervisors and clerks who receive and weigh the bamboos brought by Reddis to the riverbank. The fixed rate according to which the labourers should be paid is seven paisa (i.e. Rs 0.07) per kilogram, but I was told that in practice the labourers receive only six paisa per kilogram. The quantity of bamboos individual labourers, a few of whom are women, can deliver each day varies from 50 to 150 kilograms, and thus the daily earning should be between Rs 3.50 and Rs 10.50, but is in fact considerably less. First, the representatives of the firm pay only at a rate of six paisa per kilogram, and second, they pay the labourers only once a month, or sometimes even only once in two months. Being illiterate the Reddis lose count of their deliveries by the time they are paid, and this enables the clerks to divert some of the wages to their own pockets. If between pay-days the labourers need payment in order to purchase food, the clerks give them slips of paper which some of the local shopkeepers will accept in place of cash. Although there is in Koida a store of the official Girijan Corporation, where the Reddis could obtain grain at cheaper rates, the vouchers issued to the Reddis can be cashed only at shops whose owners are in league with the employees of the Sirpur Paper Mills. Thus the Reddis get in fact much less payment than they should receive according to the fixed rates. Not all Reddis own bullocks, and those who have to hire a pair must give to the owners of the bullocks half of their earnings. It is virtually impossible for a Reddi to purchase a pair of bullocks with borrowed money, for the local merchants exact 50 percent interest per annum.

Bamboo cutting is seasonal work, which continues from mid-September throughout the winter until the beginning of the monsoon in June. Some provident men save cash for the lean months when there is no forest work, whereas others take loans from merchants. In villages with a large non-tribal population, such as Koida, Reddis have largely lost the habit of gathering wild roots and tubers and borrow grain from shopkeepers when their own store has run out and they have no earnings from wage-labour. In this way they remain indefinitely indebted, and merchants encourage this habit in order to maintain their control over the tribals, whom they require for work in their tobacco and chilli plantations.

In villages where there are few or no non-tribals, Reddis still collect roots for their immediate consumption, and in Kakishnur, where I spent some time in December 1977, I saw every evening groups of women returning from the forest carrying digging sticks and baskets full of edible tubers. But my suggestion to the Reddis of Koida that they might free themselves from indebtedness if they reverted for some time to the eating of jungle roots fell on deaf ears. They said that they had become used to eating rice and had no more taste for their old diet.

Even in Gogulapudi, one of the most conservative villages, which has outwardly changed little since 1941, people rely less than they used to do on jungle produce, and buy some grain with the cash they earn by forest work. There the young headman told me that from October 1978 to January 1979 he had earned Rs 310 by cutting bamboos in the pay of the Forest Department, which in that area did not auction coups but worked them departmentally.

The economy of the Reddis in the high hills of East Godavari District differs from that of the Reddis of Khammam District because of the lesser importance of forest work. There are no bamboo coups leased to contractors, but the Forest Department occasionally employs Reddis for plantation work, and pays daily wages of Rs 5.50 for men, Rs 4–4.50 for women, and Rs 3 for children. Unpaid labour is exacted for the clearing of forest lines.

In this area slash-and-burn cultivation (*podu*) is still one of the pillars of the economy, but in recent years many Reddis have in addition developed the cultivation of rice on irrigated fields. Land and climate are also suitable for the cultivation of oranges, and the recent improvement of road communications facilitating the transport of this perishable crop has stimulated the expansion of horticulture. The *muttadar* of Kakur, Pallala Jiappa Reddi, is a good example of a successful tribal entrepreneur. He lives partly in Kakur and partly in the new block headquarters, Marudimilli, where he stays in his father-in-law's house. In Kakur he owns 300 orange trees, and when the oranges ripen he brings them to Marudimilli and sells them to traders who come with trucks from Rajahmundry. The oranges are sold by numbers at an average price of Rs 100 to Rs 125 per 1,000. In normal years Jiappa Reddi reaps 800–1,000 oranges per tree, and his gross income is

Rs 20,000–25,000. The carriage by head loads to Marudimilli is Rs 2 per 100 oranges. In years when not all trees bear fruit, his net income is about Rs 4,000, but there are also years of complete crop failure. In Kakur every family owns some orange trees, but there are other villages where the number of those owning orange groves is small. Some of the fruit growers transport the oranges to such markets as Marudimilli, while others sell the crop on the trees to traders, but usually only when the fruits have formed.

Most of the traders operating in the area are Valmikis, also known as Konda Mala, a community believed to have originated in the lowlands but settled in the hills for several generations. The symbiosis of Reddis and Valmikis has on the whole been to the latter's advantage, and some Reddis speak nowadays with some scorn of the exploitative practices of their Valmiki neighbours. Previously Valmikis bought up most of the minor forest products collected by Reddis at low prices and resold them at vast profit in distant markets. Similarly they often bought the whole orange crop of a Reddi, paying only a fraction of its value. Valmikis owned ponies and pack bullocks, and could thus transport such goods more easily than Reddis, who would have had to move them by head-loads. Since the construction of motor roads and the establishment of a weekly market at Marudimilli, Reddis are no longer in need of Valmiki middlemen and can sell their produce directly to lowland traders. Yet some exploitation continues, and Valmikis who are averse to manual labour employ Reddis to build their houses, paying them derisory fees, and even get their *podu* fields cleared by Reddis, whom they often give only one rupee and a midday meal for a day's work. It would seem, however, that this type of collaboration is on the way out and that many Reddis, becoming aware of the changed economic circumstances, are no longer prepared to let themselves be exploited by Valmikis, whom they have always regarded as untouchable and socially inferior notwithstanding their material successes.

DEVELOPMENT PROJECTS

Although large amounts of government funds have been spent for tribal welfare, the number of schemes aimed at transforming the economy of tribal communities in a radical way is very small. Such measures as the provision of wells and the distribution of plough bullocks have certainly had beneficial effects, but did not bring about fundamental changes. The cooperative society through which Reddis and Koyas were enabled to exploit the forest wealth of their ancestral environment was one of the few schemes which had achieved such a change, but we have seen that it was unceremoniously disbanded by the Andhra Pradesh government, probably because at that time the Forest Department preferred to deal with a large organization such as the Sirpur Paper Mills and had no compunction in sacrificing the interests of the Reddi and Koya labourers.

In some cases well-intentioned innovations could not be sustained because the tribals were mentally not adjusted to economic pursuits different from their traditional way of gaining a livelihood. An example for this was the attempt to turn the foodgathering Chenchus into plough-cultivators. In Kurnool District, which in the days of British rule belonged to Madras Presidency, the first efforts in that direction were made in the 1930s, and when I visited the settlements of Peddacheruvu, Bairluti, and Nagerluti in 1940 about 10 to 20 percent of the families living there were cultivating on a small scale. However, on my return visit in 1978 I found that for various reasons, including perhaps the less than helpful attitude of the Forest Department, cultivation by Chenchus of these villages had virtually come to an end. In Peddacheruvu I was told that in 1943 ten men had been supplied with plough bullocks, and that by borrowing these bullocks six more men used to cultivate. But when the bullocks became old or died of disease the Chenchus could not replace them. An old man, who himself had cultivated, explained that those who had bullocks and hence could cultivate never sold grain but distributed any surplus to those villagers who had no cultivation, a practice in accordance with the old Chenchu custom of sharing the meat of any game brought down in the chase. Hence the Chenchus could make no provision for replacing their bullocks by buying calves, and the whole move towards settled cultivation ultimately collapsed. Yet, the Chenchus have not completely given up the idea of growing grain crops, and on small plots near their huts some of the previous cultivators till the land with the help of a light plough drawn by hand. The old man who showed me the use of this plough said that he grew mainly maize and even now distributed part of his meagre crop among his friends. This example shows that it is easier to introduce a new technology than to develop a sense of providence. Whereas even the poorest peasant, rooted in the traditions of an agricultural society, makes every effort to provide for a replacement of the plough cattle so vital for his economic survival, the Chenchu, used to the hand-to-mouth existence of the foodgatherer and hunter, has no such innate care for the morrow, and any scheme aiming at a transformation of his economy would have to extend over a very long period during which sympathetic guidance would have to nurture the growth of a sense of economic realism.

Where the traditional economy has already necessitated long-term planning, as every developed agricultural economy does, it is relatively easy to persuade people to devote their energies to novel projects which require sustained application. An example of such a project is the transition from conventional farming with an emphasis on grain crops to extensive fruit farming. In Chennur Taluk of Adilabad District members of various backward classes have been assisted in the development of mango orchards on a large scale. The beneficiaries are Manevar (a Telugu-speaking Kolam sub-tribe), Bestas (a caste of tribal fishermen), Netakanis (untouchable weavers), Banjaras, and various other members of backward communities. The project owes its inception to a private citizen, namely N. V. Raja Reddi, a prominent landowner and businessman of Bhimaram in Chennur Taluk. In 1971 Raja Reddi distributed a substantial part of his own land to local Manevar, Netakanis, and other landless families, and helped the recipients to plant their plots with mango saplings, which he had obtained from suppliers in the coastal region. Moreover he persuaded the Tribal Welfare Department to sponsor a mango orchard collective farming society located in the village of Dampur. The department provided an initial development grant of Rs 100,000 for a scheme covering 102 acres and benefiting thirty-seven tribals, five Harijans, and six members of backward classes. This grant enabled the newly formed society to purchase 3,080 mango plants, agricultural implements, and bullocks and carts. The latter were allocated to the members of the society so that they could earn cash wages by transporting timber for contractors, and thus make a living during the five years before the mango trees would bear fruit. For three years the young trees had to be laboriously watered by hand, and to facilitate this irrigation wells were dug. While from the fifth year onwards a small cash income was derived from the sale of the first mangoes reaped, a substantial yield occurred only in the seventh year. Similar schemes, partly financed by an agricultural development bank, were started in other villages, and in June 1979 twenty-five more villages were incorporated in the project. Subsequently 70,000 mango saplings, each costing Rs. 5, were planted by 450 farmers. Of these 20,000 were purchased for cash, and 50,000 were bought with the help of bank loans which in the case of tribals were subsidized to the extent of 50 percent by the Integrated Tribal Development Agency. During the first five years of the loans, the borrowers have to pay only the interest, and after that period they have to repay the loans in twelve annual instalments, a condition the farmers can easily comply with once their mango trees bear fruit. The land utilized for the mango groves is almost useless for the cultivation of cereals because of the nature of the top-soil, but mango trees can sink their deep roots to a stratum containing humidity throughout the year.

When I visited the area in January 1979, I spoke to many villagers participating in the project, and their experiences demonstrated how successful the venture had already proved. In the seventh year after planting the saplings, i.e. when the trees were mature enough to bear substantial quantities of fruit, the farmers had derived profits varying from Rs 500 to about Rs 1,800 per acre, according to the care the trees had been given, the quality of soil, and above all the method of marketing. For some farmers sold the crop to traders for a lump sum before the mangos were properly formed, while others sold the ripe fruits by weight, the latter method proving more profitable.

One Manevar had planted 250 saplings with the help of a loan of Rs 1,000. Of these 220 survived the critical first hot season, and in the fifth year after planting the owner leased the trees to a trader for Rs 930. In the sixth year, which was a bad one, the income was only Rs 350, but in the seventh year, when the trees were approaching maturity and promised a good crop, he accepted an offer of Rs 5,000 for the entire crop even before the mangos had ripened. He told me that in the future he would not lease out the trees for a lump sum paid in advance but would sell the fruit by weight. The joint family of this particular man also owned some paddy land, which yielded enough rice for domestic consumption. Hence the profit of Rs 5,000 did not have to be spent on buying food; part of the money was used to defray marriage expenses, and Rs 700 was spent on installing electricity in the family home.

A Besta owning 145 trees had earned Rs 200 in the fifth year, Rs 250 in the sixth year and Rs 8,300 in the seventh year. In that year he had not leased out the trees but sold the mangos by weight. Rs 8,300 is a fabulous sum for a low-caste villager, but the amount was not frittered away. Rs 2,000 was used to pay off all debts, Rs 2,000 went for hospital expenses after an accident involving the man's old father, Rs 500 was used as part payment for an oil-driven irrigation pump, Rs 500 went for the installation of electricity, and Rs 1,000 was used for the purchase of food grain.

Even more successful was a Harijan of weaver caste who owned 600 mango trees, some of which he had planted as early as 1967, before the beginning of the official scheme. In the tenth year of their life he had earned Rs 10,000, and in the eleventh year the profit was once again Rs 10,000. Most of this money was invested in improvements of his land, such as the construction of an irrigation well at a cost of Rs 7,000. The only luxuries bought were a radio and a watch for his son.

Such successes have acted as a powerful advertisement for the productivity of mango orchards, and many requests for loans and technical advice are being received from villagers in neighbouring areas. At the beginning of the project there was strong opposition from local landowners, who feared that they might lose part of their labour force if landless tribals and Harijans could be turned into successful fruit farmers. They tried to sabotage the scheme by insidious rumours about the intention of government and the cooperative society, and this propaganda initially led to the wilful destruction of hundreds of saplings, but was ultimately defeated by the obvious success of the venture.

One of the lessons learned from this horticultural enterprise is the urgent need for help and encouragement by leading local personalities in all movements which aim at a radical transformation of the economy in tribal areas. Governments can do much by giving financial aid and technical advice, but in view of the frequent transfers of officials, one of the gravest weaknesses of the present system of administration, only local non-official personalities of imagination and integrity taking an active interest in the development of backward communities can guide a programme of innovation from its inception to its final fruition.

Another pilot scheme for the development of novel cash crops is being conducted in the tribal areas of Vishakapatnam District. There coffee plantations are established by the Girijan Corporation, and during the first five years local tribals are employed as labourers and trainees to learn the care of coffee bushes. After these five years the plantation will be handed over on loan to the same tribals who worked on it as labourers in the expectation that they will be able to manage the coffee cultivation by themselves. The coffee bushes would then have a further life-span of about ten years. The scheme is only in its beginning, and the outcome is hence still uncertain.

A totally different attempt to modernize the tribal economy is at present underway in Srikakulam District. There Jatapus and Saoras have been encouraged to grow sugar-cane, and every cultivator switching to the cultivation of this crop is given a one-time, non-returnable subsidy of Rs 400. Near the village of Rastukunta Bai a modern sugar factory has been built, and 250–300 tribals, both men and women, work in this mill every day in three eight-hour shifts, earning a daily wage of Rs 4. The work suits the Saoras and Jatapus, for it is largely in the open where the cane is being unloaded and cut and in large, airy halls. Expert workers and mechanics are being imported from Uttar Pradesh, but there is a scheme for the training of local tribals. The factory is not yet self-supporting, and depends on government subsidies, but the experiment of furthering the tribals' cultivation of a profitable cash crop and at the same time creating opportunities for industrial work suitable for tribal men and women is certainly worth supporting.

The only other instance in Andhra Pradesh of the employment of numerous members of tribal communities in industry is in Khammam District, where Koyas have been working in the Singareni collieries ever since the beginning of mining operations in the early years of the century, when the first mine was established at Yellandu in the heart of the Koya country. Most of the Koya miners lived in villages close enough to Yellandu to enable the men to walk to work whenever they were free from agricultural activities. Particularly in the months of March, April, May, and the first half of June, the collieries could count on the Koyas from the vicinity, who at times constituted more than 25 percent of the total labour force. However, when the collieries were shifted to Kothagudem some twenty-five miles away the employment of Koyas fell off, for those in the villages near Yellandu could no longer walk daily to the mines, and did not like to stay away from their villages for weeks at a time. Various efforts of colliery officials to persuade experienced labourers to move to Kothagudem and live in labour lines had little success. In the vicinity of Kothagudem there were few large Koya villages, and even from those not many men went to work in the mines. When I investigated the situation in 1943, I found that there were only 497 Koyas among a total labour force of 8,000; about 70 percent were men and 30 percent women. Of these, 384 Koyas, both men and women, worked underground and 113 worked on the surface; 454 were living on company ground, and very few walked to work from villages. At that time the company could have employed 1,500 more Koya labourers, but it seems that no one found a solution to the problem of transport from the villages near Yellandu.

In 1978 I revisited the area of Yellandu, particularly the village of Sudimalla, where in 1945 I had been instrumental in establishing a Koya teacher-training centre similar to the Marlavai centre in Adilabad. Among the people who gathered there were several who are employed by the Singareni collieries. Most of them go to work on bicycles, and there is now also a good bus service. Conditions of work have greatly improved, and men employed permanently receive a monthly salary averaging Rs 400, while those on piece-work can earn even more. Koya supervisors in underground work earned Rs 700–800 per month. Fifteen villages in Yellandu Taluk provided then a labour force of some 400 Koyas, and in some of the mines 75 percent of those employed were Koyas. There was a reversal of the situation on the labour market. While in the 1940s the company sought more Koya workers, being generally short of labour, in 1978 the Koyas I spoke to complained about the difficulty of getting employment in the mines. They were particularly unhappy about the termination of the company's earlier practice of giving priority in recruitment to the sons of retired miners. Now all applications for employment in the mines are processed by the labour exchange, and Koyas feel that the new system erodes their communities' old connection with the mines.

The same company now also operates mines at Bellampalli in Adilabad District, but there tribals do not constitute a significant proportion of the labour force, as the local Gonds and Kolams have not been able to establish themselves in the industries of that district.

In a national situation of increasing unemployment in many branches of the economy, it is unlikely that in the foreseeable future significant numbers of tribals will be able to earn their livelihood in major industries. It appears, therefore, that concentration on the improvement of tribal agriculture is still the most promising policy for governments and unofficial agencies concerned about the welfare of tribal populations to adopt.

5 The Problem of Tribal Education

THE VULNERABILITY of tribal populations to exploitation by minor government officials, as well as moneylenders, landlords, and other agents of vested interests, can largely be traced to their illiteracy and general ignorance of the world outside the narrow confines of their traditional environment. Their inability to cope with the many novel forces impinging nowadays on tribal villages and on an economy which had remained virtually unchanged for centuries is by no means due to any innate lack of intelligence. As long as they operate within their familiar atmosphere, tribals evince as much perspicacity, skill, and even true wisdom as any other population, but as soon as they are faced by social attitudes rooted in a different system they become insecure and often behave in a manner detrimental to their own interests. Brought up in a system in which all communications are by word of mouth, and hence used to trusting verbal statements, they get confused by constant reference to documents and written rules, which increasingly determine all aspects of rural life. Unable to read even the receipt given by an official and obliged to put their thumb impressions on documents which they cannot understand, they are easy victims of any fraud or misrepresentation which more educated exploiters are likely to devise.

It is obvious, therefore, that a modicum of literacy is indispensable as a first step towards enabling tribals to operate within the orbit of the advanced communities dominating the economic and political scene. The disadvantages under which illiterate tribals labour are multiplied in the case of those who do not even speak and understand the language of the dominant population, and hence cannot communicate with officials except through better-educated fellow tribesmen acting as interpreters.

Many of the tribal groups of Andhra Pradesh long ago lost their own language and speak Telugu as their mother tongue. In their case there is no language barrier, and hence no need for any special type of schooling. Other tribes, however, speak languages unintelligible to most outsiders, and it is imperative for them to learn Telugu if they want to communicate with members of the majority community. This is the case of the Gonds and Kolams of Adilabad, of some groups of Koyas of Khammam, and of several of the tribes of Vishakapatnam and Srikakulam.

Among the Gonds there are still many who speak no other language than Gondi, a Dravidian tongue closer to Kanara than to Telugu, and many Kolams speak Kolami and Gondi, but neither Telugu nor any other language understood by officials and members of the advanced ethnic groups. Hence they are handicapped at every step as soon as they move out of the small circle of their fellow tribesmen.

Education for tribals who normally speak their own tongues is beset with difficulties, because the acquisition of literacy has to be combined with the learning of a language other than the mother tongue. Yet the average teacher available for tribal schools has had no training whatsoever in the technique of imparting to children what is to them a foreign language.

The first major educational experiment launched among any tribal community of Andhra Pradesh was the Gond Education Scheme in Adilabad District, initiated by the Nizam's government in 1943. At the time, when there was a determined drive to improve the position of the Gonds, Pardhans, and Kolams, it was realized that no advance could be maintained unless it was accompanied by the emergence of at least a small number of literate tribals. But what was to be the medium of instruction? The vast majority of Gond children did not speak or understand any language other than Gondi, but there were no teachers who knew Gondi and could communicate with Gond children. Hence there was no other solution to the problem than to produce Gondi-speaking teachers before any schools for Gond children could be established. There existed at that time a few young Gonds who had privately learned the rudiments of reading and writing Marathi, the language spoken by many of the Hindus of the western part of the district. A small band of such semi-literate Gonds were assembled at Marlavai, a village in the hills of Utnur Taluk, and initially given systematic training in the reading and writing of Marathi and in arithmetic.

It was hoped that this training centre established in Marlavai would

Gond boys practising writing on slates in front of the school building of Marlavai village.

produce enough Gondi-speaking teachers to make it possible to start within a few years a network of primary Gond schools extending over the greater part of the district. The medium of instruction in the first two classes of these schools was to be Gondi, and to provide teaching materials the headmaster of the Marlavai Training Centre and I composed Gondi primers and readers printed in Devanagari script. The idea was that once the children had learned to read and write Gondi in this script, they could more easily be taught Marathi, the script being the same. From the fourth standard onwards Urdu, then the official language of Hyderabad State, was to be added, and in order to make this possible the teacher trainees were also taught Urdu.

By 1946 thirty primary Gond schools were functioning, and by 1949 their number had more than trebled. In order to improve gradually the standard of the Gond teachers, all of them were annually assembled at Marlavai for a course of instruction lasting one month. In this way the level of their competence was raised, and they were familiarized with new developments in the sphere of tribal welfare. In addition to the training of teachers, the Marlavai centre was used for the instruction of literate Gonds in the basic knowledge of revenue matters required for village officers, and some of those trained were subsequently appointed as *patwari*.

Girls of Marlavai being taught to read Gondi with the help of a chart prepared in 1943 for the instruction of adults.

By 1951 the Marlavai Training Centre, which in 1943 had begun with the training of five semi-literate Gonds, had produced ninety-five teachers, five village officers, one revenue inspector, five clerks, and seven forest guards. One of the trainees of Marlavai, Atram Lingu, subsequently became *patwari, sarpanch* of the Sirpur *panchayat*, and finally in 1967 president of the Panchayat Samithi of the Utnur Tribal Development Block.

The success of this centre encouraged the Social Service Department to establish a second centre at Ginnedhari, a Gond village in Asifabad Taluk. There Telugu was the language of the non-tribal population, and hence Telugu was taught instead of Marathi.

The high hopes which had been placed in this experiment of imparting education to Gond children in the mother tongue and at the same time familiarizing them with the regional languages were subsequently disappointed. The incorporation of the Telengana districts of Hyderabad State into Andhra Pradesh was accompanied by fundamental changes in the educational system. The government decided to abandon the use of Gondi, and no further schoolbooks in Gondi were supplied to the schools. Instruction in Telugu, now the state language, replaced teaching in both Marathi and Urdu, with the result that many of the Gond teachers became redundant because they could not teach in Telugu.

Yet the young Gonds who had attended the two training centres formed for years a class of moderately educated tribals. Apart from those who worked as teachers, there were some who found employment in minor government posts.

In 1972 the character of tribal schools was changed. Many single-teacher schools were closed and staff and children grouped together in so-called ashram schools. These provide boarding facilities for children from other villages, while children from the same locality can attend as day scholars. The expense of these boarding schools is considerable, for to maintain and educate a child in one of them costs the government approximately Rs 1,000 per year. There is no coordinated control over the tribal schools, as some are supported by the Tribal Welfare Department and others by the relevant Panchayat Samithi. In 1975 there were 269 primary schools, 46 ashram schools, and 10 Tribal Welfare hostels for children attending upper primary schools and high schools outside the area covered by the Integrated Tribal Development Project. The government also provided scholarships, books, slates, and clothes to tribal pupils. Despite all these facilities only 31.2 percent of the tribal children of school age were enrolled in educational institutions, and the literacy rate of the tribals of Adilabad District, which had been 2.52 percent in 1961, had risen to no more than 3.28 percent. According to the 1971 census there were then many villages the entire population of which was illiterate, and I learned by personal observation that even in 1979 there were still entirely illiterate village communities.

The numbers of the various types of educational institutions in all the tribal areas of Andhra Pradesh in 1979 were as follows:

Ashram schools	399 with 26,746 students
Primary schools	1,740 with 37,729 students
Upper primary schools	115 with 4,052 students
High schools	75 with 3,630 students
Junior colleges	6 with 305 students

The number of teachers in ashram schools was 1,171 and that of teachers in other schools 1,821. Despite the existence of all these schools, the percentage of tribal children who pass the tenth standard, i.e. matriculation, and are thus qualified to proceed to intermediate courses in colleges is very low, and in thirty-six years of tribal education only five Gonds and two Pardhans have been awarded university degrees.

What is the reason for this disappointing lack of educational progress, which contrasts so dramatically with the rapid advances achieved by most tribal communities in Northeast India (see chapter 11)?

One of the causes is undoubtedly the very low standard of teaching and facilities in tribal schools. About 75 percent of all schools are housed in thatched huts, many of which leak during the rains, a defect making their proper functioning extremely difficult. There are, moreover, no quarters for the teaching staff, and rented accommodation is unavailable in most tribal villages. The lack of basic comforts discourages non-tribal teachers from taking on jobs involving residence in remote villages, and among those posted in such villages there is a high rate of absenteeism. While non-tribal teachers are reluctant to work in tribal villages, few Gonds are nowadays available for such posts. The reason is that the Education Department has raised the required standard, so that only persons who have attained intermediate standard are eligible for teaching posts. Gonds who have reached that standard are few; those who have done so can continue their education with the help of scholarships, and if they are successful they have a good chance of obtaining more attractive posts owing to the system of reservation of posts for members of scheduled tribes. Hence, qualified tribals are not very interested in appointments as teachers, and those tribal matriculates who would be glad to take up such posts are not acceptable to the education authorities.

Among the teachers working in tribal schools at present, those of non-tribal origin generally have higher educational qualifications than their tribal colleagues. Nevertheless, their efficiency as teachers is not necessarily higher than that of tribal teachers. Their appointment to schools in a tribal area is usually purely accidental. Few of them have expressed any preference for such a posting, and they are given no orientation or training for work among tribal children. Their difficulties begin with their inability to speak and understand Gondi, the only language most of the younger children know. Moreover, they are total strangers to tribal culture and the values of the society within which they have to operate. Those who persevere in tribal schools usually pick up a working knowledge of Gondi, but their own cultural background stands in the way of an understanding and appreciation of tribal culture and traditions. As quarters are not provided by government and rented accommodation is usually unobtainable, most non-tribal teachers are separated from their wives and children, with the inevitable result that they take every opportunity of leaving their posts and visiting their families. The majority of these teachers try to obtain posts outside the tribal area as soon as possible.

As a result of the shortage of efficient teachers, as well as of the inadequate facilities in most schools, few tribal boys and girls pass the tenth standard, and the majority of those enrolled drop out long before. The reasons for this wastage are many. At the age of ten to twelve, boys and girls are useful for work on their parents' farms, and many Gonds are unwilling to spare their children, particularly if they see that the schools are not well run and the teachers' frequent absences condemn the children on many days to virtual idleness. Perhaps more important is the realization among parents, as well as the older pupils, that school education is of limited usefulness. While those who have passed the tenth standard are eligible for minor jobs in government service, by no means all have obtained such jobs, and there is, moreover, the large category popularly described as "tenth failed." Boys who have read up to the tenth standard but failed to pass the final examination have few chances of employment in government service, and as nearly all commercial activities down to small village shops are in the hands of non-tribals who employ on principle only members of their own caste or community, there are no other openings for such youths. Yet ten or more years at school have given them the ambition to find an occupation other than the ordinary farm work for which they are no better qualified than their illiterate contemporaries.

In the tribal societies of Northeast India, superior educational institutions allow many young people to obtain good academic qualifications which enable them to compete even outside their own sphere on equal terms with men and women of other communities. There many tribals have been appointed to gazetted government posts, and others have proved successful in the professions and in commerce. Hence education has so high a prestige that a few failures do not marr its image. But the Gonds see hardly any of their fellow tribesmen elevated to respected and lucrative positions, and numerous school-leavers are without any jobs. Their disillusionment with school education is therefore understandable. The advantage of having some literate persons in the village does not weigh heavily with the individual family which for years has forgone a son's help on the farm without enjoying any financial reward for the time he spent at school.

A certain disenchantment with the results of school education prevailing among many of the illiterate tribals accounts for the fact that in villages where tribals and non-tribals live side by side the latter are much keener on making use of educational facilities. In an investigation conducted in 1977 by Y. B. Abbasayulu in nine villages of Utnur Taluk, it was found that 62.28 percent of the non-tribals, but only 33.72 percent of the tribals, sent their children to school. Of the tribals interviewed, 22.15 percent gave poverty as their reason for not sending their children to school, 12.5 percent claimed the children's involvement in agricultural activities, and 3.75 percent gave as an excuse their general inferiority complex vis-à-vis non-tribals. Some of the non-tribals also claimed poverty as an excuse, but none invoked the need for children to do farm work, and reference to a feeling of inferiority did not figure in their replies. Interestingly, more tribals than non-tribals replied positively to the question of whether they thought of education as good and valuable; 98.46 percent approved of school education, whereas only 76.3 percent of the non-tribals professed so positive an appreciation. Abbasayulu interprets this surprising result of his inquiry by pointing out that non-tribals, engaged mainly in making money, were confident of their ability to be economically successful even without formal education, whereas tribals realized that their depressed status could be bettered only by education, despite the disappointing results of the schooling of so many of their children.

As an illustration of the impact of education on individual villages, we may consider the situation in Marlavai and Kanchanpalli. The former was the first centre of Gond education and is still the site of an ashram school, and the latter also has some tradition of literacy as the seat of a raja family literate for at least three generations. At Kanchanpalli, too, there is at present an ashram school.

Among the fifty households of Marlavai, there were in 1977 eleven literate adults and fourteen children attending the local school. Apart from one retired school-teacher, no one in the village had ever held a paid post.

Among the sixty-four households of Kanchanpalli, there were in 1977 twenty-two literate adults and twenty-four children were attending the local school.

In both villages there were among the literate adults men who had attended school for only three or four years, and had only a very limited knowledge of reading and writing.

By the beginning of 1980, the educational scene in both villages had considerably improved, probably because of the Gonds' general increased awareness of the need for education. Forty children of Marlavai were attending various schools. Twenty-one of these went as day pupils to the local ashram school, 15 were boarders in other ashram schools, and 4 attended schools in two taluk headquarters and stayed there in hostels for scheduled tribes where they got free food and lodging. In the Marlavai ashram school there were then 139 pupils, including 21 girls. Attendance in the Kanchanpalli ashram school had also increased: there were altogether 89 pupils, including 50 boarders and 39 day pupils.

There can be no doubt, however, that part of the money and effort devoted to the teaching of tribal children is wasted because many children leave school after the third or fourth year and soon relapse into virtual illiteracy. This is borne out by the relatively small number of literates in Marlavai. This village has had a primary school since 1945, and in 1943–44 it was the focal point of an adult literacy project for which special charts in Gondi had been printed. Yet thirty-four years later there were only eleven literate adults among the villagers.

In a study of tribal education in Adilabad District, E. V. Rathnaiah investigated the attitude of Gonds to school education.[1] In the course of this investigation he found that in the opinion of the teachers interviewed 13.7 percent of parents were positively cooperative, 56.3 percent were favourable to education but not active, 23.7 percent were indifferent, 1.3 percent were unfavourable, and 5 percent were antagonistic. The reasons given by parents for not sending their children to school were as follows:

Need for help in household work	35.7 percent
Occupation with herding cattle	30.0 percent
Children's lack of interest in education	25.3 percent
Ill health	6.6 percent
Don't know	2.4 percent

In the opinion of the teachers questioned, the reasons for the poor enrollment of tribals in schools were:

Lack of interest in education among parents	64.5 percent
Poverty	31.5 percent
Lack of interest in education among children	4.0 percent

Even more important factors impeding the spread of education among tribal children are the distance of many villages from the nearest school and the limited places in ashram schools. There are many villages whose children would have to walk five or six kilometers to attend a school, and there are not enough boarding schools to accommodate more than a fraction of the children from villages without primary schools in a vicinity.

For tribal children who are eligible for admission to upper primary and high schools, most of which are situated at some distance from tribal villages, there are hostels in which pupils are provided with free board and lodging, and in some cases also with extra tuition. Without such facilities few tribal children could attend high schools, because for most parents it is economically impossible to maintain a child in a taluk or district headquarters.

Notwithstanding all the material facilities provided by government for tribal students, few progress beyond the fifth form. The following figures relating to 1976 make this clear. Of 5,599 tribal children enrolled in the schools of Adilabad District, 4,555 were boys and 1,044

1. *Structural Constraints in Tribal Education.*

TABLE 1.   *Higher Education Scholarships, 1974–75*

INSTITUTION	NUMBER OF SCHOLARS	AMOUNT OF SCHOLARSHIPS
Government College, Adilabad	4	Rs 3,400
Degree College, Nirmal	2	1,648
Junior College, Sirpur-Kaghaznagar	3	2,863
Government College, Chennur	1	364
Government College, Mancherial	14	10,371
TOTAL	24	Rs 18,647

were girls. Distribution in forms I to X was as follows: I, 3,302; II, 832; III, 363; IV, 298; V, 345; VI, 194; VII, 119; VIII, 58; IX, 43; X, 40.

The rapid drop in attendance was particularly noticeable in the blocks of Wankdi and Utnur.

There the relevant figures were as follows:

Form	I	II	III	IV	V	VI	VII	VIII	IX	X
Wankdi	284	24	9	3	4	1	2	0	0	0
Utnur	912	192	60	28	34	28	23	6	15	7

For the years after 1976, statistics for the indigenous aboriginals are not available because in 1977 the immigrant Banjaras were notified as a scheduled tribe, and henceforth counted among the tribals. But my personal enquiries in primary, upper primary, and high schools confirmed the trend apparent in the above statistics. After the first form, in which many children are enrolled, there is a dramatic drop, and between forms II and III, and III and IV, the figures are each year more than halved. Only a very small percentage of pupils reaches forms VIII, IX, and X. Of those reading in form X, many fail the Secondary School Certificate examination, and the number of Gond children attaining eligibility for college education is thus infinitesimal; this explains the disconcertingly small number of graduates. In the school year 1976–77, 797 boys and 109 girls were attending high schools in Adilabad District, but only one boy attended a junior college.

TABLE 2.   *Educational Performance of Tribals
in Government Service, to 1977*

TRIBE	DESIGNATION AND OFFICE	QUALIFICATION	HOME VILLAGE OR TALUK
Gond	Subinspector of Police, Sultanabad, Karimnagar District	Pre-University Course	Madaguda, Both Taluk
Pardhan	Radio Licence Inspector	Higher Secondary Certificate	Adilabad
Gond	Inspector of Vaccinations	VIII standard	Kapardevi, Adilabad Taluk
Pardhan	Agricultural Assistant, Parbhani (Maharashtra)	B.Sc. Agriculture	Kapardevi, Adilabad Taluk
Pardhan	Lower Divisional Clerk, Revenue Department	B.Sc. failed	Deepaiguda, Adilabad Taluk
Pardhan	Lower Divisional Clerk, Social Welfare Department	Higher Secondary Certificate	Adilabad
Pardhan	Lower Divisional Clerk, Revenue Department	Secondary School Certificate	Lakshetipet Taluk
Gond	Lower Divisional Clerk, Public Works Department	Secondary School Certificate	Madaguda, Adilabad Taluk
Gond	Lower Divisional Clerk, Forest Department	B.A.	Korstkal Taluk
Gond	Lower Divisional Clerk, Forest Department	Intermediate failed	Kapardevi, Adilabad Taluk
Gond	Lower Divisional Clerk, Forest Department	Intermediate failed	Bhutai, Both Taluk
Pardhan	Lower Divisional Clerk, Local Funds	Secondary School Certificate	Akrula, Adilabad Taluk
Gond	Lower Divisional Clerk, Post Office	Secondary School Certificate	Both
Pardhan	Lower Divisional Clerk, Girijan Corporation	Secondary School Certificate	Thendoguda, Asifabad Taluk
Pardhan	Telephone Operator	B.A. discontinued	Asifabad

TRIBE	DESIGNATION AND OFFICE	QUALIFICATION	HOME VILLAGE OR TALUK
Pardhan	*Telephone Operator*	*Secondary School Certificate*	*Ginnedhari, Asifabad Taluk*
Gond	*Lower Divisional Clerk, Police Department*	*Intermediate failed*	*Bhimpur, Adilabad Taluk*
Pardhan	*Lower Divisional Clerk, Registration Office*	*Secondary School Certificate*	*Jaturla, Adilabad Taluk*
Gond	*District Revenue Officer*	*B.A.*	*Utnur Taluk*
Gond	*Police Constable*	*Intermediate failed*	*Dhanora, Utnur Taluk*
Pardhan	*Reserve Police Constable*	*Higher Secondary Certificate failed*	*Adilabad*
Pardhan	*Lower Divisional Clerk, Cooperative Office*	*Intermediate failed*	*Adilabad*
Naikpod	*Lower Divisional Clerk, Post Office*	*Intermediate*	*Thami, Adilabad Taluk*
Naikpod	*Lower Divisional Clerk, Public Works Deptartment*	*B.A. failed*	*Nirmal*
Naikpod	*Lower Divisional Clerk, Forest Department*	*B.A. failed*	*Manoor, Adilabad Taluk*
Naikpod	*Lower Divisional Clerk, Forest Department*	*Higher Secondary Certificate*	*Mancherial*
Pardhan	*Market Inspector*	*Pre-University Course*	*Asifabad*
Pardhan	*Market Inspector*	*Higher Secondary Certificate*	*Thari, Adilabad Taluk*
Gond	*Market Inspector*	*Secondary School Certificate failed*	*Dharampuri, Adilabad Taluk*
Gond	*Market Inspector*	*Secondary School Certificate failed*	*Dharampuri, Adilabad Taluk*
Pardhan	*Salesman, Daily Requirement Depot*	*Higher Secondary Certificate failed*	*Dehgaon, Adilabad Taluk*

TABLE 2.   *(continued)*

TRIBE	DESIGNATION AND OFFICE	QUALIFICATION	HOME VILLAGE OR TALUK
Pardhan	Salesman, Daily Requirement Depot	Secondary School Certificate failed	Jaturla, Adilabad Taluk
Gond	Salesman, Daily Requirement Depot	Higher Secondary Certificate failed	Godumalle, Adilabad Taluk
Gond	Excise Constable	Secondary School Certificate failed	Jatuarla
Pardhan	Vaccinator, Health Department	Higher Secondary Certificate failed	Indravelli, Utnur Taluk
Gond	Vaccinator, Health Department	Secondary School Certificate failed	Bhutai, Both Taluk
Pardhan	Vaccinator, Health Department	Secondary School Certificate failed	Tantoli, Adilabad Taluk

There is no shortage of scholarships for those eligible for higher education, and this may be seen from Table 1.

In the Government Degree College, Adilabad, the enrollment in the first-year intermediate course from 1969–70 to 1975–76 was twenty-five, out of which only six students completed their courses. The high degree of wastage was probably due to the students' inadequate previous education, which did not enable them to compete with non-tribal students in a course demanding not only learning by rote but also independent judgement.

The standard of educational performance by tribals, i.e. Gonds, Pardhans, and Naikpods, is reflected in the qualifications of those who succeeded in obtaining employment in government service up to 1977. The fact that no Kolam figures in this list indicates the exceptionally low educational level of that tribe.

The columns of Table 2, from which individual names are deliberately omitted, contain information on the tribe, the type of employment, the educational qualification, and the home village of the tribal employees in 1977.

This list of tribal government employees illustrates both the successes and failures of tribal education in Adilabad District. Among the successes must be considered the fact that thirty-seven tribals received an education which enabled them to enter the ranks of government service at all. Seventeen of them acquired sufficient skills to enable them to attain and hold positions as lower division clerks in a variety of offices. Their qualifications range from secondary school certificate to B.A., but a number of them failed either in the intermediate or in the degree examinations and had to content themselves with minor clerical positions though success in their examinations might have made them eligible for gazetted posts. Thus one Gond graduate has recently attained the elevated position of district revenue officer. The number of those who failed in the examinations for which they had studied is relatively large, but even they managed to obtain such minor government posts as market inspector, salesman, or vaccinator. But there must be many more who failed to attain the secondary school certificate and who did not manage to secure even the humblest of government posts.

A further fact emerging from this list is the disproportionately large representation of Pardhans among government employees. They out-number Gonds, even though the total Pardhan population is less than 10 percent of the number of Gonds. As traditional bards and chron-iclers they were always the "intellectuals" among the local tribesmen, and it is hardly surprising that they could overtake the Gonds in the competition for jobs which require some intellectual gifts.

The list further reveals the advantages enjoyed by tribals in the more progressive areas, such as Adilabad Taluk, and the more back-ward status of the tribal population of Utnur Taluk. Proximity to dis-trict headquarters seems to have had a positive influence both on education and on the people's awareness of the opportunities for en-tering government service.

A study of tribal manpower resources in Adilabad District under-taken in 1977 by the Tribal Cultural Research and Training Institute, Hyderabad, has diagnosed some of the factors which impede the re-cruitment of young tribals to government service and private indus-try. Both in government enterprises and in industry there are numerous vacancies for posts requiring technical skills, but the num-ber of tribal candidates with such qualifications are few. There is an Industrial Training Institute in Mancherial, entry into which is open to candidates with a pass in the eight standard. In the year 1973–74 one tribal joined one of the courses but dropped out, and in the years 1971–72, 1972–73, and 1974–75 there were no tribal students. In the year 1975–76 six tribal candidates joined this institute; three in the course for fitter's trade and three for tractor mechanic's trade. In 1976–77 three candidates joined the course in mechanic's trade, and in 1977 altogether six tribal students were enrolled in the institute. This is a very small number considering the fact that the Singareni Collieries Company Limited alone has an annual requirement of three thousand candidates to fill vacancies in all grades and has to import labour from other districts because of the lack of sufficient qualified local persons. In 1977 there were seventeen vacancies for holders of certificates of the Industrial Training Institute on the register of the employment exchange, but there were only two tribal candidates.

As early as 1946 I advocated in my pamphlet *Progress and Problems of Aboriginal Rehabilitation in Adilabad District* the systematic training of Gonds and other tribals in mechanical skills. I wrote:

> I believe that Gonds could be trained as skilled workmen, and I would suggest that the training of young literate Gonds as carpenters, mechanics, fitters etc. should not be deferred until the industries of the new towns have come into being, but should be taken up at once. If we can build up a small stock of trained Gond workmen of fairly high qualifications . . . these young men can become the nucleus and leaders of an industrial Gond colony and serve as an example that for the aboriginal industrial employment does not necessarily mean casual labour at low wages and life in an uncongenial, squalid environment, but that an industrial worker can enjoy as high or higher a standard of living and as good housing as an independent cultivator. (P. 54)

Had this proposal been taken up, the involvement of tribals in the industries of Bellampalli and Mancherial might have begun when these industries were still in an early stage of gradual development and hence capable of integrating small groups of tribal workers. Today Gonds can enter industry only as individuals and only at the cost of total alienation from the traditional life-style of tribal society.

In the course of the study of manpower resources quoted above, tribals in various boys' hostels were questioned about their career preferences. The results of the interviews showed that 40.9 percent wanted to become teachers in arts subjects; 22.7 percent wanted to become science teachers; 18.2 percent wanted to study medicine and become doctors; and 18.2 percent wanted to enroll in technical courses and become engineers. Of those interviewed, 82.8 percent hoped for employment in Adilabad District, preferably near to their home villages. An interesting feature of this enquiry is the preference for such familiar professions as teaching, medicine, and engineering, while none of those asked mentioned careers as veterinary surgeons or agricultural extension officers. More surprisingly none of the boys stated that he wanted to become a *tahsildar* or superior revenue officer, an interesting contrast to the aspirations of tribal students in Arunachal Pradesh, many of whom told me that they hoped to join the administrative service and to attain ultimately the position of deputy commissioner or another post involving responsibility and authority. The tribals of Adilabad have for so long been ruled by outsiders that they cannot envisage the possibility of occupying positions of authority and power, although one of them was recently appointed to the prestigious position of district revenue officer.

The situation in other tribal areas is similar to that prevailing among the Gonds of Adilabad. In the 1940s teacher training centres identical to those at Marlavai and Ginnedhari were established in Koya villages of Warangal District, and in 1979 some Koya teachers trained in those institutions were still in service. Most of the Koyas have the advantage of speaking Telugu as their mother tongue, and Koya children therefore face fewer difficulties than the Gondi-speaking children of Adilabad. The absence of a language barrier accounts perhaps for the fact that among the tribals of Khammam District the literacy rate was 5 percent, compared with 3.28 percent in Adilabad District, both figures relating to the 1971 census. Another explanation may be the inclusion in Khammam District of some areas which in the days of British rule belonged to the Agency Tracts of Madras Presidency, where educational standards were more advanced than in Hyderabad State. In the area of Sudimalla, one of the Koya training centres established in 1946, several Koyas have had fairly successful careers. In 1978 there were two Koya subinspectors of police, and one Koya who had entered the central police service held the appointment of district superintendent of police at Imphal in Manipur State, a highly responsible position in a sensitive frontier region.

In recent years special efforts have been made to develop educational facilities in Srikakulam District, where the administration is anxious to regain the confidence of the many tribesmen who were involved in the Naxalite uprising (see chapter 2). Saoras, Jatapus, and various minor tribal groups number a total of 213,928 and thus constitute 8.2 percent of the population. Most of them are economically backward and, dwelling in remote hill villages, had until recently no access to any kind of schools. A further obstacle to the spread of education was the fact that such tribes as Saoras and Gadabas speak Munda languages, whereas teaching was available only in Telugu, even where schools had been opened in the vicinity of tribal settlements. By 1978 there were 227 primary schools, 5 upper primary schools, and 4 high schools, in which nearly 12,000 children were enrolled. In addition, there were 61 ashram schools, 25 of which had been opened in 1977, and altogether 6,000 tribal children were maintained as boarders in ashram schools and hostels. The annual expenditure on education was then Rs 5,000,000. Some of the results seem to have been rather better than those from Adilabad quoted above. Thus, between 1974 and 1979, 35 tribal pupils of the high school at Bhadragiri succeeded in passing the matriculation examination. Even in some Saora and Jatapu villages situated on high hills and accessible only by footpaths, ashram schools have recently been opened and seem to be well attended.

Chenchus of Kurnool were taught ploughing and supplied with bullocks; when the bullocks died the Chenchus fashioned hand-ploughs and continue to cultivate on a small scale. A woman walking behind the plough is dropping maize seeds.

The overall literacy rate for all the tribal areas of Andhra Pradesh was 5.34 percent in 1971, and had risen to 8.62 percent by 1978. The system of ashram schools providing boarding facilities for tribal children extends to all the districts containing tribal populations, including Mahbubnagar and Kurnool, where school education is provided even to the children of the semi-nomadic Chenchus.

It appears that the low economic level of the foodgathering Chenchus has no adverse effect on the children's ability to absorb the instruction provided in schools, and in the ashram school at Mananur some Chenchu girls are studying in the tenth standard.

In Kurnool District, where education for Chenchus was started in the British period, there are a few families of educated Chenchus who have obtained positions in government service, but in Mahbubnagar District there are as yet no adult Chenchus who have gone through the school system. It remains to be seen whether those Chenchus who have spent several years in boarding schools will be able to readjust to the forest life of their parents. If they have lost the skill of gathering marketable forest produce or have developed wants which cannot be met from the income Chenchus derive from the sale of such produce, education may be a mixed blessing except for those young people who

Chenchu pupils of the boarding school at Pulajelma during the midday meal.

obtain jobs outside their traditional habitat.

The educational backwardness of most of the tribal populations of Andhra Pradesh is a correlate of the generally adverse economic conditions under which the tribesmen labour, and cannot be attributed to a lack of funds available for educational institutions. In the financial year 1978–79, a total of Rs 56,340,000 was allocated for tribal education, and of this total budget Rs 52,245,000 was provided by the Tribal Welfare Department.

The number of educational institutions in 1978, together with the number of pupils within the area covered by the plans for tribal development, is shown in Table 3. The boarders accommodated in hostels were also given special coaching. The number of teachers in ashram schools was 1,171, and the number of teachers employed in primary, upper primary, and high schools was 1,821. The number of students in receipt of post-matric scholarships was 1,950, 468 tribal students were admitted to reputable private schools and public schools, and 90 students were enrolled in the special residential Kinnarsani school for tribals.

In Andhra Pradesh the funds spent on educational institutions accessible to tribal populations have not yet brought about a fundamen-

TABLE 3. *Pupils Covered by Tribal Development Plan, 1978*

NUMBER OF EDUCATIONAL INSTITUTIONS		PUPILS WITHIN THE AREA	
Ashram schools	399	*Boarders enrolled*	26,746
Hostels	343	*Boarders enrolled*	24,383
Primary schools	1,740	*Students enrolled*	37,729
Upper primary schools	115	*Students enrolled*	4,052
High schools	75	*Students enrolled*	3,630
Junior colleges	6	*Students enrolled*	305
Aided schools	375	*Students enrolled*	24,970

tal change in the tribals' unfavourable position, largely because the social, political, and economic forces arraigned against them have so far prevented all real progress. In chapter 11 we shall see, however, that in Northeast India educational progress among tribals has played an important role in securing for them a position of political equality and growing economic prosperity.

6 Processes of Social Change

THE DRAMATIC changes in the economic and political environment of tribal populations described in the preceding chapters have had a profound influence on the social order prevailing among most of the tribes of Andhra Pradesh. While even thirty years ago many tribesmen still lived in clusters of villages with an almost completely homogeneous population of Gonds, Koyas, or Reddis, as the case may have been, today such areas of compact aboriginal populations have been split up by the intrusion of numerous newcomers of different cultural background. The social order which used to regulate the interaction of tribesmen rooted in the same or related traditions could not withstand the presence of intruders motivated by aims and a value system entirely distinct from those of the indigenous population. The disturbance caused by this admixture of novel elements to the social scene is all the greater as the newcomers are almost invariably economically and politically more powerful, and in no way inclined to fall into line with the old order. In areas where massive immigration of advanced populations has caused a complete fragmentation of tribal communities, next to nothing is left of the latter's indigenous authority system, but even where tribal villages have so far escaped the infiltration of outsiders, the effectiveness of traditional authority systems has sharply declined because of the tribesmen's increasing dependence on economic forces over which they have no control.

CHENCHUS

It would seem that the extent of recent changes in the social order stands in an inverse relationship to the complexity of the traditional authority system. The group whose social organization has undergone least change since 1940 is the Chenchu tribe in the forests of Mahbub-nagar District. As of old, Chenchus live in small hamlets of four to twelve huts and move at certain times of the year to temporary jungle camps put up in the vicinity of whatever collecting grounds are at the time likely to yield most forest produce. There has been little change in the structure of the small communities sharing a common territory. The descendants of the families whom I encountered forty years ago are still living in the same localities in much the same life-style. Deci-sions about moves from one camp to another are taken in informal discussions. The headman of the group, know as *peddamanchi,* has no other function than to preside over any gathering discussing a dis-pute, and has no decisive voice. As all Chenchus are now used to deal-ings with government officials, forest guards, and other outsiders, the *peddamanchi*'s role of spokesman for the members of his small group is of very little importance. One Chenchu expressed this by saying that the *peddamanchi* of his small group had no other task than to "sit like a statue" in the council whenever a dispute had to be settled. While in most other tribal areas *gram panchayats* have been organized by gov-ernment, no such institutions exist among the Chenchus in the forests of the Amrabad Plateau.

The Chenchus of Kurnool, who inhabit the wooded hills south of the Krishna River, have been subject to official intervention for a much longer period than those of the former Hyderabad State. In the days of British rule the government of Madras Presidency pursued a policy of concentrating the scattered groups of semi-nomadic Chen-chus in large villages, which were administered by the Forest Depart-ment. The experiment of compulsory settlement was on the whole not very successful and led to unexpected results. As long as they had lived in small groups Chenchus had settled their own disputes by in-formal discussions, and the practice of opponents going out of each other's way and joining other groups was effective in preventing out-breaks of violence. The procedure of placing spatial distance between those who could not live in peace was no longer practical when large numbers of families were compelled to live in one permanent village, and this resulted in the frequent occurrence of cases of violence, murder, rape, and theft.

When I revisited the Chenchu settlements of Bairluti, Nagarluti, and Peddacheruvu in 1978, I found that the compact villages controlled by the Forest Department had been disbanded, and the Chenchus allowed more freedom in the choice of settlement patterns. While only a few families had left the Forest villages altogether, most Chenchus constructed their houses in small family groups, similar in type to the traditional hamlets of a few closely related households. In such places as Bairluti the Forest Department has appointed paid functionaries, chosen from among the men of the group, whose responsibility it is to settle disputes among Chenchus and to see that no thefts are committed. This system seems to work reasonably well.

The main occupation of the Chenchus in this area is forest labour under the control of forest officers, and this does not require any coordination of activities by the Chenchus themselves. Attempts to develop permanent cultivation have yielded only patchy results. (See chapter 8.)

Even the more settled Chenchus lack any tribal authority which might enable them to organize themselves for a more advantageous relationship with government and those non-tribal settlers with whom they now have to share their habitat. In Kurnool there are a few educated Chenchus, mainly employed in government service, who could provide their community with some leadership, but the members of this Chenchu elite do not identify with their illiterate fellow tribesmen and are not inclined to act as their spokesmen or to provide any kind of leadership. Like many other educated tribesmen, they are more interested in as close as possible an assimilation to the caste Hindus with whom they have to work in their employment. Even should any of them have political ambitions, the Chenchu communities, whose loyalty and support they could probably gain, are too small in numbers to provide sufficient votes even in local elections.

KONDA REDDIS

The traditional social order of the Konda Reddis was conditioned by an economy based on slash-and-burn cultivation, which favoured settlements of very limited size. Groups of ten to twenty-five families used to claim ownership of a tract of forest land, the slopes of which were cleared and cultivated in rotation. Social contacts were usually confined to the inhabitants of a few neighbouring settlements. Although the Reddis extend over a large territory, there is no unifying social organization comparable, for instance, to the system of phratries and clans which comprises all Raj Gonds wherever they may dwell. Reddis of one region have little knowledge of their fellow tribesmen in other parts of Andhra Pradesh, and even the recent improvement of communications between the various districts and taluks inhabited by Reddis has done little to make the individual localized groups aware of each other's existence and to create a sense of tribal solidarity. To some extent, modern developments, far from forging any links between dispersed groups, have eroded indigenous institutions which used to give some cohesion to clusters of Reddi villages. Thus in the 1940s there lived in the riverside village of Katkur a Reddi by name of Zogreddi, who acted as *kulam pedda* ("caste elder") for all the Reddis in Hyderabad State. Zogreddi's father and grandfather had been police *patel*s of Katkur, but now a non-tribal has been appointed to this post, and there is no headman who can be called upon to adjudicate in disputes between Reddis of the Godavari region. Until some twenty years ago there was in Jiddiguppa, on the left bank of the river, a Reddi who held a leading position within a group of villages. He was literate and a teacher, and people trusted his judgement and brought cases to him for decision. Since his death there has been no one who could fulfil the role of *kulam pedda*. The Reddis in the hills south of the Godavari, who in the 1940s had recognized Zogreddi of Katkur as their tribal headman, have now lost contact with the villages on the Godavari bank, and have developed some social and economic ties with nearby villages in the West Godavari District.

A different situation prevails among the Reddis of the East Godavari District, most of whom are concentrated in the Chodavaram and Ellavaram taluks. There the feudal system of *muttadar*, hereditary local chiefs, existed until its abolition in 1969. These chiefs, whose authority was confirmed by *sanad* ("patents") issued by the British administration, were responsible for the collection of revenue and the maintenance of law and order. Most of the *muttadar* belonged to one clan, known as Palal, and although they were not debarred from intermarrying with ordinary Reddis, they had the status of a socially superior class. Each *muttadar* controlled a number of villages, but there was some flexibility in the limits of *mutta*, and it is said that in the old days a wealthy *muttadar* might give a whole village as a dowry, presumably only if a daughter married the chief of an adjoining *mutta*.

Today Reddi *muttadar* have ceased to enjoy any formal privileges, but their former subjects still give them respect and call upon them to decide disputes. Most of the newly established *gram panchayat*s unanimously elected the former *muttadar* as *sarpanch*, an exception being *muttadar* who had made themselves unpopular with the local people. In all those *mutta* which I revisited in 1979 the former *muttadar* were still the leading personalities and had retained some of their wealth, such as orange groves and some plots of irrigated land. This enabled them to maintain the custom of feeding the whole population of their village on festival days, even though not in the same lavish manner as in the old days, when the feudal chiefs were relatively better off. Despite the withdrawal of recognition by the government, the *muttadar* still provide a measure of leadership. Such economic innovations as the commercial growing of oranges and the construction of irrigated paddy fields were introduced by members of *muttadar* families, and *muttadar* also lead in sending their sons to schools. Among the few Reddis who have attained university degrees are two sons of the *muttadar* of Musirimilli. Their mother is of Kapu caste, and the whole family has adopted the life-style of Hindu plainsmen.

Unlike the Valmikis, an originally untouchable caste of tradesmen, who share the habitat of the Reddis of Chodavaram Taluk, the Reddis of that region have not entered district or state politics. Some of the reserved seats in the Legislative Assembly have been won by Valmikis and Koyas, but the Reddis have so far evinced little political ambition.

Compared with the situation of tribals in many other parts of Andhra Pradesh, that of the Konda Reddis of East Godavari District is still relatively favourable. In the hill regions, at least, there has been no massive alienation of tribal land, and even roadside villages have largely retained their tribal character. It may well be that the tradition of the agency administration of British days has had a restraining influence on the influx of non-tribal new-comers.

Within the Reddi community there have as yet been no major changes in social customs. The endogamy of the tribe is largely being maintained, and Reddis entering illegal unions with members of lower castes, such as Valmikis or Kammars, are considered automatically excommunicated. Marriages with "clean" Hindu castes, such as Kapus, are tolerated, and so are those with Bagatas, a community claiming tribal status. A special case is that of the Jangam community, which has furnished some *muttadar*. Jangams perform death rituals for Reddis, and regard themselves as purer than ordinary Reddis. There are some cases of Jangam men living with Reddi women without having undergone a formal wedding ritual, and of Jangam girls living with Reddi men. In either case the children belong to the community of the father.

There seems to be a relaxation of the ban on marriages between members of the same Reddi clan. Such unions, regarded as incestuous, are still punished by the imposition of a fine, but once this fine has been paid the couple is permitted to live together. This attitude suggests that the clan is gradually losing its character as an exogamous unit of crucial importance for the regulation of marriages.

Increased contact with non-tribals and the intensification of economic dependence on outsiders is undoubtedly leading to an erosion of the cohesion of Reddi communities. In such villages as Koida (see chapter 2) the dominance of Hindu settlers has virtually destroyed the self-sufficiency and freedom of action of the local Reddis, and they no longer constitute a cohesive social entity. Where the former *muttadar* have retained their position as pivotal figures in the local communities, there is still a focal point for concerted action, but once the men who acted as feudal chiefs until 1969 have passed away, members of their families are unlikely to continue in this role for very long. The Reddis themselves seem to have a strong desire to live in communities separate from other populations, and wherever it is possible they choose isolation even at the expense of economic advantage. The most significant example of such preference for isolation is provided by the small Reddi communities in a range of hills known as Kutturgatu near Kunavaram in Bhadrachallam Taluk.

There several small hamlets consisting of between six and ten houses are located close to the top of hill ranges, wherever there is a source of water. Access from the lowlands is by extremely steep and partly overgrown footpaths, and the difficulty of the arduous ascent serves to deter outsiders from disturbing the peace and isolation of such Reddi hamlets. Shifting cultivation on the surrounding hill slopes provides the Reddis with the bulk of their supply of grain and a few vegetables. When I visited two of these settlements in 1978, I was told that no government official had passed through these hamlets since time immemorial, though recently some of the Reddis had been called to a camp at the foot of the hills where a small school for Reddi children has been established. This contact was of very recent date, and the older people, particularly older women, in the hill settlements gave me the impression of being quite unused to dealings with outsiders. The desire to avoid all such contact finds expression in the Reddis' rigid enforcement of dietary rules designed to prevent any kind of ritual pollution. Young Reddi boys whom our party had employed as porters and guides refused to partake of any of the food they had carried because it had been in contact with members of Hindu castes. The life-style of the Reddis of Kutturgatu resembles closely that which I observed in 1940 and 1941 among the inhabitants of the hill settlements in the former Hyderabad State, such as, for instance, Gogulapudi. Like the inhabitants of these hill settlements, the Reddis of Kutturgatu keep pigs and chickens, but no cattle, and they supplement the grain reaped in their fields with wild plants collected in the forest. Their isolation is not complete, however, for now and then the men visit some weekly markets in nearby villages of the plains and barter baskets and minor forest produce for such commodities as salt, spices, oil, and woven cloth. Occasionally some of the men go to the Konta area, where contractors engage them to cut bamboos in the high hills of Bastar, which is now part of Madhya Pradesh. They are paid Rs 20 for one hundred bamboos, and usually stay fifteen to twenty days in a camp where the contractors supply them with provisions, the cost of which is ultimately deducted from the wages they have earned.

These occasional ventures into the world below their isolated hills show that, despite these Reddis' preference for isolation, they have to some extent been sucked into the money economy. Cash earnings also enable them to emulate some of the customs of the non-tribal people. Thus during a recent wedding at Pulsimamidigondi, one of the Kutturgatu hamlets, half a bag of rice costing Rs 180, one bag of sorghum at Rs 200, six kilograms of dhal, one pig, Rs 40 worth of country liquor, and two saris had been provided. This was possible because the bridegroom had saved wages earned by bamboo cutting. Here at least the Reddis are not yet indebted, for moneylenders fearful of the forests and inaccessible hills are wary of lending money to people who have no tangible assets and can easily hide in their mountain fortresses.

The social advantages of a measure of isolation or at least only limited contact with outsiders also become apparent if we compare the atmosphere in hill villages such as Gogulapudi with that prevailing in the large riverside villages. In Gogulapudi, where the Reddis live much in the same style as their parents lived some forty years ago, I found the same cheerfulness and relaxed mood which I had observed in 1941. In Koida, on the other hand, where the Reddis now dwell side by side with caste Hindu immigrants from the coastal districts, all joie de vivre seems to have evaporated, and Reddis and Koyas have turned into sullen and dispirited drudges, resentful of the tyranny of merchants and moneylenders but incapable of any concerted action which might lessen their dependence on these newcomers.

GONDS OF ADILABAD DISTRICT

While neither Chenchus nor Konda Reddis had ever developed a complex social and political structure of their own and lived basically in small groups which did not represent the constituent elements of a larger whole, the Gonds had attained quite a different level of tribal organization. For centuries they enjoyed the leadership of their own feudal chiefs, some of whom had risen to positions of political power comparable to that wielded by Hindu rajas ruling over minor states of Middle India. The Gond rajas of Chanda and Garha Mandla were not only the hereditary leaders of their Gond subjects, but also held sway over substantial communities of non-tribals who recognized them as their feudal lords. The subjection of these tribal rulers by the Mughal emperors left their position within the tribal social structure largely unaltered, and in *The Gonds of Andhra Pradesh* I have described the relations between Mughal emperors and Gond rajas in some detail. In the middle of the eighteenth century, large parts of the Deccan came under Maratha rule, and Chanda was annexed by the Bhonsle kingdom. However, Maratha rule over parts of the present Adilabad District did not last for more than half a century, and in A.D. 1773 the region was ceded to the Nizam of Hyderabad. Even then there was little interference with the feudal system of the Gond rajas, and until the very end of the nineteenth century Gond chiefs remained the effective rulers of those regions where Gonds constituted the dominant population. With the establishment of a district administration modeled on the British system by the Nizam's government, the power of Gond rajas waned, but as late as 1941, when I began my study of the Gonds, and Chanda Raja Akbar Shah was still recognized as the supreme tribal authority, and though resident in British India, he occasionally toured the Gond villages of the Nizam's Dominions and was called upon to adjudicate in disputes which the local tribal heads had failed to settle.

At that time there were in Adilabad thirty-seven chiefly families who maintained in varying degrees the traditions of feudal times and enjoyed the allegiance and respect of the tribesmen within their former estates. Only a few of them bore the title raja, while others were styled *mokashi* or *deshmukh*. A reconstruction of the jurisdictions and functions of these tribal chiefs is contained in chapter 5 of my *The Gonds of Andhra Pradesh*, where I have also shown that in the early 1940s some of them, above all the Utnur raja, still exerted considerable influence, even though their political authority had been replaced by that of the Nizam's district officials.

Rajas and *mokashi* were then the linchpins of a system of tribal jurisdiction in which the village headmen *(patla)* played a vital role. Some of them belonged to raja and *mokashi* families, and all derived their authority partly from their ritual role as village founders or successors of the village founder. In chapter 8 Michael Yorke shows how the authority of these village headmen has declined because under the present system of land allocation they no longer control the acceptance or rejection of potential settlers in their villages. Yorke's observations in the eastern part of the district are confirmed by my own findings in Utnur Taluk. This region had for long remained a bulwark of traditional Gond culture and tradition, but it has recently been subjected to drastic and sudden changes in the population pattern and the Gonds' economic position.

As late as the 1940s most Gond villages were dominated by headmen who provided real leadership and enjoyed a considerable measure of authority. Land holdings and settlements were then still flexible, for only a minority of Gonds had title deeds *(patta)* to land

and it was still relatively easy to obtain land for cultivation on temporary tenure. Hence, mobility was considerable. A strong and popular village headman would attract new settlers, and with the growth of the village his prestige and influence would increase. Conversely, the village of an inefficient or unfair headman would shrink, as the villagers could move away and find land elsewhere. At that time it was still possible to establish new villages, and the man taking the initiative in the founding of a village automatically became the headman of the group of families which had joined in the venture.

The strength of the institution of village headman was put to the test when in the middle 1940s the Hyderabad government instituted tribal *panchayats*, each based on a group of villages. The headmen of these villages were nominated as *panchayat* members, and they met once a month to settle disputes and discuss current events. The *panchayats* had been invested with judicial powers, as described in detail in chapter 1. Although there was a right of appeal to a government officer dealing with tribal affairs, this right was hardly ever resorted to, for the parties to a dispute usually had confidence in the fairness of the members of the tribal *panchayat*. These tribal councils replaced in practice the courts of the rajas and *mokashi*, but where a member of a chiefly house acted as village headman he could serve on the regional *panchayat* like any other headman. Thus statutory tribal *panchayats* functioned in almost exactly the same way as in previous days village and neighbourhood *panchayats* had functioned.[1]

The repeal of the Hyderabad Tribal Areas Regulation in 1963 terminated the functioning of the tribal *panchayats*, and with their demise ended an institution which had regularly brought together the headmen of groups of villages. The repeal of the regulation also ended any recognition by government of the settlement of disputes according to the rules of tribal customary law. Since then the traditional system of authority of the Gonds has been rapidly declining. A retired headmaster of one of the teacher training centres, intimately acquainted with Gond practices, remarked that since *panchayats* of the old type are no longer held tribal solidarity has disappeared: "Nowadays Gonds exploit Gonds—the father will exploit his son, and the son will exploit his father."

Today the erstwhile tribal chiefs have no more power, and even the prestige which some of the members of raja families used to enjoy is gradually evaporating. The role of village headman has also changed, for with the enormous increase in the bureaucracy and the number of government employees visiting villages on various errands, the head-

---

1. For a detailed description of their procedure, see chapter 10 of my *The Gonds of Andhra Pradesh*.

Meeting in the Gond village of Ginnedhari in 1948, when tribal panchayat *exercised jurisdiction in both civil and criminal cases.*

man is no longer an essential link between the villagers and the administration. This change in the headman's function seems to have had a deleterious effect on the sense of responsibility of many village heads. No longer are they mainly concerned with the welfare of the entire community, whose growth and contentment guaranteed an access to their own prestige and influence, but they think primarily of their own short-term material advantages. Thus there are many cases of village headmen leasing out some of their own land to non-tribal settlers, even though Gonds living in the village may be short of land or totally landless. The shortsightedness of many of the leading Gonds, who obtain various benefits by secretly or even openly supporting wealthy newcomers, is one of the causes of the alienation of much of the tribal land. The breakup of village cohesion is undoubtedly a direct result of the commercialization of the local economy, which favours individualistic tendencies antagonistic to the traditional esprit de corps of a Gond community.

A good example of such a development is the situation in Netnur, a Gond village in Utnur Taluk. Netnur lies in a part of the central highlands which until thirty years ago was inhabited exclusively by a rather sparse population of Gonds. In 1942 it consisted of twenty Gond homesteads scattered in small groups of three or four houses. At

Polling booth in a Gond village of Utnur Taluk during elections for the Legislative Assembly of Andhra Pradesh.

that time the community was headed by a strong *patel* who enjoyed the complete confidence of all the villagers. By 1977 Netnur had grown to a compact village of forty-four Gond and Pardhan houses. There were, moreover, two shops run by Muslims and a quarter inhabited by Banjaras. The growth of the village had been made possible by the allotment of previously vacant land to Gonds from other parts of the district during the campaign of resettlement of landless tribals in the 1940s. When I visited the village in 1977, I found not only the total scene transformed but the village deeply divided. Ten villagers, including the police *patel*, had leased part of their land for periods of one to three years to recently arrived Banjaras, who were paying relatively high rents. At the same time there were eighteen landless Gonds, only six of whom had been able to obtain land for cultivation, either on share or by paying rent to the owners. There was a faction of Gonds who recognized the danger of giving land to Banjaras on lease, suspecting rightly that the Gond owners would never be able to recover their land—a suspicion which was proved fully justified when a year later the Banjaras were notified as a scheduled tribe. The members of this faction proposed that the villagers should club together and repay the Banjaras all the money which they had paid in advances for the leases of Gond land. The village headman, however, opposed this move, and when the further proposal was made that the *panchayat* should impose on any Gond giving land to a non-tribal a fine of Rs 50, the headman initially agreed but later sabotaged the plan.

This development contrasts sharply with the action a united village can take to keep unwelcome outsiders at bay. When in Marlavai two non-tribals put up huts to be used as shops and tea stalls, the villagers, on the initiative of Kanaka Hanu, the leading man of the village, dismantled the huts and thereby prevented any non-tribal from settling in the village.

Unfortunately such strong action is nowadays a rare occurrence, and public declarations urging the Gonds to show a united front and prevent the disposal of any land to non-tribals are seldom followed up by deeds. The discrepancy between professed intentions and actual conduct became very clear during a public meeting held at Pithaguda in December 1976 and attended by some 1,200 Gonds, who had gathered to welcome me on my return to Marlavai after an absence of several years. On that occasion several leading men, such as the still highly respected Raja Atram Bhagwant Rao, the ex-president of the Panchayat Samithi Atram Lingu, and Kotnaka Suruji Maharaj, the widely revered protagonist of a religious reform movement, addressed the meeting in lengthy speeches. The following verbatim extracts from these speeches, which I was able to record on tape, reflect the mood of the Gonds at this time, and apart from certain laudatory references to myself, they represent the type of statements Gond leaders are used to make in public.

The most practical speech was that of Atram Lingu, the former Panchayat Samithi president:

Today more than a thousand of us Gonds have assembled in this meeting in order to strengthen our cooperation. Our condition is bad and therefore we should work together from wherever we hail. In past years a number of people came from various taluks, such as Kinwat, and obtained land here. This land will remain ours for ever if we hold on to it. We should not sell land under any circumstances. If we find anyone selling land we should come together, hold a *panchayat*, and fine him. The very purpose of this meeting is to decide on this. Yet, although I myself and the Gond members of the Legislative Assembly have tried hard to see that *patta* rights to land are granted to Gonds, thousands of acres are now being cultivated by non-tribals. For this reason we face many difficulties. Agriculture is the only occupation by which we can earn our living, and therefore you should promise in front of Haimendorf Sahib that you will neither sell nor lease any land to non-tribals. Anyone who has sold land has sold his own mother. There is no other land for us—neither in Maharashtra or Madhya Pradesh, nor in any other part of India. Many non-tribal people have come from Osmanabad, Nander, and other places with the intention of getting land here. By bribing the *patwari* they have obtained land for cultivation. We are weak-minded people, but for the sake of our children we should cooperate to avoid being destroyed. Just now Haimendorf Sahib advised you not to permit any non-tribal to keep a shop in a Gond village, yet you don't help your own brothers and community members, but you have helped Marathas and Muslims to establish shops in your villages, and soon they also got some land. By their tricks these outsiders can get land easily, whereas we are not clever enough to match such tricks. I can tell you how in Dhanora and Indraveli non-tribals tricked the Gonds by entertaining them with beer and good food, and when they were drunk made them sign away their land. Thus all the tribals were pushed out by non-tribals who settled in their villages. Thus the Gonds are losing their land due to a lack of foresight. Drink is the main cause of our downfall, which has also led to the downfall of our rajas, *mokashi,* and other leaders. People who own shops and lorries can afford to drink without ruining themselves, but poor tribals cannot do so. Yet though they may not have sufficient food and eat watery curry, they still drink.

We are Raj Gonds, descended from the original Dravidians of India, but now we are called Girijan, because we are backward.

This plea of Atram Lingu of Sirpur would have been more convincing if at the time of his term of office as *sarpanch* of Sirpur and subsequently Samithi president numerous non-tribals had not been permitted to settle down and open shops in Sirpur. While in 1942 Sirpur was a pure Gond village of nine houses, it is now a large place with a mixed population, including five Kachi shopkeepers from Gujarat, two Komtis, and ten Muslims from Maharashtra working as tailors and artisans, some of whom have also bought land. Atram Lingu, who was a poor man before he entered politics, now owns the largest stone house in Sirpur, and his critics connect his present wealth with the settlement of so many non-tribal merchants in his village.

Raja Atram Bhagwant Rao, who leads a simple life and has succeeded in keeping his village, Kanchanpalli, free of non-tribals, in his speech also called for more cooperation among Gonds:

In previous days the *mokashi, patels,* and other leading men were cooperating, but nowadays such cooperation is not to be seen among the tribals—if any Gond is in trouble, no one helps him. When we compare our previous fortunes with our present condition we may say that we have now better clothes, but in order to get fine clothes we fall into the bondage of moneylenders. We did not keep our religion intact, and even at ceremonies for the worship of gods, people drink, and this leads to quarrels. The old honesty and discipline is vanishing. We are trying to educate our children so that they will become intelligent, but when a boy is sent to the bazaar to buy supplies for his home, he will spend the money on cigarettes and other useless things and will return home without the goods he was told to buy. Such boys should change their ways in order to become helpful to the Gond community, for those who behave in this manner will never be of any use. Years ago Haimendorf Sahib provided schools for Gonds and organized the allocation of land to Gonds, but we have not gone along the path he showed: through lack of cohesion and cooperation we failed to take advantage of all the facilities provided. This gathering has been called to promote cooperation and you should decide to make an effort to stand together.

In a brief address, Suruji Maharaj also emphasized the need for cooperation and hard work, and he warned the assembled Gonds of the danger of drink and extravagant spending on inessential luxuries.

Whenever there is an occasion for public speeches similar sentiments are expressed, but the results of such admonitions seem to be minimal. In a situation of inescapable contacts with numerous outsiders, every Gond tries to look after his own interests, and the old feeling of tribal solidarity goes by the board. A concomitant of this diminishment of cohesion is the now frequent occurrence of rival headmen causing the split of a village community. This happened in Daboli, one of the oldest and most famous Gond villages of Utnur Taluk, whose *patel* had once held a *sanad* from the Chanda raja.[2] In the 1940s Mesram Devji of Daboli was one of the most respected village headmen of the hill region, and his son Jangu was also a strong man who kept the village together. Jangu's only son was killed by a tiger, and his kinsmen quarrelled about the succession to the headship. One of them was appointed police *patel*, but three others set up as leaders of separate groups of households, each performing the ritual functions of the *patel* at Durari and other ceremonies. Thus the village was practically split into four, very much to the detriment of its ability to ward off the designs of non-tribals on village land.

The imposition of a democratic system designed for the more advanced regions of rural India has had the effect of undermining the old authority structure without replacing it with a practical alternative suitable for Gond society. Whereas previously the village was the basic unit, the smallest element of the system of Panchayat Raj is the *gram panchayat* ("village council"), and such a *gram panchayat* must have a predetermined size far exceeding that of an average Gond village. Consequently, several villages, each with its own traditional headman, are grouped together in one new *gram panchayat*.

The Marlavai *gram panchayat*, as it was constituted, exemplified this situation. It comprised the villages Marlavai, Ragapur, Pithaguda, Burnur, Sirpur, Dubbaguda, and Suinur; of these, Sirpur contained many

2. See *The Gonds of Andhra Pradesh,* p. 125.

non-tribal residents, and in Dubbaguda and Suinur there was a majority of Banjaras. A *gram panchayat* is divided into a number of blocks, each of which should contain about one hundred households. At the time of *panchayat* elections the people of each block elect one *panchayat* member, and according to the original rules, modified in 1978, these members then elect one of their number as *sarpanch*. In a *gram panchayat* consisting of a large compact village, such as hardly ever exists in a tribal area, the division into blocks is of little consequence, but in a case such as the Marlavai *gram panchayat*, the constituting villages extend over a large area, with some of them at distances of as much as six miles from one another. Hence, the elected members seldom meet and have little sense of solidarity, particularly if there are tribals and non-tribals among them. An additional complication is created by the manner in which the blocks of one hundred households are made up. In 1977 the composition of the blocks of the Marlavai *gram panchayat* was as follows:

> Block I: Marlavai, Ragapur
> Block II: Pithaguda, Burnur
> Block III: Half of Sirpur, one third of Dubbaguda
> Block IV: Half of Sirpur, one third of Dubbaguda
> Block V: One third of Dubbaguda, one third of Suinur
> Block VI: Two thirds of Suinur

The splitting up of villages and the formation of blocks from parts of different villages not even particularly close to each other looks like an almost deliberate attempt to undermine village cohesion, but is probably due to bureaucratic convenience, some clerks in the *tahsil* office putting together neat units of one hundred houses each without any regard to the divisive social effects.

Although this *gram panchayat* is registered as Marlavai *gram panchayat* and a small building was built in Marlavai with *panchayat* funds, the *sarpanch* and the paid secretary (*karbari*) resided in Burnur, where the records of the *panchayat* were also kept.

The income of a *gram panchayat* is derived from a house tax, which is the major item, licenses for shops and tea stalls, fines for cattle trespass, fines for giving short weight, and some minor fees. The Marlavai *gram panchayat* collected in 1976 Rs 3,569 as house tax and Rs 917 as fees and fines. The expenditure was Rs 2,105 and related to such items as the improvement of local roads and the construction of cattle compounds for animals apprehended for trespass on cultivated land. Sometimes *panchayat*s are burdened by expenditure which the members had neither desired nor authorized. Thus in 1976 government officials dumped on the Marlavai *gram panchayat* one hundred mango saplings with the order to plant them along roads and later charged the *panchayat* Rs 545. As no instructions about the care of the saplings were issued and no one felt responsible for watering them, all the saplings perished in the first hot weather.

In 1977 there were in Utnur Taluk forty *gram panchayat*s, and in twenty-nine of these the *sarpanch* was a Gond or Pardhan, while in seven *gram panchayat*s a Banjara held that position. In those days the Banjaras were not yet notified as a scheduled tribe, and hence they could not compete for seats reserved for tribals. The few Hindu or Muslim *sarpanch* served in *gram panchayat*s of areas with a predominantly non-tribal population. Even in *gram panchayat*s with a tribal *sarpanch*, non-tribal members often exerted a far greater influence if they happened to be economically powerful.

According to rules introduced for the *panchayat* elections in 1979, the *sarpanch* is no longer chosen by the members of the *panchayat*, but is elected by popular vote. The effects of this innovation are not yet known at the time of writing, for local elections have been repeatedly postponed, and are not likely to be held before April or May 1981.

Unlike the old tribal *panchayat*s consisting of the headmen of an organic group of villages, the *gram panchayat*s have no judicial function, and it seems that disputes are never referred to the *sarpanch* and the *panchayat* members for adjudication. As not only Gonds but also non-tribals may be elected by the people of a block, the *panchayat* cannot serve as a body deciding cases on the basis of traditional tribal custom. Under these circumstances it is not surprising that the *gram panchayat*s do not fulfil the function of organizing the Gonds for concerted action and that they play no role in supporting tribals in their struggle against the incursions of non-tribal settlers.

The Gonds are very conscious of their lack of effective leadership. They have seen their traditional leaders, rajas, *mokashi*, and *deshmuk* stripped of all privileges and authority, and the headmen deprived even of the power to influence the acceptance of new settlers in their villages. While the *gram panchayat*s and their chairmen, the *sarpanch*, have no constitutional power to intervene in any of the conflicts which affect the interests of individuals or communities, the elected president of the Panchayat Samithi could undoubtedly exercise considerable influence if he knew how to utilize his authority to the best effect. In theory, if not in practice, the officials, such as the block development officer, have to carry out the decisions of the president. However, without experience and a high degree of literacy it is impossible to direct a bureaucratic machine in any effective way, and so far there has been no tribal Samithi president who could exert his authority to benefit his tribal constituents. When *panchayati raj* was first introduced in such areas as Utnur Taluk, the Gonds still formed the majority of the population, and it was only natural that Gonds had a good chance of being elected to the post of Samithi president. The first tribal incumbent was Atram Deo Shah, eldest son of Jagpat Rao, the last Utnur raja who still played a role as tribal chief and who was certainly the most respected Gond in Adilabad District in the 1940s. When faced with the possibility of electing a man to preside over the newly created Panchayat Samithi, the Gonds turned to one of the traditional aristocratic families and elected Raja Deo Shah to the prestigious post of Samithi president. Subsequently, Raja Deo Shah contested one of the two reserved tribal seats in the Legislative Assembly of Andhra Pradesh and was duly elected, defeating another Gond candidate. But in the elections of 1978, when Banjaras could contest seats reserved for tribals, he was narrowly defeated by a Banjara politician who had infinitely greater financial resources and the support of many non-tribals. His defeat in a constituency in which Gonds, Pardhans, and Kolams still had a slight majority over other ethnic groups was undoubtedly also due to his ineffectiveness as a tribal spokesman while he held a seat in the assembly. Being educated only in Urdu, he could not make an impact in a body most of whose business was conducted in English. In Hyderabad he had to adjust to a life-style very different from that of his Gond kinsmen, and his many social and political contacts with non-tribal Congress politicians detached him more and more from the ordinary tribal villagers of Adilabad District. Over-confident in his position as a member of the most prominent chiefly family, he neglected nursing his constituency and gradually lost the confidence of the Gonds, whom he had given scant support in their struggle against the flood of immigrant non-tribal settlers.

Another Gond politician who gained a seat in the Legislative Assembly was Kotnaka Bhim Rao, a member of the prominent and once affluent family of the Bambara *mokashi*. He was one of the few Gonds holding university degrees, spoke fluent English, and at one time rose to the position of minister of tribal welfare. Owing to the early dissolution of the ministry in which he served, he lost this position and subsequently failed to do much for his constituents. In 1978 he lost his seat because his constituency was transformed to one reserved for Harijans, and in the constituency for which he stood he had no local base. Thus from 1978 onwards the true tribals of Adilabad—in contrast to the Banjaras—have no longer been represented in the Legislative Assembly of Andhra Pradesh.

In chapter 9, Michael Yorke discusses the emergence of Gond and Pardhan school-teachers as a political force, rivalling the village headmen. This is perhaps more noticeable in the relatively more progressive and politically conscious eastern region of the district than in Utnur Taluk, but it is certainly a phenomenon which may gain in importance as the Gonds' struggle against the incursion of outsiders, particularly of Banjaras, intensifies. The *panchayat* elections originally scheduled for April or May 1978 were postponed because of the unstable national situation and the dissolution of parliament. But it is significant that among the candidates for the position of Panchayat Samithi president were two school-teachers, one Gond and one Pardhan, while previously no teacher ever stood for political offices. The fact that among seven candidates four were Gonds, one was a Pardhan, and two were Banjaras demonstrates the disunity among Gonds. If they could agree on one candidate they might succeed in capturing the important position of Samithi president, and as early as April 1979 there occurred the first of several tribal meetings which seemed to indicate a political awakening among the Gonds. Marskola Kasiram, a former member of the Legislative Assembly of Andhra Pradesh, organized a meeting of Gonds, Pardhans, Kolams, and Naikpods from twenty-seven villages to discuss the position of tribals created by recent developments and, in particular, the inclusion of the Banjaras among the scheduled tribes. The meeting was held under a banyan tree which was the traditional scene of the clan rites associated with the Keslapur *jatra,* and it was attended by about six hundred tribals, including several leading men. Kasiram asked the participants to commit themselves to strengthening tribal solidarity and to the retention of their ancient customs. He said that they should swear in front of their god Nagoba that they would neither sell their land nor give it to non-tribals on lease, and that they would desist from incurring debts. He also admonished them to give up drinking, which was the cause of much indebtedness, resulting in the loss of land.

One month later there was a similar meeting at Marlavai to which Gonds, Pardhans, and Kolams of the hill circle *(pahar patti)* were invited. Some 150 people turned up, and most of the headmen attending spoke in favour of Kasiram's proposals. Kanaka Hanu cited Marlavai as an example of how a united village could keep out all non-tribals provided it had determined leadership.

On May 26 there was a similar meeting in Khairdatwa, attended by 380 tribals. There were twenty-seven speakers, among them several prominent headmen, who urged that in the next *panchayat* elections only one Gond candidate should stand for the position of Samithi president. The fourth of these meetings was held on June 7 in Ramjiguda, Asifabad Taluk. Kasiram was not present, but all the Gond teachers of Ginnedhari and several members of the family of the Bambara *mokashi* attended.

As late as November 1980, when I last visited Marlavai, there was still no agreement on a joint Gond candidate to receive general support at the next election, and it would seem that the repeated postponements of the *panchayat* elections had deprived the movement towards unity of its impetus.

In the general parliamentary election of January 1980 the Gonds had not presented a united front, and while some had supported the candidate of Indira Gandhi's Congress Party, others had canvassed for the Janata candidate. The former had won the seat with a large majority, but as neither of the candidates had been a tribal the election had not aroused strong feelings. The Gonds had known, moreover, that as a small minority within the general electorate they were unlikely to influence the result. In an election for the state Legislative Assembly with reserved tribal seats, the unity of the Gonds would be of greater importance, and in *panchayat* elections it is even more vital.

A different political situation prevails in the region of Maharashtra adjoining the eastern part of Adilabad District. There the *zamindar* of Aheri, a relation of the Gond raja of Chanda, has retained much of his old prestige and influence. Though even in British days not recognized as a ruling prince, he was in possession of a *zamindari* as large as the states of some rulers, such as the Gond raja of Sarangarh. Like other nobles he lost his *zamindari* in 1947, but he still has considerable private wealth and political pull. Locally referred to as Maharaja Vishveshwar Rao, he represented the area for several years as member of parliament, even though his constituency was not one reserved for scheduled tribes. He usually stood as an Independent because he believed that he could represent tribal interests more vigourously if he was not hampered by party loyalties. He was defeated, however, in the elections of 1980, when Indira Gandhi's Congress Party attained a landslide victory. Maharaja Vishveshwar Rao's residence in Aheri is a large house furnished at least partly in western style, and far grander than any Gond house I have ever seen in Adilabad District. He has his own party; the symbol of his followers is a black cap of the same style as the white caps of Congress workers, and he and his supporters wear black waistcoats. Though the position of Gonds in Aheri is vastly better than that of their fellow tribesmen in Andhra Pradesh, the Maharaja is not very optimistic about their future prospects. He deplores the infiltration of many non-tribals into Gond country, because he sees them exploiting local tribals and monopolizing business. According to Vishveshwar Rao, it is difficult to organize a united tribal lobby in the Indian parliament because the tribal members come from many different parts of the country and belong to a variety of parties, which have little common ground. Yet touring the tribal villages of what used to be the Aheri *zamindari* one feels that here the Gonds are more self-confident and less dispirited and harassed than in Andhra Pradesh. Some village headmen have large, well-built houses and huge stores of paddy kept in great bins plastered with mud. It is said that in years of scarcity they use these stores to feed the poorer villagers, who otherwise would have to take loans from merchants or moneylenders.

The spirit of solidarity and mutual help which has declined so drastically in Adilabad is here still fully alive. It is hardly surprising that non-tribal representatives of business interests criticise the Maharaja as old fashioned and as standing in the way of progress.

After this digression into the neighbouring state, we may return to our analysis of social developments among the tribals of Adilabad District. We have seen that in public speeches prominent Gonds deplore the lack of cooperation and solidarity among the people of the present generation. Whatever the reason for this failing, it cannot be denied that Gonds have become self-centred and are not easily aroused to any concerted action in defense of their interests. One of the causes for this change in character is said to be a decrease in the number of large joint families, in which several adults cooperate in cultivating their land under the direction of an older, experienced man. No doubt the atmosphere in such a joint family was conducive to the development of the habit of cooperation and discipline in the interest of the common good. Today young married couples tend to set up their own households as soon as possible, and the children of such nuclear families grow up in an atmosphere very different from that of a large joint family.

It would seem that the early breakup of joint families has also resulted in an increase in inheritance disputes between close kinsmen. A factor contributing to the greater frequency of such disputes is undoubtedly the general shortage of land created by the population increase and the large-scale occupation of Gond land by non-tribals. The fall in the death rate has been dramatic, and there are now many families in which four or more sons all live to adulthood, marry, and have sons of their own. An extreme case is a family in Kanchanpalli in which nine brothers have a share in a modest property and have founded separate families. A scrutiny of old genealogies shows that two generations ago it was quite common that of five brothers two would be killed by tigers and one die in an epidemic before reaching maturity. Today tigers no longer keep the population down, and epidemics have also become rare. Although individual medical attention is not always easily available, preventive medicine is fairly advanced, and the incidence of epidemic diseases is much reduced. With more people surviving it is not surprising that quarrels over the division of property are more likely to occur than previously. One of the reasons for the frequency of such disputes is the absence of clear traditional rules regarding the right of daughters to a share of the paternal property. In the old days, when land was plentiful and mobility great, there was no need to prescribe who should inherit a man's land. There was then no permanent right in land, and Gonds could move freely to any locality where there was vacant land for the taking.

Hence it was the movable property, such as cattle, household goods, ornaments, and other valuables, which was handed on from generation to generation, and no one was greatly concerned about the inheritance of land. Daughters received substantial gifts from their parents when they married, and sometimes even after marriage, and many myths and legends refer to the generosity of parents towards their daughters. The land actually occupied by a man was usually taken over by his sons, who had shared in its cultivation in their father's life-time, but there was no need to give any shares to married daughters, because their husbands had no difficulty in finding sufficient vacant land if they did not want to continue cultivating land cleared by their own fathers.

Today the situation has totally changed, for land is a Gond's most precious possession; hence, many a father is tempted to leave some to a daughter, particularly a daughter whose husband had moved into his house as a *lamsare*, i.e. a resident son-in-law. In such cases there may be a dispute between the daughter and her father's kinsmen, who claim that immovable property should be inherited only in the male line. A village *panchayat* called upon to adjudicate between the claimants finds no clear guidance in traditional customary law, because until two generations ago land was not considered a vital part of a man's estate.

In marriage customs and the whole sphere of relations between men and women, only minor changes have occurred in recent years. Gond women have always been very independent, and it seems that, if anything, they have become more self-reliant. The present market economy enables women to earn small amounts of cash by selling vegetables or even cotton in a weekly market or to non-tribal pedlars who wander from house to house. I have heard it said that "nowadays marriage partners often select each other," while previously more marriages were arranged by the parents, but I have no statistical data to indicate the extent of such a change in customs of courtship. There is, however, a fairly general view that, whereas in the old days marriage by capture (*pisi watana*) usually occurred without previous agreement between all the parties concerned, nowadays the capture of the bride is frequently staged as a mere formality in order to avoid the expense of the full wedding ceremonies necessary in a marriage by negotiation. As the economic position of the Gonds declines, expensive weddings become more and more a burden, particularly if the bride arrives with a large party from another village. If both bride and bridegroom are from the same village, costs can be cut, but if a bridal party comes from a village lying at some distance, large numbers of people must be fed for three days, and the total cost of the wedding borne by the groom's parents may amount to Rs 4,000 to 5,000. This includes the cost of several bags of millet and of a fair quantity of rice, Rs 400–500 for goats to provide meat, Rs 500 for cloth, and perhaps Rs 1,000 for jewelry.

There is now a movement to cut such costs, and the speakers at the Pithaguda meeting pleaded for a simplification of weddings. But there is still much resistance from traditionalists. Thus, in Netnur, the village split by factional dissension, the party opposing the headman proposed to reduce the expenditure on marriages, but the *patel* opposed this move, and when a *pat* marriage was celebrated without the sacrifice of a goat, the *patel* and his kinsmen stayed away in protest.

On the whole, tribal endogamy is being preserved. Marriages between Gonds and Kolams are tolerated, though not approved, but such inter-tribal unions have always occurred, even if only very rarely. But a union between a Gond and a girl considered untouchable is clearly an innovation. Such an event occurred some years ago when an educated Gond of Keslapur, who at the time was a member of the Legislative Assembly, entered into a union with an educated Christian girl of Mala caste, hence regarded as a Harijan. When his liaison became known, he was boycotted by the Gonds and excluded from any marriage celebration or other social occasion. Finally it was decided that his Mala wife could be purified by the performance of a *nau handi* ("nine pots") rite, and a member of the Mesram *patel* family of Daboli, traditionally entitled to perform purifications by permission of the Chanda raja, agreed to minister at the rite. Seven model huts of small branches were built, and the Mala girl had to crawl through the middle one. All these huts were burnt. Then a golden ring was heated and the girl's tongue was burnt with it. Finally seven pits were dug near a stream bed, and the Mala woman had to wash in the water collecting in these pits. The husband had also to bathe, and finally both he and his wife were declared purified. In 1977 they had two children, but it was not known whether it would be possible to find Gonds prepared to marry the off-spring of such a mixed union. The couple now leads a normal life among Gonds, but it is believed that the husband's romance with a Mala woman did cost him the votes he would have needed for his re-election. Yet the very fact of his social re-acceptance is proof of a considerable change in the attitude towards unorthodox conduct. Thirty years ago a Gond openly consorting even with a Pardhan woman would have been excommunicated without mercy.

Gond social life has always been closely connected with religious ideas, and in the next chapter we shall see that unmistakable changes in these ideas have inevitable repercussions on the nature of social relations.

7 Changes in Beliefs and Rituals

HISTORY DEMONSTRATES that significant changes in a people's social and economic climate usually bring about new developments in ideology and in religious practices. The exact nature of the correlation between economic, political, and religious transformations is nevertheless still a subject of controversy, and observations among the tribal populations of Andhra Pradesh have certainly not revealed any uniform reaction to the impact of increased contact with non-tribal populations and the resultant erosion of tribal economic and social autonomy. It would seem, however, that complex religious and mythological systems, such as that of the Gonds, are more liable to change than the simple beliefs and religious practices of more primitive tribal communities.

One of the reasons for this phenomenon may be that a tribe such as the Chenchus even now interacts with other populations only superficially, so that there are few occasions for an assimilation of religious ideas. Nor do the Chenchus have traditional customs, such as cow sacrifice, which are objectionable to Hindus and thus come under attack. Their principal ritual practices—for instance, the first fruit offerings given to Garelamaisama, the deity of the forest and the chase—are so inconspicuous that non-tribal settlers in Chenchu territory are unlikely to have any occasion to comment on their merits. With the exception of those Chenchus who live in close proximity to the Shiva temple of Sri Sailam, Chenchus are also unlikely to be drawn into participation in the ritual activities of other ethnic groups.

Ironically, the recent rebuilding of the temple of Sri Sailam and its re-establishment as an important centre of pilgrimage have damaged   *167* the Chenchus' interests. As long as Sri Sailam was difficult of access, largely derelict, and served only by a few Brahmin priests, the community of Chenchus living in the vicinity had hereditary rights to a share of the offerings given by pilgrims. They served in the temple as palanquin bearers and as sweepers, and also acted as watchmen of the temple treasures. In 1978 one of the Chenchus at Sri Sailam told me: "Our grandfathers had all the keys of the temple store where the gold and silver ornaments were kept, but now the priests treat us as thieves if we go anywhere near the store-room. Yet it is we who have worked in the temple from the time of the birth of the god."

In the old days all the Chenchus of the small settlement of Sri Sailam were feasted at the four main temple festivals, i.e. Shivaratri, Sankranti, Ugadi, and Khumbam, but since 1977 this happens only at Sankranti. They also complain that previously each Chenchu man received annually at temple expense one turban and one loin-cloth, and every woman received a sari and a bodice. All such benefits were stopped when the temple finances were taken over by the government Endowment Department. On the other hand, a few Chenchus are now employed in the temple and paid cash wages. Those men who carry the palanquin with the idols of the deities also get a part of the rice thrown at the idols by the pilgrims, but part of it is now taken by the priests, whereas originally the entire amount belonged to the Chenchus.

This attachment of a primitive community of foodgatherers to a major Hindu shrine is an unusual phenomenon, and it is remarkable that despite a long symbiotic relationship the basic economy of the group of Chenchus has not significantly changed.

Among the Reddis of the Godavari region there was also a small community which came somewhat fortuitously into contact with a centre of Hindu worship. In *The Reddis of the Bison Hills* I described in detail the ashram of the Swami of Parantapalli and the effects of this hermit on the Reddis of the nearby village. On returning to Parantapalli in 1978, I found that even though the ashram continued to function on a reduced scale after the Swami's death, it had had no lasting impact on the ritual practices of the local Reddis.

In other villages, such as Gogulapudi, where I talked to men who had been children or had not yet been born at the time of my stay among the Reddis in 1941, I found that their views on religious matters differed only in some details from those of the previous generation. They were convinced that shamans (*veju*) could see the hill deities (*konda devata*), and they had no doubt about the reality of those gods and goddesses. One *veju* told me that there were 101 hill goddesses, 92 village goddesses, and 70–80 spirits who caused disease. Another *veju* told me that there were 150 female and 100 male deities, and he described in detail how they were dressed. It is not unlikely that increased contact with outsiders has made Reddis familiar with higher numerals, and that this new knowledge is now being applied to their ideas about the supernatural world. It also seems that their ideas about the departed and their fate have become more explicit or that the *veju* have grown more articulate, perhaps because they are now used to talking to strangers. They told me that they could see the departed, who worked like men in this life, prepared hill fields (*konda podu*), and reaped the crops. When a *veju* calls them they come and sit in a packed crowd in the narrow space before him. The hill deities also come and sit side by side with the dead. But only the deity or spirit who possesses the *veju* speaks and says what should be done to cure the sick person on whose behalf the *veju* has gone into trance. One *veju* told me that for each village on this earth there is a corresponding village in the land of the dead, an idea which I had found among the Wanchus of Arunachal Pradesh, but never among the Reddis. As any such notion is foreign to the local Hindus, it must be an original Reddi belief, which I failed to discover in 1941, but which may be wide-spread among different tribal societies. The Reddis' belief that dead men and women may be reborn again in the same family is more likely to be an adaptation of Hindu beliefs in reincarnation, and this idea, too, I did not encounter in 1941.

The ritual at agricultural ceremonies has remained unchanged. Pigs and fowls are the principal sacrificial animals and are obligatory victims in the worship of Bhu Devi, the earth deity. Goats are sacrificed only if they have been promised as a propitiatory offering to a spirit who has afflicted a person with illness.

DEVELOPMENTS AMONG GONDS

In contrast to Chenchus and Reddis, the Gonds of Adilabad have experienced so many external interventions in diverse spheres of their social and cultural life that it would be surprising if their religious ideas and practices had remained unaltered. The very basis of their social order rests on an elaborate mythology which explains and sanctions the manner in which the different sections of Gond society function and interact. Each of the four phratries (*saga*) is linked with a deity or a pair of deities, whose cult unites its members and provides the various clans with regular occasions for cooperation in ritual activities. The clan deities (*persa pen*) are thought to have acted as the protectors of the members of each clan throughout its long history, and the ability of the Gonds to hold their own in battles with various other ethnic groups justified their faith in the power and benevolence

of these deities. Hence the Gonds had no incentive to seek the protection of alien gods and to divide their loyalties between different cults.

Today, however, a new situation has arisen. The Gonds have become an underprivileged minority in their own ancestral homeland,
now infiltrated and largely taken over by members of various advanced communities. Appeals to the old clan deities for succour in
their misfortune have obviously been of little avail, and the Gonds
have begun to look elsewhere for divine assistance. One young man
of Marlavai told me in so many words that he had gone on pilgrimage
to Tirupati, a centre of Vishnuite worship, because the Gond gods
could offer no help in the present emergency.

The cult of the tribal deities stands outside the world-view with
which Gonds become increasingly familiar through the teachings in
schools and through contacts with officials and traders, and hence appears to the young Gonds as out of date and in need of reinterpreta-
tion. Various reform movements, to be discussed presently in greater
detail, attract men and women in search of an ideology and ritual
practices in accord with Hindu thought. This attraction coincides with
a weakening of the old tribal tradition through the erosion of the role
of the Pardhans, the hereditary bards of the Gonds, who in the old
days passed on the knowledge of myths and legends from generation
to generation. By their recitations at ritual occasions they instructed
young Gonds in the sacred lore of their clans, and they also kept a
watchful eye on the proper performance of the clan rites. Today many
Gonds do not have the means to support a class of bards and enter-
tainers, and Pardhans, who can no longer rely on the gifts and lavish
hospitality of their patrons, have taken up agriculture or moved on to
other occupations, including teaching and government service.

Although the art of the Pardhans is not yet dead, and there are still
middle-aged and old men who retain a good knowledge of the myths
and can recite them in the traditional manner, their numbers are
dwindling, and not all of them pass on their skills to their sons. The
time may be near when young Gonds will have little chance to learn
about their tribal gods and the mythological events which provide the
ultimate charter for social customs and ritual performances. Such attempts as are being made to record parts of Gond tradition in writing
have been connected with reform movements which aim at constructing links between Gond and Hindu mythology. The efforts to record
and publish some oral literature in the original Gondi made in connection with the Gond Education Scheme of the 1940s have not been
continued. Although modern technology would make it easy to record
the Pardhans' recitations on tape, so far no one has taken any steps in
that direction, and the sacred oral literature of the Gonds may well
disappear without leaving much trace.

Apart from the dilution of the body of religious knowledge, there have been changes in the performance of the rites to honour the clan deities. The most important of these changes is the abandonment of the sacrifice of bulls and cows under the pressure of Hindu public opinion. The slaughter of cattle and the consumption of their flesh by the worshippers was always an essential feature, not only of the clan-god feasts, but also of memorial rites to honour departed kinsmen. As long as the Gonds lived under Muslim rulers, such as the Nizam of Hyderabad, there was no official interference with cow slaughter, and local Hindus were not bold enough to agitate openly against the slaughter of animals universally eaten by the ruling class of the state. A change in this situation came about with the incorporation of Hyderabad within the Republic of India and the replacement of the old regime by an administration dominated by Hindus. It was not until 1978 that cow slaughter was formally forbidden by the Andhra Pradesh government, but long before that local opposition to the sacrifice of cows grew, and the Gonds were made to realize that to continue the practice would be detrimental to their social status, for as eaters of beef they would ultimately be equated with untouchables. Gond politicians who mixed with high-caste Congress men were the first to become aware of the strength of the Hindu prejudice against cow slaughter, and they prevailed upon their fellow tribesmen to renounce a custom which marred the Gonds' image in the eyes of the new ruling class. Thus the sacrificing of cows was given up—not suddenly, of course, but gradually as the conservative older men died or lost influence and a new generation conscious of the need to compromise with ideas held by the society at large took their place on the councils of villages and clans. The most crucial question was how the cult of the clan deities could be properly conducted without the sacrifice of cows. The clan myths explicitly describe, after all, how at the inauguration of the cult of the clan deities by the culture-hero Pahandi Kupar Lingal and Hiraman Guru a cow had to be brought, sacrificed, and given to the clan gods, and that the Gonds' ancestors promised the gods to repeat such sacrifices as part of their cult.[1] Similarly, legendary accounts of the history of individual Gond clans contain frequent references to cow sacrifices.[2] Thus the omission of such sacrifices was as serious a break with tradition as the replacement of communion wine by orange juice would be for Christian churches.

Cows also used to be sacrificed at funerals and memorial rites, and their flesh was an essential part of the meals prepared for the many mourners who had to be fed on such occasions. The substitution of

1. For the relevant text, see *The Gonds of Andhra Pradesh,* p. 231.

2. *The Gonds of Andhra Pradesh,* pp. 250, 270.

goats as sacrificial animals creates great difficulties for the hosts, for the meat of one goat does not go far, and few Gonds are now rich enough to provide several goats for such an occasion.

The abandonment of cow slaughter has to be rationalized, and an extract from a recent speech by a prominent Gond politician, Atram Lingu of Sirpur, ex-president of the Panchayat Samithi (see chapter 6), illustrates how this is being done:

> The original Gonds and Pardhans were cutting cows and this is why they were called *Koitur,* which means "cutter." Because the cow is an important animal we should not slaughter it, for this is a sin. The four Vedas of India do not mention such sacrifices, and because of the sinful practice of cow slaughter we Gonds are backward and we do not cooperate with each other. Therefore you must promise that you will not eat beef, neither of cow nor of bullock. You may have heard, and the old men among you have seen it, that in previous years up to twenty cows were slaughtered at the time of the Keslapur *jatra.* Now this slaughter has been stopped, because it is sinful.

This speech, made by a man who in his youth must have participated in many cow sacrifices, demonstrates very clearly the complete reversal of ideas in regard to ritual practices. What was once considered a duty, prescribed by sacred texts, is now described as sin because Gonds in close touch with non-tribals have adopted Hindu notions at the expense of their traditional beliefs. In the forefront of the propaganda against cow sacrifice were such reform movements as that of Suruji Maharaj, to be described presently. In the area affected by this movement, not only the sacrifice of cows but also an important part of the traditional funeral ritual has been abandoned. This part, known as *jagurla* and described at length in *The Gonds of Andhra Pradesh* (pp. 375–80), involved the cremation of the corpse and a ritual dance around the burning pyre to the accompaniment of drums and wind instruments. While the flames consumed the corpse a cow was sacrificed, its head was placed close to the pyre, and part of the flesh was cooked as *niwot* ("sacrificial food") and then offered to the *sanal* ("soul") of the departed with the words: "See, this is given to you, to you the cow is given; may it reach you." Subsequently all the mourners consumed the cow's flesh.

Without cow sacrifice the *jagurla* rite loses much of its significance, and while in some villages a goat is substituted, others omit the *jagurla* altogether. Thus the Gonds of Kanchanpalli, Chudur Gumnur, Netnur, Jamuldhara, Dhanora, and Chiklaguda no longer perform this rite, nor is it done by the new settlers in Mahagaon, who came from Kinwat and are devotees of Suruji Maharaj. The original inhabitants of Mahagaon still perform it, though without cow sacrifice, possibly to demonstrate their opposition to Suruji Maharaj and the new settlers, whom they regard as innovators lacking in dedication to the cult of the Gond gods.

The reform movement of Suruji Maharaj is one of several attempts to steer Gond religion in the direction of Hinduism without effecting, however, a total break with all traditional beliefs and practices. In the 1940s a similar movement was active in some parts of Kinwat Taluk, but this was confined almost entirely to Pardhans. It seems that it originated in the then British-administered territory of Berar, and that a Pardhan guru from that region spread the message in Kinwat. Some of his followers were settled in the village of Patoda, the home of a Pardhan sadhu by the name of Wika Deoba. By 1943, when I visited the locality, many Pardhans had become his followers, and some of them had given up their work as bards and musicians. They no longer played at Gond rites, and professed to worship only one god, whom they knew under the name of Bhagavan. Wika Deoba had been several times to Keslapur and had tried to persuade the Gonds to desist from cow slaughter, but at that time without much success. He taught his followers to sing *bhajan* (Hindu devotional songs) and to worship the *tulsi* plant.

Suruji Maharaj, whose Gond name is Kotnaka Suru, also came from Kinwat. His guru was Geram Joti Ram, a Gond of Bahmanguda, who in turn was a disciple of a certain Narsimlu, who was not a Gond but presumably a member of a Hindu caste. When the Nizam's government allocated land in Utnur Taluk to Gonds, Kotnaka Suru, along with many other settlers from Kinwat, was granted *patta* on vacant land in Mahagaon. He and thirty-two other Gond families settled there, and formed a hamlet of their own at a little distance from the old village of Mahagaon. The newcomers, who had previously been landless, came from different villages in the taluks of Kinwat and Adilabad, and their only unifying link was their common allegiance to Suruji Maharaj. Thanks to his influence with some government officials, he obtained for the new settlement funds for the construction of so-called "colony" houses, i.e. houses with tiled roofs and mud walls rather more solid than those of ordinary Gond houses. Yet in the material sphere his efforts did not go any further. The agricultural methods of the Gonds of the new hamlet of Mahagaon are not more advanced than those of other Gonds of the area.

Mahagaon has attained a certain fame because of a shrine built on the initiative of Suruji Maharaj in the style of a Hindu temple on top of a hill close to the village. It contains a Shiva *lingam*, and at Shivaratri a *jatra* is held there, attended by Gonds from Adilabad, Kinwat, and even Yeotmal in Maharashtra. Significantly, few people from nearby villages attend, and in 1979 the only prominent Gond from the vicinity to come to the *puja* was Raja Bhagwant Rao of Kanchanpalli.

However, Suruji Maharaj has a considerable following in Asifabad Taluk, and, as Michael Yorke explains in chapter 9, his devotees are recruited mainly from among educated Gonds, particularly schoolteachers. He moves about a good deal, visiting villages where he has made converts, and this is facilitated by the fact that he owns a jeep bought with the help of the donations of devotees, who include some non-tribals. Suruji Maharaj usually attends the Keslapur *jatra*, and there he spends the evenings surrounded by *bhajan*-singing followers.

Despite the range of his influence over a large part of the district, he gives the impression of a kindly and modest man rather than of a powerful leader; hence, his ability to recruit followers is surprising. The limitations of his message can be gauged by the following taped extract from a speech he made at a meeting in Pithaguda mentioned in chapter 6:

> I am only a simple man and have nothing much to say. I never went to school. I am a poor orator, but I came here to speak because I was urged to do so by Lingu [the ex-president of the Panchayat Samithi]. I came here to see Haimendorf Sahib and you people as suggested by Lingu. I have always been a poor man. I herded the cattle of others; I laboured for other people, for my parents were poor. By the grace of Haimendorf Sahib I came from Kinwat and was given land in Mahagaon. You must work hard and you will get good results; if you work hard you will be finding God (*pen*). Without work you will go to waste, you will get into the habit of drinking. Hence, even if you kill me, I shall go on to ask you people not to drink.

This is certainly not the rousing speech of a charismatic leader, and the loyalty Suruji attracts may simply be due to the Gonds' longing for some anchor to enable them to hold their own in a new cultural climate, contrasting sharply with a religion centred in the dramatic rites of clan god feasts when the blood of cows and goats was spilled in honour of divinities who possessed priests and shamans and spoke through their mouths to the assembled devotees.

The sect led by Suruji Maharaj is not the only movement leaning towards Hindu ideas, nor is he the only guru who has emerged in recent years. Mesram Jevant Rao was, like Suruji Maharaj, a disciple of Joti Ram of Bhamanguda in Kinwat, but he gathered round him a different circle of followers. They are found in Chudur Burnur, Chudur Koinur, Dubbaguda, Polasar, and even in one hamlet of Mahagaon. They form an endogamous group and intermarry neither with the followers of Suruji Maharaj nor with traditionalist Gonds. A Pardhan guru living in Kandiguda has both Pardhan and Gond followers, and Torosam Marothi of Jatarla in Both Taluk, who was also a disciple of Joti Ram, has organized a similar group of devotees searching for new religious expression. All these gurus accept the invitations of individual Gonds to come to their houses on full moon days and perform *puja* for Satya Narain.

TRANSFORMATION OF A TRIBAL FESTIVAL

The change in the whole tone of religious expression becomes most apparent in the way in which the Keslapur *jatra*, the most popular religious event in Adilabad District, is now being celebrated. When in 1941 I first attended that feast, at which Gonds from all parts of the district and even from neighbouring British India used to assemble, the performance of the rites to honour the clan deity of the Buigoita branch of the Mesram clan was central to the occasion. Numerous sacrificial animals, from fowls and goats to calves, cows, and bulls, were brought from all directions, and the earth near the shrine of the clan ancestors was soon soaked with their blood. The fair, where a few dozen shopkeepers exhibited their wares and Gond women bought the odd piece of cloth, a brass pot, or perhaps a ring, necklace, or belt made of silver, was incidental, and certainly less important than the appearance of the Atram raja of Utnur, who arrived, carried in a palanquin, to adjudicate in disputes which throughout the year had resisted peaceful resolution in *panchayats* of lesser status.

The ritual focal point of the entire celebration was a simple *sati* shrine, erected on a mound close to a huge banyan tree, and made of no more permanent building materials than a few wooden posts and a low roof thatched with grass. Near this shrine animals were sacrificed throughout the night, and the blare of shawms and the roll of drums accompanied each climax of a sacrificial rite. Open fires and the moonlight filtering through the foliage were the only sources of light. At intervals the sound of the strings of a Pardhan's fiddle and his singing and reciting could be heard, but there was no other music than that required by the liturgy.

Today all this has changed. A whole town of tents and shops, tea stalls, and make-shift restaurants with crude wooden benches and tables grows up on the eve of the Keslapur *jatra*, a cinema is installed in a canvas hall, and loudspeakers blare out film music long before the show begins. There are exhibitions mounted by government departments displaying all the progressive techniques supposed to be available to the local tribal populations, and a huge *pandal* where, on one of the days of the *jatra*, district officers and local politicians address a crowd of tribesmen, often promising benefits which everybody knows are unrealistic and will never be delivered, not because the speakers are insincere but because vested interests oppose any substantial improvement in the tribesmen's conditions. As dusk falls the whole chaotic accumulation of commercial enterprises and official window dressing is enveloped in a blaze of electric light, blotting out the flames of the few small fires lit by tribal families, who have come by old habit to worship their clan deities in some corner of the traditional sacred site. But the old shrine of wood and thatch has disappeared. It has been replaced by a modern temple building, constructed of stone and cement, and painted a brilliant white.

How did this happen, and who decided to construct a modern temple? The sanctuary at Keslapur, which Gond tradition equates with Bourmachua, the original home of the Seven Brother Folk,[3] had always been under the control of the men of the Buigoita branch of the Mesram clan, and the clan priest (*katora*) and the guardian (*patla*) of that branch lived at Keslapur. In 1960 officials of the Endowment Department came to attend the *jatra*, which by that time had become widely known through the sponsorship of the district officials, and, realizing its potential as a centre of pilgrimage, they proposed that a permanent shrine be built and registered with their department. They promised funds for the construction and maintenance of the temple, and persuaded the local Gonds to consent to these plans. The clan priest, Mesram Nagu, as well as the Pardhan Mesram Soniya, objected to the plan, but the village headman and *patla* of the shrine, Mesram Chitru, pressed for the construction of the temple, and being a rich and influential man he overruled clan priest and Pardhan. Most of the money required for the construction was collected from Buigoita Mesram men and from men married to Buigoita women. There were also contributions from the Endowment Department and from the trustees of the wealthy Vishnu temple at Tirupati in southern Andhra Pradesh.

In 1962, the main building was completed, and as the Gond deity worshipped at Keslapur was Sri Shek, the serpent god who plays an important role in Gond mythology, the temple was dedicated to Nagoba, the cobra deity with whom Hindus, too, are familiar. Subsequently, both a brass sculpture representing an enormous cobra and several ritual objects were installed in the temple.

At first the new temple stood on its own, but in 1976 a stone wall enclosing the whole temple complex, together with a large courtyard, was built at a cost of Rs 17,000. A committee, which at first was under the chairmanship of Raja Atram Deo Shah of Utnur, applied to the Endowment Department for support, and this application was successful. This meant that official funds became available for the new temple, but also that the donations received at the time of the *jatra* had largely to be paid into the endowment fund, a development which the

3. See *The Gonds of Andhra Pradesh*, pp. 270–80.

local Gonds had not fully foreseen. As Raja Deo Shah, who had won a seat in the Legislative Assembly, could not give sufficient time to the affairs of the temple, the committee subsequently elected as chairman Marskola Kasiram, an ex-member of the Legislative Assembly who had many contacts in Hindu circles and who seems to have approved a far-reaching Hinduization of the ritual.

At the time of the *jatra*, crowds of Gonds as well as non-tribals enter the temple and in Hindu style place offerings of rice, flowers, coconuts, and cash in front of the serpent idol. In 1977 the cash offerings amounted to Rs 1,911, and this sum went to the endowment fund. In addition, Rs 238 was given as offerings at the altar of the clan ancestors (*sati*), and this sum was divided between the clan priest, the guardian (*patla*), and the Pardhan. The Pardhan musicians who at times played and sang in the courtyard were given Rs 105 in small coins. Their singing was often almost inaudible, for the committee had sanctioned the installation of loudspeakers, and some young men thought to contribute to the festivities by playing tapes of cinema music considered suitable as background for religious ceremonies. Garlands of coloured electric lights used as decoration gave the temple an appearance totally at variance with traditional Gond ritual structures. Indeed, in the whole performance of the ritual there remained few truly Gond elements. The essential animal sacrifices, such as the offering of *tum*-goats necessary for the rite of joining the souls of departed kinsmen with the clan god, were not allowed to be performed inside the temple compound, but had to be executed rather furtively at the back of the temple, outside the surrounding wall. Until a few years ago, these sacrifices were performed in the courtyard in front of the temple, but in view of the present Hindu prejudice against blood sacrifices the ritual is considered inappropriate for the courtyard. A similar banishment of animal sacrifices from the inner temple courtyards has been reported from Kerala, but there they had not been as central to the temple ritual as the offering of animals to the clan deities is in Gond religion. The only part of the ritual performed at Keslapur in traditional style is now the introduction of the newly married brides of Mesram Gonds and Pardhans to the clan ancestors, described in detail in *The Gonds of Andhra Pradesh* (pp. 527–29).

The transformation of the Keslapur *jatra* from a tribal gathering devoted to the traditional worship of Gond deities to a great fair attended by thousands of non-tribals reflects the submergence of Gond culture in the ocean of Hindu practices. What is the Gonds' own reaction to this change, imposed on them by events which are largely outside their control? The older and more conservative Gonds, particularly those from villages in the central highlands, seem to be perturbed, for they no longer feel at home at a *jatra* which they remember as a function enacted by Gonds and exclusively for Gonds. Even the guardians of the sanctuary of Shri Shek, i.e. the Mesram men of Keslapur, who took the fateful step of allowing the construction of a temple in Hindu style and accepting funds from the Endowment Department, are uneasy about losing control over the style of worship and the use of donations received. A certain pride in the development of the Nagoba shrine as a regional and not a purely tribal religious centre is mixed with the fear that non-tribals may ultimately take over the organization of the cult, just as the organization of the secular part of the *jatra* has already slipped from Gond hands. Some of the younger Gonds, especially those educated in schools with non-tribal teachers, seem to applaud the establishment of a Gond shrine which in outward form can vie with Hindu temples and thereby gain respectability for Gond religion in the eyes of the wider Hindu society which is inevitably engulfing the Gonds of Adilabad, today already a minority in their own country. Similar sentiments have caused some Gonds to seek connections between their own mythology and Hindu scriptures and to interpret the former in the light of Hindu ideology, as the movement inspired by Suruji Maharaj is attempting to do.

In 1977, the committee of the Nagoba temple at Keslapur consisted of Marskola Kasiram (chairman); Raja Atram Deo Shah, member of the Legislative Assembly; Atram Lingu of Sirpur; Kinaka Bhir Shah of Pithebangara; Mesram Chandu, *sarpanch* of the Keslapur *panchayat;* and Gadana, member of the Legislative Assembly, a man of Golkar caste from Mudol Taluk. The treasurer was an official of the Endowment Department. The Mesram men had clearly lost control, and this confirmed the fears of the clan priest, who knew that in other places the use of the same shrine by Gonds and Hindus had led to conflict.

One such conflict occurred in Bhadi, the old seat of a *mokashi* of Jungnaka clan. In Bhadi there is a sanctuary with a stone sculpture of a Nandi. Traditionally, Gonds acted as priests of the shrine, but then a sadhu came and acted for some years as *pujari*. When a Gond of the Jungnaka clan resumed the role of *pujari*, a local Brahmin objected, and there was a court case which went as far as the High Court. In the end the Jungnaka men won the case. They get contributions of grain from all the villagers, including non-tribals, but there are now no animal sacrifices.

Another conflict over the right of worship at a shrine occurred at Jheri village. There some Hindus of Reddi caste had settled, and together with the local Gonds and Pardhans built a temple and installed in it a Hanuman image which had been at the locality long before the Reddis had settled. But when in 1960 the Gonds and Pardhans wanted to worship in the temple at the Dassera festival, the Reddis tried to prevent them from entering it. A fight broke out, and one man was killed. Since then the Reddis do not dare to obstruct the tribals' worship.

A different outcome of a joint enterprise in building a temple occurred in Chandhuri, near Hasnapur. There all the villagers, Hindus as well as Gonds and Pardhans, contributed to the construction of a temple. When it was completed, some Telugu Gollas did not allow Gonds and Pardhans to enter it. A Mesram man, who told me the story, said that he feared that the Nagoba temple at Keslapur might ultimately also be taken over completely by Hindus, and that the Gonds might be deprived of their role as priests and guardians of the sanctuary.

Not all constructions of shrines are due to cooperation between Gonds and non-tribals. In Sirpur the initiative for the rebuilding of an old temple came from the local Gonds, who undertook the repairs unaided by outsiders, at least insofar as financial support was concerned.

In Sirpur there was an old Shiva temple, stemming probably from the time when there was a Maratha fort nearby. The temple had fallen into disuse and was partly in ruins. But the stones were still lying on the site, and in 1969 the Gonds of Sirpur, on the initiative of Atram Bhimji, rebuilt the temple at a cost of Rs 5,000. As it was believed—probably erroneously—that the temple originally belonged to the Atram rajas, who were *watandar* of Sirpur, one of their descendants, who now lives in nearby Pamelawada, was designated *pujari* of the reconstituted temple.

On a stone platform in front of the temple, which must once have been covered by a roof resting on columns, there is a collection of stone Nandi and *lingam* in *yoni* of different sizes. They have probably been collected from various sites. The temple itself is built of large stone blocks, and its roof is in the form of a stepped pyramid. As one enters one finds oneself in a small entrance hall, and a low door leads from this into the inner shrine, in the centre of which there are two stone *lingam*. On the walls several stone sculptures have been arranged.

According to Atram Bhimji, the temple is in reality not a Mahadeo shrine but a sanctuary of Rajasur, the house god of the Sirpur rajas. This, however, is probably a chimera of the imagination, and the temple is quite rightly devoted to the cult of Mahadeo. About two weeks after the Keslapur *jatra*, a minor *jatra* is held near the newly rebuilt temple of Sirpur. The impulse to hold a *jatra* came from Atram Lingu, then *sarpanch* of Sirpur, no doubt with the idea of raising the prestige of the village and benefiting the local shopkeepers. It is a small affair compared with the Keslapur *jatra*, but nevertheless some 200–300 shopkeepers, who pay between Rs 300 and Rs 500 in tax, come and open stalls, and the donations to the temple average Rs 150. The total turnover of all the shopkeepers at the *jatra* in 1977 was Rs 250,000.

On the eve of the *jatra* the clan priest of the Sirpurkar clan deities first worships the village goddesses, represented by three stone images under a tree, and then performs a simple *puja* in the interior sanctuary of the temple. The Shiva *lingam* are bathed, anointed, and decorated with leaves. The worshippers then enter the shrine, and each scatters rice grains on the *lingam* and on the sculptures on the walls.

Whereas in Keslapur a Gond sanctuary has virtually been transformed into a Hindu temple, in Sirpur we find a different type of amalgamation of tribal and Hindu cults. Here the Gonds have taken over an abandoned Hindu temple and instituted a ritual combining Gond and Hindu elements.

CHANGES IN PERSONAL PRACTICES AND BELIEFS

Quite apart from adjustments of ritual affecting Gond society in general, such as the abandonment of cow sacrifice under the pressure of Hindu opinion, there are also more spontaneous innovations arising from personal decisions. Thus the *katora* of the clan deities of the Sirpurkar branch of the Atram clan took the symbols of the *persa pen* to Parsewara and performed the annual rites there, whereupon the clansmen left behind in the Sirpur area started a rival cult.[4] In the 1970s the clan priest and a group of supporters in Parsewara joined one of the reform movements which had originated in Maharashtra, and according to the new faith gave up the slaughter of animals and the eating of meat. Consequently, the ritual was altered and the *katora* broke and offered coconuts instead of sacrificing goats to his *persa pen.*

Individuals, too, take up new practices even if no other member of their local community shares their beliefs. Thus Atram Bhagwant Rao, the senior member of the raja family of Kanchanpalli, has adopted many Hindu rituals, which he performs as part of his private worship. In the courtyard of his house he grows a *tulsi* plant, and this he circumambulates every morning reciting prayers and sprinkling water. He also worships every day at the sanctuary outside the village, where an image of Hanuman, a stone Nandi, and a *lingam* stand on a small platform under a shelter. Apart from performing these rituals, he also observes various prescriptions of high-caste Hindus. Thus he no longer eats any meat and shuns alcoholic drinks, two taboos for which there is no justification in Gond tradition. Though Bhagwant Rao is highly respected and popular, there is no indication that any of the

4. See *The Gonds of Andhra Pradesh,* p. 112.

villagers of Kanchanpalli follow his example. His religious views and observances are regarded as his personal affair, and he does not try to convert others to his beliefs, nor does anyone criticize him for what Gonds might easily regard as eccentricities. While the breach of a taboo compulsorily observed by the entire village, such as the taboo on leaving village land on certain days of communal rites, would expose the offender to being fined or at least seriously upbraided, no one cares if a member of the community observes extra restrictions.

A certain laxity in the observance of customary taboos is, however, noticeable. Thus tradition prescribes that before the celebration of Holi, known to the Gonds as Durari, no one should begin ploughing. Yet men who employ farm servants on an annual basis have developed a tendency to make them begin the ploughing even before Holi, allegedly because they do not want to waste labour for which they have paid.

The celebration of Holi itself has changed. Nowadays the young men and the children throw red powder at each other and also squirt coloured water at anyone who comes their way, just as is done in Hindu villages and towns. The younger people do not even know that this is an innovation, but old men confirmed my impression that it is a new practice insofar as Gonds are concerned. Previously they used the red petals of *Butea frondosa* blossoms to decorate the frames put up for Matral and Matri, then pounded the petals and threw the resulting red paste at each other.[5]

As long as changes are neither drastic nor rapid, the actors themselves often do not realize that their conduct is altering, and few Gonds are able to say how far religious ideas have diverged from the traditional pattern. Yet one of the old headmen told me how he saw the developments which have taken place in Gond ideas and behaviour:

> The worship of the gods remains the same, but now there is less devotion, and the prescribed procedure of the ritual is not observed as rigidly as it was in my youth. The young people do not follow our instruction with sufficient attention. Once tigers used to kill people, but since we are mixed up with Banjaras and Marathas men kill men, and we have to defend ourselves against people. In the old days by sheer force of devotion we could protect ourselves against tigers, but now there is not enough devotion to serve as protection against people.

Some changes in the traditional cult have been made necessary because of the intrusions of non-tribals. Thus in 1970 the immediate vicinity of the famous sanctuary of the goddess Jangu Bai at Parandoli

5. See *The Gonds of Andhra Pradesh*, pp. 437, 438.

was forcibly occupied by Hatkars, Mahars, and Mangs, who had come from Udgir and Ahmedpur. As Parandoli lies in Rajura Taluk of Maharashtra, the many devotees of Jangu Bai in Andhra Pradesh could not prevent this defilement of sacred ground. All they could do was to move some of the sacred objects to Dodunda near Chorgaon, and there they set up a subsidiary cult centre which for the time being is safe from pollution.

A cult like that of the Gonds, which is not concentrated in a few great centres, but dispersed over innumerable small shrines and sanctuaries, each of which is of enormous sentimental importance for individual groups, is clearly vulnerable once tribesmen no longer live in compact tracts of country. Non-tribal newcomers, ignorant or even unmindful of the susceptibilities of the Gonds, often interfere by sheer accident with places and objects which appear inconspicuous and ordinary and are yet of vital importance to the religious feelings of the local tribesmen.

Whereas Hindu and Muslim settlers are almost totally ignorant of Gond religion, many Gonds are becoming increasingly familiar with Hindu ideas and practices. This is due not only to the influence of reform movements inspired by Hindu values and even of such concepts as *moksa* ("salvation"), but also to the Gonds' growing interest in pilgrimages to distant Hindu shrines. Encouraged by local Hindu entrepreneurs, many Gonds of Utnur Taluk have in recent years undertaken journeys to Tirupati, the great Vishnu temple in the extreme south of Andhra Pradesh. These entrepreneurs hire buses for the entire trip and charge the Gonds about Rs 120 per head for the return fare. Two people can visit Tirupati, do some sightseeing on the way, and get the god's blessing for about Rs 250. This is a substantial sum even for a well-to-do Gond, and it is surprising how many people go on such pilgrimages. No doubt the sense of adventure and the desire to gain prestige are motives as powerful as purely religious considerations. As the Gonds have never believed that their fate in the land of the dead depends on merit acquired in this life, the wish to gain merit can hardly rank high among the incentives to incur the expense of such a trip, but there is a belief that a deity as famous and powerful as the god of Tirupati can render his devotees assistance in their difficulties in this life.

The extent of the religious knowledge gained on such a pilgrimage is probably next to zero, but there are other channels through which some information on Hindu deities and mythological figures reaches the Gonds. Wandering sadhus occasionally visit Gond villages, and though they seldom preach, they do tell some stories in exchange for the food which they consume or are given as alms. Thus most Gonds have for some time been vaguely familiar with the main figures of the

Ramayana and the Mahabharata. It is only in recent years that extracts from these epics have been translated into Gondi; for example, Atram Ramu and Kotnaka Jalim Shah of Gunjala translated a simplified version of the Ramayana from the Marathi of a printed pamphlet into Gondi and distributed handwritten copies to several villages. The same two Gonds also invented new terms for the numerals above seven, for which no words exist in Gondi, and another Gond of Gunjala, the headman Kumra Gangu, developed a special Gondi alphabet. Yet neither the new numerals nor the alphabet attained currency outside the village where the experiments were made. Far more successful is the Gondi translation of a Marathi folk drama based on the Ramayana, made by a Gond of Mahagaon. The translation is written in Devanagari characters, and sufficient copies, all written by hand, were made to enable actors of an amateur troupe to memorize their parts.

While I stayed in Kanchanpalli in 1976, I saw a performance of this troupe. The courtyard of the ashram school was used as a stage, and the school building as back stage, where the actors dressed and changed when they had to take over different parts. A band of drummers and cymbal players, established on the verandah of the school, accompanied the action throughout the play. At times the musicians sang *bhajan*-like songs, and the actors often joined in these songs. The musical side of the performance was somewhat repetitive and monotonous; there was no variation in tune or expression whatever episode was being enacted.

The actors were dressed in colourful costumes, and gods and kings wore sparkling headdresses, which in the light of a pressure-lamp looked expensive, though they were made of very cheap, glittering materials. The play lasted without interruption from 9 P.M. to 5 A.M., and the audience, made up of the villagers of Kanchanpalli, persevered in watching, impervious to the chill of the December night. As each actor took the stage, he began by singing a song in a *bhajan* tune, accompanied by the musicians and a small chorus. The parts of women were invariably taken by young men, and no woman joined in any of the dances which formed part of the drama. A joker who engaged the characters in bantering conversation provided a comic element throughout the play. There were long stretches of dialogue, but the actors never faltered. As it would have been a prodigious feat to memorize completely the parts of a play lasting eight hours, it must be assumed that there was a good deal of improvisation. Gonds are used to improvising, and the skits enacted at the Dandari festivities give them practice in enacting a known scene even if they do not remember the precise text.

Such folk dramas familiarize the Gonds with various themes of

Hindu mythology, but it would seem that the wholesale adoption of the Marathi pattern of a musical play is a mixed blessing. There is little spontaneity in either music or dialogue, and in expressiveness the acting is inferior to that of the actors in the improvised skits enacted at Dandari time. A displacement of the indigenous musical style of the Gonds by Marathi songs must result in an impoverishment of Gond artistic taste, but it is doubtful whether the Gonds themselves are aware of this danger.

As vehicles for the spread of Hindu ideas, such dramatic performances of parts of the Ramayana and Mahabharata certainly have an educational value, for if Gonds want to move as equals in Hindu society they must be able to understand references to figures and events depicted in the great Hindu epics.

Hindu missions, such as the Rama Krishna Mission, do not operate among any tribal societies of Andhra Pradesh, and there is no question of a formal conversion of any of the tribes to Hinduism. In the eyes of the Hindu majority, such a conversion would serve no purpose, for rightly or wrongly it is assumed that without any special effort the tribal populations of the state will in any case be assimilated to Brahminical Hinduism.

Even at the time of Muslim rule, Islam never attempted to proselytize either Gonds or any of the other tribes. Christian missions, on the other hand, particularly the Catholic Kerala Mission, have opened schools in Adilabad, and although so far few converts have been made, it is not unlikely that some of the children now in Christian schools will ultimately be converted and form a small Christian community within the tribal population. So far Gond reaction against such a possibility has been outspokenly negative, and in one case parents whose children had gained free places in a mission school were put under pressure to remove them, under the threat that in the event they did not do so, they and their families would be barred from intermarriage with other Gonds. Such intolerance is not general, but it indicates an anxiety that any prolonged influence of representatives of a foreign religion on Gond children might erode the cohesion of Gond society, already weakened by the economic domination of non-tribals.

8 Relations with Non-Tribal Populations

IN THE PRECEDING CHAPTERS we have seen that most of the changes in the economic condition and life-style of tribal people have been caused by contacts with materially more advanced and politically more powerful populations. Such contacts are not an entirely novel phenomenon, for few of the tribesmen of Andhra Pradesh have ever lived in total isolation, but the intensity of their impact has grown enormously within the past forty years, and it is growing all the time. The improvement of communications, particularly the construction of motorable roads, as well as the intensified intervention of government agencies in more and more aspects of citizens' activities, have combined to undermine the independence of tribal societies. The degree of interaction with non-tribals varies according to both topographical and economic factors. Small groups in out-of-the-way places are less likely to be affected by contact with outsiders than settled communities close to a commercial highway or in the midst of agriculturally rich country. Where there are few resources to attract settlers or traders, primitive tribes may be left in peace even though access to their habitat is not difficult, while in other areas the prospect of growing lucrative cash crops rapidly leads to fierce competition between the local tribesmen and rapacious immigrants.

Among the Chenchus of the Nallamalai Hills, true competition with outsiders occurred only recently. For a long time, probably several centuries if not longer, their contact with more advanced populations was focussed on a primitive barter trade. The Chenchus were in need of knives, axe heads, and iron for arrow tips, and the com- *185*

modities they gave in exchange were honey, wax, berries, and sometimes perhaps venison. When they discarded the leaf dress of their
ancestors, they needed cotton material for scanty pieces of clothing,
and with the adoption of a more settled mode of life, they also sought
to acquire such household goods as pots and mill-stones. By the time
the Forest Department of Hyderabad State began to exploit the Chenchus' habitat and contractors started to fell trees and bamboos, Chenchus had an opportunity to earn cash wages, with which they could
buy some of the novel commodities and occasionally also small quantities of grain. At the same time merchants of the plains began to purchase increasing quantities of minor forest produce, such as aromatic
resin, kernels of *Buchanania latifolia,* and corollae of *Bassia latifolia,* the
so-called *mahua* flowers used for the distillation of liquor. Contacts resulting from such barter remained, however, rather fleeting. There
was little occasion for Chenchus to entertain any lasting social relations with the plainsmen who bought or bartered such jungle produce, for all the transactions were seasonal and involved contacts with
a variety of plainsmen. Though in such transactions the Chenchus
may sometimes have been cheated, there was little interference with
their life-style, and no outsider had any desire to settle in their densely
wooded habitat. Such was still the case when I lived with the Jungle
Chenchus in 1940, but since then various changes have occurred, as
discussed in chapter 3.

When I returned to the same area in 1977 and again in 1980, I found
that the Chenchus were no longer the sole inhabitants. In various localities non-tribals had settled and begun to cultivate on a small scale
in some clearings where a few plots of land had been allocated to
Chenchus. But the Chenchus had shown little perseverance in
cultivating, even though the government had distributed some
plough bullocks. They preferred to let out such land to Banjaras and
other plains people, who cultivated and gave them a share of the
yield.

In some localities there is another type of cooperation. In Pulajelma,
for instance, there are several families of Banjaras who come with
large herds every year in the month of May. They graze their cattle in
the forest until the following January, and throughout the eight
months of their stay they live in a kind of symbiosis with the Chenchus of the locality. The Chenchu women draw water from a well
close to their own huts, and carry it to the Banjara camp. In return for
this service they get butter-milk from the Banjaras, and this they consume mixed with millet gruel. The Chenchus insist that every Chenchu household must get some of the milk, irrespective of the work its
members have done for the Banjaras.

A more complex situation, involving members of several different castes, has arisen in Vatellapalli. In 1940 this was a Chenchu settlement of eight huts, but herdsmen from villages of the lower Amrabad Plateau used to bring their cattle for grazing in the surrounding forest, moving from camp to camp. Social contact with the Chenchus was then minimal.

Subsequently, several families of Waddars settled for a time at Vatellapalli and started cultivation. Because of friction with forest officers, they left after some time. In order to make the local Chenchus learn how to cultivate, the Social Service Department then settled eighteen families of Harijans of Mala caste at Vatellapalli. Both Chenchus and Harijans were allotted some land and plough bullocks, and the idea was that by their example the Harijans would teach the Chenchus agriculture. At first the project was reasonably successful, and several Chenchus learned to plough and reaped some grain crops from their fields. But with the exception of one man, who in 1978 was still cultivating, all the Chenchus gave up cultivation when their plough bullocks became old and died. They then hired out their land to the Harijans, and were quite content to get a share of the produce, while they themselves engaged in the collection and sale of minor forest produce. The latest arrivals are Banjaras, who keep cattle but also cultivate some land which they have been allotted. Harijans and Banjaras alike describe the Chenchus as hopelessly inefficient cultivators, and it seems that most Chenchus subscribe to this assessment and leave agriculture to others while concentrating on the gathering of forest produce. In this occupation they no longer have a monopoly, however, for Harijans and Banjaras have also started to collect marketable forest produce, though they do not range over as large a forest area as the Chenchus do. In 1977 the number of Chenchu households had grown to twenty-four. There were no newcomers among them, but all were descendants of the eight families who had lived in Vatellapalli in 1940.

A similar situation has arisen in Sarlepalli, an old Chenchu settlement which now has a mixed population. Besides twenty-one Chenchu households, there are thirty houses of Harijans, Gollas, Waddars, and Muslims. The houses stand between kitchen gardens and give an impression of permanence. Here, too, the Chenchus were allotted plough bullocks and encouraged to take up agriculture. But when the bullocks died in a cattle epidemic, they gave up cultivation, and leased out their land to the many non-tribals who had settled at Sarlepalli. Only a few of those newcomers have obtained *patta* land. Most are content to cultivate land belonging to Chenchus and to pay the owners rent in either cash or kind. The Chenchus, too, seem to be satisfied with getting a rent of about fifty kilograms of grain per acre. They are now free to collect forest produce for sale and seem to be quite well off. Some have even been able to buy buffaloes, but most of them own neither cattle nor poultry. Here I had the impression that there is no animosity between Chenchus and non-tribals, and that the symbiosis of foodgatherers and agriculturists is far more successful than the symbiosis of ethnic groups with similar, and hence competitive, economies in Adilabad District.

The Chenchus on the lower Amrabad Plateau are in a very different position. Here they have lived for some generations in close contact with non-tribal agricultural populations. The Chenchus of some communities, such as Mananur, were able to acquire land and learn to cultivate before there was great pressure on land, and some have retained their holdings despite periodic indebtedness to merchants and moneylenders. The proximity of the forest enables the Chenchus of Mananur to supplement their income by collecting forest produce and selling it for cash to the local depot of the Girijan Corporation.

In the villages east of Amrabad, the condition of the Chenchus is much less favourable. They depend entirely on agriculture, but most are short of land and of plough bullocks, and work mainly as farm servants or casual labourers for landowners belonging to the higher Hindu castes. The most impoverished group of Chenchus in this area lives in tiny huts built on an outcrop of rock near the large and prosperous Hindu village of Venkeshwaram. Only one of the Chenchus owns a little plot of land, but as he has no bullocks he lets it out to a Mala cultivator, who gives him as rent only one quarter of the yield. An old woman told me that when she came to the village as a young girl there were plenty of roots and tubers in the jungle, but that now the forest has receded because of the expansion of cultivation, and forest produce has become scarce. Here and elsewhere the Chenchus also complained that the competition of non-tribals restricts their earnings from the collection of forest produce. Real income from agricultural wages has also decreased. In 1940 I had noted that the average daily wage in these villages was 3 kilograms of grain, but now landlords pay Chenchus only 1½–2 kilograms of grain for a day's work.

In the large village of Jangamreddipalli near Amrabad, nineteen Chenchu families form a small minority, and in 1977 they were entirely dominated by a Reddi landlord, who paid male farm servants an annual wage of Rs 600 without giving them food or clothes. By 1980 their condition had slightly improved, for most of the Chenchus had been allotted some land by government, and the Tribal Welfare Department had provided them with plough bullocks.

Despite such occasional assistance by government, symbiosis with advanced populations has not proved beneficial to the Chenchus of this area. They appear on the whole less well fed than the Forest Chenchus and enjoy less independence and freedom from exploitation. But whatever the material prospects of the Village Chenchus may be, they have at least the ritual status of a non-polluting caste, whereas in South India many primitive jungle tribes became low caste and untouchable when assimilated within the caste system. The Chenchus' relatively good caste status may be due to their early association with hermits and priests of outlying temples, as well as to their conformance to the Hindu prejudice against beef eating. Hence they may draw water from the same wells as Brahmins and have free access to all Hindu temples. Yet their houses never stand inside the villages where the higher Hindu castes and Muslims dwell, but are situated in hamlets on the outskirts, very much like the settlements of such Harijans as Malas and Madigas. And while the latter play a traditional and by no means unimportant role in rural Telugu society, the Chenchu is still an outsider and does not participate to any great extent in the social and ritual life of the villages.

The relations of the Konda Reddis with non-tribals who settled in their country have already figured in chapter 2, where the problem of land alienation was discussed in detail. Similarly, the effect of exploitation by timber and bamboo merchants on the Reddis' economy has been dealt with in chapter 4. Reviewing developments throughout the Reddi country during the period from 1940 to 1979, we cannot come to any other conclusion than that on the whole the Reddis have not benefited from their contact with materially and politically more advanced populations. The only ethnic groups whom they meet on a basis of equality are such tribes as Koyas and Bagatas, as well as certain communities of craftsmen. The Kammar blacksmiths of the Godavari region, for example, live in a style similar to that of the Reddis and despite their low ritual status participate in many of the latter's festivals.

Between Reddis and the merchants and cultivators from the coastal region who settled in riverbank villages, on the other hand, there is no social meeting ground. The newcomers, most of whom belong to Hindu castes of middle status, look down upon the Reddis, feeling both socially and economically so superior that they regard them in no other role than that of potential victims of exploitation. Settlers intent on purchasing or leasing a Reddi's land may fraternize with the vendor and ply him with drink till they can persuade him to put his thumbprint to a piece of paper which gives the settler rights to his land in return for a derisory sum or other insignificant benefits. As soon as the deal is completed, the settler loses interest in his drinking companion. The surest way of making a Reddi pliable is to lead him into debt, and we have seen that one of the first non-tribal settlers in Koida opened a liquor shop and sold drink to Reddis and Koyas on credit as the first phase in his campaign for the acquisition of land suitable for growing tobacco and chillies. In *The Reddis of the Bison*

Hills I have shown that in the 1930s and 1940s timber merchants used
the system of debt bondage as the easiest means of acquiring a docile
labour force, and while the exploitation of forest coups by large firms,
such as the Sirpur Paper Mills, has done away with this type of
abuse—though by no means with all forms of corruption—indebtedness of tribals is still the most important factor in the perpetuation of
the Reddis' economic domination by outsiders.

Apart from merchants settled in riverside villages and dealing with
large numbers of tribals, such as the many Reddis earning cash wages
by bamboo cutting, there are also petty traders who periodically visit
Reddi hamlets and peddle a limited range of goods. While I camped in
Gogulapudi, a small hill settlement, a woman of Kapu caste with two
young girls carrying some baskets arrived. She was selling salt, sugar,
oil, vegetables, and some other supplies, and extended credit to those
Reddis who had no cash in the house. She seemed on familiar terms
with the Reddi women and spent the night in one of their houses. I
was told that she was a frequent visitor in out-of-the-way villages and
made a living by her petty trade. It is partly through such pedlars that
Reddis become aware of events outside their villages and learn to understand the people in the more advanced villages. Thus, modes of
dress and behaviour change imperceptibly through the example of the
few non-tribals who are on friendly terms with Reddi families.

In the hills of East Godavari District, specifically in Chodavaram
Taluk, Reddis have for several generations lived in symbiosis with
members of an untouchable caste known locally as Valmiki, or Konda
Mala. In chapter 4, in which I discussed the economic relations between Reddis and Valmikis, we have seen that, although of socially
lower status than the Reddis, the Valmikis have succeeded in dominating and, indeed, exploiting the Reddis. Recent changes in the pattern
of trade have diminished the possibility of exploitation, but developments in the educational sphere now work in favour of the Valmikis.
As many of them have been converted to Christianity, they have had
many opportunities to obtain a relatively good education in mission
schools, and this is expressed in a high literacy rate. Superior educational qualifications now give Valmikis great advantages in the competition for employment in government service. Many Valmikis have
been appointed as teachers and to clerical posts, whereas the number
of Reddis in government employ is minimal. Even more important is
the success of Valmikis in the political field. Valmikis are now represented in the Legislative Assembly of Andhra Pradesh, holding seats
reserved for tribals, while Reddis have so far shown little political ambition. As long as the *muttadar* represented their people vis-à-vis the
officers of government, lack of interest in politics was of little consequence, but since the abolishment of the system of feudal chiefs the

Reddis are undoubtedly at a disadvantage compared with educationally more advanced populations such as the Valmikis, particularly as the latter also profit from the reservation of jobs and seats for tribals.

In Vishakapatnam District, which adjoins the Reddi country to the north, Valmikis also form a substantial population in such tribal areas as Paderu Taluk. There they live in large villages side by side with Bhagatas and Konda Doras. Neither in house-style nor in dress is there much difference between Bhagatas and Valmikis. Both communities appear to be relatively prosperous, their houses are well built, and their irrigated rice fields are carefully tended. The situation of Paderu Taluk at an altitude between 2,000 and 3,000 feet and the difficulties of communication have so far prevented a massive immigration of non-tribals from the coastal region. People from the lowlands find the low temperatures of the winter months troublesome, and until recently there was no all-weather motor road between Vishakapatnam and Paderu. In 1978 many villages of Paderu Taluk could not be reached by jeep, and during the monsoon even access on foot was often difficult. Hence, so far advanced populations from the lowlands have not been attracted to settle in remote valleys where they would be cut off during part of the year. Along the motor road which leads from Paderu to the northern part of East Godavari District, however, members of various Telugu castes have settled during the past twenty years. Though they arrived mainly as traders and moneylenders, they did acquire some land, but not to an extent which seriously jeopardized the landholdings of the local tribals.

In the neighbouring Srikakulam District, different conditions prevailed. There Jatapus and Saoras are the principal tribal communities, and in the hill areas adjoining the state of Orissa, these tribes used to be the main population. As in East Godavari District, there were some tribal feudal chiefs with the title *muttadar*, and judging from the *sanad* documents some of them still possess, their authority was recognized by the British administration as early as 1848. During the last two or three generations, members of Hindu castes infiltrated into the hills both from the coastal lowlands and from Orissa, and their settlement led to the usual alienation of tribal land. In Bhadragiri Taluk, for instance, much of the flat land in the valley bottoms passed into the hands of newcomers, while the indigenous tribals practised shifting cultivation on the hill slopes. The community mainly responsible for the alienation of tribal land throughout the hill regions of Srikakulam District is the Sundis, or Sondis, originally a caste of toddy sellers and distillers of arrack, many of whom have turned into moneylenders. As early as 1909, E. Thurston referred to this caste in the following passage:

The Sondis are gradually getting much of the best land into their hands, and many of the guileless hill ryots into their power. Mr. Taylor stated in 1892 that the rate of interest on loans extorted by these Sondis is 100% and, if this is not cleared off in the first year, compound interest at 100% is charged on the balance. The result is that, in many instances, the cultivators are unable to pay in cash or kind, and become the gōtis or serfs of the sowcars, for whom they have to work in return for mere *batta* (subsistence allowance), whilst the latter care to manipulate their accounts in such a manner that the debt is never paid off.[1]

It is a sad reflection on the inability of successive governments, British and Indian alike, to protect tribals against exploitation that the conditions graphically described in the above passage have continued to prevail over nearly a century, although they were clearly known to the authorities. The fact that they were not remedied, even when in other parts of Andhra Pradesh steps were taken to eliminate land alienation and debt bondage in tribal areas, ultimately led to the insurgency under Naxalite leadership mentioned in chapter 1. This was clearly an act of desperation in the face of intolerable oppression by non-tribals, and it proved effective in bringing about a change in government policy. Under the new policy much of the land usurped by Sundis, Oriya Brahmins, and other non-tribals was returned to Jatapus and Saoras, and the relations between tribals and non-tribals were placed on a new basis. Some of the non-tribals, such as numerous Oriya Brahmins, who had acquired land in Srikakulam without giving up their holdings in Orissa, returned to their original home villages, but others had been settled in Srikakulam for long periods, and stayed on, making the best of the new, and for them unfavourable, situation and undoubtedly hoping that a change in government policy would enable them to recover some of the lost land.

Mondemkallu, a large village in the Bhadragiri area, is a good example of the multi-ethnic society which grew up during the years of unrestricted immigration. This village comprises about 500 households, and of these 200 are of Oriya Brahmins, Sundis, and other trading castes. There are Jatapu streets and at some distance from them an entire Saora settlement, which is noticeably poorer than other parts of the village. There is also a potters' street and a quarter of Oriya-speaking gardeners, who rank as tribals and have retained their plots of land.

The Sundis and other non-tribals are now lying low and try, apparently not unsuccessfully, to make a living by trade and possibly by moneylending. When in 1979 I enquired whether, despite the vig-

1. *Castes and Tribes of Southern India* 6:400.

ilance of government officials, cases of illegal transfer of land between tribals and non-tribals occurred, I learned that a few cases have indeed come to the notice of the authorities, most of them related to arrangements of sharecropping which enable non-tribals to regain a foothold in land officially re-allocated to the original tribal owners.

In villages such as Mondemkallu, some Jatapus live in a style similar to that of Sundis, and it would appear that the self-confidence they gained at the time of the Naxalite movement, as well as the resulting change in government policy, is now enabling them to hold their own in their interaction with non-tribals. I noted a similar attitude of self-assurance on the part of tribals at a weekly market in Sitampeta. Jatapus and Saoras arriving with their wares, mainly goats, pigs, fowls, and large bunches of bananas, were by no means ready to accept the prices offered by traders, who tried to tempt them with bundles of banknotes as soon as the villagers arrived at the market. The tribals bargained very vigorously, and managed to sell goats for as much as Rs 110, rejecting all lower offers. This is certainly a considerable change in attitude compared with that which had prevailed as long as most tribals were deeply indebted to merchants and had no choice but to deliver their produce to their creditors at rates arbitrarily fixed by the latter.

The relations between tribal communities and non-tribals in Adilabad has been dealt with at some length in my book *The Gonds of Andhra Pradesh* (pp. 27–35) and insofar as the eastern part of the district is concerned, there are also references to this problem in the analysis by Michael Yorke contained in chapter 9. In this context it will therefore suffice to concentrate on those aspects of the problem which have undergone major changes in recent years. There are two major causes of such changes. One is the sudden influx of non-tribals, who have occupied large parts of the district which a generation ago were purely tribal territory. While this development occurred without encouragement by government and partly even in the face of some rather ineffective opposition by local officers, the other major change in community relations is the result of a deliberate reversal of policy by the Government of Andhra Pradesh.

As long as small numbers of non-tribals lived among the Gonds and Pardhans of taluks such as Utnur, relations between tribals and non-tribals were fairly amicable. Here and there some Marathas owned a few acres of land in a Gond village, possibly a relic of the brief time when the Maratha kingdom extended as far as the Adilabad highlands. The Maratha owners of such lands either let them out to Gonds, charging a moderate rent, or lived in small clusters near Gond villages and cultivated the land themselves. In either case they maintained a low profile, and were so small a minority that they did not threaten in any way the social and economic order of the tribal people among whom they lived. Quite a different situation arose when the demographic pattern was reversed and the erstwhile Gond majority turned into a minority. In extreme cases such as in Jainur and Indraveli, nontribal newcomers occupied the central parts of villages and established a bazaar street with modern houses, while the Gonds were confined to hamlets situated at the periphery of the locality.

In such places the new settlers imported the house-style and manner of living of the lowlands, and the Gonds continued to build dwellings of wood and wattle, seldom having the means to copy the houses of those who had taken over most of their land and profited from the trade in newly introduced cash crops. So great is the gap between the Gonds' living standards and resources and those of the Hindu and Muslim settlers that there would be no real basis for social relations even if differences in language, ideology, and traditions did not present obstacles in the way of personal, in contrast to purely commercial, contacts.

The members of the immigrant communities are not content to dominate the region economically, but they are ambitious to gain influence in the local system of authority. This can be done most effectively by achieving appointments as *patel* and *patwari*. The position of *patwari*, in particular, makes it possible for an incumbent to manipulate the allocation and transfer of land, a power which in the present social and political climate also facilitates the collection of very substantial bribes.

Unlike Gonds, who seem to have lost the ability to cooperate for their mutual protection, most of the immigrant communities have set up networks of members in economically and politically influential positions, and through these networks exert a power which the Gonds can no longer match. A few examples of clusters of influential nontribals will demonstrate the composition of such networks.

Utnur has been a centre of influential Muslims ever since the days of the Nizam's government, and even today, when Muslims are no longer a privileged community, a network of locally powerful Muslims remains. The doyen of one of these networks is Tajuddin, *sarpanch* of Utnur. He served at one time as revenue inspector, and his father was head constable in the Utnur police station. He has large landholdings in Utnur, Dantanpalli, and Birsaipat, and he also operates as a moneylender. Among his close kinsmen are Abdul Rahim, who at one time held the position of *patwari* for Jainur, Daboli, Jendeguda, Ragapur, Pithaguda, and Burnur, having replaced the Gond *patwari* of these villages. Abdul Rahim's younger brother, Khalil Ahmed, is *patwari* of the important village of Hasnapur. The mother's sister's son of Abdul Rahim is Mohamed Ali, *patwari* of Dubbaguda, Daboli, and Jamni.

Another Muslim family, remotely related to Tajuddin, consists of Hasham, *patwari* of Salevada and Shampur, his brother-in-law Ismail, *patwari* of Tosham, and Sheik Husain, son-in-law of Ismail, who is *patwari* of Kando and Rampur. The latter is also secretary of an informal association of *patwari*, and maintains close contact with the so-called *asaldar patwari*, who are all Brahmins and were hereditary *watandar* whose consent had to be obtained—and often bought—when anyone was to be appointed as *patwari*.

There is also a network of Reddis (a Telugu Hindu caste different from the Konda Reddis), and the leading figure of this cluster is Linga Reddi, a landowner with holdings in Utnur and Darmasagar, who also owns a liquor shop at Indraveli, while his wife runs a moneylending business. He is closely related to Hanmanth Reddi, who in 1978 was deputy forest ranger at Janaram and who owns a liquor shop in Utnur. His wife lives in Utnur and also lends money.

Another cluster is made up of Mahars, members of a Maratha caste of low status but considerable business skill. This cluster centers around the village of Narnur. There Lokhandya Soma owns a great deal of land and in 1977 had 200 head of cattle. He is a great moneylender, lending money at an interest rate of 25 percent per annum on the security of mortgages of land. He is considered the richest man in Utnur Taluk. His son Baba Rao is *patwari* of Tadi Harapnur and five other villages, and Lokhandya Soma's two mother's brother's sons are Raja Ram, *patwari* of Chorgaon, Sungapur, Doranda, and Pipri, and Linga Rao, who is *patwari* of Malangi, Umri, Sangwi, Rumankhassa, and Ganeshpur. Finally there is Nam Deo, the classificatory brother's son of Baba Rao, who lives in Tadi Harapnur but is *patwari* of Babijheri, Bopapur, and Khairdatwa.

There are similar clusters of families of Rajputs, Hatkars, Komtis, Kalals, and Banjaras, all of whom combine economic power with the authority some of their members exercise as *patwari*.

The role played by such networks in the alienation of tribal land for the benefit of immigrant Muslims, Hatkars, Marathas, or Mahars, as the case may be, explains to a great extent the inability of the Gonds to resist the massive onslaught of newcomers on their ancestral land. For the combination of financial resources and the key position of *patwari* in the system of land rights enabled such clusters of powerful families to outwit illiterate Gonds of modest means at every step and to sabotage even the campaign of the government to restore alienated tribal land. Yet as long as the transfer of land from Gonds, Pardhans, Kolams, and Naikpods to members of any other community remained

Banjara women who had immigrated from Maharashtra into the highlands of Adilabad. In race, language, and customs they differ fundamentally from the indigenous tribals. Their characteristic dress, made of multi-coloured materials and heavily embroidered, betrays the Banjaras' North Indian origin.

strictly illegal, there was always the possibility of counteracting the tricks and falsifications of corrupt *patwari,* and all hope was not lost for tribals if a sympathetic officer took the trouble to investigate cases of land alienation in depth.

However, in 1977 a decision by the Government of Andhra Pradesh removed one of the most important safeguards against the transfer of tribal land to new settlers. In that year the Banjaras, also known as Lambaras, were notified as a scheduled tribe, and this notification invested them with all the privileges hitherto enjoyed only by the truly aboriginal tribes of Andhra Pradesh. The reason for this move on the part of the government was basically political, for Banjara leaders had been pressing for some time for their inclusion in the list of scheduled tribes, and as some 600,000 votes were at stake, the political party in power finally yielded to this pressure. The Indian parliament endorsed the proposal made by the Government of Andhra Pradesh, even though in the neighbouring state of Maharashtra the Banjaras do not have the status of a scheduled tribe.

In Adilabad District, the Banjaras are among the most recent immigrants. Their homeland is undoubtedly North India, and in physical

Muria Gond girls of Bastar wearing solid silver necklaces and many strings of glass beads; their saris are invariably white.

characteristics, language, and traditional dress they are akin to the population of Rajasthan. Originally they were engaged both in cattle breeding and in the transport of goods on the backs of their pack bullocks, and it was in their capacity as carriers that they served the Mughul armies and moved in their wake as far south as the Deccan. When modern means of transport outstripped the Banjaras' bullock caravans, many of them took to farming, with particular emphasis on the raising of live-stock.

In Adilabad District, the settlement of Banjaras is of very recent date, and in the 1940s there were still many old Gonds who remembered the time when the first immigrants arrived with their carts and cattle from the neighbouring districts of Berar. They first settled in the taluks of Kinwat and Adilabad, but when no more land was available in the riverain plains south of the Penganga, they pushed into the highlands and ultimately occupied a great deal of land in the heart of the Gond country. Generally more dynamic than the easygoing Gonds, hardworking, and shrewd, they succeeded in displacing the indigenous tribals in many villages of Utnur Taluk, and in the early 1940s there were already Banjaras who owned several hundred acres, but cultivated only a small part themselves, hiring out the rest at high rents. In their relations with Gonds they were on the whole oppressive and employed their greater business sense and their powerful physique to bully and intimidate their Gond neighbours. As early as 1948, I wrote in my *The Gonds of Adilabad* (p. 62): "Once Banjaras gain a foothold in a village, it is generally lost to Gonds or Kolams." Subsequent events proved this sentence to be truly prophetic, for by 1976 numerous old Gond villages had been taken over by Banjaras, and the acquisition of Gond land by new Banjara settlers progressed at a steady pace. When special revenue officers probed into cases of alienation of tribal land, it was found that many of them involved the illegal acquisition of Gond land by Banjaras. After the notification of the Banjaras as a scheduled tribe, the Land Transfer Regulation could no longer be invoked to restore such land to the rightful Gond owners, and it can be clearly foreseen that more and more tribal land will pass into the hands of Banjaras. As in neighbouring Maharashtra they do not enjoy the privileges of a tribe, it is only natural that many Banjaras cross into Andhra Pradesh and avail themselves there of facilities to which they are not entitled in their home state.

In Utnur Taluk, where in the 1940s Gonds, Pardhans, and Kolams still formed the overwhelming majority of the population, in the years 1978 and 1979 alone some 20,000 acres of land were assigned on *patta* to Banjaras. This is more than the entire allocation of land to tribals in the previous twenty-five years, and can be explained only by the strong pressure Banjara political leaders and their allies in the ruling party were able to exert on the revenue authorities of the district. Seen against the background of a situation in which many Gonds and Kolams had for years vainly tried to obtain *patta* for land they were already cultivating (see chapter 3), this massive operation indicates that the Banjaras have suddenly become the most privileged community in the district. But the ability to acquire tribal land is only one of the privileges recently gained by Banjaras. In addition, they now have the right to occupy seats in the Legislative Assembly reserved for tribals, and we have seen in chapter 5 that both the tribal seats previously held by Gonds have now been gained by Banjaras. As soon as the long-deferred *panchayat* elections are held, Banjaras will undoubtedly also displace many Gond chairmen of *gram panchayats*. As the Banjaras have for some time been the main competitors of the Gonds throughout the western part of the district and in the central highlands, it is obvious that their notification as a scheduled tribe has made the existing protective legislation virtually ineffective insofar as the indigenous tribes of Gonds and Kolams are concerned. Land-hungry Banjaras are now moving into the tribal area not only from Maharashtra, but also from the Telengana districts of Karimnagar and even Warangal, where most land is in the hands of advanced communities, from whom it cannot be wrested as easily as from the tribals of Adilabad.

Seen from a wider historical perspective, the infiltration of the tribal regions of Adilabad by Banjaras appears as yet another phase in the Aryan conquest of Peninsular India. For, while Gonds and Kolams represent the aboriginal, dark-skinned, Dravidian-speaking population of the Deccan, the light-skinned Banjaras of North Indian racial type, who speak a Sanskritic language, are just the latest wave of Aryan conquerors replacing an indigenous people. It is not without irony that the Muslim ruling class of Hyderabad State, though themselves largely of North Indian origin, had passed legislation protecting the Gonds from such immigrants from the north as the Banjaras, but the "Dravidian" members of the Government of Andhra Pradesh have opened the floodgates in the face of an invasion of such "Aryan" populations as Marathas and Banjaras, who are now posed to establish themselves as the dominant communities in the northernmost district of the state.

The expectation that with the progress of education Gonds and other tribals would gradually move into a position in which they could meet members of other communities on equal terms has so far not been fulfilled, and in the next chapter Michael Yorke explains very clearly why, despite an increasing flexibility of cultural barriers, the Gonds are very far from being accepted as integral parts of greater Indian society.

POSTSCRIPT TO CHAPTERS 1–8

An anthropologist's work is normally one of the most enjoyable tasks falling to the lot of social scientists. It is exhilarating to probe into the functioning of societies other than one's own, and to discover that there are innumerable ways in which human beings can attain harmony with their environment and can model universal desires in such a manner as to allow the members of their community to adjust to each other for their mutual benefit. Any one who had the good fortune to share over long periods the life of tribal societies undisturbed by the influence of self-seeking outsiders must have experienced the sense of well-being prevailing in such societies, and it is pleasant to describe and analyse the working of communities living in an atmosphere of contentment and cheerfulness.

All the more depressing is the duty of the chronicler to recount the decline and ultimate disintegration of tribes which only a generation ago had appeared secure in the maintenance of their traditional lifestyle. In much of my earlier fieldwork, such as the study of the Konyak Nagas in 1936 and subsequent research among the tribes of Arunachal Pradesh, I was dealing with homogeneous societies which had not yet been subjected to the infiltration of alien elements and were thus free of the corrupting impact of economic exploitation.

The tribal populations of Andhra Pradesh, to whose re-study I devoted the greater part of the years 1976 to 1980, present a very different picture. Here the change that has occurred during the past thirty years has been mainly for the worse. Few of the tribes I studied in the 1940s have been able to preserve their economic and social independence. Hence the foregoing chapters make depressing reading, and the fieldwork on which they are based was a far from pleasurable experience. The strong emotional ties which linked me with such communities as the Gonds of the Adilabad highlands and the knowledge that I was no longer in a position to redress or even mitigate their grievances made it hard to observe the turn in their fortunes in a spirit of detachment. Indeed I often wished that I had preserved the memory of the far happier tribal life which I had known in earlier years.

Comparing the present atmosphere among the Gonds and Kolams of Adilabad with that still prevailing among the tribes of Arunachal Pradesh, to be discussed in chapter 11, I assumed it was only in the highlands of Northeast India that tribesmen had been able to retain their economic independence and joie de vivre. But this assumption was misleading, as I learned soon after completing the larger part of the manuscript of this book, for it was then that I had the unexpected opportunity of revisiting a tribal area not far from Andhra Pradesh which has been saved from the ills afflicting the tribes of that state. This unblemished tribal haven lies in the Bastar District of the state of Madhya Pradesh, and though my visit was a brief one, it convinced me that in Peninsular India, too, there are still regions—rapidly shrinking, unfortunately—where tribal people lead a life in accordance with their own traditions and inclinations.

In the days of British rule, Bastar was a princely state whose dynasty, though claiming descent from the Kakatiya kings of Warangal, felt close to its tribal subjects and favoured the retention of the customs and life-style of their forefathers. There may have been little "development" in the modern sense, but communities belonging to a variety of Gond tribes were free from the harassment of unsympathetic petty officials, and their land was not threatened by the greed of alien immigrants.

Travelling by jeep from the eastern border of Adilabad District across a belt of Maharashtrian territory towards Narainpur in Madhya Pradesh, I passed for many hours through almost unbroken stretches of high forest. Only here and there patches of slash-and-burn cultivation or ploughed land surrounded a small hamlet of thatched huts. This was the kind of scenery I remembered so well from the highlands of Adilabad in the days before the forests had been ruthlessly felled and waves of non-tribal settlers had swamped the original inhabitants. In Bastar there was no sign of such a process, and even in the vicinity of Narainpur, the taluk headquarters, tribals secure in the possession of their land coexisted peacefully with a few families of artisans and traders who made a living by close economic interaction with the local Muria Gonds.

The weekly market in Narainpur contrasted sharply with all the markets in the tribal area of Adilabad. While there nearly all the stalls are manned by non-tribal traders, in Narainpur the local tribals, predominantly Murias in their tribal dress, establish their stalls and offer substantial quantities of vegetables, fruits, pulses, and various grains for sale. Their customers are mainly the non-tribal residents of Narainpur, many of them government servants, who buy their domestic requirements from the tribal stall-keepers and casual traders. Hence there is hardly any likelihood of tribals buying on credit and becoming gradually indebted to shopkeepers. On the contrary, the Murias sell their products for cash, and this serves them for the purchase of the few manufactured goods of which they are in need.

In the Muria villages I visited, there was a relaxed atmosphere indicative of well-being and prosperity, and in my conversations with the villagers no cases of harassment by officials or moneylenders were even mentioned. There is still enough cultivable land to go round, and nearly all the Murias have their own plough bullocks. Those who work the fields of neighbours or friends are paid in grain, never in cash. I was explicitly told that no one buys on credit and no one borrows from moneylenders. In times of need villagers borrow from each other.

The cohesion of the village communities also finds expression in the persistent vitality of the institution of the *ghotul*, the youth dormitory made famous by Verrier Elwin's book *The Muria and their Ghotul* (Bombay, 1947). In Nayanar the *ghotul* was not only well maintained but had been enlarged by annexes, which had not been there when I visited the village in 1948. Boys and girls continue to sleep in the *ghotul*, and in Malignar village I was able to observe the preparations for a triannual feast at which the boys and girls entertain all the villagers. The young people were pounding and cleaning the rice to be cooked, and the zeal and cheerfulness with which they worked betrayed an esprit de corps hard to find among the much more subdued tribal populations of Andhra Pradesh.

I found the same spirit in a remote village of the Abujhmar Hills, where all the people, men, women, and children, had gathered to thrash the newly reaped grain, a task which the setting of the sun and the rise of the full moon did not interrupt. This work, too, was done in a festive mood, with singing and laughing and the inspiration of ample quantities of home-brewed beer.

The Gonds' favourable position in Bastar can perhaps be explained by the long tradition of a liberal tribal policy in the erstwhile princely state and the one-time involvement of high-powered and anthropologically minded British administrators such as Sir Wilfrid Grigson, followed by equally dedicated members of the Indian Administrative Service such as Dr. B. D. Sharma. The young subdivisional officer of Narainpur, Rakesh Bansal, who accompanied me on my tour, was a worthy successor to those outstanding personalities. He clearly had a good rapport with the tribals, and his obvious sympathy for their way of life in turn inspired confidence and explained the success of the present policy.

The experience of those days spent among the Gonds of Bastar confirmed me in the view that the welfare of tribal populations depends not only on the laws under which they live, but even more on the spirit in which such laws are implemented.

9 The Situation of the Gonds of Asifabad and Lakshetipet Taluks, Adilabad District

by Michael Yorke

LAND ALIENATION

PROFESSOR FÜRER-HAIMENDORF has detailed the problem of land alienation throughout Adilabad District during the 1930s and 1940s, the efforts to prevent further incursions into tribal land which led to a period of economic security during the 1950s and 1960s, and, lastly, the influx of Marathi-speaking immigrants into the central area of tribal population in the 1970s and the subsequent decline and economic subjugation of the Raj Gonds and other tribals up to the present time.

In this chapter I shall concentrate on socio-economic developments which I observed in a limited area within the taluks of Asifabad and Lakshetipet during 1976–78. In the early part of the twentieth century, Telugu landlords, usually of Velma caste, extended their sway over the plains running south of Asifabad as far as the Godavari, and also into the broad valley of the Pedda Vagu. With well-established links to the administrative machinery, these Telugu landlords took advantage of an uneducated group of mobile agriculturists, who could be evicted from their land either by legal manipulation or by simply occupying land that they had left fallow in accordance with their method of cultivating their land by rotation.

The interesting difference between the eastern area, which I will now be discussing, and the central area is that in the former the structure of landlordism became established and entrenched as early as the first half of the century, while in the central highlands Gonds and Kolams remained undisturbed until much later.

The history of the development of predatory landlords in the eastern plains began with the large-scale granting of title deeds to land which was either vacant or cultivated by tribesmen whose ownership was not documented. This took place when the Nizam of Hyderabad's government decided to maximise land revenues in the area. Grants of land, known as *watan*, were offered to anyone with political influence who would undertake to extend cultivation and raise revenue, and such *watandar* also had the right to appoint *patel* and *patwari*. Subsequently, some of the remaining land was auctioned by government, usually in a manner which gave the local tribesmen no opportunity to obtain title deeds to the land they were cultivating. Changes in the right to land were often kept secret by those in locally powerful positions. Thus, such cases as that told by the residents of Venkatpur village in Lakshetipet Taluk were common occurrences:

> We have been cultivating our land in this village since the time of our great-grandfathers without any title deeds. Since the earliest time we can remember, a certain Chokka Rao of the Velma caste has claimed that he holds the title deeds to the entire 400 acres of our village. Today his son, Puskur Narsing Rao, the *sarpanch* of Ajipur and Venkatpur, still claims that he is the *pattadar*. So each year the government *patwari*, who also works for the *pattadar*, collects Rs 10 from each of us as rent for every acre that we cultivate. But he has never given us any receipts. In 1972 the deputy *tahsildar* and the *girdawar* came to our village and told us that we had no right to cultivate our land. They threatened us with force, saying that we would have to leave our homes. Then they went from house to house bargaining with each man, saying that if we paid anything between Rs 200 and 600 we would be allowed to continue farming our land. Many of us paid as much as we were able. Some of us had to borrow the money. Some of us were unable to pay, and we had to leave. Our land, which our grandfathers had cleared from the forest, was then given to other castes who were able to pay more money than we. Again in 1973, 1974, and 1975 the same thing happened, and in 1976 again they demanded the rent of Rs 10 per acre, but they also said that if we paid more money we would be given the title deeds to our land. This is because under the Land Ceiling Act the *pattadar* has to give away his land. But none of us are able to pay anything, and we are now due to pay this and are frightened that we will lose all our land.

The few tribals that live today on the plains around Asifabad or on either side of the road south from Asifabad through Tandur, Mancherial, and Bellampalli to Lakshetipet are now either landless labourers living on the periphery of large, caste-Hindu villages, or else they live in small hamlets totally dominated by landlords. The landlords of Asifabad are largely Marathi-speaking Vaishnava Brahmins, who worked as *patwari* in the government at the time of issuing titles and managed to get large tracts of land registered in their names. In the south of this eastern area, Lakshetipet Taluk, the land became the property of two brothers, one of whom had been the police *patel* to the Narsapur rajas who had held this area as *jagir*.

This penetration by non-tribal landlords had two main effects. First, it meant that the tribal occupants of the land had to pay cash rents, which in turn meant they had to grow some cash crops. With the new road built during the 1920s from Asifabad to Lakshetipet and the rapid increase in traders entering the area and opening markets, these became increasingly profitable. Forty years ago, there was only one weekly market in the Vatti Vagu and Moar valleys; today there are six weekly markets and one daily market. The need to pay cash rents stimulated the cultivation of cash crops, and these in turn made the purchase of consumer goods possible. This vicious circle gave rise to a further penetration by traders and a shift from a relatively self-sufficient economy to one dependent on outside products and credit facilities, provided by moneylenders, a well-known trend in most tribal areas of India which has always resulted in exploitation and further land alienation.

Due to this period of oppression and to the alienation of their land, many tribals left the plains area and moved westwards and northwards into the intermontane zone where the headwaters of the Vatti Vagu River cut into the escarpment of the central Adilabad Plateau. This is an area less dominated by Telugu-speaking landlords, who feared its wildness and were not accustomed to its heavier, black cotton and mixed, sandy soils. This is an area of *kharif* (monsoon) crops rather than *rabi* (winter) crops. Thus all twelve households of the Talapet hamlet of Mangi village left the plains village to the south, called Talapet, and settled in Mangi in the 1950s. Similarly, the villagers of Gangapur, near Tilani, were migrants from just west of the main road from Asifabad to Lakshetipet, where a large Muslim landlord had oppressed them. This wholesale migration from the plains was further encouraged by government, which offered grants of 15 acres of land in uncleared forest under its policy of encouraging a reconsolidation of tribals in the interior areas, where they could be afforded a new economic security and be protected from economic penetration by non-tribal communities. In this way, the village of Bhimrelli was consolidated under a grant scheme, and the hamlet of Ginnedhari began its expansion from some twelve households to more than sixty.

The intermontane zone had never received the full brunt of land alienation, mainly because Telugu-speaking landlords were not interested in ousting the tribals from their land and populating it with caste-Hindu dependents or in farming it themselves with hired labour. Yet they dominated the area for two purposes: rent farming and cattle grazing. Until overgrazing largely destroyed the excellent natural grass cover in the broad, flat valleys and on the hillsides, the plains cultivators used to send their stock herds into this area for summer grazing. Even today, the tribal inhabitants of such hamlets as Gutaguda and Tokeguda of Mangi village depend for a large part of their economy on grazing the cattle of plainsmen. For this reason, the previously tribal village of Mankapur in Lakshetipet Taluk is still dominated by one of the most rapacious of the Velma landlords from Mandamari, a locality near the road between Asifabad and Lakshetipet, which was once a purely tribal village but since the 1920s has slowly grown into a trading town with only a few households of Gonds, who live as wage labourers or by gathering firewood for the nearby mining towns.

The condition of Mankapur village is very interesting because it shows the indirect hold that the landlords have over this area. Some fifty years ago, two Kolams came and cleared some land in Mankapur. However, after a few years of bad harvests they mortgaged the land to the Velma landlord of Mandamari. Learning that this was an area of highly fertile soil, this landlord sent his bailiff, who was also the government *patwari,* to the villages of Selvella and Irkepalli. As *patwari* he encouraged eight families of Raj Gonds to move to Mankapur and clear as much land as they wanted on the promise that they would be given the title to this land. The *patwari* then registered this land in the name of the landlord. The village has now grown to twenty-four Gond and forty Pardhan households. Twelve of these households have title deeds to about eight acres of land, but they do not know where this land is. They now all live either by renting land at Rs 20 an acre or by farm labour. Almost all the population is in debt to the resident shopkeeper, who is an agent of the landlord. When it was heard that a special social service officer was giving tribals titles to fifteen acres of land, many residents cleared new forest and were encouraged to apply for the title. Though *patta* were granted to the villagers, the *patwari* withheld the certificates, and forty years later the Gonds still do not know what land is in whose name. In 1968, when illicit cultivation in reserved forest was regularized, every villager was to receive the title to eight acres, but none of them have yet been given these papers. So far the villagers have sent seven joint petitions to the government in order to discover the true status of the title ownership. Each time that they have done so, orders have come to the *patwari,* who is also the landlord's bailiff, to make an inquiry. Each time he has threatened the villagers, and the matter has been hushed up. Not only is the landlord rent farming the land, which the tribals see as their rightful inheritance for having cleared the forest, but he is also over-riding their legal rights. When communist and Naxalite ideology percolated into this district in 1975, many of the tribals began to clear new forest land in an area of some 300 acres which the landlord had used for grazing his cattle. To stop this process, the landlord took advantage of the conditions which at the time had been created by the Maintenance of Internal Security Act passed by the government of Mrs. Indira Gandhi to trump up against three household heads false accusations of holding political meetings and inciting the villagers. False charges of Naxalite adherence were produced, and only after one year in prison and considerable efforts by concerned tribal supporters were the three released with the charges against them dropped.

However, the main force of land alienation in the intermontane zone has not been due to the large, absentee Velma-caste landlords, but rather to smaller local landlords, who are distant cousins of the absentee landlords but live under the same umbrella of corrupt links through the large landlords to government officials to preserve their dominance as Velma *doralu*, or landowning "big men," within a caste framework. These small landlords moved into tribal villages and slowly took them over, initially using tribal land and then encouraging the Gonds to clear more land and moving non-tribals onto the original land. In this way Tilani, which was once a small tribal village, the seat of a Gond raja, the ruins of whose old mud fort can still be seen, and which on the ordinance survey map of 1929 appears as a small clearing in the forest, now has 580 caste-Hindu households and is a major marketing centre lying at the centre of an open cultivated plain. However, the small landlords had to operate in an area dominated by the political control of their distant cousins, and their expansion was limited to control over the villages in which they lived. The surrounding villages remained tribal but were under the domination of the absentee landlord, who may have visited the area once or twice a year, while his *gumashta*, or bailiff, who was usually also the *patwari*, collected the rents.

The rents charged by landlords in this intermontane zone were not as high as in the plains. The absentee landlords were not interested in maximising their revenues from this area or in ousting the tribals in favour of non-tribal cultivators. The existing pattern of tribal leadership was not replaced, and no non-tribals were brought in to create typical caste-Hindu villages. Yet the position of tribal leaders was undermined, as all relations with government were dominated by the landlord's network. In particular villages such as Mankapur, where the landlord had his forest grazing, a stranglehold on the tribal leadership was maintained, and one hears stories of village headmen being poisoned for standing up to the landlord's authority. But, in the majority of villages of this zone, the tribals continued to cultivate the land they had cleared as tenants, lease-holders, or sharecroppers. The major threat to their landholdings came not from the landlords, but from the ever-expanding population of new castes introduced by the smaller landlords. Here we are particularly concerned with the Perka cultivating caste. Through lending cash and grain to tribals, Perkas managed to obtain large quantities of tribal land, illegally registered in their name in breach of the Hyderabad Tribal Areas Regulation of 1949, under which all tribal-held title land was inalienable. A notorious case here is that of the village of Goegaon, which was originally a purely tribal village but has now lost all its tribal cultivators. Some seventy years ago, a group of Raj Gonds settled in Goegaon and cleared land for themselves. They soon discovered that the land had been given as a gift, *inam*, to the Muslim Abdul Qayyum Khan. They paid him a nominal rent of Rs 5 a year and were happy in the knowledge that they had the rights of a protected tenancy. After the demise of the Nizam's government, the landlord vanished, and the cultivators were granted permanent title to their protected tenancies. However, the *patwari* has continued to tell them that they must pay him Rs 200 before he can give them their certificates. None of them has ever discovered the official position as to who owns what land, though they continue to cultivate the land and to mortgage it at times of bad harvests. Pendram Jangubai told me the following story in October 1977:

> Maravi Jangu mortgaged all his land to Pettem Enkaiah, a Perka of Perkapalli hamlet of Tilani, for four years. In 1972, after the mortgage agreement was finished, Maravi Jangu tried to re-occupy his land, taking men and ploughs to the field. That evening Pettem Enkaiah came with a party of more than fifty Perkas and dragged and beat the Gonds brutally with sticks. Five of our villagers rushed to help them. They were all set upon by the Perkas and badly kicked and trampled and had chilli powder rubbed in their eyes. The next day I took them all in my cart with my son Jaithu to Asifabad. First we went to the police *amin*. We showed him the wounded. He told us to wait outside. Then he came back with the Samithi president and our *patwari*. Later many Perkas also went into the office, while we were kept outside. After some time, the *amin* came out and, threatening us, told us to go back to our village and keep quiet. We left, saying we would appeal to the district collector. As we were departing, our carts were directed to the hospital, where our wounds were bandaged. A month later Maravi Jangu died, after lying on his cot in great pain. Then his wife, Mangu Bai, went to Adilabad to see the collector. She was told that an order would be given to the *patwari* to return their land to them. *Patwari* Sattaiah later showed them only half their land, saying they could cultivate it. The other half was shown to Pettem Enkaiah. Some nine months later, Mangu Bai also died, after continually spitting blood,

since she was beaten. Today we are frightened to make any approach to our *patwari* or our *sarpanch,* and none of us have done anything to reclaim our land. However, in 1976 we heard that a special collector was appointed to return land to tribals. Many of our villagers submitted petitions to the *tahsildar* for the return of our lands from the hands of non-tribals. Whenever we attended the hearings, the defendants and our *patwari* did not come and our cases were dismissed. We were told to go away and bring our *patwari.* We presume there was connivance between the *patwari* and the *tahsildar* to dismiss our just case.

Such stories as this are typical of the oppression and alienation of tribals by caste cultivators brought into the area by the Velma landlords.

Once the network of landlords became established in Asifabad Taluk, a political economy developed quite distinct from that prevailing in the central and western areas of tribal population, where no landlords existed.

By the early 1960s, landlordism was not only firmly entrenched, but its period of predatory expansion had come to an end with the government's policies on land reform. The first and second generations of oppressive landlords were succeeded by the present third generation of highly educated people involved in politics, the legal profession, business, and contracting.

The change in the character of landlordism has been brought about by two main factors: the reduction in the rate of income from land and the implementation of land regulations. The reduction in the rate of income has been due mainly to the inability to charge rents as high as those charged previously, and also to the abolition of the landlord's right to collect revenue on behalf of the government. It has also been caused by the inability of the increasing population to make a living off the land available to it. The surplus from the land has had to feed more mouths, leaving less to be syphoned off by the landlords. As the cultivators become less wealthy (or perhaps more involved in the losses occasioned by a cash economy and the purchase of consumer goods), it is less possible for the landlord to live off the wealth of his tenants. This relationship operates because the traditional Indian system of land tenure tends to maximise, not the agricultural output for commercial gain, but the number of human dependants for political and social gain. Such a system is typical of the pre-industrial feudal structure of India.[1] However, the main factor curtailing the predatory activities of the landlords has been the implementation of land regulations and the expansion of administrative machinery, which makes it less easy for them to act as the only law in their local areas. The gradual creation of a whole package of laws relating to the power of the

1. R. E. Frykenberg, *Land Control and Social Structure in Indian History.*

landlords means that their influence can no longer be wielded directly over the cultivator, but must be exercised through government agents. This means that much of their influence has to be marshalled to deal with the new bureaucracy of the land records office, the land reforms office, and the collectorate. Building up relations and playing power politics with the administrative machine through expensive and time-consuming legislative channels means a greater expenditure of energy by the landlords to achieve the same predatory ends.

The penultimate blow to the feudal rights of the landlords came with the implementation of the protected tenancy regulations of 1973. Under section 38E of this amendment to the Andhra Pradesh Land Transfer Act of 1950, all protected tenants were given the *patta* to their land *suo moto*, or automatically, by the government. This meant that the landlord lost all control over ownership and over his revenue.

Gradually the commercial capability of the landlords has been diminished. The final blow came with the government's attempts from 1975 to 1978 to get all land illegally transferred from tribal tenants to non-tribal tenants transferred back to the original tribal. A special officer was appointed to deal with this problem. Potentially, vast acreages were involved. It is not possible to estimate their extent, but in 1977 and 1978 the government put a team of clerks to work going through every record to find out what land had been illegally transferred since 1948, the date of the original Hyderabad Land Transfer Regulation. In cases brought in petitions by tribals who were aware of illegal transfers, 13,000 acres of land were restored to tribals by October 1977. However, if and when the programme begins to restore land *suo moto*, that is, automatically and without petition, many tribals will find that land they were never aware of owning is being taken away from the landlords.

The implementation of this act gave rise to a storm of protests by the landlords. At each hearing, witnesses were suppressed and land records officers paid not to attend so that cases could be dragged out in the courts. All this proved not only tiresome but expensive to the landlords, and the large ones became the prime targets of the special officer dealing with these cases. It was felt that if the power of the large landlords could be broken, the implementation of the act would go ahead smoothly and without much opposition from smaller landlords and owner-occupiers, who had acquired land illegally from tribals through the agency of the large landlords. The landlords had to resort to expensive litigation in the High Court to get stay orders and appeals.

The end result of this process has been that the landlords' direct control over the land and their ability to live off their revenues has largely been broken. Very few of them now rely on revenue from land to maintain their standard of living. Indeed, those who try to do this usually fail. The houses of many landlords are now in ruins. The vast courtyards which were formerly filled with the grain of their dependants now lie bleak and empty at harvest time. The landlords themselves often live amid crumbling furniture, with one or two old retainers in one wing of what were once ornate and spacious mansions.

The outcome of the economic factors that reduced the income of the landlords and the legislation that curtailed their powers is that their period of predatory expansion has ended. They are no longer the same wealthy power, though they still preserve a wide range of social functions as local "big men," or Velma *doralu*, as they are known in Telugu. Many now feel that if they are tied to the land as a class their future lies in the actual cultivation of their land as farm managers maximising their agricultural output rather than their human dependants. They are using modern techniques of irrigation and fertilizers to become capitalist farmers. Most have given up living on rent farming. Those who have been unable to adjust to this new economic and social climate and still cling to a mode of life based on farming by human dependants have resorted to the technique of moneylending and of taking large acreages of land under mortgage schemes from cultivators who are in their debt. This is today a highly complex game. In order to avoid having land registered in the name of the landlord, it remains in the name of the cultivator so that, in effect, the owner becomes a labourer on his own land. This involves oppressive political manipulation, the maintainance of a vigilante force, and the perpetual "squaring" of government officials, which drains the landlord's income. Such landlords are looked on as old fashioned, but the extent of their power can still be felt in such villages as Rompalli in Lakshetipet Taluk, where out of 217 households only 3 have not lost some land to the landlord under debt-repayment mortgage arrangements.

Although by the late 1970s the power of the landlords had been largely curtailed, their earlier period of predatory expansion had pushed the tribals off the plains and into the intermontane zone and onto the plateau. The ordinance survey map of the area made in 1929, when compared with the present situation, clearly demonstrates the vast movement of people into the intermontane valleys which must have taken place. Where previously there had been only small clearings with tribal villages scattered sparsely about the valley floors, now almost the entire valley bottoms are under cultivation.

While the penetration of Telugu domination took place on the eastern fringe of the tribal area of Adilabad until the beginning of the 1960s, the upland plateau remained a largely untouched tribal heartland, as Fürer-Haimendorf has reported. But immediately after this there was a vast influx of Marathi-speaking agriculturist and other castes, who alienated tribal land and decimated the natural forests, terrorising the tribals and totally undermining their way of life.

A concomitant of this experience in the east was that by the mid-1960s a number of reform, revitalisation, and political movements had swept through the eastern area as a response to oppression, but had not affected the central area. The first of these was the development of the Shri Guru Dev Seva Mandal. Although this started in the village of Mahagaon on the central plateau under the leadership of a Gond called Kotnaka Suru, nearly all its earlier adherents were in the east in such villages as Ginnedhari, Tilani, Gangapur, Guddipet, Mankapur, and Gundela, where the worst effects of landlordism were felt. This was a sanskritising religious reform movement that involved all the educated tribals and many village headmen, though not many of the ordinary cultivators initially followed it. It was based on the teachings of Kotnaka Suru, who styled himself Maharaj, having been the pupil of a Maharashtran guru. He had supposedly become an ascetic hermit propagating a mixture of tantric, yogic, and ascetic Hinduism totally alien to the traditional tribal beliefs, though numerous scurrilous stories exist as to the true nature of his mission. He founded a society called the Shri Guru Dev Seva Mandal of Mahagaon, which now manages considerable sums of money and runs a jeep, the only tribal-owned jeep in the entire eastern area. His teachings involved ideas of *moksa* ("salvation"), totally alien to Gond religion, a ban on spilling blood, smoking, and drinking, the encouraging of new ideals of femininity and the worship of the *tulsi* plant, and the bringing in of Brahmin priests for the performance of a whole new calendar of Hindu *puja*. This has now caught on to such an extent that many Gonds in the intermontane zone have adopted *bhajan* singing, and the traditional village dramas of the Gonds have now become performances of the Ramayana and Mahabharata.

In the early 1960s, a brief wave of communist adherence spread through the eastern area under the leadership of a Gond from a village in the region of Ginnedhari. He drew his adherents from the villages which had suffered most from the oppression of Forest Department officials. He even stood as a communist party candidate in the elections, and a few villages raised the red flag. But in the end nothing came of the movement.

Also, there were two abortive attempts to set up an Adivasi Seva Sangh, or Tribal Social Council—a tribal self-help society within which the new, educated tribal leadership could develop a representative lobby for tribal demands and a cooperative movement for self-help. However, this foundered not merely on internal rivalry and corruption (all the funds were stolen by one headman), but also due to intense pressure to undermine it from the landlord class. Once, when some members went to make a representation to the deputy collector in Asifabad, they were set upon by paid thugs in the back streets. And at another time when the leader was organizing a meeting in the village of Irkepalli over a particularly unpleasant case of oppression by Perka cultivators, they were again beaten into submission.

However, the most interesting element of the difference in the histories of social change in the eastern and central areas is the fact that the widespread alienation of land by Marathi speakers that occurred in the central area hardly affected the eastern area, other than in a few small villages around Kosara, ten miles east and some fifteen miles north of Asifabad on the borders of Maharashtra in the area of Savati, where the immigrants are Kunbi cultivators. How is the eastern area's relative immunity from Maratha incursions to be explained? To successfully settle in new areas, an immigrant needs influence over the local lower-level and middle-range government officials, which is developed through informal networks. In the eastern area, such networks were already dominated by the entrenched landlord class, who jealously guarded their domain against competition from other groups. Village officers, *patwari* largely under the control of the landlords, were unlikely to allow land to be registered in the names of recent newcomers. The paradox, therefore, appears to be that the previous usurpers of tribal land reached an equilibrium, even if an oppressive one, and subsequently protected the tribal population from further penetration. In the eastern intermontane zone, the only major force still operating to alienate tribal land is the internal expansion of the Perka cultivating castes, but this does not compare in degree with the Banjara and Maratha incursions in the central plateau zone.

In the eastern area, government is now achieving some success through a special tribal welfare officer in returning land that was alienated from the tribals after 1948. Although the real quantities of land may not be large (1,867 acres in Asifabad Taluk and 810 acres in Lakshetipet Taluk between 1973 and 1977) what has been established is that the government regulations on the inalienability of tribal land can be and are being enforced, and the value of land that was original tribal *patta* land has dropped. In order to retain that land today, it is necessary to go to the expense of litigation in the High Court or else to mortgage the land to nationalised banks for agricultural development loans.

THE CHANGING COMMUNITY PROFILE

The second point that I want to consider is the social effect of the penetration of Telugu culture into the tribal population in the intermontane area of the eastern region. In considering this, I will bring into perspective the overall "tribal" category applied to the Raj Gonds and associated tribal groups.

In the foregoing discussion we have seen how the economic relations of the tribal groups have changed and that, by becoming increasingly dependent on other social groups both in terms of a cash economy and in terms of the alienation of their land, the Gonds have moved away from the tribal end of the tribe-caste continuum that S. F. G. Bailey proposed.[2] Here movement is towards role specialisation, social stratification, and ethnic heterogeneity in social interaction, involving enlargement and diversification of the network of relations. Also, given Bailey's criterion that "the larger is the proportion of a given society which has direct access to the land, the closer is that society to the tribal end of the continuum" (Bailey, *Tribe, Caste, and Nation*, p. 14), the economic changes must be seen to have moved the Gonds further towards the caste pole of the continuum, in that they are now thrown more into a relationship of interdependence with, rather than one of isolation from, Telugu culture.

Given this increasing interdependence and contact, it is important to determine whether or not changes have occurred in the way the Gonds see themselves in relation to other cultures and if so, what is the nature of the change. In passing I have already noticed the development of a sanskritising reform movement mimicking Telugu culture, but more important is whether and how intercommunal boundaries have altered.

The Gonds, with their rajas, were once the dominant agricultural group. Their community of daily intercourse was limited to Kolams, Naikpods, Wojaris, Pardhans, and Totis. As we have seen, this has now been greatly extended, and with the effects of modernization produced by schools and the reform movement, various communal boundaries have changed though the primary communal identities have been preserved. Linguistic unity remains at this time, though the influence of schooling may yet achieve a change. And there is no reason to expect that intermarriage has increased. In fact, if anything, tribal identity has been strengthened by the relatively greater degree of daily intercourse with other groups and by the administrative reification of tribal status.

Fürer-Haimendorf, writing in 1948, identified a tripartite division in the social groupings in the area:

> The so-called "aboriginals", who have been settled on the land since time immemorial and subsisted principally on agriculture; the associ-

2. S. F. G. Bailey, *Tribe, Caste and Nation: A Study of Political Activity and Political Change in Highland Orissa.*

ated castes of bards, musicians and craftsmen who are economically dependent on the aboriginals and regard agriculture as a secondary occupation; and finally the castes of Telugu and Maratha extraction—cultivators, artisans and traders—the Mussalmans and Banjara (Lambada) tribes, all of whom have their own origin and cultural connections in adjacent districts and have settled among the "aboriginal" population during recent generations without being absorbed within the social system that embraces the first two groups.[3]

While this basic configuration is unchanged, to what extent have the boundaries taken on different qualities in the thirty years since Professor Fürer-Haimendorf carried out the original fieldwork? Using this tripartite division into (a) aboriginals, (b) associated castes, and (c) recent arrivals of mainly Telegu and Maratha extraction, we can compare the intercommunal regulations that traditionally apply with what is happening today.

The Gonds themselves, both from their mythology and from ruined sites of past civilisations in the area, realise that they are not the first people to have lived here. But the fact remains that they see themselves as the people who cleared the forests and, along with the other aboriginal groups, have first claim to be the original occupants. In the past, Gonds saw themselves as ritually separate from the surrounding groups, from whom they would not accept cooked food. The Gonds had no caste of priests comparable to Brahmins to perform religious rituals. Each clan-deity cult group had its own hereditary priest (*katora*). Worship of the numerous other deities at various shrines could be performed by any Gond of reputation, though it is common for Kolams, another aboriginal group, to be called in to perform rituals for Gond deities other than those connected with the clan cult. As their own ritual practitioners, the Gonds see themselves as a group which must preserve its purity by avoiding contact with others. As one reputable Gond once told me:

> In the days of our grandfathers we even washed our feet on returning from market. But now who washes? For that reason our clan god is weak. Before we were advanced (literally "out in front"), now we are backward. We are not following the way of our clan gods. We are mixing.

Even the mainstream-Hindu immigrant populations see the Gonds as having attributes of purity. If a Hindu is asked how he evaluates the Gonds' status in the *varna* system, he will say that Gonds seem to be perpetually performing rituals themselves and must therefore be considered as high caste.

3. *The Raj Gonds of Adilabad,* p. 31.

In general status, the Gond considers himself superior to the Kolam. They will not sit on the same *charpoy* together, and initially at least the Gond will expect to sit in the presence of a Kolam, though frequent and friendly intercourse between them gives rise to an assumed status equality. Fictitious kin relations exist between them, and the Kolams have the same clan names as the Gonds, though marriage regulations are different and the Kolams do not have the same clan cult underlying their clan system. The Kolam will often act as a priest for the Gond, though there is no system of patronage or payment in this. It is merely a matter of respect towards a people who are idealised as more traditional and in closer touch with the forces of nature.

The other important aboriginal group is the Naikpods, referred to by the Gonds as Mache. They have a language of their own, like the Kolams, but in the area that I studied they all speak Telugu as their mother tongue and know Gondi, which is the lingua franca among all the aboriginal groups. Naikpod clan names bear no similarity to the Gond or Kolam model, and again intermarriage is not allowed. Their clan and lineage names are the same as those of Telugu speakers. Whereas Naikpods have been shifting-cultivators within living memory, they have now taken up plough cultivation, though they tend to be less successful than the Gonds, because they live in small hamlets on stonier ground just off the valley bottoms. The few large Naikpod villages in the valley bottoms have been entirely taken over by Telugu castes, and the tribals are now landless labourers. A traditional occupation is the making of bamboo mats for a variety of purposes; Gonds pay for such mats in grain. Once again there is no patron-client relationship along a typical *jajmani* pattern with enduring ties of interdependence. Rather than a relationship of mutual cooperation, as between the Gonds and Kolams, there is competition and resentment between Gonds and Naikpods; the Gonds often refer to Naikpods as thieves and untrustworthy, whereas Naikpods assume greater purity than Gonds because they do not eat beef and pork. Both parties refuse to accept cooked food from each other and recognize this refusal. Each assumes a higher status. On the whole the Gond avoids entering a Naikpod hamlet, and he seldom needs to. But the Naikpod, being numerically less dominant and often doing bamboo work for the Gond, often enters Gond villages, where he is forced to accept an inferior status. Generally both Gonds and Naikpods are cultivating groups and therefore equivalent, but the Gonds are wealthier.

Traditionally associated with the Gonds are seven servicing groups (I shall not describe them all in detail here), some of which can be replicated among Telugu-speaking agricultural communities. Three of these groups have specific reference to the Gonds; their occupation is tied to religious service, and, since Gond religion has a different social organization from Hinduism, these three groups are distinct from equivalents in the Hindu *jati* system.

The most important of these three groups are the Pardhans, as they call themselves, or Pataris, as they are called by the Gonds. The symbiotic relationship between communities of Gonds and Pardhans has been established by centuries of co-existence. The Pardhans are the hereditary bards of the Gonds. They have a clan and kinship system that is an exact replica of that of the Gonds, and each Pardhan household is bound by a patron-client relationship similar to that of a *jajman* to a number of Gond households of its own clan. Pardhans receive yearly payments and dues at specific rites of passage from their hereditary patrons or *dhani*. While the Pardhans' mother tongue is Marathi, they are guardians of Gond oral tradition and ritual music, which they sing in Gondi. The Pardhan is often called upon as an arbiter of Gond custom, and I have seen Pardhans, on their own initiative, object to infringements of Gond marriage regulations. While they are not the priests of the Gond clan cult, its operation is dependent on their role as messengers and arrangers of clan rituals among the clan group, which is dispersed across the entire area of Gond population. They are the maintenance men of Gond tradition.

In a similar position vis-à-vis the Gond and performing exactly the same role and function is the Toti. Certain Gond clans have Toti bards and musicians rather than Pardhans. The number of Totis is much smaller than that of Pardhans, but as they speak Gondi as their mother tongue, it is possible to argue that they have been associated with the Gonds for longer. Having a parallel clan and kinship system, the Pardhans and Totis like to claim a brother relationship to their Gond patrons, but while many Gonds are prepared to accept this superficially, they fundamentally oppose it in serious discussion. Both Pardhans and Totis are minstrel beggars and dependants of the Gonds with a lower status, though not in the Hindu sense of a different *jati* backed up by the complex rationale of a *varna* system. While travelling with Gonds I have slept and eaten in Pardhan houses, but the Gonds have had no sense of transferred pollution through me, though no Gond will eat anything other than tea with cow's milk and food fried in ghee from a Pardhan or Toti for fear of having to pay a symbolic fine and having a lock of his hair cut off. Equally, no Pardhan would think of entering his patron's house beyond the verandah. As economic dependants, both Pardhans and Totis frequently take cooked food from Gonds.

Theoretically, at least, both Pardhans and Totis share a similar relationship to their patrons, but between them there is a gulf of acute competition and resentment. Each claims to be of higher status than the other; they do not accept food from each other; and both beg equally from their Gond patrons, in front of whom they observe mutual avoidance.

The last aboriginal service group that I will mention here is the Wojaris, referred to by the Gonds as Oja. They are few and far between and by pure omission are not registered as a scheduled tribe like the Pardhans and Totis. They are nomadic brass founders using the *cire perdue* method. A family unit arrives in a village, takes up temporary residence in an outbuilding, verandah, or under a tree, and makes cheap jewelry, cattle and cart ornaments, the mouthpieces and trumpet ends for Pardhan and Toti wind instruments, and, most important, the votive offerings and ritual objects used in the worship of various deities. This work is paid for in grain or other foodstuffs. Whereas the Wojaris have a place in Gond mythology as *pen de Wojalir* ("the founders for the Gods"), their mother tongue is Marathi. Those who work in constant association with the Gonds have adopted Gond clan names, though they are not involved in the clan-cult complex. To all intents and purposes, the position in which the Wojari stands vis-à-vis the Gond appears to be similar to that of the Kolam.

Outside this group of aboriginal service groups, there are a number of Telugu-speaking service castes which are also found living in mainstream-caste villages. Important here are the Vishwabrahma-caste blacksmiths, gold and silver workers, carpenters, stone-workers, and brass workers. This caste wears the sacred thread of the twice born and does not eat pork or beef. They claim a high caste status within the *varna* system and will not eat the food of the aboriginals, who in turn treat them as non-aboriginals and dependants with whom they will not eat. But in matters of respect there is a great deal of ambivalence as to whether the Gond or the Vishwabrahma should stand in the other's presence. Later we will see that with the start of Hindu reform movements, Vishwabrahmas are often used as priests by the Gonds.

The last three groups of Telugu castes that have lived alongside the aboriginals are three untouchable castes. Whereas all the groups mentioned so far share the same wells, though often at different times, these three groups live in separate hamlets outside the main ambit of the village and wash and draw their water separately. So far we have not found any highly developed concepts of casteism in relations between the Gonds and the other communities, but for these three communities, the Gonds immediately adopt a caste model of behaviour comparable to that of Telugu-speaking mainstream Hindus, even though the overall hierarchical principle which structures the Indian *varna* system is absent.

Highest among the three untouchable groups are the Inkars, known in Marathi as Mahars and in Telugu as Netakani. They are low-caste weavers brought in by the Gonds for their skills, though now their profession has been totally eclipsed by mill-made cloth, and they have become an ordinary cultivating caste. Beneath them are the Bhoyars, known in Telugu as Manyepu and in Marathi as Mala, who are low-caste agricultural labourers. At the lowest level are the Madgi, known in Telugu as Madiga, who are leather workers. All three are categorised as scavengers who eat the flesh of dead cattle. While these three groups stand in a hierarchical relationship to each other, for the purpose of the Gonds they are all classed as Harijans. The Gond will not greet them, and all three are expected to remain standing in the presence of a Gond and to get off the pathway to allow any other person to pass. Gond children are often heard berating each other as "dirty Madgis."

Where these untouchable communities are found in association with Gond villages, they have been founded and have flourished under the leadership of influential Gond village headmen. In the past two or three generations, it was common for a *patel* who had accumulated wealth and influence to emulate the pattern of multi-caste villages of Telengana and employ Harijan village servants.

These untouchable communities must be distinguished from the aboriginal service castes of the Pardhans and Totis. The Pardhans and Totis do not beg for alms, but ask for their traditional dues as a servicing group with a long-term symbiotic relationship. This is a deeper relationship than the mere matter of economic dependence. The untouchable, in contrast, has no standing in the mind of the aboriginal; he does not perform any traditional ritual service, as in a caste-Hindu village. His position is simply a matter of status and caste emulation on the part of the Gond. The untouchable in the tribal village accrues only the negative aspects of his low status. To equate the Pardhan and Toti with the untouchable would be to adopt a castelike model that cannot apply in the dyadic relationship between each of them and their Gond patron. Rather, we have a not untypical relationship of two specialised groupings of agriculturists and traditional bards in the Indian environment, where intercommunal barriers are, not surprisingly, affected by Hindu concepts of ritual purity.

So far this has been a brief summary of the groups which have a long-standing tradition of interaction. I am not saying that the Gonds have not had contacts with other communities, which I will shortly mention, but rather that contacts were infrequent and were characterised by a mutual barrier against intimacy. Among the groups that have traditionally associated, there is no model of ranked hierarchy to cover all interactions. The only form of hierarchy that exists is the simple dyadic one between the Gonds and the two groups of bards. Both these groups are actively involved in clan-cult worship and see themselves as sharing the same gods—"we are the people who worship *persa pen*" (the clan gods). To this extent they are part of the Gond culture complex. And this degree of closeness necessitates the most intense and consciously sanctioned idioms of separation.

To summarise this traditional set of community interrelations, it is necessary to distinguish the aboriginal groups which have had a long experience of interaction: the Kolams, Naikpods, Wojaris, Pardhans, and Totis. In this group, a set of neo-caste principles operates. The three cultivating groups—the Gonds, Kolams, and Naikpods—are basically equivalent though separate. This equivalence is affected by the fact that the Naikpod can now be marginally included in the Telugu caste ideology and can claim greater ritual purity by not eating beef and pork. The Gond and Kolam are more or less of equivalent status, but the Gond assumes the status of the dominant group, not only because of historical precedent, but also because the Pardhan and Toti depend on him but not on the Kolam; this is balanced for the Kolam by his being considered a truer and more traditional aboriginal who often acts as a non-dependent priest. Pardhans and Totis are considered quasi-untouchable by all groups as traditional bards and maintenance men to the dominant Gond culture.

The Gond dominance in the economic order is symbolised by the deity Anesirar, the giver of food, who is seen as a divine Gond, the son of Bhui Lakshmi, the wealth of the land. The Gond makes the analogy that he "is Anesirar. He ploughs the land and feeds the Pardhan, Toti, and Wojari. Many communities enjoy the food of Anesirar—i.e. of the Gond. The Gond's hand is above and the others hold their hand below to receive the gift of the Gond."

But the most important message which we get from this, and the reason that I have referred to a neo-caste system, is that it is not a systemic model. The traditional model is based on a series of dyadic relationships that lack any overall organization or covering ideology. What will be interesting is to see how, now that the economic order has changed and the Gonds are in an environment of interdependence with the Telugu castes, the model becomes more systemic and more and more castelike.

The earliest Hindus with whom the Gonds came in close contact were probably Brahmins. During the brief period of Maratha rule in the second half of the eighteenth century, some Marathi-speaking Brahmins obtained grants of land (*watan*); most of the Brahmin *patwari* of later ages are probably descendants of those early Brahmin settlers. Their positions as *patwari* gave them considerable power over the aboriginal landowners, and large tracts of land became the property of the Brahmins, particularly in Asifabad Taluk. These Brahmin landlords were mainly town dwellers and absentee landlords, whom the aboriginal cultivator would meet once or twice a year at most, though the Brahmin *patwari* would have been more frequent visitors to the interior villages.

While the Maratha Brahmins had come from the north, much later Telugu-speaking Velmas came from the south. While the richest among the Velmas were absentee landlords, others settled in the district and built up caste villages around them. The castes that they brought in included the Komti, the Banias of Telengana, who initially set up stores and moneylending agencies in the caste villages but have now spread to almost every tribal village of more than thirty houses. Also, the higher-caste Kapu cultivators and the lower-caste Perka cultivators were brought in to work the newly acquired lands of the Brahmins and Velmas, and have now taken land from the aboriginals and developed their own independent villages with their own Komtis. Along with these came a high-caste group of weavers called Sale. At the time, when their traditional profession was being undermined, they were taking up agriculture and were in search of new land. Also, the toddy tappers, called Gaur by the Gonds, the barbers, called Dandvi, and the washermen, called Wartal, arrived. As their population expanded, many of them took up agriculture on alienated tribal land. Only among a few wealthy tribals are the services of barber and washerman used. Otherwise the aboriginal groups perform this service for themselves.

Without exception, in the pre-modern phase the aboriginal groups treated all these communities as complete outsiders. All social intercourse was minimised, and neither party would take food from the other or even make physical contact. Any intercourse that took place was in public places, and neither party would have entered each other's house. Although the aboriginals eat beef, they were not treated as untouchable but enjoyed a status approaching that of Kshatriyas because of their position as the dominant agricultural group and their past history as rajas of the area. Here it should not be forgotten that the Gond raja of Chanda had considerable traditional authority until the 1940s, and the local caste Hindus are conscious of the history of the Gond rajas in Asifabad.

The interesting overarching aspect of this traditional Gond-centred model of interaction is that it is not systemic. The position of each group is established on dyadic principles, so that it is difficult for the analyst to find an overall model or system. In order to describe them, I have had to rely on simple descriptive categories of historically established intimacy with, in the case of long-established contact, certain subtleties more involved than a simple "them and us" model based on the criterion of adherence to a clan cult. There is no reason to believe that this model would not continue to structure intercommunal relations well into the future were it not for the advent of factors that have accelerated social change, such as the increasing degree of inter-dependence with outsiders. In this area in the past, there have been both tribalisation and Hinduisation. Many commentators on social change on the tribe-caste frontier in India only notice the process of Hinduisation, but Adilabad was dominated by the agriculturist Raj Gond community and experienced the immigration of people from the surrounding mainstream-Hindu areas who frequently adopted the tribal model of intercommunal relations which was firmly established for the Pardhans, Totis, and Wojaris, and which appeared to be starting to establish itself for the Vishwabrahmas. However, in the recent past, after the willing introduction of three untouchable communities, there was an apeing of casteism by influential members of the dominant tribal community, which appears to have been dependent purely on individuals and not to have percolated down to the community at large. By the time of my fieldwork in 1977, the process of tribalisation appears to have been reversed to one of Hinduisation. I now want to establish this at the level of intercommunal relations, before going on to look at the factors which created it and at its broader implications.

The classical tribal model in Indian sociology is one of "them and us." That is, the so-called tribals see all other communities as equally "them" and equally to be avoided in all social intercourse. But what happens to the tribal view of "them" under conditions of social change, increased communication across the "them and us" barrier, alienation of tribal land, and geographical mixing of populations? Is there simply a greater degree of intercommunal familiarity, in which the equality of other communities is preserved but the degree of social distance and avoidance reduced, or does the tribal develop a view of "us" encompassing a wider community, in which concepts of ranking give the tribal community a positive place in a hierarchy—the Hin-duisation model? Among the Gonds it is not altogether easy to pin-point which model is being adopted.

The Gond himself does not have a conscious model of his relations with other communities other than the traditional one of "them and us," which, judging from the statement that "we are mixing" already quoted, is already redundant, although commonly stated. In the arena of national and district politics, the Gond is increasingly aware of his status as a member of a scheduled tribe. Regulations and the privileges that go with them are becoming known and are being capitalised on by the tribal. But that is different from the view that the Gond may have in his everyday intercourse with the other communities that live in the same valley as himself, although, no doubt, the two concepts affect each other.

Very briefly, I now want to look at the way in which the Gond's perception of his relationship to the new spectrum of communities can be said to have altered. It must be said that what changes exist are not to be found uniformly spread throughout the population, but only in those sections which are experiencing increased intercommunal familiarity. Whereas previously the Gonds treated the high Telugu castes, such as the Brahmins, Velmas, Komtis, Kapus, Perkas, and Sales, as outsiders from whom they would not accept food, this has been reversed, and all Gonds admit that they will accept food from members of such castes. The fact that a form of hierarchy exists is shown by the Gonds' understanding that Brahmins, Velmas, Komtis, and Kapus will not accept food from them, whereas Perkas and Sales are at least partially understood to do so. This implies a degree of equivalence between the Gond, the Perka, and the Sale, overlain by an understanding that the non-beef-eating Hindu will not eat with the tribals. (An important thing to remember is that the real opportunities for dining together are in fact minimal, so that answers to questions are hypothetical and idealised.) Whereas a large number of Gonds see the same equivalence as agriculturists applying between themselves and the Naikpods, they see the Naikpod as still standing on his traditional dignity of not eating with the Gond. The Naikpod takes the classical position of the marginal man, trying consciously to identify with the caste order and to reject his tribal background. Such a conscious move cannot be said to exist among the Gonds. The Naikpod therefore actively wishes to treat himself as separate from the beef-eating tribal in his attempt to climb the caste hierarchy, a process in which the Gond has not become involved, except for Gonds who follow the teachings of the reform sect.

Relations with the two Telugu-speaking groups that are dependent on the Gonds, the Dandvi and Wartal (barbers and washermen) have adopted a more castelike appearance. Whereas the traditionalists saw these groups and Gonds as not taking food from each other, Gonds now look on them as of lower caste and will not accept food from them, while some people believe that they will accept food from Gonds. Relations with the three untouchable groups, the Inkars, Bhoyars, and Madgis, remain unchanged, with the same caste model as before. However, it is interesting that the Vishwabrahma is now seen as of a higher group than the Gond, as the idea of the twice born and the Vishwabrahmas' occasional role as priests among the new Gond reform sect are becoming apparent. Many Gonds are therefore prepared to say that they will eat from a Vishwabrahma, while he will not accept food cooked by a Gond.

The overall pattern of change in relationships between the Gond and the Telugu castes is that whereas before the Gond would not have eaten with any of them and would have assumed that they would not have eaten with him, now the Gond will accept food from those he considers superior and is beginning to understand that those who are inferior will eat his food—a basically hierarchical model in which the Gond finds he has a relative position among other groups rather than outside them.

Generally, among the aboriginal groups and the associated servicing groups there is a greater degree of familiarity. Today it is more acceptable for Gonds and Kolams to share food. The Wojaris were previously considered to be a servicing group with whom the Gonds would not eat, and this distinction has not been relaxed. One group of Wojaris has taken up permanent residence near the village where I was doing fieldwork; its members have become avid followers of the reform sect and have therefore adopted a vegetarian diet. One of them is even a leader in the sect, and as such he is frequently seen eating with Gonds.

The Gond attitude towards the Pardhans and the Totis, the traditional bards, is virtually unchanged, although both Pardhans and Totis are less dependent on their Gond patrons than they were before. Many Pardhans have now acquired land and are not dependent on their traditional bardic dues. Also, knowledge of Gond custom and oral tradition is rapidly declining among the younger generation.

There has been a change in the Gond's view of himself vis-à-vis other communities. The concept of a loosely knit clustering of groups in which each pair had a dyadic relationship, that is, an ethnocentric view with a main ideology of "them and us," is becoming redundant. Today each group has a position in an overall framework relative to its role in the society. This is not merely the result of a lessening of cultural and economic isolation, but results from an enlargement and diversification in the network of social relations following greater economic interdependence. This castelike model of society based on role specialisation and ethnic heterogeneity in the overall grouping of Indian society, rather than a model of cultural separation, is now becoming the principle of orientation and group identity for the Raj Gonds.

But this is not applicable throughout Gond society. First, I am speaking only of the eastern area, in cultural contact with Telugu society. Also, in this area penetration by outsiders became established some time ago, and now that the period of predatory expansion of outsiders has ended, a period of mutual co-existence is developing. This probably cannot be said of the central area, with its more recent history of penetration and its present situation of virtual intercommunal warfare. Second, these changes are only true of a certain section of the eastern area. Typically, these changes are strongest among the new, school-going section of Gond society. Whereas the education system that was created by the Social Service Department of the 1940s aimed at Gondi as the medium of instruction in order to strengthen tribal identity and the idea of "them and us" as a model for development, the independent Indian model for development is one of education in regional languages, here Telugu, aimed towards national integration. Also, the education is aimed towards an urban, literate, and employment model of society in which anyone who leaves school fit for employment looks to the civil service for work. With this set of expectations, he wants to identify with urban values and the modified caste system that now operates in urban India. One feature that is particularly powerful is the ashram, or boarding, school concept of education being practised under the special system of education in tribal areas. In this system of education, the tribal child is seen as presenting a greater educational problem than children in other areas. That is, his home background is assumed to have a discouraging influence on his schooling. Schools for tribal boys under the new ITDA attempt to create a total educational environment in which the child boards at the school, where he is fed and clothed. This new environment is one in which boys and girls from all scheduled tribal communities and even a few untouchables live in intimate contact with each other, so that, in addition to creating a set of urban and employment-oriented aspirations, the traditional concepts of "them and us" are undermined by the circumstances of school life. In their search for an alternative structure, school-going children are adopting the dominant Hindu caste model.

But the forces of social change do not come only from the new generation. As in many tribal societies, periods of relative deprivation and oppressive exploitation have spawned millenarian, revivalist, and reform movements and sects. The most influential of these today is the Shri Guru Dev Seva Mandal. Followers of this sect attempt not to drink, smoke, or eat meat. Adherents are found outside Gond society among the Kolams, Wojaris, Pardhans, Totis, and Vishwabrahmas, but generally the majority are Gonds. The interesting feature of this movement is that it has attracted members from the progressive element of Gond society. The leaders of the movement are all tribal schoolmasters and progressive village headmen who were educated under the old Social Service Scheme of the 1940s. Indeed, most tribal schoolmasters in Asifabad Taluk are followers of the sect's founder and leader, Kotnaka Suru Maharaj. In all schools in the eastern area of Adilabad, morning and evening prayers and hymns are chanted from the songbook issued by the reform movement. Therefore, there is a tie between education and this sanskritising movement.

It is interesting that some of the strongest adherents of this sect are the women, who daily perform *puja* in front of the *tulsi* plant symbolising the longevity of their husbands. And, in villages where the sect is strong, the women gather every morning to chant its songs. Those who are influenced by this movement at school find reinforcement for it at home.

The effect of this sect has not so much been the direct propagation of a casteist ideology. In fact, being involved with gaining salvation through devotion, it attempts to reach everybody, irrespective of race or community. Firm followers say that if they meet another wearing the *malla* beads which are the symbol of sect membership, they will share the same food and the same *charpoy* even if the other is an untouchable. But fortunately for the believers, this cannot be put to the test as no untouchable has yet tried to join. The main effect of the sect, along with the cult of Tirupati Venkateshwara, followed by a growing number of Gonds, is that it involves Gonds in a religious ritual whose symbolic content they do not understand, as it is left to Brahmin priests who are hired to perform the ritual. They therefore see themselves more as an interdependent section of the wider Indian society, and find themselves in an arena of greater contact with other communities. This sect has given rise to a whole new series of religious rituals and festivals, such as Hanuman Jayanti, Shri Rama Naomi, Ganapati *puja*, Shankar Ratri, and others.

However, to say that the effects of education and reform movements are simply moving the Raj Gonds into the arena of the wider Indian society pure and simple is not entirely true. Gond identity still remains important, and, with the comforting barrier of "them and us" behind which to shelter, the educated followers of reform movements have adopted revivalist tendencies. They are aware that their oral tradition is being undermined by the growing lack of interdependence between themselves and the two traditional bardic groups, many of whom are now living by agriculture. Also, the children of the Pardhans and Totis, with their traditional training in verbal expression and in living by their skills as orators, have had more success than the old dominant cultivators in education and in obtaining civil service employment in the posts reserved for tribals. Educated Gonds and the followers of the reform movements, feeling themselves threatened by the loss of their position as the patrons (*dhani*) of a dependent group, are trying to write down their oral tradition. In the process, the myths are gaining a large number of Hindu elements which were not there before, such as elaborate validations for deifying the cow and not eating its flesh. But the ultimate aim is to build up a new ethnic identity in the plural world into which they now find themselves moving. However, this new plural world, in which a castelike hierarchy is becoming evident, is not finally crystallized and therefore contains a number of anomalies. This is exemplified by the activity of the Gondi Basha Prachara Kendra, the Society for Spreading the Gond Language.

Its main aim is to devise an original script for Gondi and to gain government approval for it. But, paradoxically, its letterheads and printed pamphlets are in Telugu, reflecting the anomalous standpoint and the frustrations of its members.

EDUCATIONAL CHANGE

Many officials and local politicians see education as the lynch pin on which progress among the tribal population now hangs. Arguments given to substantiate this are varied. Education, not being a hard gain, is a gift which the dominant non-tribals who control local politics feel will not give the tribal too great an advantage over other communities. Also, the vast quantities of aid available for tribal education are seen as worth attracting into an area because of the spill-over effect that they have for other communities. Frequent accusations have been voiced by tribals that funds available for schools did not reach their destination and that non-tribal boys are utilising the facilities notified for tribals. This seemingly harmless aid has therefore been positively encouraged on the basis of a prejudice that the tribal was "stupid and ignorant." This became an important motif in political speech-making by party workers in the game of winning political support. I remember particularly well the Panchayat Samithi president telling me that the tribal was so backward that all development aid spent was money down the drain and that what was needed was better schools to make him more intelligent and better roads so that he would have a chance to travel and see what his chances for self-improvement were. By emphasizing education, attention could be diverted from land reforms, irrigation projects, and other more directly commercial benefits. The feeling can best be summed up as a paternalistic one that says "the tribal is a backward child who does not deserve hard commercial aid until he has become more like us."

The superstructure of education has made great quantitative progress in the last forty years, though what it may have achieved qualitatively must be discussed separately. Before 1940 there were no educational services among the Raj Gonds. The only exceptions were a few wealthy village headmen who privately employed Muslim tutors for their own children and the children of friends who shared the expenses. At that time the Nizam's government was in power, and Urdu was the language and script used in all administrative dealings.

The establishment and development of two teacher-training centres in the 1940s has been described in detail, and here I shall confine myself to discussing the present situation in Asifabad Taluk, particularly in Wankdi Block, which includes most of the tribal villages of the taluk. With the creation of Wankdi Tribal Development Block and the start of Panchayati Raj in 1959, the education system was expanded. Today there are fifty-eight primary schools, two high schools, and ten special tribal boarding schools, known as ashram schools. Since the creation of Andhra Pradesh in 1963, the medium of education has been Telugu, using the Telugu script.

Whereas the early system of education was to provide the aboriginal peasant with a basic modicum of skills to deal with outside influences on his agricultural economy and to stand on his own feet, nowadays the education system has a different aim—to educate children for employment while providing a grounding in literacy for those who will continue to work the land. One of the government's main policies is that, with pressure on land, there should be protected employment for tribal and backward-caste communities. A quota of protected jobs therefore has to be filled, and tribal education schemes are under considerable pressure to provide candidates to take up the posts made available. Unfortunately, this type of targeted development program leads to quantity only. Many of the resulting candidates are promoted through the system irrespective of their abilities, and they then find it difficult to pass the matriculation exam at the end. If the tribal were prepared to take up labouring work of a semi-skilled nature in urban industries, this would be enough. However, he is seldom prepared to enter employment where he will meet very few members of his own community. Also, this requires registration at employment exchanges and travelling to interviews, which is very difficult given the poor communications in the tribal area. The end result is frustrated aspirations.

The main problem faced by the education system is that village primary schools, particularly boarding schools, provide a useful and desired service by taking children off their parent's hands at an age when they are not productive members of the household. Parents are eager and continually petition for more and better school facilities. While children rise automatically through the system up to standard seven, very few pass the examination to go on to high school. In 1975–76, only 15 percent of all students were able to pass standard seven. While the school system intends to turn out tribals capable of taking up employment, it is largely unable to do so. The recent *Study of Tribal Manpower Resources, Adilabad District* concludes that "the available scheduled tribal manpower is short of the present requirement."[4] Although statistically and in terms of planned development the educa-

4. See D. R. Pratap et al., *Study of Tribal Manpower Resources, Adilabad District.* It is interesting to note that in 1941 Fürer-Haimendorf gave a tribal literacy rate of 0.6 percent. See C. von Fürer-Haimendorf, "Aboriginal Education in Hyderabad," pp. 87–106.

tional changes that have taken place are only achieving a minimal target success, far more important are their repercussions on social organization.

One of the most interesting findings of the manpower resources report is that 63 percent of a sample of post-matriculate students, when asked what employment they would like to take up, replied "teaching in that it facilitates their appointment in their native place where they can educate their fellow tribesmen" (Pratap, *Study of Tribal Manpower Resources, Adilabad District*, p. 51). While the altruistic motivation to "educate their own tribesmen" sounds very fine, I believe that this reply in fact reflects the opportunities that a tribal teacher has in the village organization. It is these opportunities and the role that tribal teachers as a group play that is significant in motivating students to join their ranks.

I have already mentioned that tribal teachers have become the leaders of the reform and revitalisation movements among the eastern Gonds, but have not explained the reasons for this. Those who were trained in the first special tribal teacher-training centres and continued their careers as teachers are now headmasters of the tribal boarding schools. As such, they are the most senior tribal government employees living in the villages of a department that has considerable funds to dispense. Unlike the elected members of the *panchayat*, they are not involved in the machinations of politics to hold their position as the main link between village and government, and, unlike the *patwari*, (village land-revenue officers), they are not involved with the politically sensitive issue of land, which often involves *patwari* in the power politics of dominant landlords. Their work is purely involved with their own community, obviating any intercommunity competition. They have therefore become established as the main brokers between the people and the government; the boarding school is used by all government officers to sleep in and hold meetings in when they tour the villages; and because he collects supplies for the schools, the master is the only officer in the village who has to go weekly to the government offices. Besides commissions that he gets and favours that he can dispense in deciding whose children can attend the schools, he is the one person in the community who has a thorough knowledge of how government works and should be handled, an essential requirement in the lives of cultivators. Also, he knows about government schemes and aid programmes from which people can benefit. This knowledge is not only useful in itself, as he and his family can make the best advantage of all aid available, but it means that others interested must go through him. More important, again, is that, being a broker, he has one foot inside his own community and one in the outside world. He is therefore able to appraise the standing of the tribal from a broader perspective than others. It is this "other view" which enables him to criticise the standing of his community constructively, to assess what change is needed, and to be in a position to influence decisions.

With few exceptions, the tribal schoolmasters have all obtained considerable wealth and authority. They have large holdings of land gained either by purchase or by making the best of opportunities. The majority have irrigation wells and diesel pumps, and often employ labour to work their land. This wealth again puts them in competition with the traditional village headmen, *nar patla*, whose authority and home-based power they can often challenge with their own influence outside the community in government circles. Fürer-Haimendorf wrote in 1944, after the completion of the first year of the teacher-training scheme, that:

> Anyone familiar with conditions in the backward tracts of rural India, where not all land is settled and the minor Government servants, seldom controlled by touring officers, are a very real power, will realise the grave disadvantage under which this system places the Gonds. Without spokesmen of their own community, they are exposed to many a petty tyranny and exploitation by these non-aboriginals ruling their villages. The ending of this tutelage and the installing of progressive Gonds as village-officers in areas with a predominantly tribal population are as important an aim of the scheme for rehabilitation of the Adilabad Gonds as the establishment of schools. ("Aboriginal Education in Hyderabad," p. 8.)

It is interesting in the light of this that although nowadays many Gonds are educated and have taken on the jobs of village officers they find that, working in a system in which they are a weak minority, they are unable to achieve very much for themselves or for their community. The manpower resources report (1977) remarked that educated tribals generally preferred not to look for employment in revenue department posts except as lower division clerks, where they were not involved in local political machinations. The intention of the early training scheme was to create a corps of tribals working in government service who would be able to represent their community to government, but this aim has not yet been achieved. Rather, Gonds shun personal involvement in government, preferring to leave the government work to others and to build up a corps of people within their communities who know at least how to operate the administrative and bureaucratic regulations. The position of a teacher in the special tribal schools fulfils exactly these requirements.

It is then interesting that, although educational progress has many quantitative problems and, because of targeted goals, its quality is low, it has had an important effect on local leadership. At this stage of development, despite the fact that cultural barriers are changing, the overall community still looks inward, and educated Gonds do not yet feel able "to stand on their own feet."

PLANNED DEVELOPMENT

Since Fürer-Haimendorf studied the Raj Gonds in the 1940s, a major change has been the development programmes aimed at the scheduled tribes. Although India underwent considerable industrial development between 1970 and 1977, equivalent rural development was limited to the energetic programmes of the Green Revolution in the Punjab. Rural development is seen as crucial, not only to supply the towns, but also to expand a market for the consumption of industrial products. Also, the continued lack of development in rural areas, coupled with an expanding population, creates an ever-increasing pool of unemployed labour, giving rise to political instability. Under the populist policies of the Congress Party since the Green Revolution, development has been aimed at the backward minority elements of the rural population. A central agency, the ITDA, has been set up to distribute vastly increased funds to the tribals through the block development offices. In August 1976, the Planning Commission finalised the allocation of Rs 455.3 million for tribal development in Adilabad District. In total, the overall expenditure on tribal development for Adilabad District from 1974 to the end of 1977 was Rs 741.2 million, financed from a number of sources. The estimated expenditure on tribal development in the same area for 1977–78 alone was Rs 2,788 million. This increase has had a great effect on life in tribal villages, not only because of the actual development aid which has reached them, but more significantly because of the mushrooming of government and administrative attention paid to their lives.

While there is not space here to go into every aspect of the development programme, I shall look at small irrigation schemes in some detail to analyse their effect on the Raj Gonds. The emphasis placed on such schemes is revealed by the fact that in 1977–78 they received 41 percent of the overall development budget, while the general agricultural development budget was only 28 percent of the total. The rationale behind this was that in Adilabad District the scheduled tribal population has large average holdings of land. Due to the allotment of title land under the Social Service Department of the 1940s, the average holding is eleven acres per household. The type of agriculture is almost all upland, extensive cultivation of single-crop sorghums and small millets, often sown together with various pulses. New varieties of sorghum which are not drought resistant require irrigation, as does wet rice cultivation and market gardening on these very fertile, mixed, alluvial and black cotton soils. With irrigation it should therefore be possible to make the most of the large land holdings and enable at least two crops a year to be harvested. Aiming a development budget at this grossly under-utilised resource should therefore yield good returns. Such go the utopian arguments of the development economists and politicians. However, reality is often at variance.

In 1975–76, funds for irrigation projects for scheduled tribals were released through a credit institution called the Land Mortgage Bank (LMB). Under this scheme, the cultivator was loaned money to undertake the building of a well himself, using local know-how and labour at a low rate of interest to be paid back over twelve years through increased harvests. If the well was a failure, the cultivator's land was to be taken on mortgage by the government and the loan repaid over a number of years through the cultivator's harvest while holding the land in his name. Targets were set for the amount to be distributed, and officials went into the villages to get support from the tribals to take loans. Government officers approached many of the less wealthy tribal leaders, such as headmen of small villages and minor tribal officials, who all had large holdings of land and were respected members of the community but who, unlike the wealthy leaders of the community, did not have the capital to go ahead with their own schemes and had been unable to raise finance in other ways. Under this scheme, thirteen cultivators in the village of Ginnedhari were persuaded to take loans varying from Rs 1,500 to Rs 6,000 (this compares with an estimated income from an average land holding of eleven acres of Rs 3,000 in a good year). All the thirteen had to pay the junior officials of the Land Mortgage Bank between Rs 100 and Rs 200 to have their applications processed. Finally the loans were sanctioned and, without supervision, each person was given the money. Two of the applicants had bad harvests that year and used all the money for household expenses. Eight of them started work on digging wells. In two cases they ran out of cash before reaching water. In five cases they reached water but failed to line the well, either due to lack of funds or due to an inability to get cement, so that in the next monsoon season the well caved in. Only in one case was the well successful, but even then it was not deep enough to store sufficient water to actually irrigate a crop, though the well has subsequently been deepened and is operating. One person built a small dam across a stream to irrigate a small garden, but he had mixed the mortar incorrectly, and the dam was swept away in the rains. Another built a small earthen barrage dam to irrigate one acre of paddy, but the barrage over-flowed, was destroyed, and swept the soil off the levelled paddy fields. The last two applicants purchased diesel engines to lift water from perennial streams, but one was delivered incomplete and unusable, while the other broke down after three weeks' work, and the owner was unable to repair it. Due to lack of supervision and to expecting people to adopt a technology of which they had no previous experience, all but one of the projects failed, and the other was successful only because the cultivator put considerable personal investment into it. However, the tragedy was that next year the LMB officials came to collect the first installments on the repayment. All the cultivators understood that the government would take all their land until they repaid the debt. Here there appears to have been a lack of communication. As a result of this, the applicant who had made a success began his repayment, one applicant sold two acres of paddy land and paid off his debt in full, and four others mortgaged their land to moneylenders at vastly inflated interest rates and paid off the loans in full. The two with pumps had the rusting remains confiscated for auction and were told that the outstanding debt would be collected next year, and the next absconded temporarily but subsequently had all his household brassware confiscated until he attended the bank to settle the claim. Basically, twelve out of the thirteen were harmed by the development loans granted to them. The government target for distribution of loans was reached, but subsequently all the unpaid loans were annihilated by the government, and no increase of irrigated land was achieved at all. The scheme was thus considered a failure by the development office.

Subsequently, in 1977 the government again wanted to increase the irrigated land. However, due to the failure of the last scheme the contracts for the twenty-seven wells to be dug in the village were offered to an outside contractor. The villagers were very upset, saying that the contractor would be dishonest and not build the wells properly and that they would collapse after only a short time, as had the colony houses built for a nearby village after it had been burnt. They said that he would bring outside labourers into the village, who would cause trouble and probably steal from their houses.

Although this is only one example of the planned development schemes, it follows a common pattern. It is only possible to come to the general conclusion that development plans which are pushed on the Raj Gonds tend to do more harm than good and have become an integral part of the risks that backward cultivators suffer due either to the vagaries of nature or to the vicissitudes of human beings. The Raj Gonds often sum this up by saying, "Once we feared the tiger, but now we fear the block development officer." In fact, in all my travels in Asifabad Taluk I met with only one government-funded small irrigation scheme which was running successfully, and which belonged to the tribal member of the Legislative Assembly, though it should be mentioned that another one was almost successfully completed by the end of 1977. However, this does not mean that tribals are not aware of the advantages of irrigation and agricultural development. Eleven irrigation wells are successfully working in Wankdi Block, all privately financed by Raj Gonds. Overall development is making progress among the Raj Gonds, and people do want it and understand the benefits that it brings. What is lacking is the proper implementation of development programmes, a fact of which the Raj Gonds are well aware.

Beyond the question of straight economic harm done to what is an economy under stress, two further effects of the failure of planned development projects are to be considered. First, such projects have a considerable effect on the credibility of local leadership. Many argue that it is a waste of funds to give aid to tribals at all; help should be given to those in the best position to take advantage of it and to maximise the return on it as an investment. There is an understandable tendency to want to give aid where it will be put to best advantage. Many state this as an argument in favour of not giving aid to the backward and scheduled tribal groups, who are least likely to show a return on hard investment. However, within the confines of the government's policy to develop scheduled tribals, the tendency is again to give aid to the more advanced and progressive sections of the population. Here there is a complex and unconscious selection process, whereby those people who stand politically in the forefront of the community receive government aid. Typically, a village-level worker, in his attempts to get the targeted number of applications for irrigation wells to be dug, went to the headman, Pendram Jangu, of the small hamlet of Kereguda, consisting of fourteen houses, and persuaded him to take a loan to construct a well. Under this scheme, a small advance was given to Pendram Jangu to start work, and at each subsequent stage the work was to be inspected and further payments made to cover the work done. Pendram Jangu employed his villagers to do the work but the inspector never came, he never received the payment, and the well collapsed in the rains. This left the village headman indebted to his villagers and destroyed his standing in the community. The person who should have been able to mediate between the village and the outside world had introduced an unacceptable risk into the community by trusting government. In this way, his role as mediator in the village was destroyed, and the fragile structure of community cohesion was badly undermined. In this damage to the social organisation of small communities by undermining the delicate balance of social structure lies the long-term ill effect of planned development. This process is, I believe, one of the main reasons Fürer-Haimendorf says:

The most striking impression one gains of the Gonds after thirty years of absence is an incipient disintegration of the traditional structure of Gond society. Village communities led by headmen, most of whom were men of strong personality and authority, used to be characterised by a pronounced sense of solidarity and corporateness. Today there is much less cohesion and mutual helpfulness among Gonds, and many of the prominent men have learnt to seek short term advantages by cooperating with wealthy newcomers unmindful of the damage done to other Gonds, and indeed too shortsighted to see the danger to their own position.[5]

Second, one of the major spill-over effects of the planned development programmes is the degree to which the shift from an isolated economy and a social structure with a horizon of limited dependence to a wider horizon of dependence on external factors has been accelerated. This is but another aspect of the general rate of increase in economic dependence of the scheduled tribal's economy on a dominant and generally exploitative economy.

ADMINISTRATIVE AND POLITICAL CHANGE

The post-independence philosophy of developing backward areas has lead to fundamental changes in the social environment of the Raj Gonds as they become increasingly involved in the ever-expanding web of government. The political requirement of developing the area has created a need for better communications so that government can reach the areas which it intends to administer more actively. For a culture and economy based on relative isolation in the past, improved administrative protection is necessary. If you let government in, you also open the area to the forces of exploitation.

Ever since Wankdi Block was made a Tribal Development Block with special privileges and increased budgets, it has been a focus of manipulation by local power politicians. In 1959, the Panchayati Raj Act was extended to this area, and scheduled tribal leaders were appointed to positions of considerable influence in the hopes of creating a grass-roots democracy. In the system of elections adopted in Andhra Pradesh, the villagers were to elect a head of the village committee, known as *sarpanch*. These *sarpanch* in turn sat on a block council, *samithi*, and elected a *samithi* president who sat on the district council, *zilla parishad*. At the village level, the elections worked well enough, with tribal leaders being elected as the *sarpanch*. However, the elec-

5. C. von Fürer-Haimendorf, "The Changing Position of Tribal Populations in India."

tions for the *samithi* president became a vehicle for non-tribal Congress Party workers, who finally got one of their members, the brother of a wealthy shopkeeper and moneylender, a Komti, elected. The scheduled tribal *sarpanch* complained about this on the grounds that a tribal development block should have a tribal as its president. The president promptly took a tribal girl as his wife, got a stay order on his election as president, and fought the case up to the High Court on the grounds that he was a scheduled tribal. To do this he had to sell his jeep and borrow extensively from local Brahmin landlords, the financers of the Congress Party workers, whose main interest was not to support the populist policies of the Congress Party but to stifle the implementation of such policies as the Land Reforms Act by infiltrating the local administrative bureaucracy.

The president finally won his case and gained control as the representative of the tribal block. He was then in a position to control the distribution of government aid on a wide scale, from such small matters as the channelling of fair-price sugar and kerosene to the control of rural cooperative credit schemes and the channelling of funds for road building and for sinking drinking-water wells. The village *sarpanch* found themselves in the invidious position of owing support to Congress Party workers, who were financed by the landlords with whom they were in constant conflict over land rights. In their attempts to repossess land mortgaged to moneylenders their village headmen were often powerless to represent them, as the *samithi* president put pressure on them by channelling government loans away from their villagers. Indeed, when three tribals were accused of being Naxalites by the landlord and were arrested, sufficient pressure was brought to bear on two *sarpanch* to testify falsely against the accused.

The situation had reached such proportions by 1976 that the *panchayat* hierarchy was purely a vehicle of factional politics. The administrative machinery had been taken over by the politicians. The situation was appraised, and the administration decided that the only remedy was to abolish the post of *samithi* president, so the *sarpanch* were made directly responsible to the deputy collector as a special officer. As government had to admit, the creation of a grass-roots democracy had failed. But worse than this, the attempt had considerably damaged the existing structure of community leadership, which was often seen to be in league with, or at least made powerless by, the exploiters of the tribal economy. In this sense, the damage done is that dependence on other communities in the economic sphere was allowed to extend into the administrative sphere.

In the past, leadership was based on inheritance, and its dynamism had depended on the flexibility of residence patterns and the mobility of villages. As new leaders developed they hived off and started new communities, and the success of a new village depended on the qualities of its leader. The geographical mobility of villages has been a vital factor in the economic and cultural form of Gond society. The village as a symbolic, economic, and political community is centred on its headman (*nar patla*), who re-affirms his position every year at the Durari festival in March. Symbolically the *nar patla* represents the re-creation of the community every year, despite the fact that other, more wealthy individuals may develop within the village and wield greater political power; such other "big men" are loosely described as *patla* and lack the epithet of *nar*, meaning village. It is this symbolic unity of the village in the *nar patla* that has nearly always been re-affirmed in the elections of political representatives to the outside world. In the elections for government office these *nar patla* were elected rather than individual leaders, although they were frequently not the best suited as individuals to take the necessary strong stands in the factional politics that characterised the Panchayati Raj. Therefore, while there was an administrative reification of symbolic political structures, those structures were undermined by the invidious position in which these leaders were placed. When the traditional leadership is weakened in this way the entire structure of village politics founders.

In the traditional structure of Gond society, the answer to this dilemma would have been that as leadership in a given village crumbled and the village was gradually taken over by external political domination, its population would gradually have moved away and started new villages under new headmen, thus preserving the dynamic of political leadership. However, administrative regulations have prevented this geographical mobility. This has happened in two ways. First, Forest Department regulations have forbidden the clearing of new forest areas and the expansion of existing cultivation. In the past, due to various forces, including the flux of leadership, groups of individuals from a number of villages would start cultivating a new village in virgin forest or else would occupy a deserted village site. Not only have government regulations prevented the establishing of new village sites, but they have also created a shortage of land at a time when population growth has put pressure on land. Second, this pressure on land, combined with the new administrative code of title ownership, has changed the value put on land within the community. Previously, land was the property of the cultivator by right of conduct. Whoever was seen as cultivating the land was the owner, in combination with a permanent right of ownership vested in the original clearer of the land. Land was not a saleable resource but was enjoyed for the produce that it gave. It was not communal property in that it belonged to any group such as a lineage or clan. Any perma-

nent rights over land which existed were the right of the village headman, who accepted the cultivator in his village community. Without
the permission of the village headman, which was given through
symbolic representations, including the permission of the entire population of the village at the festival of Durari, an individual would find
it difficult to cultivate a piece of land. However, with the onset of
administrative and bureaucratic concepts of registered ownership,
land became a saleable resource. The village headman no longer had
right of veto over who should own the land, but rather the government exercised these rights through the issuing of title deeds. The
government rather than the community therefore became the arbiter
of village membership, and the social dynamism inherent in community life became subject to external influences.

This is admirably demonstrated by the application of protected tenancy regulation in Ginnedhari. When the village was first established
about fifty years ago, the father of Kumra Jangu cleared and cultivated
about twenty-two acres of land upstream of the village in the centre of
the valley. Some ten or so years later the absentee Brahmin landlord
from Asifabad claimed that the land which Kumra Jangu's father had
cleared belonged to him. He brought government survey officers, who
showed Kumra Jangu's father the title deeds to the land, and Kumra
Jangu's father was forced to submit to this. However, as a palliative he
was told that his name would be entered on the land register as the
cultivator of the land. From that moment on Kumra Jangu's father
became a sharecropper, and half the harvest had to be given to the
Brahmin landlord. Jangu's father found this arrangement unsatisfac-
tory and decided to vacate the twenty-two acres and clear a new area
of forest. Subsequently the land was rented out and sharecropped by a
number of villagers. However, in 1950 it was decided that all tenants
or sharecroppers should be registered as protected tenants and given
certain inalienable rights to their tenancy. The name of Jangu's father
was found on the land register as the cultivator under a sharecropping
agreement, and he was given the protected tenancy papers, not understanding what they were and not having cultivated the plot of land
mentioned for some years. Acting like most Indians would have done,
he kept this certificate and gave it to his son on his death, neither of
them realising its importance.

Between 1960 and 1962, the headman of Ginnedhari came to an
agreement with the Brahmin landlord to purchase the land. Money
was exchanged and a deed of sale transacted. The headman began to
cultivate the land and even sunk an irrigation well and installed a
pump irrigating eleven acres.

With the increase of education in the community and through the
auspices of the tribal schoolmaster, Kumra Jangu discovered that un-

der section 38E of the Andhra Pradesh (Telengana Area) Agricultural Lands and Tenancy Act as amended in 1973 all protected tenants had been declared the title owners to their land. He canvassed opinion on this to make certain that he had the backing of the relevant officials, forcibly occupied the land at the start of the 1977 ploughing season, and successfully evicted the village headman who had paid for the land. The headman lost not only his money but also his entire investment in the improvements to the land.

It is not important that the village headman was himself overridden by the law of the land; what is important is that administrative regulations have now become a significant element in defining the community. Whereas previously village membership was recognized through symbolic representations of community consensus at the festival of Durari, it is now at least partially decided through a hierarchy of government officers. Traditionally land was the main defining principle of the village. It was for the village headman to show the new immigrant an area of land which he could cultivate or an area of forest which he could clear. If a man intended to migrate to another village, he would first come to a verbal agreement with that village through the office of the village headman as to which area of land he might cultivate. Then at the festival of Durari at the beginning of the ploughing season, this would be ratified by the headman accepting his offering of two coconut kernels, some pulse cakes, onions, and sorghum seed. These offerings form an integral part of a ceremony in the name of the spirits of the village boundary, Siwa Auwal and Siwa Marke, a particular attribute of the earth mother goddess of the village, Natna Auwal. The remains of the offerings are then distributed to every householder and cultivator in the village. He takes these offerings, sanctified in the name of the earth mother goddess who is specific to each village, to the land that he is to cultivate that year. At the field he prays to his clan deity, associating it with his land, and, placing the offerings in front of any bush or shrub growing on the land, he symbolically cuts the shrub down. This ceremony, often called *podela paimar* ("striking the bush"), is referred to by its other name, *kuta mohtur*, by Fürer-Haimendorf.[6] This not only gives him the right to that land for that year, but, more importantly, the acceptance of the offering signals his inclusion in the community. If his offering had not been accepted he would be *ale:da manwal*, meaning that he could not attend any village councils or take part in village ceremonies. This is only a temporary exclusion from the community which carries no supernatural sanctions and is not a total excommunication from the tribe. However, it

6. C. von Fürer-Haimendorf, *The Raj Gonds of Adilabad*, pp. 311–13.

does mean that although the man is not physically thrown out of the village he cannot rely on any of its institutions for support.

With the present scarcity of land and the power of the administration to determine rights of ownership over land, the community is no longer so much a religiously and economically defined corporate grouping, although its symbols may still operate. The new bureaucratic element has become a significant variable which creates basic changes in the nature of community cohesion. Previously, the development of factions within the village would have been limited. Any party which wanted to challenge the leadership of the village would have either been ostracised and unable to attend the village council or participate in any of its corporate religious festivals or would already have left the village and started a new one. Traditionally each village had a single faction, and any factions that existed would be separated into different villages and their rivalry therefore minimised, though inter-village factionalism did exist. However, in the new administratively dominated environment this mobility is no longer possible, and the inevitable internal rivalries mean that the village community is now a divided entity. This implies fundamental changes in the nature of Raj Gond village political structure. Previously, the symbolic and political unity of the unifactional village was represented in the single office of the *nar patla*, which was inherited by the eldest son of the previous holder. The ability of the village headman to exercise political authority would have determined the success and the size of his settlement. Under the good leadership of prominent leaders, certain villages became large and thriving communities with many households. However, with the onset of administrative norms for community membership, the political and symbolic aspects of community leadership became separate functions. Political rivalry can no longer be accommodated by hiving off new communities, as new land is not available. Instead there is a fragmentation of the institutional structure of the village. The *nar patla* still acts as the symbolic focus of the village in his hereditary role, but the actual political power lies elsewhere, either with other individual "big men" or with various officials of the village, such as the schoolmasters. But the interesting thing is an element of cultural lag which means that the *nar patla* are still elected to the administrative office of *sarpanch* in the majority of villages, although they are no longer necessarily the people who wield the real power. Panchayati Raj did therefore theoretically bolster the traditional village institutions, but in practice the *panchayat* system was stripped of its effective powers and turned into a vehicle of inter-communal power politics, in which the traditional leaders were often ineffectual. This only further undermined their position in their villages, as they became bankrupt brokers between the people and government and in many cases lived off the ill-gotten gains of development aid channelled through party political support groups.

The problem that this creates is that the ideal channels of administration become ineffective. In traditional societies, where roles are multiplex and bureaucratic norms are not understood, the individual finds it difficult to approach a government officer when the channel of communication through his community leaders has broken down. Whatever the quality of individual officers, those that manage to do their job best are those who are prepared to spend time with people. Such officers as these are preferred by the villagers, who tend to find bureaucracy impersonal and unresponsive. Inherent in this are not merely the well-known problems of Indian bureaucracy, bound by regulations and red tape, but also the problems of the poor cultivator's narrow social horizon. He tends to see the administrator as somebody with power and influence who will only take action on his behalf as a personal favour. Therefore the petitioner is willing to give gifts to the government official to get wishes fulfilled, even though he does not know the regulations well enough to understand whether or not his demands can be carried out according to the rule book. Under these circumstances, the gift is an attempt to create a bond between the petitioner and the official. The official often expects payment for his services, and the villager is prepared to pay in the hope that the official is then bound under an obligation. The gift gives the villager some means of leverage over the official, which he otherwise feels is lacking. It is essentially an attempt to create favour, though by the bureaucratic rules it is defined as corruption. Whether it is corruption or an attempt by people who do not understand the inherent obligations placed on the civil service, it gives rise to a new form of community management based on patron-client relations and the buying and selling of favours, which further undermines traditional forms of leadership as it becomes entrenched in village life.

While it is a mistake to say that favours and patron-client relationships based on economic gain have never been a part of the political activity of a community, the fundamental change that has taken place is that these are now dependent on an external force. In effect, there has been an increase in dependence and exploitation in the field of economics. The resulting increase in relations across cultural barriers has affected intercommunal relations, as we have already seen.

The resulting administrative reification of the village is a new feature of Gond society. The days have passed when villages divided, new settlements were started, and abandoned village sites were left to be overtaken by the forest. A new element has been imposed on the village from above. The village is now a permanent institution which must be able to deal with internal division and dissension. Couple this with the new reform and revitalisation movements, the new avenues for leadership, and the influx of other communities into the arena of village life, and it is clear that Raj Gond society has undergone great changes in the last thirty years.

INTERNAL COHESION—THE SYMBOLS OF UNITY

The early policies of tribal development planned by the Social Service Department in the late 1940s and early 1950s intended to delimit a geographical area in which the tribal population would be administratively separated from other populations. Within this area non-tribals would not be allowed to own land. The idea was that the unity and strength of Raj Gond culture should be allowed to continue within this protected zone, which would artificially recreate the conditions of relative isolation that had been destroyed by the penetration of caste peasants. By preventing land alienation, it was hoped that the traditional economy of the Raj Gonds would be allowed to continue and that the cultural distinction between the Raj Gonds and caste-peasant societies could be preserved. This has not happened, and the basis of Raj Gond economy has changed to one of interdependence on others. I have described the effects that this has had on intercommunal relations and on the Raj Gonds' perception of themselves within a new plural society. It now remains to look at internal perceptions and symbols of unity and to see how the social structure of Raj Gond society has itself undergone transformation.

I have discussed how, due to economic changes, Raj Gond society is beginning to assume a place within the plural structure of hierarchically arranged social groups that defines the form of Indian society. Given this, it is important to see how this new position affects the internal structuring of Gond society. In this section I therefore want to discuss changes in the religious and kinship system of the Gonds, which are closely interlinked. One fundamental aspect of the Gonds is a clan system bound up with complex religious motifs that define "Raj Gond" as a separate entity. Raj Gonds define themselves as the people who worship *persa pen*, the Great God, a term applied to all the varied clan deities. To be a Raj Gond is therefore to be a member of a clan and to be identified with a clan cult.

The Gond descent system is based on the vertical division of Gond society into four phratries, each of which worships one particular clan deity or one particular pair of deities. But the phratry is not the corporate religious group. Corporate worship of the clan deity is carried out by each of the clans which make up the phratry. Each clan has a shrine to its clan deity at which ceremonies are performed twice yearly. As the clans are dispersed units with a membership scattered throughout the area of Raj Gond population, the clan cult forms the main mode of unity of the clan. The descent system, defined by the clan cult, is the structure around which the Raj Gond kinship system operates. Being a Dravidian-speaking people, the Raj Gonds have a Dravidian kinship system, with all the connotations of an alliance system which L. Dumont has described.[7] Each clan group is allied with other groups through a system of preferential marriage between the children of close affines. Thus the descent system, activated by the corporate worship of clan deities, binds the society together through a system of marriage alliances. The continuance of the Raj Gonds both as an identifiable system and as a system able to unify its membership structurally is therefore dependent on the continued operation of the clan cult. It is thus important to look at the changes that have been wrought in this cult. The importance of the clan cult to Raj Gond cohesion based on a "them and us" model can be seen from the statement of one reputable village headwoman who told me, as I have already quoted:

> In the days of our grandfathers we even washed our feet on returning from market. But now who washes [to preserve the purity of the clan deity?] For that reason our clan god [*persa pen*] is weak. Before we were advanced, now we are backward. We are not following the way of our clan gods. We are mixing.

As an agnatically defined cult group, the clan is divided into any number of lineages (*kita*). Most of the lineages only have importance as local lineages, the descendants of a particular ancestor who lived in one locality. Such lineages are called *kutma kita*. However, within the clan there are two particular lineages which relate to the organisation of the clan cult. First is the *patla kita*, the lineage of the keeper of the clan-deity shrine. The shrine, its environs, and the ritual objects are in his charge, and the position is inherited by primogeniture within the lineage. The second lineage is that of the priest, *katora*, and is called the *katora kita*. The priest officiates at all the rites to the clan deity. In no sense does he gain any divinity from this himself, and in all the prayers he joins the congregation, even though he is the ceremonial leader on whom devolve many of the arrangements for the highly complex rituals. However, the most important aspect of the clan cult is the role played by the traditional bards, who are either Pardhans or Totis. The Pardhans and Totis have a clan system which is parallel to that of the Gonds. Traditionally the members of each respective Par-

---

7. See Louis Dumont, *Hierarchy and Marriage in South Indian Kinship,* and M. P. Yorke, "Kinship, Marriage and Ideology among the Raj Gonds: A Tribal System in the Context of South India."

dhan or Toti clan served as bards and cultural maintenance men for the clan cult of their Raj Gond patrons. Every bard had his *dhani,* or patron, who was the head of a Gond household of the same clan as his own. The relationship between the bard and his patron is a highly complex one. The bard performs specific ritual functions for the household and is paid both annually and at specific rites of passage for each member of the household, with the service being inherited patrilineally.

The emic structure, or mythical charter, of the clan-cult system is contained in a highly elaborate oral tradition. At certain specific ceremonies the bards are paid to recite and sing the myths reflecting this tradition. They are the guardians of religious knowledge, and in the past they depended for their livelihood entirely on purveying and transmitting the oral tradition for their clan patrons. As well as being the purveyors and transmitters of the oral tradition, they also act as the communications hub of the clan-cult group and as the maintenance men for its customary regulations. In their role as bards they periodically visit the members of the dispersed clan-cult groups, performing their profession, announcing the times for ceremonials, collecting sacrificial offerings, and generally disseminating news and gossip of the affairs of the group. Not only do they bind the group together in this way, but they also act as expert arbiters of customary practice. They are often able to recite the genealogies of the lineages better than their patrons, and they are often more aware of the details of marriage regulations. I was once present at a council meeting called by the family bard, who had objected to a secondary marriage between a son of a priestly lineage and a girl of a non-priestly lineage.

In this role the bards act as maintainers of much of the fabric of the clan-cult system and of the alliances that bind it together. However, this role is dependent on their being able to gain a living from their patrons by acting as traditional bards. What has happened today is that the Raj Gonds no longer seem prepared to patronise the bards in the way that they did before, and the bards have also gained a wider horizon so that new generations find opportunities for making a livelihood outside their traditional role. The economy of the few Gonds who still live in the plains, have largely lost their land, and are now landless labourers has suffered to such an extent that they can no longer support a non-productive activity, and their ritual life has lost much of its symbolic content and form. However, it is not easy to say the same for the Gonds in the intermontane and plateau areas to the west of the eastern region I am discussing. The change in the economy is not so much one of a movement from wealth to poverty as a greater dependence on the wider economy of India. Today surplus in the economy is more likely to be expended in paying debts to moneylenders, gaining vital favours from government officials, and, above all, in purchasing consumer products, such as cloth, soap, radios, and more varied foodstuffs than are available locally. But a more important factor than changes in the economy of the patrons is changes in the rural economy of India. The growing sense of insecurity in peasant economies occasioned by the shortage of land and the rise in population has set off a counter-reaction in a rush for land as the only available form of lasting security. Many of the Pardhans and Totis have also felt this as they have seen their traditional role being eroded. The emphasis is no longer on making a living from learning the traditional skills as bards and maintainers of Gond social regulations but rather is on the skills of peasant agriculture. This move away from the traditional profession has also been assisted by the new educational facilities open to tribals and by reserved jobs in government posts. The traditional bards have been able to take greater advantage of the educational opportunities available than have the Gonds. Their background in verbal skill enables them to get higher qualifications than their patrons, whose home environment is oriented towards agriculture. This ability and the reserved opportunities open to them as tribals means that they now aspire to education and government employment, for which they are preferred above the other tribal communities.

All these factors have meant that the main mechanism for the maintenance of the central symbol of tribal identity is no longer operating with the same efficiency as in the past. The result is a clear lack of deep understanding of the ritual and symbolic tradition that existed in the past. Knowledge of the oral tradition is already deteriorating. Many of the myths which Fürer-Haimendorf collected in the 1940s are no longer fully understood. Group identity and cohesion, insofar as they are maintained by oral tradition and ethno-history, are weakening. The Gonds themselves are well aware of this, and many educated Gonds are beginning to write their myths down. However, the written myths lack a great deal of the detail that exists in the spoken versions. Also, as these versions are recorded by the Gonds who have greatest contact with the wider Hindu culture of India to which they aspire, many previously non-tribal elements are being introduced, such as reasons for worshipping the cow, which was formerly a sacrificial animal. These ideas are being particularly encouraged by the Shri Guru Dev Seva Mandal reform sect.

This weakening of clan identity is most powerfully indicated by a relaxation of concepts of ritual purity. The clan cult acted as a symbol of separation between the Raj Gonds and other communities. Worship of the clan deity involved the preservation of the individual's ritual purity and the purity of the entire household. In the 1940s only a Gond was allowed to enter the house of a Gond, and on returning from a place where non-Gonds gathered, such as marketplaces, every Gond used to wash himself ritually with water as an act of respect for the clan deities. However, such symbols of separation have now fallen into almost total disuse. And, as I have quoted, traditionally minded Gonds see this lowering of standards as a cause of the relative increase in the backwardness of their people. Although the relative backwardness may or may not be greater, their perception of it indicates the relaxation of the formerly held symbolic indices of ritual separation between "them and us."

The greater economic interdependence between the Raj Gonds and other communities has clearly lead to a lowering of cultural barriers and to increased social interrelations. What were previously powerful symbols of internal cohesion are no longer being observed with such rigidity.

Although the symbols of unity are being relaxed, the more critical structures that bind the Raj Gonds together as a social group remain unchanged. Language remains a unifying force, and the existence of a separate ethno-history allows them to see themselves as separate. There is no perceivable movement towards intercommunal marriages. As such, Raj Gondness remains a symbol of identity, but the degree of cultural and economic isolation has greatly lessened, though within the plural structure of Indian society Raj Gonds are now more able to see themselves as one group among many rather than as a particular group closely associated with a few other similar groups such as the Kolams, Naikpods, Wojaris, Pardhans, and Totis.

CONCLUSION

Change in social relations is largely initiated by changes in economic environment. The end product is due to what A. R. Beals calls "the interplay of many factors."[8] The forces which activate the dynamism of society are finally only a contributory factor in determining the resulting social configuration. Patricia Caplan, in her study of the changing relations between high and low castes in a village of western Nepal, writes, "Economic change is most likely to take place when the village is not a self-sufficient unit."[9] This model of social change follows the pattern for most of caste India, where each community and village is linked with a complex network of ties of interdependence.

8. A. R. Beals, "Interplay among Factors of Change in a Mysore Village."

9. Patricia Caplan, *Priests and Cobblers: A Study of Social Change in a Hindu Village in Western Nepal*, p. 85.

However, this model cannot be applied to the Raj Gonds, for whom the antithesis of interdependence, isolation and separation on a "them and us" model, operated. The economic change that has occurred is not a relative change in the environment but rather is an enlarging of economic networks with the outside world and the development of interdependence—a radical and absolute change in the economic environment, not a relative one; in fact, a change-over from isolation to interdependence.

The baseline model for the ideal type of traditional Raj Gond society is of the quasi-dominance of the Raj Gonds, relatively isolated in the vast and underpopulated Mughal Empire. Increased wealth, the building of large forts, and the employment of various caste service groups brought in Hindu influences, which were tribalised by the Raj Gonds, who preserved their dominant position. However, with the exponential increase in India's population, pressure was put on their relative isolation. The rise in population occasioned an influx of caste peasants, requiring an extension of centralised authority. This authority was more amenable to influence from, and more easily manipulated by, the more powerful immigrants. In the competition for resources the immigrants, backed by the power of government, managed to alienate the primary means of production—land. This reached a crisis point in the 1930s when the government also reserved the forests, so that Raj Gonds were caught between their land being taken away and not being allowed to clear new forest land. Improved communications and government policies of improved land registration and revenue collection increased the requirement for cash. As the Raj Gonds mortgaged or sold their land, or had it illegally registered in the names of Brahmins and Velma landlords, they found themselves moving into economic dependence on powerful outsiders. The landlords who obtained land from the tribals farmed their dependants for rent and invested the proceeds in moneylending. If loans could not be repaid, the land was given to immigrant cultivating Telugu castes. The situation gave rise to the Babijheri uprising of 1939 (see chapter 3) and later to sympathies with the Communist and Naxalite parties in the 1960s and 1970s.

In the 1940s, as a result of the fortuitous coincidence of the unease created by the Babijheri incident and Fürer-Haimendorf's anthropological investigations, the Nizam's government adopted a policy of trying to restore the Raj Gonds to a position of economic independence. Numerous landless tribals were granted new land to cultivate, existing holdings were registered on inalienable title, and parallel programmes for social development were initiated. The intention was to preserve the tribals' economic and cultural independence and to develop them to a level on which they could compete with the immigrants. Due to the historical circumstances of national independence and state re-organization, the tribal development policy was not properly implemented, and the process of economic subjugation returned. Cultural concepts such as "them and us" were no longer applicable, as the Gonds found themselves more and more dependent on the new dominant communities, and they began to see themselves as having an integral position in a new economic and class-based hierarchy.

The domination of the Raj Gonds in the eastern area of Adilabad District by Brahmins and Velma landlords and their interdependence in the new economic order did protect them from the onslaught of small peasant farmers from Maharashtra who came later into the central area. This domination by caste-Hindu landlords is the main feature of the new structure of interdependence; a structure in which the Gonds have a new role as cultivators in an economic arena where trade and cash cropping have involved them in increased relations with other communities. New nation-building policies of integrating minority groups, while affording them protected development, encouraged this interdependence. Thus social change has taken the form of a breakdown of local self-sufficiency and an opening up of frontiers with the outside. This has not modified the character of existing social relations, but is a radical move creating new social relations in a hierarchical caste model.

However, it is not as simple as this. Identity is not affected only by external factors of economic change. Faced with these changes, the Gonds themselves have actively tried to direct their changing identity. The administrative concept of "tribal" rather than the indigenous one of *adivasi*, or aboriginal, with all its connotations of a privileged minority, has become a new banner to wave. The more modernised Raj Gonds who have adopted this new identity as tribals within an Indian hierarchy have resorted to the cultural mechanism of a semi-reform and semi-revivalist movement with new norms of behaviour and social interaction to allow them to operate in the enlarged network of social relations in which they find themselves.

One of the major changes in the area has been the development of the special tribal development programmes, around which the new administrative concept of "tribe," as opposed to *adivasi*, has developed. Government improvements in the national infrastructure have opened the area up for cash cropping and the purchase of consumer products, increasing dependence on outside economic factors, including the ubiquitous moneylenders. Education has attempted but so far has largely failed to provide alternatives to cultivation as a means of livelihood. The main effect of education has been to create a new elite leadership at the local level and to create greater social interaction across previously rigid intercommunity barriers. Agricultural development programmes themselves have achieved little progress, though they have shown the way for enterprising individuals to intensify and rationalise their farming techniques. And the new techniques are gradually being taken up.

However, the inability of the traditional leaders to operate in the new local political structures has largely undermined their position, while the previous dynamism of local leadership, which was based on mobile residence patterns, has broken down. This has taken place along with a combined shortage of land to clear and the imposition of legal parameters to land ownership. The traditional population pattern of small, isolated villages which often moved or at least had a mobile population has begun to change, so that today certain tribal villages are becoming large and permanent settlements of a multi-ethnic composition, in which the pattern of local leadership is based on factional politics similar to those found in the multi-caste villages of the Indian plains, with strong links to and involvement in the national political framework.

Along with this general movement towards greater economic interdependence and a broader horizon of intercommunal contact, the special relation between the Raj Gonds and their traditional bards, the Pardhans and Totis, has begun to break down as the bardic groups begin to rely on cultivation for their livelihood. This in turn has affected the position of the Raj Gonds, who were previously the politically dominant land-owning group, but are now becoming another group of less-advanced peasant cultivators in the nexus of the plural society of India. While castelike parameters are beginning to become the determinants of social identity among the educated young, revitalisation and reform movements which are closely associated with the special tribal educational system are beginning to reshape the mythical basis of group identity.

The new identity that the Gonds are developing as one community in a wider, more integrated society, while having a castelike character, is developing into a reformed version of their identity of a tribal group. The Raj Gond language and clan cult, while being mixed with many Hindu elements, are being emphasized as an important element in a new identity of tribal ethnicity. This new tribal status is gaining further reality under the special regulations for tribal development. Land reforms, boarding schools, and privileges in agricultural development schemes all reinforce this identity. Whether or not such schemes actually achieve their aim of altering the economic structure of society, they are preserving a politically defined cultural identity in which the Raj Gonds see themselves as a tribe within an integrated Indian society.

10 Konda Reddis in Transition: Three Case Studies

by Jayaprakash Rao

THE KONDA, or Hill, Reddis are a primitive tribe of Andhra Pradesh, whose strength was 43,609 according to the 1971 census. Konda Reddis are distributed over a large part of the Eastern Ghats, and their habitat extends from the Sileru River in the north to the Sabari River in the west and the plains of coastal Andhra in the east. In the south it straddles the Godavari River, and there are settlements of Reddis in the districts of Khammam and West Godavari. Although they are spread over a large area, the majority of the Reddis (31,000) are concentrated in Maredumilli and Addateegala community development blocks of East Godavari District.

On the basis of physical features the Reddis' habitat can be divided into three distinct zones: (1) the hill settlements, (2) the riverside settlements, and (3) the settlements of the lower Agency Tract and plains.

The hill settlements, as the name suggests, are mainly in mountainous country, and even to this day a large number of these settlements are inaccessible by road. Only during the last ten years have the Reddis of these settlements come in contact with the outside world, mainly due to the penetration of the agents of paper mills, who are organizing the extraction of bamboos as raw material for their factories. For all practical purposes the normal administrative machinery of government is absent, except for the activities of forest guards. Contact with the outside world is only peripheral, and the Reddis of these settlements have remained foodgatherers and shifting-cultivators.

Riverside settlements are situated on both banks of the Godavari. They are found between the confluence of the Sabari and the Godavari at Kunavaram and in the area around Devipatnam. The Reddis of these settlements are plough cultivators, tilling the narrow strips of alluvial, flat lands found between the hills and the riverbank. Because of the communications afforded by the river traffic, these settlements have for long been in contact with the outside world, and this contact with non-tribal populations increased with the introduction of motor-boats in the late 1920s.

The third zone, the smallest of the three in terms of population and number of settlements, consists of the lower agency of East Godavari District and the scattered settlements of Reddis in the plains adjoining the hills in West Godavari and Khammam districts. These settlements came in touch with outsiders much earlier than the hill settlements, and these contacts have increased in the last two decades due to the migration of non-tribals into tribal areas. The Reddis of these settlements cultivate flat land with ploughs, like the Reddis of the riverside settlements.

In this chapter I present three case studies, (1) Gogulapudi, (2) Pandirimamidigudem, and (3) Koruturu, selected from each of the three zones and showing the changes in Reddi society which have taken place in the last four decades.

GOGULAPUDI

Gogulapudi is a small Konda Reddi settlement in the hills south of the Godavari River. The village is in Sattupalli Taluk of Khammam District, and is located on the boundary between Khammam and West Godavari districts. The efforts of the government in the last thirty years to develop the tribals have not reached this settlement at all. Gogulapudi was studied by Fürer-Haimendorf in 1941 and is described in his book *The Reddis of the Bison Hills,* but when I went to Ashwaraopet, the headquarters of the community development block in which Gogulapudi lies, I was surprised to find that none of the staff of the Tribal Development Agency knew of its existence. The revenue officials were also surprised when I enquired about its location and the route to reach it. However, after six days of persistent enquiries, an old and retired *patwari* ("village officer") of the Samasthan of Paloncha came to my rescue.

Gogulapudi is situated about forty-five kilometers northeast of Ashwaraopet. To reach Gogulapudi from the block headquarters, one has to travel about forty kilometers through West Godavari District. During the dry season it can be reached by jeep from Ashwaraopet and Buttayagudem, the headquarters of the community development block of the same names in West Godavari District. For the last four or five years, the State Transport Corporation has been running buses from Eluru to Doramamidi, a big, non-tribal village about seventeen kilometers southwest of Gogulapudi. During the rainy season, however, even travel on foot between Gogulapudi and the plains is rendered difficult by the swelling of numerous hill streams.

Gogulapudi village lies on the slope of a hill and is surrounded by lush forest. For all practical purposes there is no flat land in or around the settlement. The villagers subsist by shifting cultivation (*podu*), foodgathering, and forest labour. The Reddis are simple folk, and their necessities are few. They dress as they used to forty years ago, and no one in the village is literate.

The story of Gogulapudi during the past four decades is a story full of woe. In 1941, the Reddis lived in two small settlements, Gogulapudi and Dornalpushe, a mile apart from each other. Four families lived in Gogulapudi, and its population was twenty-eight souls. There were five families in Dornalpushe, and its population was twenty-seven. Smallpox broke out in this area in 1943, and a large number of Reddis and Koyas of neighbouring villages died. The smallpox did not spare the secluded Reddis of Gogulapudi and Dornalpushe. All the members of two families in Dornalpushe perished in the epidemic, and someone or other died in the remaining three families. The epidemic reduced the population of Dornalpushe to nineteen souls. Gogulapudi was more fortunate, and there were only four smallpox deaths. The surviving members of the three families of Dornalpushe were so shocked by their losses that they deserted the village. Two families migrated to Gogulapudi, and the third went to Chintakonda.

After the smallpox epidemic, for about seven or eight years the Reddis led a peaceful life cultivating *podu* fields, gathering wild roots, bamboo shoots, and mushrooms, and drinking caryota wine. This peaceful and secluded life received a jolt when, soon after independence, communist troubles started in the Hyderabad State. To contain and suppress the communist movement, the Government of India began resettling the population living in isolated forest villages in and around big villages, where it had set up special police camps. During this period in the late 1940s, the police raided Gogulapudi, beat all able-bodied males, and reduced the village to ashes on the suspicion that the Reddis were helping the communists. Then the entire population of Gogulapudi was forcibly settled in Vinayakapuram, a big, non-tribal village about twenty miles west of Gogulapudi, where there was a special police camp.

The Reddis were not allowed to go back to their village for about one and a half to two years. For the first month or so, the Reddis were fed by the police at state expense; later they were asked to look after themselves. The Reddis survived either by working as farm hands for non-tribal landlords or by making baskets and winnowing fans and selling them. The traumatic events had so unnerving an effect on the Reddis that they did not return to Gogulapudi to re-establish the village even when they were permitted to do so. Instead, three families migrated to Motagudem, another Reddi settlement in the hills across the border between the then Hyderabad State and Madras State. The other three families settled down in Kamaram, a Koya village in the plains, also on the other side of the state border.

All those who went to Motagudem lived in usual Reddi style, depending upon *podu* fields. But those who settled in Kamaram cultivated jointly with the Koyas the lands owned by the latter, getting 50 percent of the yield. While living there, some of the Reddis learned how to handle a plough. However, they could not acquire any flat land of their own, as all the land in the village belonged to Koyas.

Around 1968 or 1969, the officials of the forest department in West Godavari District began to enforce prohibition of *podu* cultivation. This affected the Reddis living in Motagudem, and for one year they were completely stopped from cultivating *podu* fields. Consequently, the Reddis of Gogulapudi who had migrated to Motagudem decided to re-establish their old village. They proposed to the families living in Kamaram that they should join them in their venture, and the latter agreed to this plan.

It was during this time that the families of Golla Gangaya, Golla Reddaya, Boli Potaya, and Gurgunta Pedda Pandaya, who lived in Kamaram, and Kopal Potaya, Kopal Lachmaya, and Gurgunta China Pandaya, who had settled in Motagudem, all originally from Gogulapudi, re-established the village on its old site after a period of twenty years. Along with them, the families of Gogula Kannaya, Gogula Lingaya, Gurgunta Viraya, and Gurgunta Somaya came and settled in Gogulapudi from Motagudem. They appointed Golla Gangaya as *pujari* and Golla Reddaya as *pedda kapu*, for Golla Lachmaya, the former *pujari* and *pedda kapu*, had died without sons.

Later two brothers, Gurgunta Dasaya and Gurgunta Chinnaya, came to Gogulapudi from Thandigudem, and Kechela Potaya and Karapala Potaya came, along with their families, from Motagudem. The latest arrival in the village was Madakam Chinnaya, a Koya originally from a village on the banks of the Godavari River, who had been wandering from one village to another for several years. He had come in contact with the Reddis of Gogulapudi while he was living in Kamaram, and in 1976 he settled in Gogulapudi with the permission of the *pedda kapu*.

In early 1978, while I was camping in the village, there were seventeen Konda Reddi families and one Koya family in Gogulapudi. Out of seventeen Reddi families, only eight were those of either original inhabitants or their descendants. The population of the village was eighty-three souls, of whom thirty-five were males and forty-eight were females. Out of the total population of eighty-three, only eight were alive in 1941 when the village was first studied.

The troubles of the Gogulapudi Reddis, however, did not end with the re-establishment of the village. The Naxalite movement emerged in India around the time the village was re-established. The Naxalites of Andhra Pradesh used forest areas in the state as their bases and began organizing people against exploitation by landlords, merchants, and minor officials with the aim of overthrowing the existing social order. To suppress the activities of the Naxalites, the state government established numerous police camps in the forest areas, and began combing the forests for Naxalites.

Although the Gogulapudi Reddis did not get involved in the Naxalite movement, they were caught in the cross-fire as they had been in the late 1940s. A police camp was established in Kavadigundla, a big Koya village across the hills, and the police of this camp began combing the forests around Gogulapudi. The police, whenever going for combing (or rather so-called combing) operations in the forests, visited Gogulapudi and took away the chickens raised by Reddis. During 1970–74, the police took away about seventy to eighty chickens from the Reddis of Gogulapudi without paying them anything. Besides the chickens, two goats worth about Rs 250, one belonging to Kopala Potaya and another belonging to his son-in-law Gogula Gangaya, were carried off by the police. While they paid Rs 20 to Kopal Potaya, nothing was paid to Gogula Gangaya.

On one of their visits, the police snatched away a silver necklace worth Rs 200 (at current prices) from the young son of Gurgunta Somaya. During this perion, the *pedda kapu* Reddaya and a few others were summoned to the police camp four times and were badly beaten on the suspicion that they were helping the Naxalites by providing food and shelter. The police harassment, however, came to an end with the fall of Mrs. Gandhi's government in March 1977, although the police are still stationed at Kavadigundla.

Prior to the burning down of Gogulapudi and the shifting of the population to the Vinayakapuram police camp during the communist troubles of the late 1940s, the village was comparatively isolated from the outside world. The economy of Gogulapudi was more or less self-sufficient. The needs of the Reddis were very few, and most of them were met from the resources available locally. Food requirements were met by growing cereals, such as *jawari (Sorghum vulgare), sama (Panicum miliare), korra (Sataria italica)*, and pulses such as red gram ("pigeon pea") and *alasanda* ("cow pea") on the *podu* fields. As there was nothing else to do then, the Reddis began felling the forest from December onwards to prepare the *podu* fields for the next year's sowing. On an average a Reddi family cleared the forest over 2 to 2½ acres of land and prepared the fields by June, when there are the first showers of the monsoon and the seed is dibbled. As the average yield of *jawari* per acre of *podu* field is 250 kilograms, each family harvested about 600 kilograms, besides 150 to 250 kilograms of small millets.

The yield from *podu* fields, however, was not sufficient to meet a year's food requirements. The Reddis bridged this gap by gathering a variety of edible jungle tubers and roots which are available throughout the year. Besides the tubers, the Reddis depended on the pith of caryota palms and the kernels of mango stones during periods of scarcity. During the summer season, when caryota juice is abundantly available, the Reddis depended more on the fermented caryota juice than on cereals. They grew a few vegetables in *podu* fields and near their houses, besides gathering bamboo shoots, mushrooms, and a variety of leafy vegetables from the forest.

They built their houses of bamboo, timber, and grass, which were abundantly available in the forest, and they made baskets, winnowing fans, mats, such implements as digging sticks, and bows and arrows.

Their cash requirements were small, though they depended on the outside world for cooking pots and simple iron implements, such as axe, billhooks, and a few knives, used in agriculture and basket making. Cooking pots, salt and clothing, which anyhow was scanty, were obtained from markets, where Reddis bartered their baskets for such commodities. The Gogulapudi Reddis got their iron implements from a Koya Kammara of Kamaram in exchange for grain or some other goods, such as caryota palm wine or bows and arrows.

In those days the Reddis earned a little cash by felling bamboo for non-tribal farmers who came up to Kamaram. Their cash earnings were very small, as the bamboo requirements of the non-tribal farmers were modest and the wage paid was one rupee for one hundred bamboos.

The more or less self-sufficient Reddi economy of Gogulapudi and other hill settlements remained undisturbed and the settlements remained isolated until the beginning of the 1950s. The process of breaking down the isolation of these settlements began in the early 1950s when the state government began auctioning the rights to extract bamboo and timber from the forest in the vicinity of Gogulapudi. The contractors who purchased the rights to extract forest produce and their clerks from the plains were the first outsiders to come to these areas. Initially their presence did not alter the economy of the Reddis, as their activities were confined to forests in the plains. They could not extract timber and bamboos from the hills due to difficulties of transport and hence did not substantially affect the life-style of the Reddis. However, the Reddis were not left to themselves for much longer.

During the late 1950s, the contractors laid temporary roads in the hills and introduced trucks in the place of bullock carts for transporting forest produce. With the help of mechanized transport, the merchants began extracting bamboo and timber from much larger areas of the forest. With this the demand for labour increased, and for the first time the Reddis got an alternative source of employment.

In 1961, the state government leased the rights to extract bamboo from the coups of Khammam District on a long-term basis to the Sirpur Paper Mills. Similar rights over the coups of West Godavari District were given to the Andhra Paper Mills. The paper mills, with their larger capital resources, laid an extensive network of forest roads designed for the extraction of bamboo from the hills and thereby created a large market for forest labour. In 1974, the government abolished auctions of forest coups in order to eliminate the private merchants, who under duress had been making substantial contributions to the armed squads of the Naxalites. Since then the government has been extracting bamboo and timber through its logging division. This work begins in October or November and continues until the end of May or early June. Felling operations are prohibited during the rainy season in order to allow the forest to regenerate. The transportation comes to a standstill immediately after the first monsoon showers, because then the roads become impassable.

As the labour the Reddis can supply is insufficient, the paper mills import labour from outside to work in the forest. The labourers live in make-shift camps at the bamboo-extraction sites in the forest. During this period the paper mills build huts either in or near a village or sometimes in the forest itself to house their clerks and to store rice and other daily necessities. From these depots the clerks of the paper mills make "rice advances" to the labourers, whether they are Reddis or outsiders. It was the merchants and the paper mills who introduced the regular consumption of rice among the Reddis, besides breaking their isolation from the rest of the world.

Because of the extraction of bamboo from October to May and the demand for labour, the Reddis can get uninterrupted employment for two-thirds of the year. However, the Reddis of Gogulapudi and most other hill settlements work continuously only from the last week of January or the beginning of February until the end of May. Up to December they do not work every day, as they are still busy guarding their standing crops against birds and other wild animals.

When the sorghum crop is harvested, all men and women, with the exception of nursing mothers, old persons, and young children, hire out their labour to the agents of the paper mills until the forest work comes to an end. During this period, the women get up around 5:00 A.M. and prepare gruel, and by 7:00 A.M. the Reddis eat the left-over food of last night and set out of their houses with their billhooks, bows and arrows, and gourd bottles filled either with drinking water or with gruel. In the forest, men cut the bamboos from the clumps while women and adolescent children help the men by shaving off the side branches of the felled bamboos. Then all the workers drag the bamboos to the lorry tracks, where they are loaded into trucks. The Reddis return back from their work by 2:00 P.M. and rest for a few hours. As felling bamboo and dragging it to the transport point through the bush is very strenuous, none works for more than four or five days in a week.

All the three organizations make payment by piece-work, and each has its own method of calculation. The Sirpur Paper Mills pays Rs 30 to 40 for one hundred bundles of bamboo, depending upon the distance from which they are carried. Each bundle contains twenty bamboos six feet long. On the other hand, the Andhra Paper Mills pays by weight. The average rate is Rs 45 per ton of dry bamboo and Rs 40 per ton of green bamboo. The rate again varies according to the distance and the steepness of the hill from which the bamboo has to be carried. The felling rates in the case of the logging division are fixed by the state government. During my stay in Gogulapudi they were Rs 30 and Rs 20 per one hundred long bamboos of Medara and Kadembaru varieties, respectively. Labourers employed by paper mills have to fell the bamboos, cut them into pieces of suitable size, and make them into bundles. Then they carry these bundles on their shoulders and dump them by the side of the lorry track. One man makes on an average seven to eight trips to transfer the bamboo bundles from the work site to the lorry track. In the case of long bamboos, first the side branches are cut off, and then they are dragged to the road. If the slope of the hill is steep they are pushed down, gathered together, and dumped by the side of the road.

During 1977–78, the Gogulapudi Reddis worked initially in the coups of the paper mills. Later on, in February when the logging division of the Forest Department began extracting long bamboo, they began hiring their labour to the logging division. Though the logging division does not make advance payments of either cash or rice, the Reddis preferred to cut long bamboos because it was easier than felling bamboo for the paper mills. The cash earnings of each family depended upon the number of family members working, the number of days they worked, and the amount of bamboo felled by each family. Table 4 gives the cash earnings of the Reddis of Gogulapudi during the year 1977–78.

TABLE **4.**   *Cash Earnings of the Reddis of Gogulapudi, 1977–78*

NAME	ANDHRA PAPER MILLS	LOGGING DIVISION	TOTAL
	SOURCE OF EARNINGS, IN RUPEES		
Kopal Potaya	321.00	475.60	796.60
Kopal Gangaya	124.00	340.20	464.20
Kopal Lachmaya	261.00	798.60	1,059.60
Golla Gangaya	168.00	340.00	508.00
Golla Reddaya	530.00	573.70	1,103.70
Karakala Potaya	67.00	615.40	682.40
Boli Potaya	18.00	764.40	782.40
Gogula Kanaya	276.50	990.40	1,266.90
Gogula Chinnaya	—	172.40	172.40
Gogula Pendaya	—	370.00	370.00
Gurgunta Chinnaya	265.00	798.60	1,063.60
Gurgunta Dasaya	134.75	578.60	713.35
Gurgunta Pedda Pandaya	171.00	745.00	916.00
Gurgunta Chinna Pandaya	4.00	549.60	553.60
Gurgunta Viraya	130.00	602.00	732.00
Gurgunta Somaya	64.00	467.00	531.00
Madkam Chinnaya (Koya)	83.00	500.00	583.00
TOTAL	2,617.25	9,681.50	12,298.75

Gogula Kanaya's family earned Rs 1,266.90, which is the highest income in Gogulapudi, because his wife and his two sons helped him in cutting bamboos. The earnings of Gogula Chinnaya were only Rs 172.60. He was a boy fourteen years old, and he did not get help from the other members of his family because his parents were too old for forest work.

The clerks of all the three organizations cheated the Reddis by taking advantage of their illiteracy and lack of knowledge of accounts. The supervisor of the Andhra Paper Mills weighed the bamboos cut by the Reddis and the labour imported from outside by using a spring balance whose needle did not rest at zero but was adjusted to rest at 200, thereby underweighing each bundle of bamboo by two to three kilos. Further, the accounts of rice advances made were falsified to the Reddis' disadvantage.

The forest ranger of the logging division deducted 5 percent of the bamboos felled by the Reddis and paid them accordingly. But when submitting the bills to the government, he gave the actual number of bamboos felled and pocketed the difference. If the Reddis had been paid for the actual number of bamboos felled by them, they would have received a total of Rs 12,913 instead of Rs 12,298. Although the Reddis resented the deduction of 5 percent of bamboos they had felled, they were helpless because they did not know the higher officials to whom their complaints would have had to be sent, and even if they had done so it is unlikely that they would have obtained any redress.

The creation of a market for labour in the forest by government and paper mills has drawn the Reddis of these hill settlements into the nexus of a market economy. Cash transactions have replaced barter, and the cash requirements of the Reddis have increased although the use of money within the village has not yet developed. Due to the flow of cash and the easy availability of credit from the merchants of Kamaram during the bamboo-cutting season, rice, which in the past was for Reddis a rare delicacy, has become the staple food of Gogulapudi at least for six months in the year. During my stay in Gogulapudi, in hardly any of the houses was millet regularly cooked. The only exception was the house of Kechel Potaya, because he could not earn cash due to a broken shoulder. Thus the Reddis today depend for their food on outside markets for at least five to six months in a year, for rice is not grown in Gogulapudi. Besides the consumption of rice , the consumption of dried fish and tobacco, which also must be procured in the market, have increased substantially. Today each family, at least during the bamboo-felling-season, eats dried fish once a week.

In the 1940s, the quantity of tobacco consumed by Reddis was small, and they got it by exchanging their baskets and winnowing fans and by growing a few plants near their houses. Today on an average each adult Reddi male spends weekly about Rs 1.50 on tobacco.

Nowadays Reddis frequently visit markets at Doramamidi and Buttayagudem, and are gradually replacing their earthen cooking pots by aluminium and other metal vessels. The lorries which regularly ply between the bamboo coups and bamboo depots in nearby towns have enabled the Reddis to visit these towns both for enjoyment, such as seeing movies, and for making occasional purchases. These visits have widened the Reddis' horizon and have changed their social outlook.

Although the total consumption of cereals by the Reddis has increased, the yield from *podu* fields has gone down. The area in which the Reddis clear forest growth to prepare *podu* fields has been reduced to 1 to 1½ acres, partly because of the official restrictions on shifting cultivation and partly because of the diversion of labour to work for government and paper mills. With the decrease in the area of *podu* fields, the yield from them has also declined. This phenomenon increases the dependence of Reddis on the market for their food, and exposes them to fluctuations in food prices.

Although the cash income of the Reddis of Gogulapudi has increased enormously when compared with the past, they have little cash to spare because of the high cost of food. This will be seen from the following example. During my stay in Gogulapudi, the wife of Gogula Kanaya cooked daily 3 kilograms of rice, half the quantity in the morning and the remaining half in the evening, to feed her husband and four children. Thus the family consumed each month 90 kilograms of rice. If we assume that the family consumed rice during six months, then 540 kilograms of rice were required. The price of 1 kilogram of rice was then Rs 2, so the family had to spend Rs 1,080 on rice alone, out of its total cash income of Rs 1,266.90. Besides rice, the family spent money on tobacco, dried fish, and occasionally liquor and other small luxuries. In fact, with the exception of the families of Kopal Potaya, Kopal Gangaya, Boli Potaya, and Gogula Pandaya, none of the families had any savings. On the other hand, six families owed between Rs 10 and Rs 30 to the petty merchants who visit Gogulapudi during winter and summer.

The Reddis do not have much spare cash to spend on clothes, and the dress and appearance of the men and women of Gogulapudi has not changed very much since the 1940s. Three or four Reddis have acquired trousers, but even these men reserve such clothes for festivals and do not wear them otherwise. Men usually wear nothing but a small loin-cloth (*budda gochi*) to cover their private parts, and a few occasionally wear shirts. While they are in the village or working in the fields, most women wear only a sari, but when they go to other villages or to a market they usually put on a bodice. The dress of the children is scanty.

Gogulapudi is no longer isolated, and its economy has ceased to be self-sufficient. Owing to the availability of wage labour, the consumption of cereals has increased, but the Reddis of today are exposed to the inflation of food prices. In the absence of any government-sponsored development activities, their future is bound up with that of the organizations exploiting forest resources, and in the event of the cessation of their activities in the region the Reddis would be faced with a serious economic crisis.

PANDIRIMAMIDIGUDEM

Pandirimamidigudem is a Konda Reddi settlement in the plains of West Godavari District. This settlement is about ten kilometers south of Gogulapudi, and is surrounded by Koya villages. Buttayagudem, the headquarters of the community development block in which the settlement lies, is situated at a distance of about twenty kilometers.

Prior to the smallpox epidemic of the early 1940s, the village was about half a kilometer south of the present site, to which it was shifted due to the large number of deaths. About two kilometers north of the present site, there are still remnants of huts under a tamarind grove at the base of a hill suggesting an earlier settlement of Reddis there. However, no one in the village, not even the oldest living person, ever lived on that site.

Although the Reddis of this settlement have been in touch with the outside world for a long time, their contact with the non-tribal population has increased since the early 1950s. It was during this time that the forest coups in the region were auctioned and the first non-tribal, a Komti merchant, migrated to Pandirimamidigudem from Jangareddigudem and established the first small provision store. We shall discuss the role played by Komtis in the economy of the Reddis at the end of this section.

Within the last fifteen years the village has come into the orbit of the developmental activity of the government. In the past the Reddis fetched water for drinking and cooking purposes from a stream flowing about two kilometers from the village. To alleviate the drinking-water problem, a well was sunk within the village at government expense. A primary school with a single teacher was established in the village some time around 1965. In the early 1970s, two fair-weather roads connecting Kamaram and Buttayagudem with Jeelugumilli and Doramamidi were laid through the village. Since then a number of trucks heading for the forest coups in the hills regularly pass through the village during the dry season. A daily requirement depot of the Girijan Corporation, selling rice, chillies, oil, etc., at reasonable prices was also established in the early 1970s. This depot also purchases tamarind, soapnut, broomsticks, and other minor forest produce collected by Reddis and the Koyas of nearby villages.

During my stay in the village in 1978, there were thirty-seven families, and the total population was 156, of which 80 were males and 76 females. Out of thirty-seven families, seven were non-tribal families, accounting for 24 persons. Besides the Komti already mentioned, there was another family of Komtis who had come to the village four years previously. Two non-tribals were liquor merchants and sold government-supplied alcoholic drinks. Both of them had come in the last five or six years. For the last two years, one of these merchants had cultivated with hired bullocks three acres of land leased from a Reddi. There was also the family of the clerk of the daily requirement depot. An old non-tribal couple eked out a living by selling dried fish in the nearby villages. There was also a carpenter, who worked mainly for the non-tribals of nearby villages, making to order such furniture as chairs and cots from local timber, which was cheap due to the proximity of the forest. The Reddis did not engage his services, as they made wooden ploughs and cots themselves.

Out of thirty Reddi families, eight had moved to Pandirimam-idigudem from other villages. One had migrated there from across the state border about thirty years previously during the communist troubles. Other families had come and settled in the village about ten to fifteen years earlier, because they either had married girls of the village or were in search of land due to the prohibition of *podu* cultivation in their home settlements. With the exception of the family which had immigrated thirty years ago, all others had close relatives in the village.

The change among the Reddis of this settlement due to their contact with the outside world is apparent from the clothes they wear. They dress in the style of non-tribals and the *budda gochi* ("loin-cloth"), the universal dress of men in the hill settlements, is replaced by *dhoti*. They wear shirts even in the village, as well as when they visit other villages and markets. Elderly men either wear a turban or keep a towel on their shoulder. A few who are comparatively well off wear sandals purchased from markets. The younger generation of men, particularly those between fifteen and thirty years of age, wear shorts and shirts tailored in modern style. In this village I saw only two old men dressed in the style of hillmen, and these two had migrated from settlements in the mountains. All men use the services of a barber, who comes to the village regularly from Doramamidi, and pay him a small fee in cash for shaving and cutting their hair. Women wear sari in the style of non-tribals and a short-sleeved blouse (*choli*). While hill women do not feel self-conscious about leaving their breasts exposed, an entirely new concept of modesty has crept into the village owing to the long-standing contact with non-tribals, and hence none of the women in the village moves around without a *choli*. The boys wear shorts and shirts, and small girls wear frocks. The clothes worn by boys and girls enrolled in the village school are supplied by government. Cheap bangles and necklaces of glass beads are the common ornaments of the women, and even small pieces of gold and silver jewelry are occasionally worn by the more affluent women.

The Reddis of this settlement persist in the performance of all the traditional rituals. They celebrate the mango festival, hold first fruit ceremonies before eating the new crops, and perform the festival of mother earth before ploughing their fields. A few Reddis also celebrate certain Hindu festivals, visit nearby Hindu temples, and make offerings to the deities. In most of the houses there are cheap prints depicting Hindu gods, and a few Reddis burn incense to such deities.

With the establishment of a primary school in the village about fifteen years ago, literacy has spread among the younger generation. Two Reddi youths have studied up to the eighth form, and a few others have studied up to the fifth form. One youth who had studied up to the eighth form has been appointed as basic health worker ("barefoot doctor") after training at the hospital at block headquarters. In 1978, out of twenty-two Reddi boys and twenty-three Reddi girls between six and twelve years old, fourteen boys and seven girls were enrolled in the village school. Four other boys and one girl were studying in an upper primary ashram school located in a neighbouring village.

Modern medicine has largely replaced the traditional practices of healers (*veju*), and belief in such magicians has considerably declined. For common ailments such as fever the Reddis either visit the government hospital at Doramamidi or take medicines from the basic health worker. A few Reddis have visited a private nursing home at Jangareddigudem for treatment of serious complaints. During one of the family-planning campaigns of the late 1970s, fifteen men of the village were sterilized by vasectomy.

AGRICULTURE AND LAND TENURE

In the past, the Reddis used to cultivate flat land in the style of *konda podu*. They cleared the forest on a patch of land, allowed the felled trees to dry for three or four months, then burned them and in the ashes dibbled seed with digging sticks. After cultivating the land for two or three years, they shifted to a new plot. After nine or ten years, they cultivated the old patches of land, where by that time the forest had regenerated. The Reddis gave up this slash-and-burn cultivation about three or four decades ago and began plough cultivation. In 1978 only one man, who had recently moved to Pandirimamidigudem from a hill settlement, cultivated *konda podu* on a nearby hill slope.

Though only eleven of the thirty Reddi families own parts of the 300 acres of flat land available in the village, all families are involved in cultivation. The soils are sandy and of poor quality, and though the Reddis own cattle and know of the advantage of manuring, they are not in the habit of manuring their fields. This may be either due to the lack of bullock carts for transporting manure or due to the relative novelty of plough cultivation. The Reddis grow sorghum millet, kidney beans (*Phaseolus aconitifolius*), pigeon peas, and other pulses as food crops, and sesamum and castor as cash crops, which they sell to merchants.

There are no sources of irrigation for general use. Boli Soma Raju sunk a well in his land about ten years ago and cultivated tobacco and chillies until he was murdered by his brother two years later. Since then the well has remained in disuse. In 1978 Boli Mukka Reddi, the headman (*pedda kapu*) of the village, took a loan of Rs 9,000 from a commercial bank at Buttayagudem for sinking a well, which enables him to grow tobacco and chillies.

The Reddis raise sorghum millet by two methods. In the first method they prepare the soil by ploughing it three or four times and then broadcast the seed. A large area is cultivated under sorghum by this method. In the second method a smaller area is ploughed six to eight times, and a well-prepared patch is used as a nursery. When the seedlings are about four to five inches high, they are transplanted into the field in rows with the help of a rope. Between the rows a space of about nine inches is allowed. As transplanting requires a great deal of labour, only a small amount of sorghum is raised by this method, though the yield is higher. This method of cultivation has been in vogue for the past sixteen years.

The unit of consumption is the nuclear family, as it is in the hill settlements. But only in a few cases is the nuclear family also the unit of production. The unit of agricultural production in Pandirimamidigudem and in the surrounding Koya villages is known as *kamatham*. A *kamatham* consists of members of two or more families who pool their land, labour, and cattle resources for cultivation. If a *kamatham* does not have bullocks or requires an additional bullock, it hires it from others who have a surplus of bullocks and pays one bag (120 kilograms) of millet per year. If the hired bullock is yoked for the first time, no payment is made to the owner of the bullock. The *kamatham* is the unit for borrowing grain in periods of food shortage, and such grain is repaid from the next year's yield. The harvested crop is split up into shares after deducting the land revenue, hire charges for bullocks, repayment of loans taken before the harvest, and the seed for the next year's sowing. The grain yields are distributed among the members as follows: one share to each person contributing a pair of bullocks; and one share to each pair of persons, i.e. husband and wife, mother and son, or brother and sister, working on the land. The owner of the land does not receive any share for contributing the land, but only the share for his contribution to the labour. Only if the land revenue is not deducted from the common pool is he given an extra share.

The men of the *kamatham* plough the land, sow the seed, guard the field from wild animals and birds, and harvest the crop. Weeding is done exclusively by women, and they help the men in other agricultural operations, such as transplanting and winnowing the threshed grain. A *kamatham* comes into being by informal understandings between the members, and it lasts as long as no differences develop among them. The members of a *kamatham* are usually interrelated. Within the *kamatham* all are equal, and there are no hierarchical relationships, irrespective of the area of the land contributed by each member.

The Reddis of Pandirimamidigudem are organized into eleven *kamatham*, of which only three are nuclear family units. One woman leased out her land to a Koya of a neighbouring village at a rent of Rs 100 per acre when her husband died and her son was too young to handle a plough. Another widow's land was cultivated by her son-in-law's *kamatham*, and she got one out of three shares.

The largest *kamatham* of the village was that of the headman (*pedda kapu*), Boli Mukka Reddi. Besides himself, his wife, and a son, nine other members of six families worked together to cultivate twenty acres of Mukka Reddi's land. None of the other members had land, and the *kamatham* also cultivated eight acres belonging to Suppala Ramulamma, the mother-in-law of Mukka Reddi. The *kamatham* retained 2 out of 3 shares of the yield from these eight acres and gave 1 share to Ramulamma. Mukka Reddi owned seven plough bullocks, and the *kamatham* hired one plough bullock from a Komti and ploughed the land with four ploughs. The grain yield was divided into 7½ shares, after repayment of loans and deducting land revenue and charges for the hired bullock. Three shares were given to Mukka Reddi for the labour of his family members and his bullocks, and the remaining 5½ shares were divided among the nine other members of the *kamatham*.

Another big *kamatham* was that of Mamidi Pandaya. In this *kamatham* were three families besides the family of Pandaya. Two were those of his younger brothers, and the third family was that of his father's sister's son. All had contributed land and cultivated it together with three ploughs. One bullock was contributed by Pandaya, three bullocks by his brother Ganga Raju, two bullocks by his father's sister's son, while the youngest brother did not contribute any plough bullocks. The grain yield was divided into five shares, each family getting one share irrespective of its contribution of plough bullocks, and one share was given to Pandaya's mother, who lived separately.

Before the abolition of the *zamindari* system, the village was part of Gutala estate. Then none of the Reddis had individual ownership rights over the land, as all the cultivable land was held by the village community as a whole. However, during this period the Reddis recognized the right of a family over the land on which it had cleared the forest, and no one else cultivated it without the permission of that family. We do not know how land revenue was collected while the Reddis were practising shifting cultivation, but ever since they have taken up plough cultivation, the land revenue assessed for the village as a whole has been collected from each *kamatham* on the basis of the number of ploughs it used to cultivate the land.

All the tamarind trees and toddy palms of the village were also owned communally. Each family participated in the tamarind harvest and got an equal share. The village council allotted to each family a certain number of toddy palms for tapping toddy and cutting the leaves for thatching purposes. None had a right to sell either palm leaves or the trees for other purposes. This communal ownership over the land and the tamarind trees and toddy palms remained unchanged even after the abolition of the *zamindari* system, for the village as a whole was assessed for purposes of revenue collection.

The state government recently completed a surevy of the agricultural land in the village. In 1974, the revenue authorities issued titles(*patta*) of individual ownership to the Reddis for the land on which the forest was cleared either by the present cultivator or by his father. Since then, the state has been collecting land revenues directly from the individual owners, according to the acreage by each family.

Ever since individual ownership rights were granted, those Reddis on whose land there are tamarind trees and toddy palms have enjoyed the usufruct of these trees. With the exception of the tamarind trees standing on the village site, all trees have thus become the private property of the owners of the land. For the first time palm leaves acquired an exchange value, and all those who have no land or insufficient numbers of palms purchase leaves needed for thatching from those who have a surplus of leaves. As the trunks of the toddy palms are used in building houses, few Reddis have sold them to the nontribals of nearby villages. While I was staying in the village, three families sold to timber merchants five mango trees standing on their lands for Rs 100 each.

The concept of private property which has crept into the Reddi economy of this village, coupled with contacts with outsiders, is eroding the authority of the headman and the village council. Boli Mukka Reddi, the headman of the village, confessed to me that of late nobody was listening to him. There were latent divisions within the village community due to unresolved quarrels which had taken place in the recent past.

One such quarrel occurred between Mamidi Kannaya and the other villagers over the usufruct of eleven tamarind trees which were standing on the former village site. Until the year before, the usufruct of these trees was enjoyed by all the Reddi families of the village. But

Kannaya refused to share the yield of these trees because he had been given the ownership rights over the former village site, and he alone was paying land revenue for it. This infuriated all the other Reddis, but they did not take the issue to the village council because other owners of tamarind trees did not share their tamarind trees with the entire village either. Since then Mamidi Kannaya has been socially boycotted by others and is not invited to marriages or other social gatherings.

Another quarrel resulting in some sort of social boycott took place at the time of the mango festival. The youths of the village wanted to hire a record player for the mango festival and began collecting Rs 5 from each family. A few resented the collection of the money but did not object openly. Mamidi Mukkaya, though contributing Rs 5, commented that the money was being collected for the purpose of buying drink. All those who were collecting the money got angry and a quarrel took place. However, it subsided after the intervention of others. A few months later, when a pig of Mukkaya's entered the field of Boli Mukka Reddi's *kamatham*, a young man who had taken an active part in the collection of money for the mango festival and was one of the members of the *kamatham* killed it with an arrow. Mukkaya, who was convinced that he would not get justice, did not take the matter to the headman and the village council. Besides these two quarrels, there were also some disputes between members of certain *kamatham* over the distribution of the grain yields.

ALTERNATIVE SOURCES OF INCOME

The Reddis of all hill settlements weave bamboo baskets and winnowing fans during the rainy season. On an average each adult male can weave five winnowing fans in a week and can sell each winnowing fan either for Rs 2 or for 1½ kilograms of sorghum millet in plains villages. In Pandirimamidigudem only two Reddis know the art of weaving baskets, and these two have moved there from the hills.

During the summer months the women cut broomstick grass, tie it into bundles, and sell these to the daily requirement depot of the Girijan Corporation, which pays Rs 10 for every one hundred broomsticks. The women also collect small quantities of soapnut, available in the vicinity of the village. Another source of income for the Reddis of this village is tamarind. After harvesting the tamarinds, they exchange them for rice, either in the shops of Komtis or in the Girijan depot.

During the 1950s, when the forest coups were auctioned, the Reddis of this settlement worked for forest contractors. But due to indiscriminate felling and the pressure on cultivable land, the forest in the vicinity of the village disappeared. However, on the nearby hills there is still some secondary forest.

With the growth of world demand for Virginia tobacco grown on light soils, the area on which Virginia tobacco is cultivated increased sharply in the upland non-tribal areas of the district. The amount of firewood needed for curing Virginia tobacco also increased, and to meet the demand for firewood the government began the extraction of firewood through its logging division. During the winter months a few Reddis worked in firewood coups located near neighbouring villages and were paid Rs 3.50 per cubic meter of wood. However, earnings from this source were meagre because of the distance of the coups from the villages.

Due to a great demand for firewood for curing Virginia tobacco, a few merchants from the plains began smuggling the wood from this area with the connivance of forest guards and petty officials of the department. Through the carpenter who lives in the village, the smugglers employed the Reddis of this settlement for felling the wood and loading it into trucks. The smugglers paid Rs 150 per truck-load of wood felled and Rs 20 for loading it into the trucks.

In small groups, the Reddis cut this wood for the smugglers during the winter season. Initially, when there were large orders for felling such wood seventeen men formed themselves into a group and felled six truck-loads. Besides felling these six loads of wood, the members of the group loaded another forty truck-loads of wood felled by others. Later on, the group split up into smaller ones and felled wood, anticipating a demand for it, but only a few could sell the firewood cut by them because the demand had slackened.

THE ROLE OF MERCHANTS IN THE VILLAGE

The first non-tribal who settled in Pandirimamidigudem was a merchant of Komti caste from Jangareddigudem. In 1952 he established the first petty provision store in this region, and at that time he was almost a pauper. Initially he sold millet, rice, salt, chillies, and other commodities of daily use to the Reddis and Koyas in exchange for tamarind, soapnut, and other minor forest produce. Gradually he began giving grain on loan and got repaid by deliveries of minor forest produce.

Once he had established himself, he began advancing grain loans on interest, besides purchasing castor, sesamum, and other cash crops from the tribals. With the easy availability of credit, the Reddis of this settlement and the Koyas of neighbouring villages began taking millet and rice on credit during years of bad harvests and to tide them over family crises such as marriages or funerals. Later he also gave cash loans to Reddis and Koyas who pledged their future harvest of oil-seeds or kidney beans.

If a Reddi takes on loan one bag (120 kilograms) of millet from the Komti, he has to repay a bag of millet (the actual loan) in addition to half a bag (60 kilograms) of millet as interest. Often the crops are bad, and once a Reddi gets indebted to the Komti he cannot extricate himself, because he pays more than half of the current year's harvest to clear off the previous year's loan and again falls back on the Komti to bridge the food gap till the next harvest. By giving these food loans the Komti controls the entire agricultural economy of the village. An example will demonstrate this.

During 1977, the Komti settled in the village advanced 325 kilograms of rice and 2,600 kilograms of millet to the Reddis of Pandirimamidigudem alone. The Reddis would have had to repay to the Komti 490 kilograms of rice and 3,900 kilograms of millet, including interest, to clear off their debts at the time of harvest. Due to a cyclone the crops failed, and the millet yield was negligible. The Reddis repaid only 965 kilograms of millet out of 3,900 kilograms (including interest) by giving the Komti 225 kilograms of castor, 125 kilograms of soap-nuts, 1,440 kilograms of kidney beans, and 65 kilograms of millet. They still owed 2,836 kilograms of millet and 490 kilograms of rice, which multiplied to 4,260 kilograms of millet and 735 kilograms of rice by the next year's harvest.

Until five or six years ago this Komti was the only merchant in the region either to give grain loans or to purchase kidney beans and oil-seeds from Reddis and Koyas. Using his monopoly position he dictated prices whenever he purchased minor forest produce or grain from the tribals.

Until the Girijan Corporation established a depot in the village, he was the only merchant who purchased minor forest produce from the tribals living in this area. He bought such produce at rock-bottom prices and sold it at an enormous profit in the market of Jangareddigudem. Even recently, in spite of the prohibition of private purchase of minor forest produce from tribals, he bought substantial amounts of tamarind and soapnut by giving the Reddis advances of grain. With the connivance of the clerk of the daily requirement depot, he transported such produce to the nearest town.

From the early 1970s onwards, when the armed squads of Naxalites began operating in this area, he reduced the scale of his operations. But by that time he was believed to own property worth Rs 300,000—400,000 in Jangareddigudem. He told me that the Reddis and Koyas of the surrounding villages still owned him grain worth Rs 20,000. In the absence of alternative sources of credit, the Reddis and Koyas have a high regard for the Komti because he came to their rescue in periods of crisis. In spite of his exploitation of Reddis and Koyas, it must be held to the credit of this particular Komti that, unlike many other merchants in similar circumstances, he did not grab any of the Reddis' land.

KORUTURU

Koruturu village lies on the right bank of the Godavari River below the gorge area, at a distance of about forty kilometers from Polavaram, the headquarters of the taluk and the community development block of the same name. Towards the end of the nineteenth century, the government began auctioning the rights to extract bamboo and timber from the hills flanking the river, and since then the Reddis of this settlement have come in contact with the non-tribals of the coastal plains. Communications between Koruturu and the outside world are excellent when compared with those of the hill and other plains settlements of the Reddis. The village can be reached throughout the year from Rajahmundry, a big market town in the coastal plains, and by motor-boats which ply up to Bhadrachalam, an important Hindu temple town. During the dry season one can also reach the village from Polavaram by jeep, as a fair weather road was built in the early 1960s.

The inhabitants of Koruturu were exclusively Reddis and Koyas until 1936. Then there were about twenty-five to thirty houses. In 1937, the first non-tribal, a clerk of one of the bamboo and timber merchants by name of Satyam, settled in the village, and has been living there since. The second non-tribal came to the village to establish his permanent residence fourteen years later. The composition of the village population has undergone substantial changes in the last two decades, and in 1978, when I was in the village, there were seventy-four households, with a population of 236. The Reddis were the major ethnic group, with a population of 129, and lived in thirty-four households. There were fourteen Koya families, and their population was 43. The rest of the families, numbering twenty-six, were non-tribals. With a total strength of 64, they represented 27.6 percent of the village population.

The influx of non-tribals had already begun when the village was brought into the ambit of the tribal development activities of the goverment in 1961. In that year a primary school was established, and in 1972 this was turned into a ashram school. In the early 1960s a forest guard and a forest watcher were posted in the village, and a forest rest house was built. In 1969 the postal department opened a sub–post office in the village with a postmaster and a postman to assist him. In the same year a health worker was posted in the village to dispense medicines for malaria and other common ailments. Around this time a maternity and child care centre was established, and an auxiliary nurse-midwife was posted to advise the pregnant and lactating women. The Girijan Corporation set up a daily requirement depot in the village to make available cereals, salt, chillies, and other commodities at reasonable prices. A veterinary dispensary with a livestock inspector was opened in the village in 1973. I was told that during the years when bamboo is extracted from bamboo coups of the Papikonda reserved forest, the Andhra Paper Mills establishes its rice depot in the village, and a large number of non-tribal labourers imported by the agents of the paper mill reside in or near the village.

In the past the Reddis and Koyas of this village had a subsistence economy like that of any other Reddi settlement on the riverbank. Then the Reddis depended for food mainly on sorghum millet and other small millets raised on *podu* fields. Although the Reddis owned flat land and were cultivating it, they still paid great attention to their *podu* fields. During the bamboo-felling season, the Reddis worked for timber and bamboo merchants and were paid wages in kind. In lean periods the Reddis bridged their food gap by gathering a variety of wild roots, caryota pith, and mango kernels, and hence they did not have to take loans of food grain, a practice which is now the main cause of indebtedness.

In the past the Reddis who hired their labour to bamboo merchants received their wages mainly in the form of grain. They depended for all other commodities, such as clothing, salt, chillies, earthen pots, and iron implements, on the timber and bamboo merchants. Professor Fürer-Haimendorf in his book *The Reddis of the Bison Hills* described vividly the nefarious and exploitative activities of the timber and bamboo merchants. The tyranny of these merchants ended with the establishment of a labour cooperative society by the Swami of Parantapalli in the early 1940s. The Swami introduced payment of wages in cash to the Reddis who hired their labour to the cooperative society. During the years when the labour cooperative society was active, the society procured rice from Rajahmundry and made it available to the Reddis at reasonable prices. However, the grip of the timber merchants over the Reddis was only temporarily removed, for the labour cooperative society functioned only for a few years. In the early 1960s the government excluded these merchants from the bamboo and timber trade, and gave the Andhra Paper Mills a monopoly on the extraction of bamboo from the forests of this region. Since then the Reddis have been paid cash wages for work in the bamboo coups.

Due to long-standing contact with the outside world and particularly to the later influx of a large number of non-tribals into the village, the outlook and the value system of the Reddis of this settlement have changed substantially. Nowadays the Reddis name their children in the style of plains people, and educate them by sending them to school. When I was in the village, almost all the children between six and fourteen years old were enrolled in the ashram school. A few boys and girls who had completed their studies in the village school went to Kandrukota village a few miles further downstream and sought admission to the upper primary school. Some Reddis now employ the services of a Brahmin priest to officiate at marriage ceremonies and pay him a fee. The hiring of record players and the decoration of houses with paper flowers have become common practices.

In the last fifteen years major shifts in dietary habits have taken place, and now Reddis rarely dig for wild tubers. For all practical purposes, they have given up eating wild roots, caryota pith, and mango kernels. Only those six families who still have *podu* fields consume sorghum millet, that, too, for only a short period in a year, for rice is widely available and is generally preferred to other food grains. At funerals and weddings rice, as the more prestigious food, is served to the guests, and the serving of sorghum millet on such occasions is looked down upon. These changes in the dietary habits, the engaging of the services of Brahmin priests for the performance of marriage rites, and the hiring of record players, coupled with general inflation, have pushed up the cost of marriage and death ceremonies and have made the Reddis vulnerable in periods of a crisis in the family. The impact of these changes on the Reddi economy will be discussed below.

With the increasing monetisation of the economy, cattle, goats, and pigs, which in the past had only a use value, have acquired an exchange value. Raising goats for sale in the market has become a common practice. Occasionally, surplus plough bullocks and cows are also sold by Reddis.

Based on the role they play in the economy of the Reddis and Koyas, the non-tribals of the village can be classified into three categories: (1) government and semi-government employees, (2) traders, agricultural labourers, and others rendering services, and (3) cultivators.

There are ten families of government employees in the village. Three of these are Koyas and one is a Reddi. With the exception of the forest guard and the forest watcher, none of the non-tribal government employees has any role in the village economy. All these employees are outsiders, and they stay in the village only as long as they are not transferred to some other place. Both the forest guard and the watcher regularly extort cash and chickens from the Reddis and Koyas on the plea that the tribals illegally use timber for making ploughs, and in addition they collect money whenever a Reddi or Koya builds a new house. Such fees are collected even though government orders allow tribals the use of forest produce for domestic purposes.

In the second category of non-tribals there are eleven families, but among these only one, a single woman, plays a significant role in the economy of the Reddis and Koyas. She was the concubine of a motor-boat owner and was brought by him to the village a few years ago. She is involved in the firewood business, and is an agent of the fire-wood smugglers of Rajahmundry. She purchases rice, chillies, and to-bacco from Polavaram and advances them to needy Reddis and Koyas. They gather firewood from the forest, cut it up, and make it into bun-dles, which they supply to her at a rate of half a rupee per bundle weighing fifteen to twenty kilograms. This woman sells the firewood for Re 1 a bundle to the merchants of Rajahmundry, who come in sailing boats once in a week or ten days to collect the firewood and smuggle it to the markets of Rajahmundry by bribing the forest guards and other petty officials posted in riverside villages.

Every third year the bamboo coups in the vicinity of Koruturu are not worked, and during these years, when no regular forest labour is available, most Reddis work mainly for the agents of firewood smug-glers. On an average each worker cuts sufficient firewood for fifteen bundles in a day if he works from morning to evening and for about five bundles if he works for only a few hours. In the year in which I stayed in Koruturu, the forest guard collected one bundle of firewood once a week from all the Reddis and Koyas engaged in cutting fire-wood and sold it to the same firewood smugglers for Re 1 per bundle.

Out of the remaining ten non-tribal households, two are those of single women who run tea shops; their customers are mainly the other non-tribals living in the village. Occasionally the Reddis, too, buy tea and other eatables from these shops. Another non-tribal in this category is a Muslim from Kerala who came a few years ago and set up a provision store. Ten years ago an evangelist of the Christian mission at Narsapur was posted in the village, but he has failed to convert any of the tribals. He does not have any stake in the village economy and depends for his livelihood exclusively on the salary which he receives from the mission. One of the non-tribals is a car-penter cum smith, whom the non tribal cultivators employ for mak-ing agricultural implements, such as ploughs and harrows. The Reddis employ him for affixing plough-shares to the ploughs made by them and for making arrow-heads. Two non-tribals are washermen, who launder the clothes of the non-tribals for a small fee besides engaging themselves as casual agricultural labourers. All the other non-tribals in this category are casual agricultural labourers.

The third category of non-tribals, the cultivators, though only five in number, plays an important role in the village economy, for they control the major part of the cultivable flat land. In 1978, out of 150 acres of flat agricultural land available in the village, 119 acres were cultivated by them. They raised tobacco on 36 acres, chillies on 35 acres, kidney beans on 23 acres, black gram (*Phaseolus mungo*) on 15 acres, and paddy on 18 acres. However, none of these five cultivators owns any land in the village.

Although non-tribals lived in the village in the past, they were basically interested in the bamboo and timber trade, and none of them had any interest in agriculture, as then the price of sorghum millet and other pulses in the markets of the plains was not attractive. In the early 1960s, the period when private merchants were displaced from the bamboo trade coincided with an increasing demand for chillies in the outside markets. During this time many clerks of the former bamboo and timber merchants living in the riverside villages switched over to commercial agriculture.

Although the first non-tribal settled in Koruturu as early as 1936, he did not engage in cultivation until the 1950s, when he began to raise paddy for consumption and kidney beans on a small area for sale. He took up the growing of cash crops in 1968, after having failed in some business enterprise in the plains. The second non-tribal, who came to the village in 1954 to set up a provision store, was the first non-tribal to cultivate part of the village land. He told me that then he used to raise black gram, kidney beans for the market, and paddy for consumption. Between them these two non-tribals cultivated not more than twenty-five to thirty acres of land in the village. During this period, some other non-tribals who lived in the village for shorter periods did not cultivate any land, as they were exclusively engaged in the bamboo business.

The first non-tribal who migrated to this village with the sole intention of cultivating chillies and tobacco arrived in 1967. Later other non-tribals took up the cultivation of tobacco and chillies, and by 1978 two Reddis began raising those cash crops. Although none of the non-tribals owns land in the village, in the past ten years they were never short of land for cultivation. In fact, in the early 1970s, when the demand for Virginia tobacco increased phenomenally, they had invested substantial amounts of money by building six tobacco-curing barns in the village.

The following examples will show the process by which the land passes from the Reddis and Koyas into the hands of non-tribals.

Katmuri Virapa Reddi owns 5 acres of land, a pair of bullocks, and two cows. His son-in-law migrated to the village, as Virapa Reddi had only a daughter. Until 1973, he, along with his wife, daughter, and son-in-law, cultivated his land and raised sorghum millet, kidney beans, and green gram. Then the family consumed sorghum millet and green gram and used to sell black gram for cash. Once Virapa's crop failed, and he borrowed Rs 75 from a non-tribal for consumption. He gave half of his land for three years to that non-tribal cultivator in lieu of this loan. After three years when the lease period was over, Virapa's wife died. This time he had to borrow Rs 400 to celebrate the death ceremony. To repay the amount he again leased out this land for four more years. A year later in 1975 his brother passed away. Once again he had to borrow money for performing his brother's death ceremony. This time he leased out the remaining 2½ acres of his land to another non-tribal for four years for Rs 300. Since then the members of the family are surviving by hiring their labour to the paper mills in the bamboo-felling season and to the non-tribal cultivators at other times. In 1978, Anna Rao, the grandson of Virapa Reddi, was working as a permanent farm servant for one of the non-tribal cultivators on a salary of Rs 1,000 a year.

Konla Chinnabhai and Somi Reddi are brothers. Though they live in separate houses they together own three acres of land. They own neither plough bullocks nor cows. Until 1970 the land was cultivated by them jointly along with their father. To celebrate Somi Reddi's marriage, the father then borrowed Rs 560 from one of the non-tribal cultivators and leased out his land for nine years. The lease period ended in 1978. But in 1977 two acres of land had been given for share-cropping to another non-tribal cultivator for the agricultural year 1978–79. The father died in 1977, and to celebrate the death ceremony they had borrowed a bag of rice worth Rs 175 and Rs 70 in cash for purchasing a goat. The non-tribal who was cultivating the land on the basis of sharecropping raised chillies on it, retaining 1½ shares of the yield and giving them 1 share, after deducting the costs of cultivation. Ever since the land was given on lease, the brothers have eked out their livelihood by hiring their labour to the paper mill, the non-tribal cultivators, and the agent of firewood smugglers. For the last two years, Chinnabhai's two sons, aged nineteen and twenty-one years, have worked as permanent farm servants in the employ of non-tribal cultivators for annual wages.

Kechala Chinna Reddi owns 1½ acres of land. He does not have plough bullocks but owns two cows. About ten years ago he leased out the land to a non-tribal, initially because he had to borrow money to celebrate his father's death ceremony. Before the lease period was over, he borrowed again to bridge the food gap in the lean season by giving the land on lease for a further period. Since then, every year he has been borrowing grain from the same non-tribal in the lean season and has never resumed cultivation. His wife works as a casual labourer in the fields of the non-tribals, and he cuts bamboo during the bamboo-felling season and transports it to the riverbank by yoking his cows. In 1978 he was hewing firewood and was selling it to the agent of the firewood smugglers.

The three examples cited above show that in periods of crisis in the family, such as marriage or death, the Reddis borrow money from non-tribals to tide over their difficulties by leasing out their land. There is an increasing discrepancy between the Reddis' resources and the expenditures which contact with more advanced communities encourages them to make at social occasions, such as weddings and funerary rites. At these times they now have no other choice than to borrow money or grain. When a Reddi or Koya approaches a non-tribal with the request for a loan, he has to mortgage some of his land, and the period of lease is fixed by the lender, depending upon the amount asked and the urgency of the borrower's need. In the past, also, the Reddis used to mortgage their labour to merchants, who at that time were interested in hiring as many Reddis as possible for work in forest coups. In the lean season the Reddis used to depend heavily on wild mango kernels, caryota pith, and tamarind seed to bridge the food gap. In 1978 only three families did not lease out their land, and five other families leased out part of the land they owned. These eight families cultivated only 19 out of 150 acres of flat land owned by them in the village. All the rest of the families owning land had either leased out their land or were sharecropping with non-tribals.

One might think that the Reddis would resume cultivation of the land owned by them upon the expiration of the lease period. But in practice, the Reddis are unable to resume cultivation because their savings from wages earned from forest labour are negligible, and they are short of food during the rainy season when no wage labour is available. The change in their dietary habits forces them to depend on the consumption loans readily made available by the non-tribal cultivators. Although the demand for wage labour has increased with the extension of the cultivation of tobacco and chillies, not all the adults in the village get employment even for six months in a year. Furthermore, the demand for agricultural wage labourers is seasonal. The agricultural practices followed by the non-tribal cultivators are described below and indicate the months during which the Reddis are employed and the number of days they are employed.

This area receives one or two pre-monsoon showers in the month of May. From this time on, the non-tribal cultivators begin preparatory tilling of the land. During May to August or September, the land in which tobacco and chillies are raised is ploughed five or six times, depending on the moisture in the soil, in order to control the growth of weeds. Transplanting of tobacco seedlings begins in the first or second week of September and extends up to the first week of October. Chillies are transplanted from the last week of October until the end of November. The land is tilled again crosswise four or five times just before the transplanting. Ploughing the land is the exclusive task of men, and they plough in the forenoons from 6:00 A.M. to 11:00 A.M.

For transplanting, both men and women are employed. The task of the men is to mark the soil into rows and to make small holes with digging sticks, into which the women transplant the seedlings. Care is taken in maintaining a definite spacing between each row and each plant. Both men and women are employed to carry water from the nearby hill streams in pots for watering the transplanted seedlings. Chemical fertilizer is mixed in the water carried in the pots before watering the plants.

A week or ten days later, by which time the seedlings are well established in the soil, the land is ploughed between the rows to control the growth of weeds. This operation is repeated after an interval of approximately a week or ten days. Each time the land is ploughed between the rows, two women are employed to replant the plants uprooted by the plough.

In addition to the time of ploughing between the rows to control the growth of weeds, women are twice employed for weeding in both tobacco and chilli fields. Ten days after transplanting, tobacco fields are watered once again, employing female labour. The chilli fields are only watered once in December if there are no rains at all. Towards the end of November or the beginning of December, diesel engines are fixed for lifting water from hill streams, and the tobacco fields are watered in between each plucking of the leaf. A man is employed to channel the water each time the field is irrigated. During this period, only men are employed for plant protection measures, such as dusting or spraying of pesticides.

Harvesting of tobacco begins in the middle of January and extends until the end of February. The leaf is plucked five or six times with an interval of eight days. During this period, male and female labour is imported from Guntur District, and the plucking of the leaf is given to these labourers on a contract basis. For curing the leaf, also, the experts from Guntur are employed. After the leaf is cured, Reddi and Koya men and women are employed for grading.

Harvesting of chillies begins at the end of January and extends up to April. On an average, each field is picked eight times, and only female labour is employed for this purpose. After each picking, the chillies are dried and graded before being packed in bags.

The total labour required for the cultivation of one acre of Virginia tobacco is about forty-four man-days and forty-nine woman-days. This estimate includes thirteen ploughing operations extended over six months , transplanting, watering of seedlings, weeding, and grading the cured leaf.

The total labour required for the cultivation of one acre of chillies is estimated to be 35 man-days and 103 women-days, covering thirteen ploughing operations performed at various times, transplanting of seedlings, watering of young plants, weeding, replanting of plants up-rooted during weeding with ploughs, picking the chillies, and grading them.

The labour employed to grow tobacco on thirty-six acres thus adds up to 1,764 woman-days and 1,584 man-days, and the labour required for the cultivation of thirty-five acres under chillies totals 3,605 woman-days and 1,355 man-days. The figure 1,355 includes 130 man-days required for the preparation of five nurseries in which the seedlings are grown. Out of the total village population of 236, 67 men and 61 women hire their labour for wages, and among them 7 men and 6 women are non-tribals. If we exclude the labour employed by the non-tribals for cultivating paddy, kidney beans, and black gram, which is negligible, then on an average a woman gets employment for about 90 days and a man for about 45 days in a year. During the months when bamboo is extracted in the vicinity of the village, men hire their labour mostly to the paper mills. As the demand for both agricultural and forest labour is during the winter and summer seasons, the Reddis of this settlement are unemployed in the rainy season. Because of the change in their dietary habits, they approach the non-tribal cultivators for consumption loans. In order to retain the land of the Reddis and Koyas for cultivation, these non-tribal cultivators advance the loans and ask the Reddis to extend the lease period.

In the past few years, the Reddis of this settlement have become conscious of the Andhra Pradesh (Scheduled Areas) Land Transfer Regulation of 1959 due to the activities of the Naxalite armed squads and to conflicts among the non-tribals. Now they know that the non-tribals cannot grab their land. The presence of the armed squads of the Naxalites in the area also instilled fear in the non-tribals and acted to deter attempts to acquire ownership of tribal land. In the past few years, the non-tribal cultivators have adopted a novel method for retaining the land of the Reddis and Koyas for raising tobacco and chillies. On the expiration of the lease periods, these non-tribals enter into agreements with the Reddis for sharecropping, on the condition that the entire cost of cultivation be borne by them and the yields be distributed according to a ratio of 1½ : 1; 1½ shares to the non-tribal cultivator, and 1 share to the tribal landholder. The other conditions are that the landowner pay the land revenue, that the non-tribal give first preference in the employment of labourers to those families from which he has taken the land, and that he advance grain and cash whenever required by the Reddis and settle the accounts after the crops are sold.

I could not estimate how much the Reddis have benefited from these agreements, as they did not remember the grain they took as advance in a year, and they also did not know the cost of cultivation of the commercial crops raised in their fields. The non-tribal cultivators evaded showing me their accounts whenever I requested them to let me see the books. Under these circumstances, I suspect that the non-tribals are cheating the Reddis by falsifying the account books.

In 1969, the wages paid to the agricultural labourers were very low. A woman received Re 1.25 for a day's work, and a man received Rs 2 per day. The Naxalites, who became active in this area in the late 1960s, began organizing the forest labour working in the hills for increasing the wages for felling bamboo. They also organized tribals in nearby villages and gave a strike call for increasing agricultural wages. Though the Reddis of Koruturu did not go on strike, the non-tribals increased the wages paid to women from Rs 1.25 to Rs 4.00 and for men from Rs 2 to Rs 5 due to the fear of reprisals from the armed squads of the Naxalites.

A timber merchant who lived in the village during a short period in the 1950s managed to get about five acres of the land owned by Chandala Lacchi Reddi's father transferred to his name in the land registers. No one in the village knows whether this merchant really purchased the land or whether he manipulated the register of land rights in his favour. None of the Reddis was aware of this transfer, and the merchant in question never cultivated the land. Lacchi Reddi's father cultivated this land as long as he was alive, and Lacchi Reddi inherited it after his father's death.

In 1966, this merchant, who presently lives in Polavaram, leased out the land for Rs 3,000 for six years to another non-tribal by name of Krishna of Purshothapatnam village in the plains. In 1967, Krishna came to Koruturu to take possession of the land for cultivating chillies. But Lacchi Reddi, who had been cultivating the land, resisted and threatened that he would kill Krishna if he attempted to enter the field.

Krishna appealed to the *pedda kapu* and the other elders in the village. The Reddis took pity on Krishna, as he had already paid Rs 3,000 for the lease to the merchant who claimed ownership of the land. They decided that Lacchi Reddi should allow Krishna to cultivate about three acres of the land for six years and that Krishna should give preference to the family members of Lacchi Reddi when employing casual labourers. Bothe Krishna and Lacchi Reddi agreed to the conditions imposed by the village elders, and Krishna began cultivating the land. Lacchi Reddi died before the lease period was over, and Lacchi Reddi's widow gave the remaining two acres of land cultivated by her husband on lease to Krishna, as her son Devi Reddi was too young to handle a plough.

The merchant who claimed ownership of the land sold it to Satyam, the first non-tribal to settle in the village, for Rs 6,000 in 1972, a year before the expiration of the lease period. In 1973, Satyam took possession of the land from Krishna. Lacchi Reddi's widow and other elderly Reddis in the village remained silent spectators when the transfer of land took place, as they did not know the procedure for appealing to the government about the alienation of land. Krishna thereupon developed a grudge against Satyam, as the land had passed from his hands.

To become popular among the Reddis, Krishna suggested that they construct a temple to the Hindu god Sri Rama by raising funds in the village and by collecting Rs 200 for each tobacco-curing barn owned by the non-tribals. He volunteered to contribute the additional amount for building the temple. To prevent Krishna from becoming popular among the Reddis, Satyam, who owns two tobacco-curing barns, refused to contribute the Rs 400 for constructing the temple. This incident further infuriated Krishna.

After failing in this attempt, Krishna continued his search for means of gaining popularity. He found that Konla Jogi Reddi, the *sarpanch* of the village, was suffering losses in arrack sales because of undermeasurement of the alcohol supplied by the tribal arrack cooperative society. He took Jogi Reddi to Polavaram and asked the president of the arrack cooperative society to correct the measures. When the president of the society refused to correct the measures, Krishna lodged a complaint about him with the excise officials.

When there was no effect even after complaining to the officials, Krishna persuaded Jogi Reddi to stop selling the alcohol supplied by the society. He organized the Reddis and the Koyas in the village into a cooperative to procure and sell liquor illicitly brewed in Kondamodalu village on the other bank of the river. The Reddis persuaded Satyam to participate in the venture also and informally selected Krishna, Satyam, Jogi Reddi, and Karukunda Mutyala Reddi, assigning tasks to each of them. Krishna agreed to contribute the initial investment for procuring the liquor, and he was asked to look after the procurement. Satyam was assigned the task of maintaining the accounts. Mutyala Reddi and Jogi Reddi were to keep the cash, and another Reddi was appointed to sell the liquor procured by this committee. The business went on smoothly for two months, and there was a profit of Rs 3,000 which was distributed among all the tribal families. But when Mutyala Reddi was ill, Satyam and Krishna fell out over the management of the accounts, and the Reddis sided with Krishna. The latter, who had been waiting for an opportunity to humiliate Satyam, drew the Reddis' attention to the Land Transfer Act of 1959 and instigated them to file a petition of behalf of Chandla Devi Reddi against Satyam for purchasing the land from the former timber merchant.

Around this time, the district collector visited the village. The Reddis submitted a petition to the collector against Satyam and on behalf of Devi Reddi. The collector passed on the petition to the special deputy collector for tribal areas for suitable action. At the beginning of the 1976–77 agricultural year, the villagers prevented Satyam from tilling the land which he had purchased. However, neither the Reddis nor Satyam cultivated the land in that year. Soon after this incident, Devi Reddi received a summons from the special deputy collector. Krishna helped Devi Reddi to engage the services of an advocate to argue his case in the deputy collector's court. The deputy collector's court gave judgement in favour of Devi Reddi and restored the land to him. When I was in the village, Devi Reddi was cultivating the land restored to him, and Satyam had appealed the judgement to a higher court. In 1980 this appeal was still pending, leaving Devi Reddi in possession.

Though the non-tribals employ the Reddis as wage labourers, the relationship between them is not that of a master and servant. They attend each others' marriages and other social functions, and on the whole the social relations between them are cordial. The Reddis approach the non-tribals for advice whenever they have personal problems and take their help in matters connected with the government or other outside non-tribals.

THE FUTURE OF THE KONDA REDDIS

In the three case studies presented above, I have shown the changes that have occurred in three villages in the past four decades. Similar changes are taking place throughout the Konda Reddi country. The forest policy of the government is a major source of change in the hill settlements, and in the Reddi settlements on the riverbank and other settlements in lower Agency Tracts the principle agents of change are immigrant non-tribals.

To increase the dwindling area of forest in the country, the Forest Department has realigned the boundaries of the reserved forests. In the process, the officials of the Forest Department drew the boundary lines closer to the villages in many places, leaving a smaller area of unreserved forest for general use by the population. In Sukumamidi village of Khammam District, while redemarcating the reserved forest boundary the forest officials included some of the flat land which had been ploughed by the Reddis for the past twenty to twenty-five years and prohibited the Reddis cultivating that land. A similar incident took place in Ankampalem village, whose inhabitants are Koyas.

Due to the restriction of the area for *podu* cultivation and the increase in the population, the cycle of shifting cultivation has shortened, resulting in the total baldness of hill slopes near a few Reddi settlements. For example, all the hill slopes around Thandepalli village have bocome completely bare due to these restrictions. The yield from the *podu* fields is likely to decrease due to insufficient time given for the regeneration of the bush.

The Forest Department, to meet the raw material requirement of the Andhra Paper Mills and the growing demand for firewood and timber in the markets of the coastal plains, began the extraction of bamboo and timber from the forests of the northern hills on a large scale starting in the early 1960s. The laying of roads in the hills to transport forest produce has broken the isolation of many hill settlements. Today most of the 370 Reddi settlements of this area can be reached by jeep during the dry season.

The state government entered into an agreement with the Andhra Pradesh Rayon Factory in Mulug Taluk of Warangal District to supply eucalyptus wood, its raw material, in sufficient quantities. To honour this commitment, the Forest Department has begun a programme of planting eucalyptus on a large area in the Northern Hills.

Although the work in these plantations provides an alternative source of employment and cash income for the Reddis, the policy of extending plantations is not free from harmful effects on the life-style and economy of the Reddis. The lure of cash income is diverting the Reddis' attention from the *podu*, as well as the flat land, fields, and this results in a reduction in grain yields. For instance, the Reddis of Bodlanka village have been engaged in forest labour for the past three years, and Pallala Ram Reddi, the *sarpanch* of the village, told me that the grain yield is falling because most of his kinsmen are paying less attention to their fields than they used to do because of the temptation to earn cash. He further told me that nowadays they have to walk longer distances to collect wild roots and tubers during the lean seasons because the natural forest is cleared in the vicinity of the village to raise plantations of eucalyptus and teak.

Another policy of the government which has seriously affected the food supply of the Reddis in this area is the granting of the right to fell mango trees in the forest to the Godavari Plywood Factory set up in Rampachodavaram. The supply of kernels of mango stones, which are a main source of food for the Reddis during the rainy season, is dwindling due to the felling of this fruit tree on a large scale. The agitated Reddis appealed to the chief minister of the state when he visited Mar-

TABLE 5. *Land Alienation in the Tribal Areas of East Godavari District*

REVENUE CIRCLE	NUMBER OF VILLAGES	NUMBER OF NON-TRIBALS OCCUPYING TRIBAL LANDS	EXTENT OF LAND UNDER THE OCCUPA-TION OF NON-TRIBALS (IN ACRES)
Rampachodavaram Taluk			
Rampachodavaram	130	1,357	6,651.07
Dcvipatnam	72	735	4,689.60
Yellavaram Taluk			
Addateegala	192	1,138	10,169.32
Rajavommangi	62	1,103	8,665.49
Pidathamamidi	174	1,094	3,667.53
TOTAL	630	5,431	38,805.01

adumilli in early 1979. But nothing had happened by the time I left the area in the middle of the year.

To protect the interest of the tribals, in 1917 the British government passed protective legislation prohibiting any transfer of tribal land to non-tribals without the consent of the agent of the government. Similar legislation was enacted by the Nizam's government in 1946 for the tribal areas of the then Hyderabad State. The Government of Andhra Pradesh in 1959 passed a land transfer regulation incorporating the 1917 act, and amended it in 1976 to prohibit any transfer of immovable property in scheduled areas by a non-tribal to another non-tribal.

Though these acts were in force, the non-tribals took advantage of the ignorance of the Reddis and grabbed almost all fertile alluvial land in the villages on the banks of the Godavari River. The process of alienation of land began quite early, and in Kondamodalu village considerable portions of plough land had passed into the hands of non-tribals by the time Fürer-Haimendorf visited these villages in 1941. Today, though most of the land is being cultivated by the non-tribals in the villages, the Koyas and Reddis have become conscious that the land belongs to them.

The condition of the Reddis in Anantaram and Timmalkunta villages in Sattupalli Taluk has worsened because the non-tribal cultivators who settled in these villages became legitimate owners of the land which they acquired from the Reddis before the enactment of protective legislation. The Reddis live on the outskirts of both these villages. Most of the adult Reddis have been working as farm servants for the non-tribals from their childhood and are much poorer than their counterparts living in the hills.

The figures in Table 5 on the alienation of land in the district were given to me by the special deputy collector (tribal welfare) of East Godavari District. The table shows the magnitude of the problem of land alienation in the tribal areas of the state.

Out of a total of 5,431 cases of non-tribal occupation of the tribal lands detected in the district up to 1 August 1977, the staff of the special deputy collector completed enquiries in 1,305 cases and filed *suo moto* suits against the non-tribals in the courts.

In the past the government never seriously implemented these acts to protect the tribals. Also, due to their ignorance a large number of tribals did not succeed in their attempts to resist the alienation of their land. For instance, when the Reddis of Teliberu village of East Godavari District filed petitions about the alienation of land by non-tribals before independence, the then deputy collector of the district did not take suitable action as he suspected that the Reddis were instigated by the nationalists. In the early 1970s, when the Reddis of this village once again filed petitions against the non-tribals, the government officials were under the impression that the Reddis were instigated by the Naxalites, and the cases had not been disposed of by the time I left the area.

The state government became aware of the need for implementing protective legislation in the early 1970s, when Naxalites began increasing their influence among the Reddis in this region, as wells among the tribes of Srikakulam, Visakhapatnam, Khammam, and some other districts.

The Naxalites organized many tribals against the exploitation of merchants and landlords. Thus, in 1969 they encourage the Reddis, Koyas, and Kammaras of Kondamodalu village and its thirteen hamlets to harvest the paddy fields occupied by non-tribals. This they did and carried away 680 bags of paddy. The police immediately swung into action, arrested large number of tribals, and filed cases against them. Many tribals were kept in jail pending disposal of the cases until 1975 or 1976. However, the government has since filed *suo moto* suits against the non-tribals of this village for occupying tribal lands in contravention of the Land Transfer Act.

In Kechaluru, another riverbank village inhabited exclusively by Kammaras, a small tribal community, in 1966 a non-tribal grabbed the tribals' land by falsifying documents. When the Kammaras resisted the land grab by killing a non-tribal, the police arrested all the adult males in the village and kept them in jail for ten months by refusing them bail. The cases against them dragged on for two years, though cases against the non-tribals for occupying tribal land were filed in the special deputy collector's court. In April 1979, the special deputy collector (tribal welfare) of East Godavari District gave judgement in favour of the Kammaras and restored their land.

Though the government has become active in restoring land to tribals, we do not know to what extent it will succeed, because most non-tribals are economically well off and are employing lawyers to defend their cases, while the tribals have no documents in their possession to prove their claim to the land and do not have the economic resources to employ lawyers to defend their cases.

Though the measures to rehabilitate the tribals were initiated by the government before independence, they were not effective. The efforts te develop them gained momentum from the third Five Year Plan on with the creation of tribal development blocks and the allocation of more funds. By the middle of 1970, a number of institutions were created in the Konda Reddi country for tribal development. During this period, the government laid 256 kilometers of road in the Konda Reddi area, besides setting up 122 primary schools and ashram schools to spread literacy among the Reddis. The state also prepared numerous plans for improving the condition of the Reddis. But lack of will on the part of the political leadership and rampant corruption prevalent at various levels of the bureaucracy have choked the flow of benefits to Reddis and other tribals.

The only ray of hope is the spread of literacy in the younger generation of Reddis due to the functioning of ashram schools. This makes them aware of the world around them and prepares them to accept innovations which may improve their lives. One must wait to see what will happen to the Reddis in the next twenty or thirty years.

11 Change and Development among Tribes of Arunachal Pradesh

REALISTIC ACCOUNTS of the fortunes and prospects of the majority of the tribal societies in Peninsular India may well create the impression that material impoverishment and the disruption of the traditional social fabric are unavoidable concomitants of the aboriginals' contact with economically and politically more advanced sections of the Indian population. Yet developments in other tribal areas of India present a very different and far less gloomy picture, and in this chapter I shall outline the emergence of Himalayan tribes from almost total isolation and their harmonious integration into the economic and political structure of the wider Indian society. The people in question are of Mongoloid race, speak Tibeto-Burman languages, and dwell in the highlands of the Subansiri District of Arunachal Pradesh. Until recently designated as North East Frontier Agency, this union territory, which extends from Assam to Tibet, always enjoyed a political status different from that of most other parts of India. In the days of British rule only a fraction of the territory was under regular administration, whereas the greater part was a political no man's land where feuding tribes lived in a state of complete autonomy.

When in 1944 I first entered the Subansiri region, so called after its main river, in the course of a mission aimed at exploring the tribal country beyond the control of the Governemnt of India,[1] I encoun-

1. The circumstances of that mission undertaken in the service of the Government of India are described in my book *Himalayan Barbary,* and my recommendations for the eventual administration and development of the area are contained in my report *Ethnographic Notes on the Tribes of the Subansiri Region.*

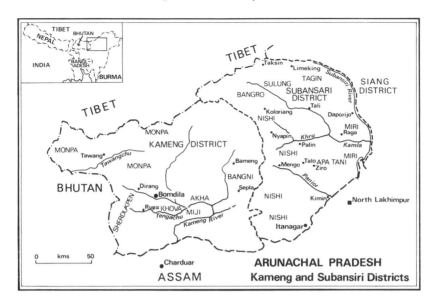

tered a tribe known as Apa Tani, which numbered then about 15,000 and had persisted for centuries in an archaic economy and self-contained social order uninfluenced by any outside power. Although the Apa Tanis had developed an exceedingly efficient system of rice cultivation which enabled them to produce a surplus of grain for barter with neighbouring tribes, they did not know the use of the plough, were unfamiliar with the wheel, and did not use their cattle for traction, carriage, or milking. Money had no place in their economy, and though a few men occasionally ventured to the fringe of the plains of Assam, not a single Apa Tani had a command of Assamese sufficient for effective communication. A few of the neighbouring Nishis had some knowledge of the Apa Tani dialect, and many Apa Tanis could follow the dialects of nearby Nishi villages, all these tongues being closely related Tibeto-Burman languages. In view of the Apa Tanis' geographical and cultural isolation, one might well have assumed that the obstacles in the path of their development and adjustment to the economic and social system of contemporary India would have been much greater than those impeding the progress of such tribal populations as the Gonds of the Deccan, who for generations have been in touch with advanced civilizations. Surprisingly, the economic and political progress of the Apa Tanis during the past thirty years belies any such supposition, and we are faced with the phenomenon of a rapid material, social, and educational development of a tribal society which has found a place in the modern world without so far losing its identity as a distinct ethnic entity.

In my recent book *A Himalayan Tribe: From Cattle to Cash*, I described in detail the transformation of the Apa Tanis during the years which followed the establishment of permanent links with the Indian administration in 1944 and 1945, and in this context I shall concentrate on the circumstances which account for the differences between the fortunes of the Apa Tanis and the fate of the tribal societies discussed in the foregoing chapters of this volume.

When the Government of India extended its administration over the region now known as Arunachal Pradesh, it continued the long-established policy of protecting the tribal populations inhabiting the hills which surround the plains of Assam against incursions and exploitative practices of people from the lowlands. Fundamental to this policy was the maintenance of the so-called "Inner Line," a boundary running along the foothills, which no plainsman was allowed to cross without a written permit. Inhabitants of the hills were free to cross this line in either direction, for there was no intention of keeping the hillmen within their territory, only of keeping the lowlanders out. In the days of British rule there was in nationalist quarters considerable criticism of the fact that Indian citizens should need special permission to enter any part of India, but it is to the credit of the leaders of post-independence India that they were realistic enough to retain the Inner Line policy in order to allow the tribesmen of Arunachal Pradesh to develop undisturbed by outsiders competing for the resources of the hill regions. The protection afforded to Apa Tanis and other tribes of Arunachal Pradesh by the Inner Line prevails to this day, and we shall see presently how great were the benefits which they derived from the breathing space provided by this policy.

The basis of traditional Apa Tani economy was agriculture, with animal husbandry and barter trade taking second and third place. The Apa Tanis are expert in growing several varieties of rice on terrace-fields irrigated by a complicated system of channels and ducts fed by streams and rivulets which flow from the surrounding wooded hills into the wide bowl of the Apa Tani Valley. At an altitude of close to 5,000 feet there is no possibility of growing two rice crops per year, but the Apa Tanis make the best of their irrigable land by planting both early- and late-ripening varieties of rice. Unlike many of their neighbours they do not grow rain-fed rice on hill slopes, but use arable dry land for the cultivation of millet, maize, potatoes, and various vegetables, many of which have recently been introduced by the administration. Apart from these they plant fruit trees, and carefully tend groves of bamboos and pine trees required as building material. The meticulous care with which the Apa Tanis have transformed the entire valley into a veritable garden, in which every square yard is put to a useful purpose, is one of the most striking characteristics of the

The Apa Tani Valley is filled with an intricate pattern of irrigated rice fields, while the villages lie on higher ground at the foot of the surrounding hills.

Apa Tani women, wearing home-woven jackets and skirts, weeding a rice field.

Street in a traditional Apa Tani village; the houses are built on piles and have verandahs in front and rear.

tribe, and one which distinguishes them from the much less systematic shifting cultivators in the surrounding hill regions.

Contact with the outside world and the growing familiarity of many young Apa Tanis with other regions of India have not led to any fundamental change in agricultural methods, and though Apa Tanis possess cows and bullocks, attempts to introduce ploughing have not met with any positive response. On the other hand Apa Tanis have eagerly taken to fish farming in the flooded rice fields, which provides the owners of fish ponds and suitable fields with a considerable cash income. Similarly, fruit farming, initially subsidized by government, has been developed most successfully. Some enterprising men have planted several thousand fruit trees and derive large profits from their orchard.

In traditional Apa Tani society a man's land-holding determined to a great extent his prestige and influence, and though new sources of wealth have developed, land is still a cherished possession, and rich men continue to invest in land though the yield in money terms is less than the rate of interest paid by the State Bank of India on deposit accounts. Previously land could be purchased only in exchange for cattle, but today Indian currency is widely accepted and most land sales are effected by cash transactions. In 1978 half an acre of irrigated

Street in Hapoli, the newly founded district headquarters in the Apa Tani Valley; shops and restaurants are frequented by Apa Tanis and Nishis.

land was worth about Rs 7,000–8,000, and for a large field near a village up to Rs 30,000–40,000 was paid. In assessing the significance of such cash transactions, it must be remembered that land can be passed only from one Apa Tani to another, for no outsider is permitted to acquire land.

When I first studied the Apa Tanis, none of them ever gave land on lease or hire, and sharecropping was unknown. Today, both leasing and sharecropping have taken root, and men engaged in trade outside the Apa Tani Valley let out their land on rent paid either in cash or as an agreed share of the crop. A novel feature of the agricultural economy is the employment of labourers paid cash wages. Previously most of the work on the fields was done by labour gangs, whose members worked on each others' fields in rotation. Rich men could hire such a gang by paying the workers in rice, but nowadays the payment is usually made in cash. The average daily wage in 1980 was Rs 5 for men and Rs 3 for women, and in either case a midday meal and ample quantities of rice beer were provided by the employer. For the heavy work of levelling fields, Rs 8 was paid, and during rush times adults earned daily wages of as much as Rs 10 to Rs 15. Wealthy landowners spent an annual average of Rs 3,000—4,000 on payments to agricultural labourers.

Apa Tani men and women on the verandah of a house; the men wear brass pins in their hair-knots.

Large sums of money are also paid for cattle, and particularly for *mithan* (*Bos frontalis*), the bovine which traditionally has the greatest prestige value, both as a sacrificial animal and as a medium of exchange. While in the latter role *mithan* have been replaced by cash, they still play an important role in ritual and as a source of meat. A full-grown *mithan* fetches nowadays a price of up to Rs 1,500. Ordinary Indian cattle (*Bos indicus*) are also increasingly kept by Apa Tanis. Many animals are bought in the plains of Assam and driven up to the Apa Tani Valley. Some are used for breeding, but all are ultimately destined for slaughter. Among the Apa Tanis there is an inexhaustible demand for beef, and many cows and bullocks are sold at a large profit to neighbouring Nishi or Miri tribesmen, who value beef no less than the Apa Tanis. There is also a flourishing trade in small pigs, purchased in the plains and brought by bus or truck to the Apa Tani Valley, where they are kept till full grown. Meat is an important item of the local diet, and there are not many parts of India where villagers eat meat as regularly as Apa Tanis do. In the old days Apa Tanis used to obtain livestock from Nishis in exchange for their surplus grain, and at the time of seasonal festivals hundreds of pigs were sacrificed, most of which had been supplied by Nishis.

There is still a limited trade between Apa Tanis and their tribal

Apa Tani women and children. The women wear nose-plugs of blackened wood, blue beads, and hand-woven cloths.

neighbours, but its economic importance has been eclipsed by the Apa Tanis' involvement in commercial exchanges with the people of the plains. They also earn cash by provisioning government employees posted in the hills and by working as contractors or in various other capacities for government agencies.

The headquarters of the Subansiri District, officially referred to as Ziro, is situated in the Apa Tani Valley on a site known as Hapoli. Since this place has been linked by an all-weather road with North Lakhimpur in the plains of Assam, Hapoli has grown into a township with a large bazaar offering a choice of goods hardly inferior to that found in any average Indian district headquarters. But whereas commercial centres in tribal areas of Peninsular India are invariably concentrations of non-tribal merchants, all the shops at Hapoli are owned by Apa Tanis, and no outsider is permitted to establish himself in any locality within the valley. The initial success of the many shops at Hapoli was largely due to the fact that hundreds of Apa Tanis were earning cash wages by being employed in road-building projects and other public enterprises. In the past twenty years there has been a great deal of construction work both inside the Apa Tani Valley and in the surrounding country, and Apa Tanis, who are disciplined and industrious, could easily compete with Nishis and Miris, neither of whom have a tradition of coordinated labour. No figures are publicly available for the total amounts spent by government on such undertakings, but one can well imagine how many millions of rupees must have been shelled out for the construction of all the mountain roads with permanent surface throughout the Subansiri District. Apa Tani contractors who could supply and control labour must certainly have earned a substantial share of the funds expended, for the experience of wealthy clan heads in directing the work of numerous slaves and hired labourers undoubtedly helped them in recruiting and controlling contract labour. There can be little doubt that it was the influx of government funds through the channels of wage payments which gave the first stimulus to the development of Hapoli as a commercial centre. The profits of contractors enabled Apa Tanis to establish and stock shops, and the wages earned by a broad stratum of Apa Tanis led to the emergence of an adequate clientele patronizing these shops. The explanation for the success of the relatively inexperienced Apa Tanis lies in the fact that government had barred outside merchants from engaging in trade in the hills. While in other parts of India Marwaris, Komtis, and members of other trading castes have infiltrated into most tribal areas and prevented the emergence of any indigenous merchant class, the Apa Tanis were saved from such competition and hence could establish their own business enterprises without being overshadowed from the start by more skilled and more aggressive traders and moneylenders.

While it is difficult to find out the volume of an individual's trading operations or to assess his capital resources, various indications suggest the general level of the trading community's affluence. In the branch of the State Bank of India in Hapoli about 1,200 tribesmen, most of whom are Apa Tanis, maintain current accounts, and in a good many of these there are balances of over Rs 100,000. Some time in 1978, a wealthy, middle-aged man who wanted to marry a young girl as his second wife was persuaded to open a joint account in his own name and that of his bride with an initial deposit of Rs 30,000. His willingness to do so indicates the affluence of some Apa Tani businessmen, an affluence which stands in stark contrast to the poverty of most tribal populations in other parts of India.

The Apa Tanis' success in the commercial field was facilitated by the rapid spread of education, which has led to the emergence of a class of businessmen capable of operating in an economy involving a measure of paperwork. While at the time of the Apa Tanis' initial contacts with representatives of government they hardly knew the meaning of literacy, as early as 1950 government schools were established in the valley, and this enabled children to obtain a sound education irrespective of parental means. In more recent years parents capable of paying fees have also sent children to independent schools outside Arunachal Pradesh. As a result of all these factors, educational progress has been rapid and literacy is now relatively high. After some years, when teaching had been first in Assamese and later in Hindi, student organizations put pressure on the Legislative Assembly of Arunachal Pradesh to adopt English as the medium of instruction at all levels of education beginning with primary schooling. This move greatly benefited those students who wanted to join universities and other institutions of higher education. Many were accepted for degree courses in a variety of subjects, and by the beginning of 1980 there were already forty-five Apa Tanis with university degrees, while many more students were enrolled in the universities of Gauhati, Dibrugarh, Shillong, and even Delhi. Most of the graduates entered government employment, and in 1978 no less than fifteen served in gazetted posts. Among them were fully qualified doctors and a pilot-officer in the Indian Air Force. If one contrasts this with the lamentable performance of the products of Gond schools in Andhra Pradesh—schools which were established a decade before the first Apa Tanis even began primary education—one realizes how disadvantaged the tribal people of Peninsular India are in comparison with the tribesmen on India's northeast frontier. It could be argued that the Government of India has provided very large funds for the development of a politically sensitive and strategically endangered zone close to the Chinese border, and that the Apa Tanis and other tribesmen of Arunachal Pradesh automatically benefited from the large expenditure in the region. Yet very substantial funds have also been sanctioned by the central government for tribal development in such states as Andhra Pradesh, but these grants were not spent in a manner conducive to bringing the intended benefits to the tribesmen.

One of the causes of the rapid economic and educational development of the Apa Tanis is their freedom from oppression and exploitation by more advanced communities. When the hill regions now forming Arunachal Pradesh were brought under the control of the Government of India, great care was taken not to disrupt the traditional social order, and from the very beginning efforts were made to build up a political structure which would allow the tribesmen to run their own affairs within the framework of the wider Indian political system. At first village and district *panchayats* were established, and local leaders emerging from these bodies were subsequently appointed as members of a Legislative Assembly which functioned on the lines of the assemblies of the Indian states. Arunachal Pradesh is at present a union territory with a political setup differing only in details

Modern Apa Tani couple; the husband, Kuru Hasang, was a fighter pilot in the Indian Air Force, the wife owns and manages a pharmacy in Hapoli.

from that of such states as Nagaland and Meghalaya. In February 1978, elections to the Legislative Assembly were held on the basis of universal franchise. Four Apa Tanis, all literate in English, stood as candidates in a constituency which included not only the Apa Tani Valley but also numerous Nishi villages. The candidate of the Janata Party won the seat and was subsequently elected speaker of the Legislative Assembly of Arunachal Pradesh. The ministry consists entirely of tribals from various regions of the union territory, and the making of policy thus lies almost entirely in the hands of tribal leaders. This situation, too, contrasts sharply with conditions in Andhra Pradesh, where the few tribal members of the Legislative Assembly, heavily outnumbered by Hindus and Muslims, are without power and influence, demonstrably unable to influence developments in the tribal areas and to protect their constituents against oppression by non-tribals.

In Arunachal Pradesh the tribesmen are masters in their own house, and after only thirty-six years of contact with government and an even shorter time when any kind of education was available, a very substantial share of government posts is already held by Apa Tanis. In 1978 there were not only 15 Apa Tani officers in gazetted posts, but 342 Apa Tanis served in non-gazetted posts. Of these 115

P. Ette, Circle Officer, Raga, and his wife, a school-teacher; both belong to the Adi tribe, which is closely akin to the Miris of Raga.

were posted in the Apa Tani Valley, while many worked in other localities in the Subansiri District, and the rest were dispersed over several districts of Arunachal Pradesh. This development, which indicates a progress not matched by any of the tribes of Peninsular India, is, moreover, cumulative, for men in government employment usually have both the opportunity and the incentive to send their children to good schools, with the result that in the next generation even more Apa Tanis will be qualified for posts demanding a mesasure of higher education.

Opponents of any special privileges for tribals, particularly of the exclusion of non-tribal settlers from tribal areas, often put forward the argument that tribals will advance only if they freely mix with other sections of the population. The experience in Arunachal Pradesh demonstrates that this argument is fallacious, for it is precisely the special protection afforded to the tribesmen by the Inner Line policy which has enable the Apa Tanis to achieve within one generation an advancement surpassing any achieved by those Indian tribals whose ancestral homeland has been infiltrated by members of the so-called progressive communities. Events such as the massive alienation of tribal land in Andhra Pradesh are unthinkable in any part of

Arunachal Pradesh, where the indigenous inhabitants are politically sufficiently conscious and powerful to safeguard their rights and to resist any exploitation by outsiders.

Some 15,000 Apa Tanis, constituting only a small percentage of the 467,511 inhabitants of Arunachal Pradesh, already occupy a position of influence and economic power completely out of reach of the more than 100,000 Gonds of Adilabad District, even though in the days of the Gond rajas the latter were a ruling race and long ago acquired such technological achievements as plough, wheel, and animal traction, which even one generation ago were foreign to the Apa Tanis and their tribal neighbours.

There have been changes in the Apa Tanis' social life, but these were gradual and none of them can be described as revolutionary. The Apa Tanis were never ruled by autocratic chiefs, but order was maintained by a system of clan elders and village councils entrusted with such tasks as the organization of seasonal rituals and feasts, mediation in disputes, and the punishment of criminals. Though this system was basically democratic, Apa Tani society was divided into two classes, which I have called patricians and commoners. These two classes were, and largely still are, endogamous, but under the influence of education and new opportunities for commoners in trade and government employment this endogamy seems to be breaking down. In recent years there have been some marital unions between patricians and commoners, though the couples involved still suffer from some discrimination. While a few commoners have become successful traders and have even gained political influence, the members of the leading patrician families have retained much of their wealth and influence. They were the first to take advantage of new educational facilities, and most of them are active in commerce. The most prominent Apa Tani politician, elected speaker of the Legislative Assembly of Arunachal Pradesh in 1978, is the son of a wealthy and highly respected clan elder, and other patrician families have also succeeded in maintaining their status. The abolishment of slavery in 1962 has deprived them of some of their captive labour force, but they received from government compensation for the loss of their slaves, and now employ many of their previous dependants as wage labourers. Some differences in wealth and power have been evened out, but others have arisen as the result of the large profits made by successful businessmen. Several of these have built homes in Hapoli and furnished them partly in modern style, while retaining their old family houses in their villages. The possession of bicycles, motor scooters, and in some cases even jeeps enables them to move freely between their two homes and between the old and the new life-style without showing any of the symptoms of alienation and disorientation so typical of tribal political leader in states such as Andhra Pradesh.

The sphere of Apa Tani life which has been least influenced by recent developments is that of religion and ritual. Apa Tanis continue to perform public as well as domestic rites in the traditional manner, and even public servants and students residing temporarily outside Arunachal Pradesh make every effort to return to the Apa Tani Valley when their village performs the triannual celebration of the Mloko, the greatest of the seasonal feasts. Unlike such tribes as Gonds and Koyas, who, yielding to Hindu pressure, have given up cow sacrifice, the Apa Tanis show no signs of abandoning their traditional ritual practices, nor has there been any suggestion that the people of the plains of Assam stigmatize them as untouchable because of their habit of eating beef. The self-confidence so characteristic of Apa Tanis and other hillmen of Arunachal Pradesh enables them to resist interference with practices which they consider their own affair and of no concern to anyone outside the tribal community. In this respect, too, the Apa Tanis' attitude sharply contrasts with that of the timid tribals of Andhra Pradesh, whose long-standing experience as victims of oppression and bullying has broken their spirit and taught them the wisdom of complying with Hindu prejudices. Among the Apa Tanis there is as yet no significant impact of Hindu ideas or customs, but it would seem the traditional belief in an underworld, where the departed lead a life identical to that they led on this earth, has been slightly confused by stories of heaven and hell brought back by students in mission schools. However, such novel ideas have not yet had any effect on the ritual practices in which even the most educated participate with undiminished dedication. These, of course, are early days in the contacts with different ideologies, and it is by no means unlikely that the traditional world-view may not indefinitely satisfy the intellectual aspirations of those who study in universities and other institutions of higher learning.

The Apa Tanis are only one of the numerous tribal groups which make up the population of Arunachal Pradesh, and in 1980 I had the opportunity of spending some time among their neighbours, known as the Nishis and the Hill Miris. When I encountered these tribes in 1944 and 1945, their relations with the Apa Tanis alternated between mutually profitable trade contacts and sporadic feuds, often culminating in the capture and holding for ransom of Apa Tanis by Nishis or Miris, or in the raiding of the latter's settlements by Apa Tanis seeking revenge. Though the loss of life was usually not very great in these long-drawn-out feuds, revenge killings did occur, and it was unsafe for any tribesman to enter the land of villages where he had no friends to offer him protection. Among the slaves of the Apa Tanis there were many of Nishi or Miri origin, usually men or women captured in raids. A few had been taken prisoner by Apa Tanis, but many more were victims of endo-tribal fights between Nishis whose captors had sold them to Apa Tanis.

Today peace reigns among Nishis, Miris, and Apa Tanis, and anyone who experienced the tense atmosphere which prevailed only thirty-five years ago in areas rent by unending feuds must be surprised by the speed with which the Government of India brought tranquillity to this region. The achievement is all the greater as the elimination of feuds and raiding was effected largely without employing armed force. Although at the beginning of the pacification of the region there were a few incidents involving members of the security forces, on the whole law and order was established more by persuasion than by police action, and this stands in sharp contrast to the interminable fights against insurgents in Nagaland. At present men and women of any tribal group can freely move from village to village without running any risk, and many have become used to visiting the plains of Assam for the purpose of petty trade.

Whereas the Apa Tanis, dwelling in large, compact villages, always enjoyed a considerable degree of security as long as they did not venture too far from their home ground, for Nishis the newly gained freedom from the fear of being raided or kidnapped is a relatively novel experience, and one which has transformed their social life. Previously, individual families sought to attain a measure of safety by concluding alliances with men in other villages, and such alliances were based either on marriage relations or on formal friendship pacts which involved the exchange of valuables. Today the need for such individual links no longer exists. Recent political events have ended the lawless state of affairs in which the members of a Nishi household had to fend for themselves, and even co-villagers were under no obligation to come to the rescue of a family attacked by raiders. Quite apart from overall control by the administration, which is capable of imposing sanctions on law-breakers, the past few years have seen the development of a judicial system resting on the authority of village elders, the so-called *gaonbura*. Among the Nishis their position is an innovation which goes back to the final phase of British rule, when the officers of government selected in a somewhat informal way prominent men as representatives of their villages. After the suppression of violent acts of self-help, which used to be the only way of obtaining redress of grievances, the tribesmen have learned to depend on the *gaonbura* for the settlement of disputes, and various steps have been taken to regularize their function. In the Raga Circle, for instance, an area which has a large concentration of Hill Miris, the circle officer—incidentally, himself a tribal—encouraged the *gaonbura* and *panchayat* members to lay down certain basic principles for the administration of justice.

In a meeting of village elders drawn from all parts of the circle which was held on 27 February 1980, a number of rules for the settlement of disputes were formulated and unanimously agreed upon. Significantly, the elders decided that anyone trying to bypass their jurisdiction by directly approaching an officer of the administration should be fined Rs 500, which for tribals is a very substantial sum. The rules laid down in the document resulting from this meeting reflect a very liberal attitude insofar as the marriage system is concerned. Thus the list of rules begins with the categorical statement that "child marriage is strictly prohibited" and that a fine of Rs 1,000 would be imposed on the parents of the immature girl as well as on the person marrying her. This is followed by the rule that "nobody can marry a girl against her will" and that "the parent giving her in marriage against her will would be fined Rs 1000." Compared to these rates the fine of Rs 600 for adultery and of Rs 500 for attempted murder seem rather small. No punishment for homicide is laid down because capital offences fall under the jurisdiction of government magistrates. Once a council of tribal elders has pronounced judgement in any of the cases within their purview, an appeal to the circle officer is permitted, but in most instances this representative of government confirms the verdict of the council.

The regulations framed by the tribal elders of the Raga Circle are the first attempt at the codification of customary law by assemblies of tribesmen. In practice most disputes have for long been dealt with by informal gatherings of elders, and it speaks for the broadmindedness and imaginative approach of the government that law enforcement by local bodies is encouraged and the intervention of government officers and courts reduced to a minimum. This policy contrasts with the much more legalistic and far less imaginative attitude of the Government of Andhra Pradesh, which abolished the tribal courts instituted by the Nizam's government, with the result that the tribals are once again subject to the jurisdiction of ordinary courts, the complicated procedures of which they are incapable of comprehending.

While the Government of Arunachal Pradesh deliberately favours the retention of the greater part of the traditional social order, it has encouraged certain changes in the settlement pattern. Unlike the Apa Tanis, most Nishis and Miris used to live in dispersed settlements, and particularly the former rarely built compact villages. Individual longhouses, sheltering under one roof several families and sometimes up to fifty or sixty people, stood on spurs and ledges, often at a considerable distance from other houses of the same village. Such a scattering

Nishi jhum *field cleared of all brush-wood; the stumps of trees are left in the ground and serve to prevent erosion. The crop will be sown in between the stumps and trunks of felled trees.*

Harvest on a Nıshi jhum *field. The ears of millet and rice are cut off the standing crop and carried home in baskets.*

Miri house in Godak, Raga Circle. The house contains one undivided hall with separate hearths for individual families.

of homesteads made the provision of public facilities difficult, and the government hence adopted a policy of regrouping villages so that as many people as possible could benefit from the establishment of schools and health centres and, above all, could gain access to piped water and of late also electricity. The regrouped villages are still not very large, the number of houses seldom exceeding forty, and there has been no change in the type of houses. These are still built on wooden piles and contain one large undivided hall with a number of hearths, each used by one unit of the joint family inhabiting the house. Regrouping has occurred mainly in areas where a motorable road acts as an incentive to move from mountain sites to the vicinity of such a line of communications.

One example of such a population movement is the Panior Valley, for the road linking the Apa Tani Valley and such large Nishi villages as Jorum and Talo with the Assamese town of North Lakhimpur runs for a long stretch through this valley. In the 1940s this valley was covered in dense tropical jungle difficult to penetrate even on foot, and several Nishi settlements were perched on the crest of hills high above the river level. The inhabitants cultivated the upper parts of the hill slopes and descended into the valley only for fishing and hunting, or when visiting settlements on the other side of the valley. Within

Nishi long-house in Talo village standing between permanently cultivated and regularly manured fields and garden plots.

the past ten years most of these hill-top settlements have been abandoned, and the Nishis have moved down into the valley, where they build houses close to the motor road. They still practise shifting cultivation on hill slopes situated within their traditional territory, but wherever the valley broadens and offers possibilities for permanent cultivation, they grow rice in irrigated fields. Those in settlements close to the plains have also begun to use ploughs and bullocks for tilling their land.

This Nishi tribe extends over a large area of diverse climate and configuration, and the altitude of settlements ranges from a few hundred feet to well over six thousand feet. In the 1940s I had found many parts of the Nishi country sparsely populated, and the frequency of feuds and revenge killings then undoubtedly acted as a check on the growth of the population. This check has now been removed, and the availability of medical services has limited the effect of epidemics, which on occasions took a heavy toll. An increase in the Nishi population is hence inevitable and will certainly be reflected in the figures of the 1981 census. Even before these figures are available one can gauge the magnitude of the problem by comparing the present size of villages with that observed in 1944. The village of Talo, whose land adjoins the Apa Tani Valley, for instance, consisted then of fewer than 40 houses. In 1978 I counted 176 houses and the number of hearths, which mirrors the number of separate nuclear families, was then 1,077, while the size of the population was estimated to be 2,076. My Nishi informants stated emphatically that few of the villagers had migrated to Talo from other places and that the expansion of the village was due solely to the natural growth of the families of old residents. Yet there has probably been a considerable influx of women born elsewhere, for the men of Talo were rich and could marry many wives by paying high bride-prices. Even in 1944 there was a man who had nine wives, and men with five wives were not unusual in Talo.

The increased population of Talo can be maintained because the village land comprises a large expanse of level ground which has been transformed into irrigated rice fields. Following the example of their Apa Tani neighbours, the Nishis of Talo have been raising wet rice for some time, but the acreage under irrigation has now greatly increased. Every side valley with a trickle of water and even narrow ravines have been adapted for the construction of rice terraces, and much hard work has gone into this transformation of the natural environment. The traditional slash-and-burn cultivation is also being practised, and there is still some land for the potential expansion of this type of tillage.

Yet not all Nishi villages are as favourably placed as Talo, with its large area of level irrigable land. In neighbouring Jorum the population has also grown but land has become scarce, and within the past ten to fifteen years four colonies have branched off and moved to sites close to the periphery of Jorum land. The members of these new settlements have converted former communal land into rice terraces, and these they now regard as their individual property. This is not contrary to Nishi custom, and as long as land was plentiful such practices were generally accepted. But with the increasing population growth, land is gradually becoming an object of conflict, and in Jorum I was told that whereas previously men used to quarrel about women and *mithan* most disputes now arise from competition for land.

A novel source of dissension among Nishis who inhabit the hills adjoining the plains of Assam is the influence of Christian missions on young people educated in their schools in places such as North Lakhimpur and Tezpur. While numerous Hindu children go to such schools without being induced to change their religion, a good many Nishi youths have been converted to Christianity. This in itself need not have created any difficulty, for Nishis, like most tribals, are not greatly concerned about the religious beliefs of their fellow-tribesmen, and if the Christian converts had been equally tolerant their rejection of traditional Nishi religion might have been ignored by the great mass of conservative tribesmen. However, the converts seem to have been lacking in tolerance and tact, and educated young men of villages affected by the ideological split to whom I spoke in 1980 complained bitterly that Christians deliberately disrupted the harmony of community life. They allegedly refused to share the houses of adherents of the old faith, and this meant that old parents were abandoned by their converted children, who claimed that they could not stay in dwellings where "devils" were worshipped and the meat of sacrificial animals was consumed. My informants insisted that the missions encouraged the establishment of separate settlements for Christians, and that the Christians refused to participate in village festivals, thereby demonstrating their dissociation from the tribal community. It was alleged, moreover, that converts, not satisfied with this symbolic withdrawal from village life, went a step further by abusing and physically attacking priests as they invoked the gods in the performance of traditional Nishi rituals. Enraged by such interference with hallowed religious practices, some Nishi youths took the offensive and destroyed some huts used by Christians for their prayer meetings.

Nishi teachers at the government high school in Yazali, who were members of a youth organization formed to promote traditional tribal culture, told me how frustrated they were because they could not match the large sums lavished by the missions on propaganda which is undermining the old Nishi life-style. The missionaries concerned are Indian nationals, and though the Inner Line rules prevent them from entering Arunachal Pradesh for the purpose of proselytization, they allegedly pay young Nishis to spread Christianity in their home villages, and a commission of Rs 200 is said to be paid to any convert who induces another Nishi to embrace Christianity. Whatever the rights and wrongs of the case may be, it is widely believed that there are young Nishis who, after having left mission schools, live in comfortable circumstances without holding any official position or engaging in any normal occupation, such as farming, teaching, or running a business. Adherents of the traditional faith resent the subsidizing of such young people, whom they regard as hostile to their ancestral ideology and social customs.

The conflict created by the impact of Christianity on the Nishis of the Subansiri District stands in striking contrast to the developments in the neighbouring Kameng District, where tribal groups such as the Khovas have come under the influence of Tibetan Buddhism. In their general life-style the Khovas, a tribe of shifting-cultivators adjoining Monpas and Sherdukpens, resemble Nishis in their economy and in the character of their traditional religion. Among the Khovas there is a spontaneous trend towards Buddhism; in two villages small *gompa* are under construction, and the villagers have invited Monpa lamas to

Monpa men of Sangti in Dirang Circle of Kameng District; they wear rain-resisting caps made of yak hair.

perform Buddhist rituals. A prominent headman of the last generation who was known to be a believer in Buddhism is said to have assisted in the establishment of a *gompa* in Bomdila. Unlike the Christian converts among the Nishis, those Khovas who are attracted to Buddhism do not opt out of the social life of their community and continue to participate in the traditional tribal rituals.

In the same way the Sherdukpens combine their adherence to Mahayana Buddhism with the communal worship of tribal deities whose cult lies in the hands of priests entirely distinct from the lamas in charge of the large *gompa* furnished and decorated in the style of Tibetan *gompa*. Among the Monpas, too, elements of the ancient Bon religion coexist with the dominant Buddhist faith, and the parallel practice of both religions within the same communities has not sparked off any conflicts comparable to those which threaten to destroy the social fabric of Nishis affected by religious rivalries.

In the field of higher education the Nishis and Miris have not yet caught up with the Apa Tanis, but their progress is nevertheless remarkable compared to the educational achievements of such tribes as the Gonds and most other tribal groups of Peninsular India. In 1980 there were some thirty university graduates among the Nishis and Miris of the Subansiri District, and several youths and girls were en-

Sherdukpen couple of Rupa in ceremonial dress; the wife wears a brocade hat of Tibetan style.

rolled in degree courses in institutions outside Arunachal Pradesh. The speed of the educational and political development of the Nishis can be measured by the fact that a member of that tribe by name of Tada Talang, born in 1944 in Nyapin, a remote village south of the Khru Valley, is now education minister of Arunachal Pradesh. He told me that while at present teachers recruited from various parts of India were still on the staffs of many schools, soon enough trained tribal teachers would be available to make the employment of teachers from outside Arunachal Pradesh unnecessary. At the same time, he demonstrated his realism by explaining that at this stage government must consolidate rather than expand primary education. In the first enthusiasm of providing education for all children of school age, numerous schools were opened and teachers appointed, but the supply of essential equipment such as books and slates could not keep pace with this rapid expansion. The minister emphasized, therefore, very reasonably, that existing schools must be properly equipped before there was any point in establishing new schools.

Having experienced how in Andhra Pradesh educational policy was drawn up and repeatedly changed without any consultation with the tribals whose children were ultimately affected by the planning of the school system, I was impressed by the sound and responsible attitude

Monpas of Tawang during a village festival involving a ritual riding display.

of a relatively young man belonging to the first generation of literate Nishis and already in charge of a ministry controlling education throughout Arunachal Pradesh.

My respect for tribal leaders grew even more when a few weeks later I had a chance to discuss educational policy with the former Chief Minister Pema Kando Thondung, M.P., who by that time had been elected to represent the people of Arunachal Pradesh in the Indian Parliament. He belongs to the numerically small but culturally advanced community of Sherdukpens and evinced a breadth of vision and a refreshing realism which I have not often encountered among Indian politicians. Though his career has been little short of meteoric, he was free of all pomposity and seemed to possess a captivating sense of humour. The Sherdukpens, whose total number was 1,639 at the time of the 1971 census, have been prominent in public life, and the success of their leaders in state and national elections shows that in the politics of Arunachal Pradesh personal qualities count for more than the size of the community which backs a candidate in an election. Pema Kando Thondung's predecessor as member of parliament was also a Sherdukpen, and in 1979 another member of the tribe, Nima Tsiring Khrime, was elected to a seat in the Legislative Assembly of Arunachal Pradesh, defeating candidates from numerically very much stronger tribal groups.

Monpa priests of the indigenous, pre-Buddhist Bon religion with a crowd of villagers celebrating a festival in honour of local deities.

The spectacular progress of Apa Tanis, Nishis, Sherdukpens, and other tribes of Arunachal Pradesh within the past thirty years establishes beyond any doubt the capacity of Indian tribal populations to attain the same level of education, economic efficiency, and political maturity as any other ethnic group within the wider Indian society. The fact that the enlightened policy of the Government of India vis-à-vis the hillmen of the northeastern frontier regions could bring about so rapid a transformation of archaic and in some respects barbaric societies highlights the failure of the tribal policies of the governments of many of the Indian states. For none of these governments provides its aboriginal tribes with facilities similar to those available in Arunachal Pradesh, nor do they effectively assist them in their struggle for an existence free of exploitation and domination by powerful vested interests. Unless we were to argue that the tribes of Arunachal Pradesh are by nature and heredity equipped with superior mental qualities, their performance, outshining most other tribal populations, must be attributed to favourable circumstances and to the historical accident of their relatively late emergence from an isolation which provided them with physical protection from subjugation by economically and politically more advanced ethnic groups. The tribesmen of Arunachal Pradesh were fortunate that at the time when their isolation finally came to an end they benefited from a liberal policy framed by the distinguished anthropologist Verrier Elwin and powerfully supported by the then Prime Minister Jawaharlal Nehru. Had a similar policy been consistently applied to the tribal areas of Andhra Pradesh, the fate of Gonds, Koyas, Kolams, and Konda Reddis would also have been a happier one, but we have seen that there measures taken for the benefit of tribal populations in the 1940s were reversed when political pressures created an atmosphere unfavourable to the indigenous tribesmen. Thus tribes such as Apa Tanis and Gonds—to take only two typical examples—stand today at opposite ends of a spectrum which reflects the various possibilities for the development of tribal societies: while the Apa Tanis are clearly set on an upward path, the Gonds are threatened by an apparently irreversible decline in their fortunes.

12 The Tribal Problem in All-India Perspective

In an industrialized India the destruction of the aboriginal's life is as inevitable as the submergence of the Egyptian temples caused by the dams of the Nile.... As things are going there can be no grandeur in the primitive's end. It will not be even simple extinction, which is not the worst of human destinies. It is to be feared that the aboriginal's last act will be squalid, instead of being tragic. What will be seen with most regret will be, not his disappearance, but his enslavement and degradation.

NIRAD C. CHAUDHURI, *The Continent of Circe*, 1965

FIFTEEN YEARS ago Nirad C. Chaudhuri, the provocative analyst of the Indian social scene, published this gloomy forecast, and readers of the foregoing chapters may well agree that the dice are heavily loaded against the likelihood of an unclouded future for the forty million Indian aboriginals. A comparison of the fate of the tribes of Andhra Pradesh, who share their environment with Hindu populations, and those in sole possession of the highlands of Arunachal Pradesh indicates the alternative lines along which tribal communities may develop. However, the choice of the road which any tribal society will take is hardly ever left to the tribesmen themselves but is imposed on them by external circumstances outside their own control.

During the last years of British rule in India, there raged a passionate controversy about the policy to be adopted vis-à-vis the aboriginal tribes. While anthropologically minded administrators advocated a policy of protection, which in specific cases involved even a measure of seclusion, Indian politicians attacked the idea of segregation and seclusion on the grounds that it threatened to deepen and perpetuate divisions within the Indian nation, and delayed the aboriginals' integration into the rest of the population. Today this controversy, though occasionally revived in newspaper articles and political speeches, has largely abated. It has become obvious that, on the one hand, a measure of integration is coming about automatically even in protected regions such as Arunachal Pradesh, but that, on the other hand, compulsory integration, even if rapidly progressing, has rarely benefited the trib- *313* als in the sense of assuring them a satisfactory place in the wider Indian society.

The protagonists of integration usually ignore the fact that there exists no homogeneous Indian society with which tribal groups could merge by adopting a standard cultural pattern. The so-called advanced Indian society, with its linguistic, religious, and caste divisions, is far from uniform, and it has never been specified into which of the numerous divisions any particular tribal group could be integrated. India's tribal population is equally divided, for its heterogeneity extends to race, language, and cultural levels, quite apart from its scattered distribution over numerous disparate environments.

Racial distinctions are superficially most obvious, though their social implications are of minor significance. As the most ancient population element in the subcontinent, some of the aboriginals belong clearly to very archaic racial strata. The oldest is formed by the Veddoids, exemplified by tribes such as Chenchus and Kadars (see the Introduction). They represent a racial type which extends from south Arabia eastwards across India, and as far as parts of the Southeast Asian mainland and Indonesia. Intermixed with other racial types, the Veddoid element is found in most of the tribes of Southern and Middle India, and its prevalence among the Gond tribes is reflected in the term *Gondid*, which some physical anthropologists apply to one of the Veddoid subtypes.

The Veddoid element is absent among the hill tribes of Northeast India, who belong to a racial stratum usually described as Palaeo-Mongoloid, which extends over wide areas of Southeast Asia, including Indonesia and the Philippines. Mongoloid traces are discernible also among some of the hill tribes of Orissa, such as Saoras and Bondos, and it is not unlikely that in prehistoric times, before the invasion of India by waves of peoples of Caucasoid race, there were some marginal contacts between the Veddoids inhabiting Middle and Southern India and the Mongoloids who occupied the Himalayan and northeastern regions.

In discussion of the prospects for the integration of the aboriginals with the majority of the Indian population, these racial factors are often overlooked. Yet many tribals differ in appearance from the dominant population of their respective regions, and even complete cultural and linguistic assimilation cannot remove the fact that an Apa Tani or Nishi looks different from the members of Assamese Hindu castes or a Chenchu from the peoples of Hyderabad City. Khasis and Nagas of Northeast India often comment on the fact that on visits to Delhi or Bombay they are taken for Burmese, Thais, or Malayans, and are asked to produce their passports.

It is all the more remarkable that, despite racial differences no less obvious than those found in countries with acute race problems, India has never experienced any serious racial tensions. While religion and language have frequently figured as factors in communal controversies, distinctions in physical make-up have never been played up as facts of political significance. One of the causes of the unimportance of the race factor may be inherent in the ideology of Hindu caste society, which accepts that humanity is divided into intrinsically distinct groups. Since the endogamy and social exclusiveness of Hindu castes are in themselves a bar to close inter-group relations, there is no need to place social distance between racially differentiated groups. The normal operation of the caste system is quite sufficient to prevent intermarriage, commensalism, and intimate social intercourse between members of different communities, and hence there is no need to bring in the race factor. There is very little likelihood of any substantial miscegenation involving persons of basically different racial groups, and whatever progress in the cultural assimilation of tribal communities may be made, there can be no doubt that for a long time to come most tribes will persist as groups with distinct racial characteristics.

Another decisive factor is language, but unlike race, this is not an immutable feature. While a tribal community cannot change its racial make-up in order to conform to the characteristics of the population dominant in a region, its members can become proficient in the main regional language. The first step in such a process of assimilation is usually bilingualism, and many aboriginals in contact with advanced populations are fluent in languages other than their mother tongue. Sometimes bilingualism is only a transitional phase, followed by the decline and ultimate extinction of the tribal tongue. A process of linguistic assimilation has gone on for hundreds and probably thousands of years, and many tribal communities have lost their original tongues and speak today one of the main languages of India.

The smaller a group is, the greater is the likelihood that it will lose its tribal language and adopt the language of economically stronger and culturally more advanced neighbours. Examples of the displacement of one language by another are numerous. Telugu, one of the Dravidian languages with a substantial literature, is steadily gaining ground at the expense of minor unwritten tribal tongues, which also belong to the Dravidian language group. This process can be observed in the Telengana districts of Andhra Pradesh. The Koyas of some groups of villages south of the Godavari still speak their tribal Gondi dialect, but use Telugu as a means of communication with their Telugu-speaking neighbours. The majority of Koyas, however, have given up Gondi altogether and speak Telugu even among themselves.

The contact zones between tribal and non-tribal populations provide instructive examples of the manner in which new languages may infiltrate the speech of small communities. The Bondos of the Orissa highlands, for instance, speak a Munda language, but in conversation with their lowland Hindu neighbours they employ Oriya. Such contact is mainly in the sphere of commerce, and the Oriya terms for the higher numerals, lacking in Bondo, and those for weights and measures have been incorporated into Bondo speech. Surprisingly, many prayers and magical formulae are also spoken in Oriya, because the Bondos think it proper that deities and spirits should be addressed in a "superior" language. Thus Oriya is fast becoming the ritual and not only the trade language of the Bondos. School education imparted through the medium of Oriya no doubt accelerates the erosion of the tribal tongue. It goes without saying that the displacement of a tribal language also involves the loss of the entire oral literature of the tribe concerned, and this in turn leads to a blurring of the tribal identity and world-view.

Whatever the results of linguistic change for the development of tribal cultures may be, there can be no doubt that in an age of rapidly improving communications extreme diversity of languages cannot persist unmodified. In some parts of Nagaland one could, even when travelling on foot, pass in a single day through three different language areas, and this linguistic fragmentation had come about because villages were isolated from each other by long-standing feuds, often involving head-hunting raids, and there was hence no occasion for people from different settlements to converse with each other. The pacification of tribal areas in Northeast India has put an end to the isolation of small communities and created a need for a common language. In Nagaland and Arunachal Pradesh a kind of pidgin Assamese partly fulfils this need, but the people of both territories have now chosen English as their official language and medium of instruction, and the educated, at least, increasingly use English for communication between members of different tribes.

The attitude of the Government of India and the various state governments to the tribal languages is ambivalent. In Andhra Pradesh, the use of Gondi as the medium of instruction in primary schools for Gond children was abandoned, and since the breakup of Hyderabad State no more books in Gondi have been printed. The avowed policy of the government is clearly to educate all children through the medium of Telugu, which is now the official language of Andhra Pradesh, even though much of the official business is still conducted in English.

Notwithstanding the fact that educational experts in most Indian states are unanimous in advocating education in the mother tongue at least up to high school level, this principle is not applied to tribal children, even in the case of such large tribal groups as Santals and Hos, who speak Munda languages not even remotely related to Hindi, the dominant language of the state of Bihar. The Scheduled Areas and Scheduled Tribes Commission set up by the Government of India in 1960 under Article 339 of the Constitution severely criticized the reluctance of state governments to satisfy the tribals' demand for primary education in their own languages. Under Article 350A of the Constitution, every state must endeavour to provide children of minority groups with adequate facilities for instruction in their mother tongue at the primary stage of education, but the commission pointed out that some of the states had taken this matter very casually, and failed to provide textbooks in even the major tribal languages. It does not appear that these admonitions have induced state governments to change their policies, and the prospects for the future of tribal languages are thus far from encouraging. The voluminous publications issued by the office of the commissioner for scheduled castes and scheduled tribes and other agencies concerned with tribal welfare contain very little information on the problem of tribal languages, and it is difficult to avoid the conclusion that politicians and officials alike regard their ultimate disappearance as inevitable and even desirable in the interest of the integration of the tribes with the majority communities.

Only in some states of Northeast India, where the growth of political consciousness has led to a new evaluation of tribal identity, is there also a revival of interest in tribal languages. Thus Khasi, an Austroasiatic language spoken in Meghalaya by one of the two tribal majority communities, has been developed as a literary language suitable as a medium of instruction. This move had the result that even the University of Gauhati, though situated in Assam, has now recognized Khasi as a language in which certain examination papers may be written. For major tribes determined to cultivate their own languages, bilingualism would seem to be a solution which would enable a people to participate in the wider national life without losing touch with its cultural heritage.

Besides differences in race and language, there are various cultural factors which set the tribesmen apart from the bulk of Hindu society. Some of these are intangible and do not lend themselves to statistical assessment or comparative analysis. For many years the factor of religion was a criterion by which the tribes were distinguished from such communities as Hindus, Muslims, Buddhists, or Christians. Until 1931 millions of aboriginals were returned in the census reports as adherents of tribal religions, but in more recent census reports tribal religions were not separately listed but were included under the head "Others." The reasons for the discontinuation of the heading "Tribal

Religions" are partly of a practical and partly of a political nature. Tribal religions are clearly not as easily definable as Islam or Buddhism, and whereas no doubt usually exists whether a person is a Muslim or an adherent of a tribal religion, it is not so easy to distinguish between some tribal cults and certain types of popular Hinduism. The political objections to the separate listing of tribal religions are based on the argument that census statistics on religion tend to perpetuate communal divisions.

The undoubted tendency to classify members of aboriginal tribes as Hindus and to play down the distinctions between tribal religions and popular Hinduism must not be considered indicative of an organized movement to convert tribals to Sanskritic Hinduism. Apart from the discouragement of such customs as cow sacrifice and the use of intoxicating liquor as an offering to tribal gods, there is on the part of local Hindu communities little desire to induce the tribals to change their beliefs and religious practices. Indeed, a cynical observer of the relations between tribals and Hindus in such regions as the highlands of Adilabad may come to the conclusion that the Hindus "want the Gonds' land and not their souls." Though in areas of close contact between Hindus and tribals Hindu ideas and customs may gradually spread to tribal communities, they usually find acceptance as an addition to tribal beliefs rather than as their replacement. "Conversions" of tribesmen to Hinduism in a sense comparable to conversions to Christianity or Islam are comparatively rare, even though in recent years Hindu missions have been active in some tribal regions of Middle India. Their efforts have concentrated more on modifying social customs than on propagating a new doctrine. Even where there are no such agencies for the propagation of the Hindu way of life, school-teachers and minor government officials, who—except in Arunachal Pradesh— are almost invariably non-tribals, tend to discourage tribal customs objectionable to Hindu sentiment, and although India is constitutionally a secular state, there have been instances of official interference with such tribal religious practices as animal sacrifices.

In this respect there are certain discrepancies between the policies advocated by the central government and those pursued by individual states. The official policy of the Government of India is one of tolerance towards the beliefs, customs, and way of life of the tribal people, whereas some of the state governments have shown themselves less sensitive to the right of tribal communities to follow their traditional pattern of life, even in matters not affecting the interests of other sections of the population.

It is paradoxical that in many areas where tribals are exposed to the influence of caste Hindus just those features of Hindu society which modern India strives to discard are newly introduced among populations to whom they had hitherto been foreign. Thus, not only the prejudice against certain occupations such as leather working and butchering, but also dietary taboos, child marriage, and restrictions on the remarriage of widows and divorcées are gaining a foothold among the hill- and jungle-folk at a time when they are losing ground in the larger urban centres. This development is almost inevitable as long as throughout rural India compliance with the puritanical precepts of Hindu morality remains the principal criterion of social respectability.

Acceptance or denial of the necessity for assimilation with Hindu society is ultimately a question of values. Are the tribals to be left to follow their own inclination in emulating or rejecting the cultural pattern represented by their Hindu neighbours, or are they to be coaxed to abandon their own cultural traditions and values? In the past Hindu society has been tolerant of groups that would not conform to the standards set by the higher castes, and in some areas, notably Kerala, the emulation by low-status groups of upper-caste fashions in such matters as dress or marriage celebrations was resented and often prevented because the higher castes saw their monopoly of certain cultural features endangered. In recent years, however, there has been a change of attitude vis-à-vis cultural divergencies, and it may be the influence of the Western belief in universal values which has encouraged attempts to enforce conformity with the standards of dominant populations. Yet India is not only a multi-racial and a multi-lingual country, it is also a multi-cultural one, and as long as Muslims, Parsees, and Christians are free to follow their traditional way of life, it would seem only fair to respect also tribal customs and beliefs, however distinct from those of the regional majority community they may be.

Hinduism is, of course, not the only ideological force which has brought about fundamental changes in tribal culture and mores. Christian missions have been active in tribal areas, with the result that about 50 percent of all Nagas and Mizos and 20 percent of all Mundas and Oraons have been converted to Christianity. The advantages of missionary activities lie mainly in the field of education, for many of the literates among these tribes were educated in mission schools, and literacy certainly aided them in resisting exploitation by non-tribal populations. By reducing tribal languages to writing, usually in Roman script, missionaries were also helpful in securing the survival and development of tribal tongues, which without their efforts might have been displaced by regionally dominant languages. On the other hand, missionary influence has eroded much of the tribes' cultural heritage, which was inseparably linked with the traditional mythology, beliefs, and rituals, and wilted when these were abandoned. Above all, the conversion of part of a community tends to destroy the social unity of the whole tribe, as we have seen in chapter 11. Today foreign missionaries no longer play a significant role, but their work is continued by Indian Christians whose tolerance of tribal customs is no greater than that of the earlier European or American missionaries. Indeed, nowhere in India has there been a merging of Christian and traditional tribal practices such as I have observed among autochthonous communities in Mexico and Guatemala, where representations of Maya gods adorn the walls of some Catholic churches, and libations to ancestor spirits are offered in the aisles.

In the political sphere the interests of tribal populations should have benefited from the introduction of a system of grass-roots democracy, known as *panchayati raj,* which was intended to take the place of the more paternalistic form of government characteristic of the days of British rule, both in the British provinces and in the princely states. In territories such as Arunachal Pradesh and Nagaland, where tribals are in an overwhelming majority, government by elected bodies, both on the local and the state level, has certainly boosted the tribals' self-confidence and has also brought them some tangible advantages. In areas where tribals are in the minority, however, such as in Andhra Pradesh, decentralization has had far from desirable results. As early as 1963, the commissioner for scheduled castes and scheduled tribes expressed in his report for the year 1962–63 the fear that, due to the existing pattern of concentration of social and economic power in the hands of a dominant section of the population, democratic decentralization may lead to a more extensive exploitation of the scheduled tribes. This apprehension was fully justified, for recent experiences have shown that the *panchayat samithi* and *zilla parishad,* which in some states took over the functions of the former district officers, were dragging their feet in the implementation of tribal welfare schemes, for the simple reason that their leading members belonged to the very classes which traditionally profited from the exploitation of the tribes. By diluting the powers of civil servants, who alone were likely to safeguard the interests of the tribals, decentralization certainly did more harm than good to the tribal cause.

A problem even more important than the introduction of *panchayati raj* is the impact of industrialization on the tribes in areas rich in mineral resources. Certain areas within the tribal belt of Middle India, and particularly Orissa, West Bengal, Bihar, and Madhya Pradesh, contain rich deposits of minerals, and their exploitation and the establishment of great steel works in the very centre of the tribals' homeland have already led to a large-scale displacement of tribal populations. Focussing on one particular incident connected with such industrialization, the Scheduled Areas and Scheduled Tribes Commission reported that out of 14,461 tribal families displaced from an area of 62,494 acres, only 3,479 were allotted alternative land. The disruption of the tribal economy and the degradation of tribals by large-scale industrialization, such as any visitor to the Ranchi area of Bihar can observe with his own eyes, is well described in the following paragraph of the commission's final report on the problem:

> The tribals were dislodged from their traditional sources of livelihood and places of habitation. Not conversant with the details of acquisition proceedings they accepted whatever cash compensation was given to them and became emigrants. With cash in hand and many attractions in the nearby industrial towns, their funds were rapidly depleted and in course of time they were without money as well as without land. They joined the ranks of landless labourers but without any training, equipment or aptitude for any skilled or semi-skilled job.[1]

Though the commission recommended that the government, as trustee of the scheduled tribes, "should not allow the tribes to go under in the process of industrialization," little was done to rehabilitate the displaced tribesmen and to train them for work in the new industries. Their eventual proletarization seems inevitable, and in the streets of Ranchi one can still see Munda and Oraon riksha pullers who not long ago were independent cultivators tilling their own land.

Destruction or alienation of tribal land as a result of industrialization is not a process peculiar to India, and it is well known that in areas such as the Solomon Islands or Melanesia or the tropical forests of Brazil the welfare of primitive tribes was sacrificed to the interests of local or multinational companies exploiting mineral or forest resources. Great as the inroads into tribal forests have been in India, some comfort may be derived from the fact that the forests are exploited mainly by local contractors and not by large companies who have acquired felling rights for long periods. Thus, state governments are still free to reverse their policies and to take up a system of forest exploitation compatible with tribal interest, such as has been suggested by Dr. B. D. Sharma (see chapter 3).

Yet the drive for modernization and industrialization pursued by all Indian governments committed to the improvement of the country's standard of living does not augur well for the future of tribal populations affected by projects promising to raise industrial output. This applies in particular to hydroelectric and irrigation projects located in hilly country inhabited by tribals whose land is to be submerged by the construction of reservoirs. One example of such a project is a great dam to be built in the 1980s across the lower course of the Godavari. This will involve the flooding of all the riverside villages of Reddis and Koyas, many of whom settled there because the reservation of

---

1. *Report of the Commission for Scheduled Castes and Scheduled Tribes for the Year 1962–63* (New Delhi, 1963), p. 271.

forests had forced them to move down from the hills on which they used to practise slash-and-burn cultivation. At a time when a growing population pressure has produced a scarcity of cultivable land throughout India, any resettlement of displaced communities is inherently difficult, and tribals, who have no political pull, are likely to remain at the back of the queue for land promised as compensation for their holdings sacrificed on the altar of India's modernization.

There can be no doubt that the establishment of vast industrial enterprises in tribal zones lends urgency to the extension of protective measures to all tribals whose rights and way of life have been placed in jeopardy. The architects of the Indian constitution were determined that, while the age-old isolation of the scheduled tribes would have to be ended, they should be saved from exploitation and from the erosion of their rights to their ancestral land. It was clear that this aim could be achieved only by special legislation, but unfortunately for the tribals the original idealism of politicians and legislators is wearing thin, and while the laws for protecting tribals are still in existence, their implementation leaves much to be desired. Even among educated Indians, there seems to be a growing unwillingness to face the fact that forty million tribal people will for a long time form a separate and unassimilated element within the Indian nation. While many may concede that there is a need for some special protection, there is also a widespread feeling that any privileges enjoyed by tribes were required only for a period of transition, and that within a span of perhaps ten or twenty years the integration of the tribes within the mainstream of the population should be completed, whereupon there would be no more justification for the continuation of scheduled areas and privileges for scheduled tribes.

This new trend in public opinion represents as great a threat to the future prospects of tribals as the greed of land-grabbers does to their present well-being. The manner of the integration of the tribals into the wider Indian society will ultimately be determined by political decisions, and these will be made on the basis of moral evaluations. It thus seems that unless the intellectually leading sections of the Indian population develop a spirit of cultural tolerance and an appreciation for tribal values, even the most elaborate schemes for the economic improvement of tribal populations are likely to prove abortive.

In conclusion I can do no better than to quote from the principles which Jawaharlal Nehru, the most idealistic of Indian politicians, formulated as a guideline for the policy to be pursued by his administration in its dealings with tribals:

> People should develop along the lines of their own genius and the imposition of alien values should be avoided.

Postscript, May 1981

This book was already in press when a massacre of large numbers of Gonds in the Adilabad District of Andhra Pradesh confirmed the author's view of the chances of survival of the Gonds and other South Indian tribes as self-contained ethnic groups.

The following account of the incident is largely based on the findings of the Andhra Pradesh Civil Liberties Committee, a non-political body consisting of senior academics, medical practitioners, lawyers, and other professional persons, and on the observations of journalists who visited Adilabad District after the events of 20 April 1981, when a crowd of unarmed Gonds was fired on by a force of police assembled to prevent a meeting of Gonds who had gathered to protest the alienation of their land and harassment by non-tribal exploiters.

The following extracts from the report of the Andhra Pradesh Civil Liberties Committee, dated 2 May 1981, speak for themselves:

> Several days before the firing incident the Girijan Ryotu Coolie Sangham had sponsored a rally, and had given it extensive publicity. One could see wall-posters spread from Nirmal town to Adilabad inviting people to join the rally on 20 April 1981. According to the posters a procession was to commence at 4 P.M., followed by a public meeting at 6 P.M., where leaders would speak. A cultural programme was to complete the meeting. Incidentally April 20 was a weekly shandy ["market"] in Indravelli, where people would gather in large numbers to buy their weekly provisions.
>
> On April 19 the police went round Indravelli in the evening announcing that section 144 Criminal Procedure Code [Cr.P.C.] was imposed in the area. As such the Sangham meeting on April 20 would not be held. The police also told the people not to attend the meeting. Four platoons of policemen occupied the local high school and camped there.
>
> On April 20 around 7 A.M. the Superintendent of Police Adilabad and the Revenue Divisional Officer [R.D.O.] were present at Indravelli. Early in the morning Gonds started pouring into Indravelli from all directions. They came in buses, in trucks, and on foot. The police encircled the village. They stopped all the incoming vehicles and the Gonds were made to get off, beaten up, and sent back. Those approaching the village on foot were chased away with *lathi*s ["batons"]. This went on for several hours. The committee met a number of Gonds who went to attend the abortive meeting. The Gonds said that:
>
> 1. They were quite unaware of the situation prevailing in Indravelli, for instance the imposition of section 144 Cr.P.C.
>
> 2. They did not know that they would be stopped by the police at the road entry. Thus they continued to pour into the village unsuspecting and unaware of what was in store.

The Gonds told the committee that they wanted to visit the village for three reasons:

1. To attend the meeting in the evening.
2. To attend the weekly shandy in the forenoon and make purchases.
3. To offer prayers to their Goddess Indarayee [the temple of Indarayee is located at Indravelli].

The Gonds were unarmed except for the sticks which they usually carry when they travel.

Some of those chased away by the police gathered at a nearby place wondering why they were not allowed to enter the village.

By 4 P.M. the Gonds continued to arrive from different directions as they were unaware of the police obstruction or of the imposition of section 144 Cr.P.C. They were chased away with *lathis*, but the police not satisfied with the *lathi* charge resorted to bursting of teargas shells and suddenly without warning opened fire. Some policemen took positions in the tops of trees and fired. An open jeep full of armed policemen ploughed through the crowd and started firing. The crowd ran helter-skelter. Some dropped dead, and the injured started running away in panic. Those who tried to pick up the dead or rescue the injured were also fired upon. Panic and commotion gripped the area. Many, including women and young boys, escaped with bullet injuries. This was at about 6 P.M. Some pelted stones at the advancing armed policemen while retreating. No one was allowed to touch the dead or the wounded. The police carried away the dead and the wounded in trucks. The firing continued for several minutes, until the crowd ran for their lives.

According to the police the dead included thirteen Gonds and one police constable. No dead body was handed over to the relatives of the deceased. The Gonds told the committee that the dead bodies were being recovered from tanks, wells, rivulets and bushes as late as April 26. They could not say with certainty the exact number of the dead, as many had come to Indravelli from far-off places. Also, dead bodies were continuing to be recovered. However, they place the number around one hundred. When asked about the death of a constable, the Gonds said that they had also heard about it, but the constable must have died after being hit by a bullet fired from the tops of the trees or from the jeep.

Our enquiry reveals that the notification of prohibitory order under section 144 Cr.P.C was made on April 19 by means of a public address system by the local police on the road between Mutnoor and Utnur. Thus only the villages situated on the roadside were aware of the prohibitory orders. Even they were under the impression that they could attend the shandy. All that was announced was that the meeting was cancelled and that nobody should come to attend the meeting. The police authorities and the R.D.O. were well aware of the fact that April 20 was a shandy day. Notification in law does not mean merely announcing the section under which the power is exercised. It should be intelligible and effective, and in a language known to the assembly. It was not announced that the shandy was also cancelled. The result is that when the Gonds were proceeding towards Indravelli the assembly could not be characterised as an unlawful assembly. Our enquiry revealed that the Gonds were under the impression that they could attend the shandy.

The presence of policemen posted on tree tops and a huge armed battalion makes it clear that the administration decided on the course to be adopted well in advance.

On 13 June 1981, the prestigious *Economic and Political Weekly* published a three-page account of the incident of April 20 under the title "Carnage at Indravelli." The reporter M. Raghuram had spent a week in the troubled area and came to conclusions very similar to those of the Civil Liberties Committee. This may be seen from the following extracts:

As the Gonds bewildered by the sudden cancellation of permission for the meeting were pleading and insisting on their right to go ahead with their meeting the Superintendent of Police forced the Revenue Divisional Officer to order firing. When they tried to run away in panic and confusion they were met head on by an open police jeep emerging from the local high school whose armed police occupants fired at point blank range upon the fleeing Gonds, the policemen hiding in the trees and haystacks nearby also opened up their trained guns to add to the toll.

How many persons were killed at Indravelli on that day? The Home Minister has stated that identification of the victims was not possible since none of them were from the villages within a five kilometre radius of the firing spot. It is however widely believed that more than sixty persons were killed on the spot that day and many of the dead bodies were burnt secretly outside Adilabad town. Many of the seriously injured were callously piled upon each other in two vans and taken to the Adilabad District hospital. When the vans reached their destination the hospital staff pulled out ten corpses from the vans, and three more died later. Some hospital sources complained of police high-handedness in preventing proper documentation, for only thirteen were shown as killed and nine injured while more than twice that number had died in the hospital itself. The number of injured persons exceeds sixty-five in the hospital records in the various towns of the district are taken into account. In Utnur town itself about thiry to forty dead bodies were picked up on the roadside by fleeing Gonds or left behind for the police to tackle, according to Congress (I) and eyewitness accounts. This excludes those left dying in ditches and rivulets and forests. To this must be added the toll in Ichoda town (twenty-five) and Muthnoor village (thirty). That many of the wounded too will die is certain, for not merely have the medical facilities been inadequate, but many of the injured have not availed themselves even of these inadequate facilities because of the deep fear of the police. Most of the jails in the district and nearby ones are now filled with Gonds arrested in the taluks or in Indravelli, including those who had come for the weekly shandy.

The local monthly magazine *Olympus* published a report on the police action against the Gonds under the heading "The Indravelli Massacre—Tribals Face Extinction." After describing the police firing, the report contains also the ominous news that "the Government has recently taken a decision to regroup tribal villages, thus uprooting the Gonds from their homes and hearths." It concludes with the following prediction:

Tribals are fighting a grim battle for survival. The depredation of forest contractors has upset their economic life. And now their lands are sought to be snatched away by the new "voortrekkers." The plainsmen with the power of the modern state behind them are moving in.

Observers in Andhra Pradesh have compared the massacre at Indravelli to the British suppression of a demonstration at Jallianwala Bagh, which has a place in Indian folklore has an example of the ruthless display of state violence meant to terrorise a population into total submission. Sentiments of protest and revulsion expressed in the above quotations from Indian publications are the only ray of hope in an atmosphere of otherwise unrelieved gloom.

Adivasi Aboriginal, member of a scheduled tribe
Alasanda A pulse; cow pea.
Asaldar patwari Hereditary village accountant
Ashram Hermitage; retreat
Ashram school Boarding school
Ayak Kolam god corresponding to the Gond god Bhimana

Ballar dhal A pulse; pigeon pea
Bewar Slash-and-burn cultivation
Bhimana Gond god
Bidi A kind of cheap cigarette in which leaves are substituted for
    paper
Brahmin, also Brahman Member of the highest Hindu caste
Budda gochi Loin-cloth

Charpoy Bedstead
Chenna dhal A pulse; horse gram
Choli Blouse

Deshmukh Marathi title of a hereditary official in charge of a
    group of villages
Devari Village priest
Devata Deity
Dhal Pulse, which is one of the mainstays of the Indian diet
Dhani Patron

Dhoti Loin-cloth worn by men, usually made of white cotton cloth
Dodomankal Kolam priest

Gaonbura Assamese term for village elder
Ghotul Youth dormitory in Bastar
Girdawar Revenue inspector
Girijan Aboriginal; member of a scheduled tribe
Gondi Dravidian language spoken by Gonds
Gompa Buddhist temple or monastery
Gram panchayat Statutory council of elected members representing one or more villages
Gumashta Bailiff; landlord's steward
Guru Religious teacher

Harijan Modern euphemistic term for untouchable

Inam Gift, particularly of land granted free of revenue

Jagir Estate assigned by ruler to landlord on special terms
Jagurla Gond cremation rite involving animal sacrifice and dancing
Jajman Patron of Brahmin priest; by extension any hereditary patron
Jangali Crude, primitive; literally, "of the forest"
Jhum Assamese term for hill fields made by cutting forest or shrub and then burning it
Jiv or jiva Soul; life-principle

Karbari Secretary; assistant
Katora Gond clan priest
Katora kita Priestly lineage
Khamatan Group of families cooperating in agricultural production
Kharif Crops grown during the monsoon season
Kharij khata Type of temporary tenure of government land
Kita Lineage within a Gond clan
Komti Member of a Telugu merchant caste, moneylender
Konda devata Hill deity
Konda podu Hill field made by cutting and burning forest
Korra Finger millet; *Eleusine coracana*
Kulam pedda Telugu term for clan or caste headman
Kuta mohtur Gond rite marking the beginning of the agricultural cycle
Kutma kita Gond lineage of agnatic kinsmen

Lamsare Resident son-in-law
Langoti Small loin-cloth

Lingam Phallus of the Hindu god Shiva

Mahua *Bassia latifolia,* a tree whose corollae are eaten and used for distilling liquor
Mansabdar Feudal chieftain
Maqta Estate assigned by ruler to landlord on special terms
Maund Measure of weight; approximately 96 kilograms
Mithan *Bos frontalis,* a variety of semi-domesticated cattle prevalent in the highlands of Northeast India
Mokashi Hereditary chieftain of a rank inferior to that of raja
Moksa Salvation
Mutta Territorial division ruled by a hereditary chief
Muttadar Chief in charge of a *mutta*

Nar patla Gond village headman
Naxalite Member of a leftist revolutionary movement
Niwot Sacrificial food offered to gods and then eaten by worshippers

Pahar patti Hill circle
Panchayat Village council, tribal council
Panchayati raj Modern system of grass-roots democracy based on elected local councils
Parampok Type of temporary tenure of government land
Pat Gondi term for secondary marriage
Patel Village headman
Patta Title deed to land
Pattadar Owner of land held on *patta*
Patti Region, revenue circle
Patwari Village accountant
Pedda kapu Headman of Telugu village
Peddamanchi Headman, term used mainly by Chenchus; literally "big man"
Pen Gondi term for deity
Penda Slash-and-burn cultivation
Persa pen Gond clan deity; literally, "great god"
Pisi watana Gondi term for marriage by capture
Podu Slash-and-burn cultivation
Puja Hindu rite
Pujari The one who offers *puja*, priest
Pungam Forest tree whose seed is used for pharmaceutical purposes

Rabi Crops grown during the winter season
Rupee Unit of Indian coinage. The symbol for the singular is Re and that for the plural is Rs; the exchange rate in 1980 approximated Rs 18 to the pound sterling and Rs 7.5 to the U.S. dollar.

Saga Phratry, largest exogamous division of Gond society

Sahukar Merchant, moneylender

Sama A small millet; *Panicum miliare*

Samithi Regional council or committee in charge of a taluk or part of a taluk, also known as *panchayat samithi.*

Sanad Patent or document, usually relating to grant bestowed by ruler

Sanal Spirit of departed

Sari Draped garment consisting of one piece of cloth universally worn by Indian women

Sarpanch Elected chairman of a *gram panchayat*

Sati Deified ancestor

Shandy Market

Shikmedar Shareholder in landed property

Tahsildar Officer in charge of the revenue administration of a taluk; also known as *tahsil*

Taluk Administrative unit forming part of a district

Talukdar Officer of Hyderabad State in charge of a district, corresponding to the present-day collector

Varna Section of traditional Hindu society, which was divided into four *varna* arranged in hierarchical order

Veju Magician, sorcerer, shaman

Watan Hereditary estate

Watandar Owner of *watan* or of hereditary right or office, hence *watandari patwari*

Zamindar Landowner

Zamindari Estate owned by *zamindar*

Zilla parishad District council

Bibliography

Only sources quoted in the text are listed here. For a comprehensive bibliography on the anthropology of tribal India, see *An Anthropological Bibliography of South Asia*, by Elizabeth von Fürer-Haimendorf and Helen Kanitkar, Vols. 1–4 (The Hague, 1958, 1964, 1970, and 1976).

Bailey, S. F. G. *Tribe, Caste and Nation: A Study of Political Activity and Political Change in Highland Orissa.* Manchester, England, 1960.
Beals, A. R. "Interplay among Factors of Change in a Mysore Village." In *Village India,* edited by M. Marriott. Chicago, 1955.
Bower, Ursula Graham. *The Hidden Land.* London, 1953.
Caplan, Patricia. *Priests and Cobblers: A Study of Social Change in a Hindu Village in Western Nepal.* London, 1972.
Dumont, Louis. *Hierarchy and Marriage in South Indian Kinship.* Royal Anthropological Institute, Occasional Paper no. 12. London, 1957.
Ehrenfels, U. R. von. *The Kadar of Cochin.* Madras, 1952.
Elwin, Verrier. *Maria Murder and Suicide.* Bombay, 1943.
———. *The Muria and Their Ghotul.* Bombay, 1947.
———. *The Religion of an Indian Tribe.* Bombay, 1955.
Frykenberg, R. E. *Land Control and Social Structure in Indian History.* Madison, Milwaukee, and London, 1969.
Fürer-Haimendorf, C. von. *The Chenchus—Jungle Folk of the Deccan.* Vol. 1. *The Aboriginal Tribes of Hyderabad.* London, 1943.
———. "Aboriginal Education in Hyderabad." *Indian Journal of Social Work* 5 (1944): 123–28.

———. *The Reddis of the Bison Hills—A Study in Acculturation.* Vol. 2. *The Aboriginal Tribes of Hyderabad.* London, 1945.

———. "Tribal Populations of Hyderabad: Yesterday and Today." *Census of India, 1941.* Vol. 21. Hyderabad, 1945.

———. *Tribal Hyderabad—Four Reports.* Hyderabad, 1945.

———. *Progress and Problems of Aboriginal Rehabilitation in Adilabad District.* Hyderabad, 1945.

———. *Ethnographic Notes on the Tribes of the Subansiri Region.* Shillong, India, 1947.

———. *The Raj Gonds of Adilabad.* Vol. 3. *The Aboriginal Tribes of Hyderabad.* London, 1948.

———. "The Cult of Ayak among the Kolams of Hyderabad." *Wiener Beiträge zur Kulturgeschichte und Linguistik* 9 (1952): 108–23.

———. *Himalayan Barbary.* London, 1955.

———. "Notes on the Malapantaram of Travancore." *Bulletin of the International Committee on Urgent Anthropological and Ethnological Research,* no. 3 (1960), pp. 45–51.

———. *The Apa Tanis and Their Neighbours.* London, 1962.

———. *Morals and Merit—A Study of Values and Social Controls in South Asian Societies.* London, 1967.

———. "The Changing Position of Tribal Populations in India." *Royal Anthropological Institute News,* no. 22 (October 1977): 2–8.

———. *The Gonds of Andhra Pradesh. Tradition and Change in an Indian Tribe.* London/Delhi, 1979.

———. *A Himalayan Tribe: From Cattle to Cash.* Berkeley and Los Angeles/New Delhi, 1980.

Grigson, Sir Wilfrid. *The Maria Gonds of Bastar.* London, 1949.

Jay, Edward J. *A Tribal Village of Middle India.* Calcutta, 1970.

Mann, E. G. *Sonthalia and the Sonthals.* London, 1867.

Mazumdar, B. C. *The Aborigines of the Highlands of Central India.* Calcutta, 1927.

Morris, Brian. "Tappers, Trappers and the Hill Pantaram." *Anthropos* 72 (1977): 225–41.

Pandey, B. B. *The Hill Miri.* Shillong, India, 1947.

Pandhe, M. K., editor. *Social Life in Rural India.* Calcutta, 1977.

Pratap, D. R. *Occupational Pattern and Development Priorities among Raj Gonds of Adilabad District.* Hyderabad, 1972.

Pratap, D. R., et al., *Study of Tribal Manpower Resources, Adilabad District.* Manpower Study Series, Project No. 1. Hyderabad, 1977.

Rao, P. Setu Madhava. *Among the Gonds of Adilabad.* Hyderabad, 1949.

Rathnaiah, E. V. *Structural Constraints in Tribal Education.* New Delhi, 1977.

Russell, R. V. *The Tribes and Castes of the Central Provinces of India.* London, 1916.

Sarasin, Paul und Fritz. *Die Weddas von Ceylon und die sie umgebenden Völkerschaften.* Wiesbaden, Germany, 1893.

Scott, Jonathan. *Ferishta's History of Dekkan.* Shrewsbury, England, 1794.

Seligmann, C. G. and Brenda. *The Veddas.* Cambridge, England, 1911.

Sharma, B. D. *Tribal Development: The Concept and the Frame.* New Delhi, 1978.

Sharma, R. R. P. *The Sherdukpens.* Shillong, India, 1961.

Shukla, B. K. *The Daflas of the Subansiri Region.* Shillong, India, 1959.

Thurston, Edgar. *Castes and Tribes of Southern India.* Madras, 1909.

Wakefield, G. F. C. "Note on a Visit to the Prehistoric Burial-Grounds of Janampett in the Paloncha Taluka of Warangal District of H.E.H. the Nizam's Dominions." *Annual Report of the Archaeological Department of H.E.H. the Nizam's Dominions for 1918-19,* pp. 24–29, Hyderabad, 1920.

Yorke, M. P. "Kinship, Marriage and Ideology among the Raj Gonds: A Tribal System in the Context of South India." *Contributions to Indian Sociology,* n.s. 13 (1979): 85–116.

Designer: Ed Pinson
Compositor: Computer Typesetting Services, Inc.
Text: APS 5 Palatino
Display: APS 5 Palatino
Printer: Thomson-Shore, Inc.
Binder: John H. Dekker & Sons